Landlords and Lodgers

Malam Bako, Founder of Sabon Zongo. Courtesy of Alhaji Yahaya Hamisu Bako.

LANDLORDS AND LODGERS

Socio-Spatial Organization in an
Accra Community

Deborah Pellow

THE UNIVERSITY OF CHICAGO PRESS
CHICAGO AND LONDON

Deborah Pellow is professor of anthropology in the Maxwell School at Syracuse University where she has also been director of Integrated Studies in Space and Place. She is the author of numerous books, including *Setting Boundaries: The Anthropology of Spatial and Social Organization*.

The University of Chicago Press, Chicago 60637
The University of Chicago Press, Ltd., London

First published in 2002 by Praeger Publishers
University of Chicago Press edition 2008
Printed in the United States of America

17 16 15 14 13 12 11 10 09 08   1 2 3 4 5

ISBN-10: 0-226-65397-8 (paper)

ISBN-13: 978-0-226-65397-6 (paper)

Library of Congress Cataloging-in-Publication Data

Pellow, Deborah, 1945–
  Landlords and lodgers : socio-spatial organization in an Accra community / Deborah Pellow.
      p. cm.
  "First published in 2002 by Praeger Publishers."
  Includes bibliographical references and index.
  ISBN-13: 978-0-226-65397-6 (pbk. : alk. paper)
  ISBN-10: 0-226-65397-8 (pbk. : alk. paper) 1. Human territoriality—Ghana—Accra.
2. Spatial behavior—Ghana—Accra. 3. Hausa (African people)—Ghana—Accra—Social
conditions. 4. Muslims—Ghana—Accra—Social conditions. 5. Accra (Ghana)—History. 6.
Accra (Ghana)—Social conditions. I. Title.
  GN645.G55P44 2008
  306.09667—dc22
                                    2008001102

♾ The paper used in this publication meets the minimum requirements of the American National
Standard for Information Sciences—Permanence of Paper
for Printed Library Materials, ANSI Z39.48-1992.

Na sadaukar da wannan littafi ga mutanen Sabon Zongo

CONTENTS

ILLUSTRATIONS

GLOSSARY

alkali	judge
aski	barbering
auren	marriage/of
auren kulle	marriage of seclusion
baban riga	the flowing gown, worn over pants and a long sleeve shirt of the same material
baƙo	guest, settler
balangu	grilled lamb
barance	clientage
biki	party
bori	spirit possession cult with adherents among the Hausa, Zabrama and Fulani
cicinga	lamb or beef kabobs
cikin gida	central courtyard
fadawa	courtiers, advisors
fufu	pounded yam or cassava or cassava and plantain eaten with soup
fura	a porridge of pounded millet, mixed with pepper and spices and eaten with milk or yogurt
gida/n	house, compound/of
haji	pilgrimmage to Mecca
hanya	road

Imam	Muslim priest
jojoma	a Yoruba word that refers to women traders who must return daily to collect payments
kayan ɗaki	dowry, lit. things for the room
kenkey	the local Ga staple, made from fermented corn
kishi	jealousy
kishiya	co-wife, lit. jealous one
ƙofar gida	forecourt
ƙosai	bean cakes
kulle	seclusion
kunya	modesty
kutare	lepers
lalle	henna
lungu	alley
magajiya	"queen mother"
mai/masu gida	patron/s, household head/s
makafi	blind
makaranta	Koranic school
makwala	a place for idlers
malam/ai	teacher/s
manyan gari	elders, big men in the community
maroƙi/maroƙiya (pl. maroƙa)	praise-singer/s
masalaci	mosque
masa	a fried cake made from corn
pinkaso	wheaten cake fried in oil
riga	gown
roƙo	praise-singing
Salla	Id il Fitr celebration at the end of Ramadan
sarauta	leadership positions
sarki/n	chief/of
Sarkin Fada	the chief's linguist or major domo
shigifa	a transitional zone
suna	outdooring party held when a baby is seven days old and is formally acknowledged and named
taliya	pasta
titi	street
tuwo	the Hausa staple, made from millet or cassava flour, or from rice

unguwa	quarter, neighborhood
uwar gida	senior wife (lit. mother of the house)
wake	beans and rice
zaure	entryway, entrance hall
zongo	Hausa word for "stranger quarter"
zongwanci	a collective identity that derives from living in and feeling attachment to *zongo* life

PREFACE

Long-term research is not easily funded, because funding agencies love projects that are new and glitzy. But it is extraordinarily satisfying to finish a monograph after spending years on a single project, in a single community, and getting to know the players, their friends, and families. The residents of Sabon Zongo have always made me feel welcome and have provided me with a sense of belonging.

I first went to Accra in 1970, to carry out my doctoral field research. I lived and worked in the popular and diverse neighborhood of Adabraka. One of my field assistants was a Hausa woman, "Akokai" Harona. She belonged to one of the then-active intra-city Muslim women's mutual benefit associations, that met to celebrate life-cycle events, especially marriages and baby outdoorings (parties held when a baby is seven days old). I often attended the women's meetings with her. The greatest number of members were Hausa, and in spending time with them, I became curious about their lifestyles: in particular, how they and the Hausa community more generally were able to maintain institutional integrity within the confines of this city that is characteristically Christian and Western and lies about 1,900 miles southwest of the Hausa homeland.

These Muslim Hausa women were my segue into Accra's Muslim community and the development of its enclaves known as *zongos*, stranger quarters, from the Hausa word *zango* or encampment. Akokai introduced me to Alhaji Ali Kadri English, chief of the Central Accra Hausa community, who took me to meet members of Accra's "first families of Islam": Alhaji Braimah, the chief of the Yoruba community; Alhaji B.B. Shardow, chief of the Nupe; Audu "Something," Chief of the Zabrama in Shukura. My friend Alhaji Safianu Hamidu introduced me to Sha'aibu Maiyaki, Hausa chief in Nima, and Alhaji Zenua, Chief of the Kanuri. I collected oral histories and stories of the power struggles among Accra's Hausa that exploded in the first decade of the twentieth century, which I corroborated through materials in Accra's National Archives.

I chose to focus on the community of Sabon Zongo for a variety of intellectual and personal reasons: it was the first *zongo* consciously created in Accra by those who would live in it, there is considerable documentation in the National Archives of Ghana of the founding Bako family's political struggles, and I had good contacts there. In 1982, I began my long-term project on Sabon Zongo. The oral histories helped trace the ties of Sabon Zongo to Accra's larger Muslim community. Various elders in the Bako family were superb sources of historical and institutional information: Alhaji Hamisu Bako, the senior member of the Bako family during the 1980s, had a memory that was clear as a bell, and he was ever-welcoming to my never-ending questions. He provided me with an extraordinarily extensive Bako family genealogy. His tales were supplemented by those of his brother, Malam "Gambo" Bako, at that time the head of the family's Koranic school, and by Sha'aibu Bako, chief of Sabon Zongo. The chief's linguist, Sarkin Fada, took me to interview every sub-chief in the community. The Chief introduced me to the lawyer representing his claim to the Sabon Zongo chieftaincy, James Glover-Amoako, an associate at Akufo-Addo and Prempeh; he gave me all of the relevant court transcripts, as well as the survey map of "Malam Bako's New Zongo," detailing names of property owners. Glover-Amoako left the firm and thirteen years later, Alex Quainoo, a member of the firm who specializes in land tenure, helped me search for other maps relevant to my research project.

My research stay in 1982 was very difficult. Flight Lieutenant Jerry Rawlings led a successful coup d'etat on December 31, 1981, and the country was placed under military rule. There was an enforced curfew throughout my stay and the necessities of daily life were either in short supply or gone altogether. A general state of fear prevailed. James Channing, the cultural affairs officer at the American Consulate, went out of his way to help me protect my notes and materials.

I did not return until 1993, and since then I have been back almost yearly. Over the years, my work has been supported by grants from Syracuse University's Senate Research Fund, the Appleby Mosher Foundation, and the American Philosophical Society.

Since 1995, I have also worked especially close with Alhaji Baba Mai Doki, son of Idrissu Bako (the first gazetted chief of Sabon Zongo), his cousin Alhaji Hudu Bako, Alhaji Sule Bako, son of Sha'aibu Bako, Alhaji Yahaya Adamu, Alhazai Alhassan and Huseini Sulley and Muhsin Barko and his sister Rukaya Abdurahaman. These individuals, and their families, have nurtured me in all ways—answering myriad questions, taking me to meet others, feeding me, giving me emotional support. Chief Sha'aibu had old letters from the colonial government to Malam Bako and other members of the family, which he allowed me to photocopy. The nineteen landlords (and their families) whose houses I surveyed were ever-gracious and responsive to my requests for help.

I knew that there was a formal portrait of Malam Bako, founder of Sabon Zongo. Finding it turned out to be far more difficult than I had anticipated. Several community people had very bad copies; in all of them, Malam Bako's face was damaged. I went from elder to elder, asking if any had the photo. When I approached Malam Hamisu's son Yahaya, he went through a moldy box of moldy books. Inserted in one was a postcard of the original photograph. Alhaji Yahaya gave me the card to take back to the United States and have it reproduced. I am ever grateful to him for trusting me with this piece of history.

Chief Sha'aibu Bako provided my initial entrée into Sabon Zongo and has always been gracious and helpful. He died on April 8, 2001. Following extensive discussions within the Bako family, Yahaya Hamisu Bako, son of Malam Hamisu Bako, was chosen to succeed Sha'aibu. However, on the observation of the fortieth day following Sha'aibu's death, his son Sule Bako contested the succession and claimed the chieftaincy. Despite arbitration by the Jamestown Ga chief, at the time of this writing, the chieftaincy remains up in the air, as there are still two men claiming to be Sarkin Sabon Zongo.

Many academic colleagues and unknown reviewers have contributed immeasurably to this research project. Professors J.H.K. Nketia, K.B. Dickson, K.E. Agovi and Kwame Arhin, each during his directorship of the Institute of African Studies at the University of Ghana, allowed me to affiliate with the Institute during my research stay and provided documentation to the Ministry of Interior making my long-term stays possible. In 1982, Professor Yangouro, a sociologist at the University of Ghana, helped me define the parameters of my investigation and those I should interview. Bossman Murey, a staff member in the Department of Archaeology at the University of Ghana, did an extraordinary job in 1995, 1996, and 1998 with a thirty-meter tape in translating the house forms onto paper. Joseph Hayford, an architect in Accra, had nothing formal to do with my project but everything to do with the final product. He has been a continuing source of information on matters architectural in Accra, pushing me to keep my Euro-American assumptions at bay. He provided me with new GIS (Geographic Information System) photography of Sabon Zongo. And he has introduced me to a wonderful group of architectural and social science professionals in Accra.

Over the past fifteen years, I have published some of the material contained in this monograph in journal articles and book chapters. The book represents more than a compilation of essays: I have gone further with the theoretical grounding, I have included more of the domestic/public socio-spatial material and the complete group of nineteen drawings and their analyses are reproduced for the first time. My analyses and conclusions owe considerable debt to my colleagues in the Space and Place group of the American Anthropological Association. I owe a particular debt of gratitude to Professor Setha Low, who has

organized paper sessions at meetings and has edited volumes in order to insti-
tutionalize studies of space and place in the discipline of anthropology. Setha
has read this manuscript in a variety of incarnations and has made crucial sug-
gestions. Others who have read and commented wisely on the manuscript include Bob Rotenberg, John Middleton, Michelle Gilbert, Caroline Tauxe, Bill
Mangin, and Michael Freedman. Denise Lawrence has been a superb critic who
has nudged me to theorize forcefully about socio-spatial realities. Beverly Mack,
Barbara Cooper, and Frank Salamone read and commented on chapters dealing
with Hausa social and spatial institutions, helping me to differentiate between
historical and cyclical continuity and change. Claire Robertson, a fine historian
of Accra, kindly read and commented on Chapter 2. Sam Spiers, Gerard Chouin,
and Francois Richard read early versions of the material chapters, commenting
through the lens of archaeology. Dr. Mark Hauser drew new maps for the book.
He and Joe Stoll, cartographer in the Geography Department at Syracuse University, used their Computer Aided Design (CAD) abilities to adapt Bossman
Murey's house drawings and maps for easy reproduction. In addition, Mark was an
invaluable advisor and aide, reliable and accurate, in harmonizing house drawings
and genealogies. He bailed me out more times that I care to remember. My good
friend Robert Rubinstein introduced me to SmartDraw, enabling me to represent
the genealogies elegantly, simply, and accurately. Jim Lance, acquisitions editor
at Heinemann, was extraordinarily thoughtful in his appraisals of the book and
his help getting it through the labyrinthine process of production. The reissuing
of the book was made possible by David Brent, anthropology editor, and Maggie
Hivnor, paperbacks editor, at the University of Chicago Press. David liked the
book and cheered it, and me, on through the process of acceptance, a process
made easier by Maggie in good humor and professionalism. Paula Duffy, a friend
of many years and a real pro in the world of publishing, advised me as I sought
to have the book reissued. I owe my final thanks to my best friend, my husband
David Cole, who has supported me through the long process that resulted in
this book.

Permission was granted to reprint material from "The Power of Space in
the Evolution of an Accra *Zongo*" in *Theorizing the City: The New Urban
Anthropology Reader*, edited by Setha M. Low (Brunswick, N.J.: Rutgers
University Press, 1999) 277–314 and from "Male Praise-Singers in Accra: In the
Company of Women," *Africa* 67, no. 4 (1997): 582–601.

1

INTRODUCTION

This is a book about a community in Accra. It was created in 1910 by Malam Bako, a local Hausa leader, as a *zongo* (the Hausa word for "stranger quarter"). A spin-off of the original downtown *zongo*, he named it Sabon Zongo, "new zongo." It started out as a place of refuge for Muslim Hausa migrants from Northern Nigeria, who were squabbling with other Muslim ethnics in downtown Accra. They stayed, and many of their children stayed. Over the years, these early settlers and their families have been joined by yet other "strangers." Many have remained, in part because they could not financially afford to move, in part for reasons of social familiarity and comfort.

My interest in Sabon Zongo goes beyond its draw as a place to live. Rather, I am focusing on the social and spatial evolution of Malam Bako's community, of its genealogical underpinnings as they have played out socially and on the ground. A resident's relation to the history of this *zongo* and to its founder affects one's social identity within this *zongo*. Over the years, residents have reproduced its social and spatial order while also incorporating change and new meanings in the process. But genealogy is a major key to Sabon Zongo, to its organization, its interconnectedness. It explains who has influence, who has status. Even as the cast of characters has grown and widened, they have reproduced a sense of a community of like-minded people as instilled by Malam Bako when he founded the *zongo* almost 100 years ago.

Community sentiment is expressed everyday through what I call zongo-ness or *zongwanci*, a notion I shall develop in the course of this study. As I shall show, in many respects Sabon Zongo continues to operate like a village-in-the-city. While anchored in Accra, it is not typical of Accra or any other West

African city. Actually, there is nothing typical about neighborhoods in Accra. Accra is a cultural mosaic of ethnic groups and physical layouts.

When we talk about the post-colonial city, we are often thinking of places with a colonial base that have evolved from a pre-colonial past. These places represent a continuation of modernist, European, monumentalist style. In Accra, established as a colonial city in the late 1870s, internationalist style carried the symbolic representations of governmental authority through the pomp and circumstance of government buildings. Rationalist modern city planning schemes influenced the reordering of Accra, with site planning of various areas within and outside of the city limits and infrastructure aimed at increasing efficient circulation and hygiene in much of the city. Post-independence, these incentives were carried forward. Sites such as Black Star Square and State House were erected. Nationalism, as in Cuba and Berlin, became the order of the day. More recently, the postmodern cognized "power of place" has become increasingly evident in the historic preservation of pre-colonial areas. In Jamestown, the old core of downtown Accra and for several hundred years one of the Ga people's hometowns, revitalization is going on to best preserve Ga ethnic identity.

Sabon Zongo is different. It is one of those communities that is culturally and spatially distinct, but that is neither being revitalized nor being signified through special construction. The migrant Hausa settlers transplanted into this one locality created in space a cultural form that incorporated a pre-colonial past from Northern Nigeria, a colonial overlay, and an adapted post-colonial form.

Does this happen elsewhere? Aspects of Sabon Zongo's social and spatial uniqueness, its zongo-ness, occur elsewhere in Accra as well as in other West African cities and throughout the colonial and post-colonial world. My thesis is that Sabon Zongo is one example of a particular kind of linking of people and space; it constitutes a type of sociospatial form found in other African cities that exemplifies the transition from the colonial to post-colonial city. Although one cannot generalize about the whole city from the microcosmic view of the *zongo* presented in this book, it helps us gain a better understanding of post-colonial urban environments.

LINKING PEOPLE AND PLACE

How do strangers cohere and create a socially meaningful world? How do they nurture a cohesive and familiar community in the city? I suggest that they do so by engaging in social practices (exchange) and spatial/temporal practices (the use of public and domestic spaces over time) linked through the social production of the spatial environment. The social system and its spatial locale are mutually constituted. Social relations are spatialized while the physical environment and its spaces are culturized.

In Sabon Zongo, as in all places, space and time are socially constituted and as such, carry meaning. The spatial meanings are cultural constructions, produced by social realities. Social values, roles, and behaviors, are embedded in this spatial environment. This is not to say that the organization of space is a direct reflection of cultural codes and meanings; rather, as Moore (1986) detailed in her study of the Maraket, it is a context developed through practice, through the interaction of individuals. The built environment, an exemplar of material culture, is socially produced. As a spatial element, it does not just exist as background or setting. It is an active setting and must be problematized to understand how it intertwines with social relations. Moreover, space itself works as a mnemonic, expressing, enforcing, enabling, maybe even structuring, sometimes engendering the social and material exchanges. Social relations are embodied in things and things (objects or artifacts) become active in relation to people (Harvey 1996:220f.). For example, houses in Sabon Zongo have social pedigrees and these are carried forward in not just memories but also bring current landlords status in the community.

At the surface level, as in Schildkrout's analysis (1978:87) of Kumase *zongo*, Sabon Zongo is not physically demarcated by a gate or a wall. There are known street boundaries. Moreover, its social constitution and coherence is differently perceived within and from without. But as I shall show, Sabon Zongo is quite distinct. It is genealogically anchored, its current chief a lineal descendant of the founder. And the community of residents is delineated through interaction and exchange—whether the dailiness of sharing space and talk, of engaging in commercial enterprises or rituals, or through acting out intangibles of genealogical entanglement and remembered histories.

Not only are social composition and physical form mutually constituted; they are also concurrently implicated in peoples' daily routines and manners of exchange. Exchange is localized and occurs through time and space, through genealogical/fictive connections of the main families (Bako, Garuba, Kariki, and Damaley), business relations with traders (local and long distance), marriage ties with neighbors or newly arrived migrants, or ritual and collective activity. The redistribution of foods at festivals and life-cycle events is one way in which people articulate the interconnections.

To say that social life is created through exchange is not particularly unique; the classics of Mauss (1967) and Malinowski (1922) elaborated on the bonds created and cemented by gift giving and reciprocity. Moreover, for years Africanists have recorded the exchanges of sociability (kinship, marriage, clientage) and materiality (food, beer, housing). What I bring to the equation is an examination of spatial practices as part of the social system and as instrumental in building a coherent community. Like Moore (1986), I believe we must look both at social actors who intend to act and place meanings on their actions, and the socio-physical structures (including social institutions and places), which enable the generation and reproduction of meanings and action, of social strategy and behavior.[1]

It is through the body, through our personal experience, that we internalize social values and meanings (Comaroff 1985). "Through routine, habitual activity, our bodies learn what is 'inner' and what is 'outer,' which gestures are forbidden and which required, how violable or inviolable are the boundaries of our bodies, how much space around the body may be claimed, and so on" (Bordo 1993:16). We learn what is up and what is down, what or who is in or is out. This order is learned everyday, by participating in daily life. Like Bourdieu's *habitus* (1977), these practices and institutions pervade one's perception. "The primacy of perception is ultimately a primacy of the lived body—a body that . . . is a creature of habitual cultural and social processes" (Casey 1996:19). Bodies inhabit space and senses of place as special or familiar register with or by the body; such dimensionalities as up/down, front/back, right/left, help cement the body with place (Casey 1996). There is no question that phenomenologically certain places evoke a special feeling of attachment and/or protectiveness for the user. Order is inscribed in the physical environment, which in turns reminds us of our roles and behaviors.

In this sense, Sabon Zongo is actively significant, it matters. It is not just a physical setting or an inert container for the enactment of life's daily dramas. Rather, as Rodman problematizes it, as a place it is "politicized, culturally relative, historically specific"; it is socially produced (Rodman 1992:641).

My study of Sabon Zongo focuses on two levels of social order over time: the public spaces of the community, that is, streets and markets; and the private or semi-private spaces of daily life, the compounds where people reside. The two levels are separate but linked through the behaviors and practices of people as they pass back and forth between them. For example, the control of "things" through trade and gift exchange links the house with the world outside (Cooper 1997b:201), as does using children as runners or as sellers (in trade) or "lending" children to households that are childless.

The two social levels also communicate spatially. The architectural element of the *zaure* or entryway in the Hausa compound house instantiates this interaction with the outside. It is a permeable element like a window that signifies transitions in use, space and social meaning (see Chapter 7), a threshold connecting the interior and exterior worlds. At both compound and street levels, we see people constructing identity out of everyday rituals (Allen 1988; Bourdieu 1977). "The culture is mostly 'lived'—in practice, and as *habitus* . . . lives are run on an unconscious mastery of the system" (Sahlins 1985:51).

Broadly speaking, Sabon Zongo residents fall into two categories: house owners (or members of families who are) and renters of rooms. For residents and especially the tenants, there are issues of belonging and localization (Lovell 1998:3); rights to community involvement are not a given if one is not a member of a house owning family. And even if one is, the compound's location matters. The landscape is conceptually divided up and valued according to association with myth and memory (genealogy) and socio-ritual performance. These have varied over time. Rights to belonging are not only linked to genealogical origins (in this case, a descendant of Bako or of one of his followers); they are also tied into exchange, such as participation in collective rituals and celebrations (Ottino 1998:103).

Thus, houses are particularly salient. And as Muhammad-Oumar observes in his research on houses in the Hausa Northern Nigerian homeland (1997), the study of the domestic compound could be a means of tracing the social history of the milieu. Yet, while they have been valued by scholars as artifacts of architectural expression, as physical structures that provide evidence of symbolism or cosmology (Blier 1987; Denyer 1978; Guidoni 1975), they have been neglected as elements that are socially and conceptually basic to the economies, kinship systems, and political organization of societies worldwide (Carsten and Hugh-Jones 1995; Humphrey 1988). Their social imperative provides an impetus for my research in Sabon Zongo. Let me further suggest that they also carry considerable weight as "inalienable possessions" (Weiner 1992), and as such, they carry information and authority. Each house with its "exclusive and cumulative identity with a particular series of owners through time" (p. 33) acts as a stabilizing force as it authenticates kinship and political histories. "Yet the possession may be the very symbol of change" (p. 10), as the people resident, the spatial layout, and the exchanges and activities contained, change over time.

To probe the stuff of exchange and its occurrence in place and time, I explore how the structure and use of public spaces (where people circulate, engage in commercial activities, and celebrate family events and festivals) and compound spaces (where people eat, sleep, and relax) carry social meaning and how they are built into the community's social organization. Because the invocation of space enters into transactions, because space implicates social bonds or ties; indeed, because place talks to people and teaches them how to behave (Bourdieu 1977), space and place matter. Weiss (1996) has shown for the Haya, Gow (1995) for Amazonia and Munn (1986) for Gawa, "specific practices create the world, or spacetime, in which they occur" (Gow 1995:60).

I suggest that Sabon Zongo has two primary spatial-social delineations, up/down and landlord/tenant. The former refers to two named physical locales in the community, which express social position; the latter refers to the two possible resident (social) statuses of community members, which are often represented in physical locale. Neither is mutually exclusive, they may impact upon one another, and their significance may shift depending upon the social and historical context (Hirsch 1995).

The locality where exchange occurs is thus relational and contextual (Appadurai 1996:178ff.), but exchange is spatial as well, insofar as memories, relations, and their social contexts play out in place, which in turn reminds people of their roles and statuses. Social identities and transactions are anchored in physical spaces. Certain kinds of practices "situate a given location as a recognizable place, and thereby establish a meaningful orientation to the space and time it inhabits" (Weiss 1996:7). Indeed, physical spaces become *places* when "given meaning through personal, group, or cultural processes" (Low and Altman 1992:5). Places are social productions that contain "memories, ideas, feelings, attitudes, values, preferences, meanings, and conceptions of behavior and experience which relate to the variety and complexity of physical settings that define the day-to-day existence of every human being" (Proshansky, Fabian, and Kaminoff 1983:59).

The built environment and material culture are powerful forces in people's lives. The physical environment reinforces social "acts" and is affected by them. They are mutually constitutive. In the scheme of social acts or transactions and physical spaces, I am exploring how social acts are reinforced, engendered, directed, facilitated, and channeled by the physical environment. Like the social, the physical can be consciously created or reinforced, and in their mutual constitution, places enculturate as they connect people to one another.

We know that material things, like houses, do not have intentions and thus cannot behave like agents, that is, have the capacity to initiate causal events; and yet, we also know that human agency operates in the material world. Here Gell's anthropological theory of art is particularly helpful. Defining art as "the social relations in the vicinity of objects mediating social agency," he observes that his theory "merges seamlessly with the social anthropology of persons and their bodies" (1998:7). Gell distinguishes between " 'primary' agents, that is, intentional beings who are categorically distinguished from 'mere' things or artefacts [*sic*], and 'secondary' agents, which are artefacts, dolls, cars, works of arts, etc., through which primary agents distribute their agency in the causal milieu" (Gell 1998:20). In other words, people as primary agents create and use, for example, houses. They encode the houses both with practical meanings for what to do where and with symbolic meanings that express status, identity, and so on (Birdwell-Pheasant and Lawrence-Zuniga 1999:9). The houses, then, are the agents that connect one person or group of persons to another. They are mediators in that they also carry messages of fame, genealogy, and so on (Harvey 1996:221). The slow to change or conservative nature of built form serves to reinforce the unchanging nature of the product, for example, the house form; it reinforces the message that is externalized in routine practices, the prevailing social life (Gell 1998:127).

But messages change, as do the habitats of meaning—the cultures and spaces—in the course of changes that occur during the life cycle and also when people and cultures travel and mix (Hannerz 1996). The parameters, contents, and contexts of exchange alter. There are changes in family size and composition. Intersections shape cultural process in which agency operates. The local and repetitive that have reinforced the habitats of meaning are jolted by new kinds of intersections with different kinds of people and may create innovation and creolization (Hannerz 1996). Like works of art, images, icons, and houses can be sources of and targets for social agency (Gell 1998:96). Their construction and destruction are due to social and cultural forces and have social and cultural outcomes. Marris detailed for the city of Lagos how spatial destruction, like the razing of a neighborhood or creation of "alien" house types, also destroyed the livelihood and way of life of the people who live there (Marris 1962).

MANAGING IN THE CITY

All societies co-produce a set of socio-spatial institutions. The social institutions realized in or built into spaces promote legitimate behaviors and gradually gain the credibility of tradition. By the same token, they operate to support the social system, providing the model for behavior, while incorporating the interactants. The hometown community is a whole, characterized by familiarity. This is what Hannerz (1992) refers to as small-scale, folk or primitive society. Face-to-face, "its members stay within the same limited geographical territory and on the whole interact only with one another, but do a great deal of that" (41). They share a community of space as well as time. In such societies, kin-based or not, kinship is the metaphor for interaction and the mechanism for incorporating newcomers. Within such a community, there are both physical and social institutions to foster a sense of cohesion. Institutions such as the market, the political system, cultural festivals and religious rituals, life cycle events, and behaviors, help tie the members together as part of an extended (kinship) network. Ethnic and lineal membership in the community provides the individual with an identity that is also reflected in and reflects where she/he lives. Thus, when one first enters a traditional area as a "stranger" (an outsider) to settle or to engage in extensive transactions, it is customary to formally greet the chief who has the power to facilitate the stranger's acceptance. Most members' daily activities and transactions are contained within the bounds of the physically demarcated community space, in effect helping to reinforce their ties. It is a shared culture.

In complex society, for example urban West Africa, life can be fundamentally different. Here, unlike in the face-to-face society, "there is nothing automatic about cultural sharing" (Hannerz 1992:44). The division of labor generates divisions in knowledge and life experience. Communication is uneven and fragmented, redundancy in information transfer less likely, specialization abounds, scale in relationships varies wildly, relationships are often narrowly defined and transient, ambiguity is common. Thus, "the full context of cultural externalizations [is rendered] opaque, rather than fairly transparent as it would be in the small-scale society" (Hannerz 1992: 44).

The colonial city (King 1995) instantiates such a culturally and spatially complex place. A characteristic of the primary cities along the coast of West Africa was that each was founded early in the twentieth century by a colonial power. Like colonial cities elsewhere in the world, the West African variety was developed by foreigners to promote their own interests and mushroomed in growth after the Second World War (Rayfield 1974:173). In such a city, the colonizer's program had a particular impact on the indigenous people's social and physical spaces and on the urban system.

The so-called "modern technologies" of planning and architecture "are employed to build these new societies and indoctrinate citizens within the spatial confines of rationally planned towns" (Low 1996:395). While urbanization has often been destructive to traditional patterns of life and thus of diversity of life, a crucial side-effect of such planning, often not planned, is that neighborhoods and communities make the city manageable for the residents. These urban places may be clearly delineated or may exist as intangible essences. Thirty years ago, Suzanne Keller wrote that such a place may be "a fluid, vaguely defined subpart of a town or a city whose boundaries are only vaguely apparent and differently perceived by its inhabitants" (Keller 1968:12). What matters is that it embodies a physical order and its social institutions encapsulate meaning, which in turn residents reproduce through their daily activities. Since, for example, Accra is large, one cannot know or use the whole city. Thus, a local neighborhood or community "becomes an area intermediate between the dwelling and the whole city, which is better known, with which one has more identification (however minimal) than the larger, unknown area" (Rapoport 1980a:71).

For many of Sabon Zongo's residents, the community is a point of orientation to the urban system. As in other cities, this developing cultural local identity is informed by the urban institutional structure. But there is also something about this particular space that has transformed it into a place of great significance to those who choose to live there, despite its material deterioration.

The social institutions, activities, and attachment of residents to the *zongo* are enacted daily: through residents' relation to the myths of origin of the place and to its "first families" through memories, social networks, and social institutions (including associations, schools, occupations, religion, and chieftaincy) evoked through the physicality of place. Hausa ethnicity was fundamental to Sabon Zongo's establishment. And unlike any other *zongo* in Accra, it was consciously founded *by* Hausa *for* Hausa. Clientage was a primary characteristic as well. In particular, it was the followers (clients) of local leader Malam Bako who were the original settlers, to whom he allocated land and whom he made the first landlords.

But Sabon Zongo is an amalgam of traditions, an urban community; while as in other West African cities, ethnicity still matters, in Sabon Zongo, it is not the defining feature of life. Ethnicity and clientelism have been powerful explanatory social constructs since the blossoming of West African urban ethnography in the late 1960s and 1970s. They were employed to explain questions relating to the migration of individuals, the impact of the city on traditional lifeways, the creation of new role structures, and responses to pluralism. Urban ethnicity became an important sub-set of the last (Cohen 1974; du Toit 1978), with even the *zongo* as a focus of study (Cohen 1969; Schildkrout 1978).

In his analysis of a Hausa migrant community (Sabo) in the Yoruba city of Ibadan, Abner Cohen (1969) presents ethnicity as an adaptive means to organizing political relationships and monopolizing long-distance trade. Sabo social organization was based upon the activities of the Hausa patrons (*masu gida*), the business landlords. For them, he wrote, Hausaness was an expression of economic control, and their command over housing (as landlords) was a command of economic power. Their customs and institutions "contributed in important ways to the formation of a closely knit Hausa community" (Cohen 1969:

15). In nearby Mushin, another Yoruba locale, Barnes (1986) also utilized ethnicity and clientelism to understand how low-status indigenous and migrant Yoruba gain and use power. Like Cohen, she revealed the advantage of house ownership as it brought in clients to the landlord and reinforced his prestige. In a third important study of a migrant community, Schildkrout (1978) focused on the Mossi living among the influential migrant Hausa in Kumase *zongo* in Ghana. Unlike the case presented by Cohen for Ibadan's Sabo, Mossi economic specialization did not follow ethnic lines, and compound life fostered the abandonment of traditional identities while Islam supported cultural integration. And yet, ethnicity persisted as a basis for Mossi social organization. According to Schildkrout, this is because ethnicity operated in the domains of kinship and politics and in fact was the glue that tied the Mossi together.

All of this fine work on ethnicity, migration, urbanization, and community formation is physically anchored, but for each, the locale is simply a backdrop. I take my cue from the more recent urban anthropological work that implicitly engages Gell's theory of secondary agency: considering place as an active participant in social life, exploring the relation between built form and culture in seeking out spatial meanings (Pellow 1991; Rodman and Cooper 1989; Rotenberg 1993; Low 2000). Such studies examine how "the organisation of space comes to have meaning and how those meanings [are] maintained through social interaction" (Moore 1986:74; see also Lawrence and Low 1990; 2002). And in these days of post-colonialism, it has become clear that any understanding of contemporary urbanism also requires an understanding of the cultural imprint of colonialism on the socio-spatial order, the manifestation of relations of power (King 1976; 1990).

The problem of power is implicit in the anthropological problem of place, "the problem of the culturally defined locations to which ethnographies refer. Such named locations . . . constitute the landscape of anthropology" (Appadurai 1988:16). The problem of place, and the intrinsic issue of power, frames this study. I examine the physical *zongo* both as an anchor and as a secondary agent: its public spaces, streets, mosques, and compounds extend human social agency. I consider how social categories cross-cut time and space and how social activities and exchange in effect produce the boundaries of the neighborhood. The Hausa cultural pattern of regulating relations among people is extended into and re-worked by the wider community of Sabon Zongo. It is the key to understanding how the community works. At the same time that Sabon Zongo has reproduced its social order based on Hausa principles, it has also produced change, it has evolved into a different kind of post-colonial urban community.

Here, patterns extracted from the cultural lifeways of numerous "stranger" groups have been melded together to create a new urban culture. Like city dwellers everywhere, the residents must learn how to negotiate the city. My earlier work leads me to believe that while the boundedness is cultural, it is not exclusively ethnic; it is based upon a collective identity that transcends Hausa ethnicity. It is a zongo-ness, which is produced and re-produced in time and space. The community is organized by genealogy and bound together by the place affiliation expressed in zongo-ness, which includes webs of exchange based on a combination of kinship, ethnicity, religion, hierarchy, and propinquity. It is born of social relationships, knit into social networks, played out in cycles of observances and activities, which are found within the community or its enclosed neighborhoods, anchored in and communicated through the material environment. This place and its meaning is represented and enacted daily, and "continually woven into the fabric of social life, anchoring it to features of the landscape and blanketing it with layers of significance . . . In large ways and small, [people] are forever performing acts that reproduce and express their own sense of place—and also, inextricably, their own understandings of who and what they are" (Basso 1996:57).

In a pioneering essay, Kuper (1972) wrote that as sites are pieces of social space that become symbols within the system of communication, social relations are differentially articulated in different sites.

There is a condensation of values in particular sites, and transactions that constitute the totality of social life may be spatially mapped with specific sites expressing relatively durable structured interests and related values. (421)

Sabon Zongo is such a site; it condenses the values of zongo-ness. In its redefinition from the traditional milieu, Sabon Zongo reveals the social production of space. Since there is a mental blueprint that guides the structure's layout, "a traditional model can, therefore, incorporate into its timelessness, structures from different times" (Kuper 1972:421).

This is not to say, however, that the *zongo* is simply a village transported to an urban space. It is part of the urban system. It shares institutions with the rest of Accra, even as its residents know that Sabon Zongo suffers because of uneven development. The social environment is flexible and adaptable: for example, Hausa is an inclusive ethnic category and the people both intramarry within and intermarry between groups. The spatial environment is flexible as well; this is clearly manifest in the public spaces (new neighborhoods, street trading and new services) and in the compound. The house particularly embodies tensions between lineage culture and urban culture. Through the commodification of domestic space, as owners alienate property by selling or renting it to make money, they destroy the localized core of the family by introducing tenants.

Sabon Zongo is not ethnically homogeneous, as such a village might be in Hausaland[2]; and unlike Cohen's Sabo (1969:36), the moral universe of the settlers is neither exclusively Hausa nor confined to the *zongo*. The meaning of this urban *zongo* community appears to derive from the realities of social relationships and cultural values. As Bestor notes, it is "the mundane, almost unnoticed but nonetheless significant institutions of urban neighborhood life—the texture and structure of social relationships" (Bestor 1989:9)—that is ethnographically compelling.

THE STORY UNFOLDS

In the course of the next seven chapters, I shall tell the story of Malam Bako's *zongo*—how it has evolved and its institutions solidified—through the intertwined dimensions of society and space over time. For heuristic purposes, I have separated the two dimensions wherever possible in order to better show how each operates. But in fact, the spatial is culturized and the social is spatialized, and the two are mutually reinforcing.

Chapter 2 explores the socio-spatial history of Accra: in a quick overview of the capital city today, I consider the cultural dimensions such as ethnic and linguistic components, the city's economic base and its infrastructure. This is followed by a historical look at the indigenous establishment of Accra, its colonization by Europeans and the colonial impact on social and physical space— the politics of spatial allocation, the delimitation of neighborhoods, and the housing designed and built—and the messages conveyed.

Chapter 3 opens at the turn of the twentieth century as Accra's Muslim enclave sought to organize itself politically in terms of secular and religious leadership. I focus on the early Muslim strangers who lived downtown in the midst of the Ga, their leadership struggles and the emergence of Malam Bako, son of Malam Idris Bako Nenu, as an important patron. As Malam Bako's followers expanded and seemingly irreparable disagreements among the different Muslim ethnic groups erupted, Bako sought to establish his new community, Sabon Zongo. He organized it along the lines of Hausa officialdom and founded his own "royal" line. But even there, leadership problems emerged. The chapter considers the early social and spatial organization of Sabon Zongo.

Chapter 4 describes Sabon Zongo in terms of its physical distinctiveness and the social implications of that distinctiveness: its separateness from the old downtown area and its boundaries, as well as internal physical boundaries, including axes of orientation and elements of the built environment. A major interest is how the community's physical layout and its constituent elements enable community organization and lifestyle.

In Chapter 5, I isolate four primary elements of identification that are the glue of Sabon Zongo. These are: kinship, which through its intertwining genealogies, carries corporate identification; Hausa ethnicity, which is expansive but still creates bonding; Islam; and, the formal ties of patrons and clients. While there are many people resident in Sabon Zongo who are not obviously hooked in through any combination of these four elements (because they are not Muslim, Hausa, or house owners), I believe that the overarching (or underlying) solidarity of such bonds enables belongingness even among them.

Basic to my thesis is the idea that community routines and interpersonal ties cross-cut and anchor attachment to the physical place of Sabon Zongo. Chapter 6 explores the lifeways of contemporary residents and the meaningful spaces, whether artifactual or conceptual, which anchor everyday activities and which along with the activities are routinized. I consider various domains of exchange or transactions that help socialize the residents of Sabon Zongo, as zongo-ites and as urbanites as well.

Chapters 7 and 8 both focus on the compound, its physical elements and its social content. In the compounds practice and exchange are also spatially and temporally transacted, reproduced and changed. Chapter 7 sets the stage. Here I analyse the socio-spatial systems of Sabon Zongo's compound housing. I begin by describing the typical housing in Northern Nigeria (provenance of the first settlers in Sabon Zongo) and southern Ghana (the location of Accra). The basis for this discussion and analysis is a sample of 19 compounds.[3] The encoding of gender is particularly important as well as how it has evolved over time, as the principles of seclusion have diminished. I have categorized the compounds as follows: the original model and its emulators; variations on the Hausa family compound; and the evolved forms of tenant and nuclear family homes.

As social systems, the compound houses in Sabon Zongo are "performative" (Sahlins 1985). In Chapter 8 I look at how the compound space is used for staging life and for socializing adults and children alike, and how the spatial transformations discussed in Chapter 7 are expressed in domestic social behavior. Chapter 8 discusses the draw of Sabon Zongo, the importance of house ownership, and the rights and status it confers, how Hausa have held onto property and how non-Hausa have acquired it. Many who live there now are renters. How do they gain housing and like owners, how do they use their domestic space? What are the social meanings that have come to characterize compound life?

In her study of ethnicity and politics in Mossi *zongo* in Kumase, Schildkrout (1978:266) speaks of a "zongo culture," of "the adoption of new values and new ways of doing things" as generated by the processes of Islamization and Hausaization. I too have come to the conclusion that the fundaments of life in Sabon Zongo reduce to a concept of "zongo-ness," what I call *zongwanci*. While *zongwanci* is a kind of northern ethos that derives from the intertwining of Islam and Hausaness, neither is it simply ethnic-based nor is it only kin-based. Chapter 9, the Conclusion, fleshes it out, to better understand it as it cross-cuts ethnicity, as an idiomatic representation of the lifeways and boundedness of this community and its residents. I suggest that it is basic to the ties that bind, to the overarching shared morality, to the attachment that residents feel for the community. It is operationalized by exchange as social practice in everyday life and defines the boundaries of Sabon Zongo.

NOTES

1. Rapoport (1980a:68) speaks of the facilitating environment and its cues.
2. Nor is it like Bestor's Miyamoto-cho—a cookie cutter-like neighborhood in Tokyo (Bestor 1989).
3. See the Appendix for details of the houses chosen.

2

THE URBAN CULTURAL CONTEXT

Al-laah Ak-baar! The electrified voice of the muezzin at Abokin Ango mosque wafts through the air at 7:00 P.M., calling Muslims for Isha'i, the last mandatory prayer of the day. The kebob sellers have their fires going, the Night Market and street-side prepared food sellers are sitting behind their kerosene lamps waiting for customers.

George, a Christian resident at Sabon Zongo, walks down the main road to The Shooters. He sits at one of the few tables, on a makeshift chair, in the tiny outdoors area, walled off from the road by wooden latticework. He drinks a Club beer and, over the noise of the Afro-beat music, chats with some friends. At Bus Stop, he catches a "tro-tro" (lorry) to Circle, one of the main termini in Accra. Once there, he threads his way through the aisles of traders selling household appliances, watches, McVitie's biscuits and Cadbury's chocolate, fresh pineapples. At the traffic light, he stops to eye the second-hand clothing market—the slacks and shirts, Italian sandals and Timberland boots. Crossing the Ring Road, he sees the prostitutes en route to Piccadilly, a popular bar/dance place. He walks toward the Overhead Bridge, past the Forex Bureau, where one can buy and sell American dollars, pounds sterling, guilder, marks, Nigerian naira and West African CFA (the currency of former French West African colonies).

He hops a taxi that drives the Osu route, gets off at Danquah Circle, and walks down "Oxford Street," the hip area of the city close-by to the tony suburb of Cantonments. Here at corner stands one can buy "European" vegetables, like lettuce and green peppers, and at Lebanese shops, cracked wheat bread and imported food items like butter, cheese and jams. There are upscale restaurants like the elegant Dynasty, a Mandarin Chinese institution, and fast food establishments like Frankie's, the white-washed build-

ing with blue neon lights, with a take-out pastry shop. The Berlin Connection has hardwood floors for dance, the chrome tables have plush leather
chairs, the ceiling has gray sponge work, on certain nights there are Salsa
lessons. Off on the side streets are boutiques that carry imported men's and
women's shoes and clothing. He sees Africans and Europeans, people on
foot and others in Benz cars, women in Ghanaian "slits" and clam digger
pants, Moschino shoes and local sandals. A few people queue at the Bar-
clays Bank ATM.

George is meeting a friend at one of the new small clubs. While he is
sitting outside waiting for the music, he buys some kebobs from an ambulatory food trader who carries them on a tray on her head. Since after an
hour, neither his friend nor the DJ have shown up, George decides to go
home, retracing his route back to *zongo*. Across Oblogo Road, the all-night
church service has just begun. He falls asleep to the sound of 100 congregants singing "Jesus Loves Me."

Accra is a cosmopolitan city. It has the only international airport in the country. It boasts one five-star and several four-star hotels. On the perimeter of the
old downtown area, there are many modern multi-story office buildings, the
marble conference center known as The Pink Lady, the boat-shaped National
Theatre. Fanning out beyond the semi-circular Ring Road, there are numerous
suburban areas. Accra is also home to a variety of so-called traditional enclaves. In the Ga areas of James Town and Ussher Town as at the "strangers"
home of Sabon Zongo, family rites of passage and ethnic festivals are publicly celebrated and family houses are steeped in memories that go back one
hundred years.

Accra's diverse lifeways are undergirded by the city's role as the administrative and commercial center of Ghana. It has been the seat of government and
the primary city of Ghana since 1877, when the British moved their headquarters
there, and the capital of the independent country since 1957, when Ghana became the first sub-Saharan African country to gain Independence. Accra consists
of three districts: Accra, Tema (the port), and the Ga District. Colonialism and
modernization in Ghana, as in much of the Third World, have affected spatial
and social differences within Accra itself. This chapter begins with a brief sense
of Accra today, before exploring its socio-spatial history: 1) the establishment
of the Ga as Accra's indigenous people, 2) the arrival of the Europeans, and 3)
how neighborhoods and housing have evolved there.

MODERN ACCRA: A BRIEF GAZE

Accra sits on the Atlantic Ocean, at the base of the Akwapim-Togo mountain
range (see Figure 1). Over the last century, it has grown from a series of Ga
fishing villages to a capital city with a population estimated to be about
2,100,000 in 1995,[1] which accounts for 13 percent of the country's population.

Figure 1
Map of Contemporary Accra. Drawn by Mark Hauser.

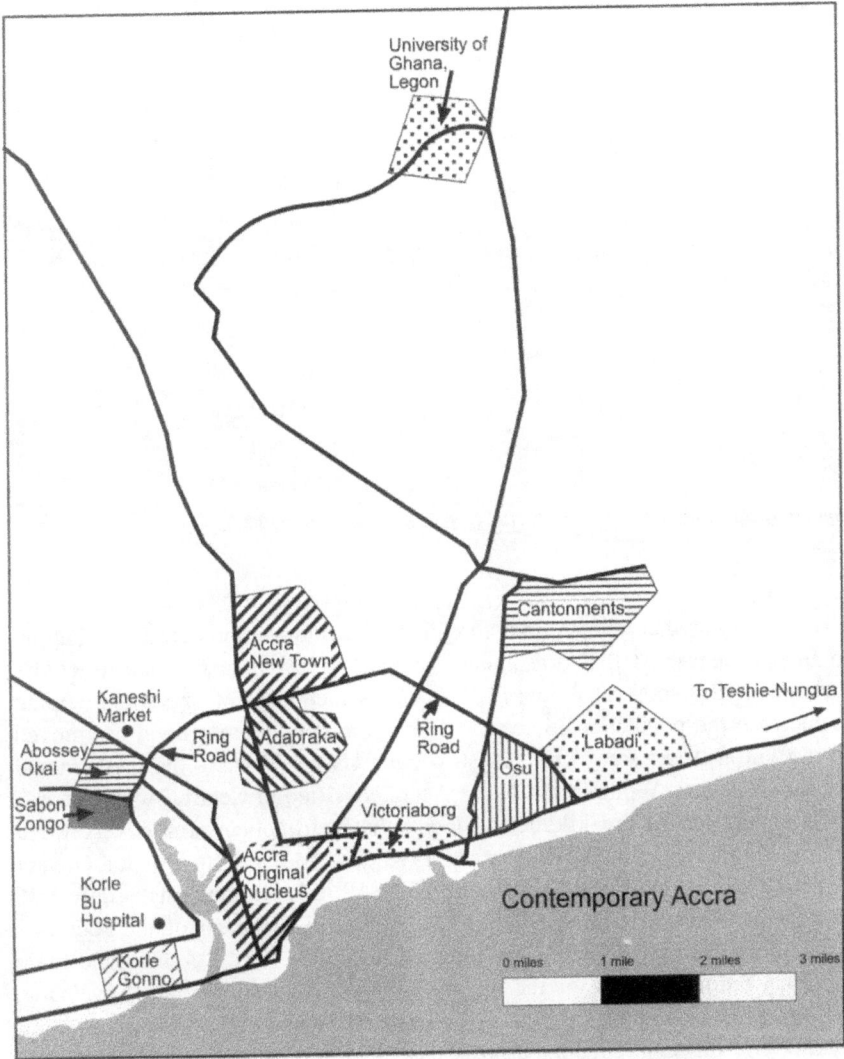

Unlike many African cities, Accra has an ancient history of authochthonous developments. For hundreds of years it participated in coastal trade and assimilated populations of different origins: Ga, Akan, Ewe, Sierra Leonean, Hausa, Europeans, and others. It thus represents a curious melange of history and migration, of European colonization and post-colonial social and economic inequalities. It has had the status of a primate city, what Konadu-Agyemang (1998:

Table 2.1
The Growth of Accra in the Twentieth Century

Year	Population
1901	17,895
1911	18,574
1921	38,049
1931	61,558
1948	135,926
1954	192,047
1960	337,828
1970	633,880
1985	1,400,000
1990	1,700,000
1995	2,100,000
2000	2,725,896

Source: Adapted from Arn 1996:433, AMA 1996, and Twum-Baah 2000.

69) refers to as that of the "favored child" at least since the decade leading up to Independence. At that time, many activists involved in nationalist activity throughout British West Africa used Accra as their base of operation, helping to increase the population. Since the 1960s, the population growth has moved from Central Accra areas like Jamestown and Ussher Town to the northern and western outskirts. While in the 1870s Accra consisted of Central Accra, an area of less than ten square kilometers, today the metropolitan area covers 1,079 square kilometers (Konadu-Agyemang 1998:69). And still, as a region Greater Accra (which includes the port city of Tema 18 miles to the east) is only 1.36 percent of Ghana's land area, while it contains 15.8 percent of the country's population. Currently, "the Accra-Tema Metropolitan Area has the highest rate of urbanization, and one of the highest in West Africa" (Konadu-Agyemang, 1998:69). Its current growth rate is 4.7 percent per annum.

This city has contradictory aspects. As an administrative center, Accra has created the necessary peaceful environment and the infrastructure that enabled the cocoa trade to thrive (Konadu-Agyemang 2001:65). It has also been derided by some as an economic parasite on the rest of the country, a bastion of neo-colonialism (Konadu-Agyemang 2001). Moreover, terrible social and spatial inequities abound and many of its residents live in deprived conditions.

Such problems fall within the purview of the governing local body. The Accra Metropolitan Assembly (AMA), one of 110 district assemblies in the country, is supposed to maximize the local government's role in raising resources, providing services, expanding linkages with the rural areas, stimulating private investment, and implementing national development policies (Mousset-Jones 1999:37). The AMA's tasks include oversight of public toilets, waste management, and city markets (cleaning, maintenance, provision of electricity and water, patrolling). "It functions as a single-tier local government authority responsible for the development of the city" (Larbi 1996:199). The AMA is battling a deteriorating and insufficient infrastructure, and impossible vehicular congestion as public transportation is inadequate (the ownership of automobiles has far outstripped the capacity of city roads, most of which are two-lane, and in the central city, are also clogged with ambulatory hawkers and traders who illegally claim the sidewalk as their stalls).

Unfortunately, the ability of the local councils to remedy these problems has been impeded by their composition. The AMA and others are made-up of

government sympathizers ... to the extent the city administration has always been an extension of the political party or military junta in power. Just as the various colonial governors appointed their supporters or at least people who were sympathetic to their cause to the council, so have the various post-independence administrations manipulated the membership even where elections were held. (Konadu-Agyemang 2001:96)

This legacy of favoritism has combined with the usual twin scourges of mismanagement and corruption. As in other African cities, "Accra's fast growth over the years has exceeded the capacity of the Accra City Council and the central government to provide adequate infrastructure for the burgeoning population and to maintain existing facilities" (Konadu-Agyemang 1998:81). These conditions have made some areas "better" than others and have led to the uneven provision of facilities and upkeep in communities throughout the city. "Perhaps most critically of all, the physical environment is suffering from gross misuse and an absence of long term planning" (Konadu-Agyemang 2001:97).

More than 60 percent of the city's population live in areas such as Central Accra, Accra New Town or Fadama, that are poorly serviced or badly deteriorated. Some have no sanitation system whatsoever. The inadequacy of garbage pick-up, in combination with indiscriminate dumping of refuse and an inferior drainage system, have led to periodic flooding. Given these problems and that of mosquito (malaria) control, the population is subject to health hazards. On the other hand, the provision of potable water has been successful; it is available throughout Accra (Addae 1997:167).

Something about Accra's social style fascinates, perhaps due in part to trade—"the involvement of a very high proportion of the populace in trade may be its single most conspicuous social feature" (Dakubu 1997:21). It is Accra's commercial functioning that has produced the city's growth and prosperity. The commercial vitality and vibrancy of the city goes back as early as the mid-seventeenth century when Accra was "the major center for the gold trade on the West African coast" (Robertson 1984:29). One hundred years later, Accra was a center for trade from Asante, the north and the east. In the nineteenth century, with the slowing down and cessation of the slave trade, the principal commercial items were ivory and gold dust in exchange for gunpowder, rum, and cloth. The second half of the nineteenth century saw a shift in the occupations of many local Ga men from farming and fishing to skilled labor. Coincident with this change was an increase in educational opportunities for the Ga men as well as positions in the civil service (Robertson 1984).

Market trade flourished under colonialism and urbanization, and with men taking specialized jobs, the market became the province of women, especially Ga women. As markets expanded, so did the women's participation in them. Trading is the largest occupational category in Ghana. Thirty-two percent of Accra's employed are traders, leading some to characterize Accra's economy as a kiosk economy. Trading still carries the greatest financial potential for an untrained or illiterate woman. Indeed according to Robertson (1984:77), "approximately 70 to 75 percent of Accra Ga women were traders in the twentieth century." While the majority of the market women today are not big earners, the market in Accra is still one of "the last realms of influence left to women" (Robertson 1983:476).

Every neighborhood seems to have its local market, though most traders operate downtown in Accra's Central Business District (CBD) bounded by the Ring Road and the coast. The core of the CBD is an outgrowth of the traditional Ga section in downtown Accra and home of several of Accra's famous markets—Makola, Salaga, and Timber Market. Makola Market, the primary wholesale and retail market in Accra, was razed in 1979 when the women traders were blamed for Ghana's economic woes (Robertson 1983). Many women prefer to shop at the downtown markets, believing they have more variety, fresher produce, better prices, than the neighborhood ones. But women also patronize the local markets, such as those at Adabraka and Kaneshie (at Kaneshie, a popular night market also operates). Sabon Zongo's Freedom Market is not particularly well-known and it is somewhat dilapidated, but given its convenient location on the southern edge of the community, Sabon Zongo women do shop there.

Most traders operate in the informal sector. When Keith Hart first coined the term "informal sector" to represent the economic life of people who support themselves outside of the wage-employment economy (Hart 1973), he demonstrated that in Accra, such a work force was large. This continues to be the case in Accra and in Ghana more generally. According to an ILO (International Labor Organization) estimate, "informal-sector employment in Ghana increased from 89% in 1970 to 553% of the total number employed in the formal sector in 1990" (Boeh-Ocansey 1997:8). And in the urban areas, 60 to 85 percent of all those employed in 1990 worked in the informal sector. Most have little or no education, earn very little, and their businesses are not registered. "[T]hese are the producers and suppliers of most of the material requirements and services needed by the rest of Ghanaian society" (Boeh-Ocansey 1997:13).

But Accra's commercial life goes well beyond the informal sector. Ghana's government has adopted the rhetoric of economic globalization while advertising the country as "a friendly, safe, cheap, gateway location for doing global business" (cited in Grant 2001:999). In 1983, Ghana was one of the first African countries to implement a structural adjustment program (SAP), known as the Economic Recovery Program (ERP), and thus became a SAP poster child for the International Monetary Fund (IMF). The goals of SAP included initiating market reform by liberalizing the economy and attracting foreign direct investment (Grant 2001:999). Social spending was curbed in favor of debt repayment. In 1999, 655 foreign companies were active in the Accra metro area; the last time foreign investment had surged into Ghana was in the 1920s during the cocoa boom (Grant 2001:1002). The government is continuing Nkrumah's policy of promoting Accra as a growth pole for the national economy by making the capital city into a connecting node with the world economy and global capital (Grant 2001:1011). The uneven spatial effects of globalization has meant that 84 percent of all foreign companies established in Ghana since 1983 are headquartered in Accra, where they engage in producer services, consumer services, trade and mining (Grant 2001:1003). Strategic to their decision to headquarter in Accra was access to international transportation hubs and proximity to financial and governmental institutions (Grant 2001:1004).

The fastest growing area for foreign involvement is producer services, one of which is "back office" computing work, chiefly data entry. Aetna Health Insurance and Keystone Mercy Health Care have moved some of their data processing to downtown Accra. There, at the U.S.-based ACS Inc., 400 Ghanaians connected to the United States by satellite are working in three eight-hour shifts. The work involves punching the raw claims data sent to them from the U.S. companies onto computerized forms and then sending it back to the United States by satellite for final processing.

You have to imagine this scene: You step off the steamy streets of Accra, go up three floors, and all you see in every direction is a sea of young Ghanaians doing data processing on computers, in air-conditioned rooms with a radio playing, "Don't Worry, Be Happy." (Friedman 2001)

According to Bossman Dowuona-Hammond, the Ghana manager for ACS, Ghana is the first African country to get into this sort of tele-computing. The company is planning to expand from 400 to 1,000 later this year, because they expect UPS and American Express to move some of their data entry there as well. The Church of Latter Day Saints now also has a tele-computing office in Accra. Other data processing firms have been scouting out Ghana for their back office computing work. Not only does this help connect Ghana globally; it is a financial boon for the workers; but it is also a boon for the companies. While the best ACS processors earn about $300 per month (just under Ghana's average *annual* income), get free transport to work, health care and meals, this is a fraction of what the companies would be paying data entry workers in the United States.

Part of promoting Accra as a gateway to the world has meant at least in theory giving priority to the city's physical infrastructure. In fact, urban planning was tackled as part of ERP because of spatial problems. Rules regulating such things as street plans and housing additions are based on favoritism because of the way social and cultural identification works: primary loyalties going to extended families and hometown kin (Larbi 1996). ERP's Urban I focused particularly on Accra:

The absence of effective governmental control led to a situation in which buildings sprang up on nearly every vacant land site in . . . Accra. Open spaces and road reservations were encroached upon by rich people and people with connections, with the connivance of public officials, who took advantage of weak planning and development controls. (Larbi 1996:195)

Residential crowding in the capital city has been high. According to the Ghana Population Censuses, between 1948 and 1960 in Accra, the number of persons per dwelling increased from 14.2 to 18.4 while the number of persons per room was 2.6. This kind of crowding has worsened since 1960 (Obudho and Mhlanga 1988:13). The most densely populated areas in Accra are still James Town and Ussher Town, the original nucleus, where congestion is terrific. In these indigenous Ga coastal neighborhoods, many people continue to maintain family houses, with room density as high as eight persons, and as many as 16–20 households in each house (Ghana 1992). Private toilet facilities are rare in the coastal neighborhoods, so that the majority rely on public latrines and some openly relieve themselves on the beaches.

The area of "Old Accra" has cultural, religious and spiritual significance for the Ga, the single largest ethnic group in Accra, who have been there for over 300 years (see the next section). Organizational membership is high in these areas, especially township, occupational (fishing) and *homowo* festival associations. By the same token, it is a deprived area, home to "one of Ghana's most vulnerable risk groups in terms of poverty, dilapidation, morbidity and mortality" (Bremer 2000).

In addition to the Ga, the city is now home to about 100 ethnic groups— including the southern Akan, eastern Ewe, northern Dagomba, Dagati, Frafra, and foreign Africans. About 70 percent of Accra's population is composed of migrants, almost an equal percentage of female as male. Their migration to Accra was generally economically-motivated (Peil 1972; Sandbrook 1977). Even as many of the migrants maintain their ethnic identity through various associations and festivals, the fluidity of ethnicity facilitates their redefinition into more encompassing regional units.

Bound up with the city's economy of trade and, according to Dakubu, another fascinating element in Accra's style, is the city's multi-lingualism. Both multi-lingualism and extreme polyglotism in Accra, characteristic also of the rest of sub-Saharan West Africa, refer mainly to the use of a variety of African languages. On the coast, urbanization does not currently imply linguistic homogenization and there is no apparent tendency toward the reduction of multi-lingualism. The polyglotism is adaptive and not due to education or travel but to the daily activities engaged in, especially in the urban context (Dakubu 1997: 24f.).[2]

This practical acquisition and use of language is in keeping with the relationship between social groups, their activities and their spatial environment. Accra's immediate hinterland is dominated by Akan speakers, which has affected the situation in Accra. Again, Dakubu reminds us that market location, goods sold, and languages used are closely related (Dakubu 1997).

There is a long-standing tradition of physical separation of strangers or foreigners, and if we look at Accra in terms of language areas, we see that Ga is a strong presence in Central Accra, especially below Ussher Fort; it has been separated out by a commercial belt, by a physical barrier, and by public facilities. Accra's settlement pattern distinguishes historically and spatially Ga and non-Ga at the first level and southern Ghanaian (Ga-Akan-Ewe) and West African (other nationals) the next level down (Dakubu 1997).

In the old Ga area of Central Accra (James Town, Ussher Town, Zongo Lane), the major first languages and major non-Ghanaian lingua francas of the resident population are Ga, Akan and English, with smaller numbers speaking Dangme, Ewe, and Hausa (Dakubu 1997:53). The acquisition of Twi (Akan) and Hausa are associated with living in Accra:

Although Hausa was spoken by very few respondents, most of those who did speak it had acquired it in Accra, contrary to the assumptions of most southern Ghanaians, who firmly believe that Hausa is spoken mainly in the north. (Dakubu 1997:60)

Akan is the dominant second language spoken in Central Accra. At Zongo Lane, most non-Ga migrants learn both Akan and Ga. Ewe speakers are present in significant numbers but fewer Ewe speak a second language than do members of other ethnic groups (Dakubu 1997:66).

As a British colony, the English language was brought in to serve as the formal language of the land and continues to be so. Thus it continues to be used in government venues, such as Parliament and the courts. Children are socialized into English usage. Primary school, which children enter at age six, is supposed to be taught in English; in fact, many schools use the local language for the first 3 or so years, but then, in addition to teaching English, they move over to teaching in English. The English language is also used and taught throughout Junior Secondary and Senior Secondary School (Boeh-Ocansey 1997).

Thus, Accra today is epitomized by contradictory impulses that play out in diverse lifeways. There are many who continue to live in ethnic enclaves, speak their own vernacular, and pursue traditional occupations; and yet, they are still part of this Western-oriented city. Few people are untouched by Accra's metropolitanism. Moreover, there is enough of a forward-looking population, who are credentialing themselves to accommodate Western ideas, that Accra has the human potential to connect with global social and economic enterprise.

EARLY SETTLEMENTS

The impact of colonialism on Accra led some observers to characterize it as a "relatively typical Black African city" (Lisowska 1984:115), but Accra is distinctive, tied to a particular social and spatial history of settlement of Ghana's coastal areas in general and Accra in particular (Ward 1948; Acquah 1958; Bosman 1967 [new edition, 1967]; Parker 2000). Until the fifteenth century, the Kpesi (a branch of the Guan, an Akan people) were likely the Gold Coast's only known inhabitants, and they lived in the Accra plains. During the fifteenth century, the Gas, of whom the Accras form one group, came along the eastern coast, in extended family groups, founding villages among the Kpesi. They established "a series of contiguous settlements" which make up the Ga whole (Robertson 1984:27). Because of the aridity of the coastal plain, agriculture was limited, so the Ga took up fishing, saltmaking, and, by the seventeenth century, trading with the Europeans (Parker 2000). They were concentrated around Ayawaso, eight miles northwest of modern-day Accra.

When the Ga moved to the coast they formed a series of villages, some of whom merged to become Accra quarters. Not long after settling at Ayawaso, the Accras moved their capital to Small Accra—the area between the not-yet-constructed James and Ussher Forts. Here, it was hoped, there would be better trade possibilities with the Portuguese, hostilities notwithstanding. Other Ga tribes accepted the Accra supremacy and moved as well. While the Accras were enjoying prosperity, the Akwamu moved into the area north of Accra in modern Akim Abuakwa. From their perch, they looked over the Akwapim ridges to the peopled plains of Guan villages and isolated Ga towns. They commanded the main trade route from Accra inland.

By the late 1600s, coastal trade had grown and its exchange with the hinterland was controlled by three states: the Akwamu, the Akim, and the Denkyira. As the Akwamu expanded, they took over control of the trade routes and in the late 1600s, the Akwamu destroyed the two areas of Great Accra and Little Accra. Their authority went unchallenged from 1680–1730.

But by the early 1700s, Accra had recovered, and it became the capital of a Ga federation, which extended from the plains to the Volta River (Ward 1948: 52). In 1733, two Akim groups and other neighboring peoples took on the Akwamu. "The truth is that, as the Akwamu themselves relate with a sort of gloomy pride, they had been thoroughly bad neighbors to all around them, and every neighboring state jumped at the chance of expelling them" (Ward 1948: 104). The war lasted fifteen months and ended with Accra having recovered her independence.

The Ga family groups reorganized themselves into nuclei of towns, of which Accra became one. After the Akwamu conquest in the 1670s, the nuclei of Ga towns invited stranger-groups to join them. These groups retained their respective traditions and helped keep up numbers and strength in the event of a hostile incursion (Amoah 1964).

The oldest Accra quarters, Asere, Abola, Gbese, and Otublohum, constitute what is known as Ussher Town. There the Dutch established Fort Crevecoeur (re-named Ussher Fort by the British) in 1650. The other three quarters, Alata, Sempe, and Akumadje are referred to as James Town, which became a British area of jurisdiction. James Fort, 500 yards from Crevecoeur, was built by the British in 1673. The Osu Ga were located three miles east. There the Swedes built Christiansborg Castle in 1657. It became the Danish headquarters and is currently the office of Ghana's President (Figure 2). Ussher Town, James Town and Osu Ga came to form the nucleus of the city of Accra; Ussher Town and James Town make up what is now known as Central Accra. All have chiefs called *mantsemei* (sing. *mantse*, literally "father of the town") (Parker 2000:9). The Ga paramount chief located his family on Okai Kwai Hill. The town which grew up around it was Great Accra, while its coastal sister was Small Accra (Amoah 1964).

In addition to the Ga and Kpeshis, Akwamu, Akim, and Fante were also living in the European-controlled areas. Then the British West African Trading Company "brought Yoruba people from Lagos [Nigeria] as servants; they came to form a relatively prosperous and respected community in Accra" (Arn 1996: 423). The various ethnic groups took the language of the Ga, adopted some of their customs and ceremonies and intermarried with them (Arn 1996).

The eighteenth century witnessed the consolidation of the great Asante empire (Wilks 1975). An Akan people, the Asante settled near Kumase, about 170 miles north of present-day Accra. They developed into an organized state with a strong military and by the mid-eighteenth century defeated the Akwamu and overran the Akim. The defeat of the Akim gave them direct access to the coast and trade. The Asante central government controlled a state trading organization, and it was prepared to go to war to open closed trade routes, such as the roads leading to Accra (Davidson 1974).

The only coastal area not controlled by the Asante was that of Cape Coast held by the Fante Confederacy, another Akan group. Fante and Asante relations improved and soured due to their respective concerns about coastal-inland trade. Asante ultimately declared war on the Fante. Asante maintained nominal rule over Accra until the mid-1820s. "For the period of peak slave exports from the Gold Coast, therefore, Accra was the only port with continuous access to the interior, becoming the main Asante entrepot for guns, ammunition, salt, and

Figure 2
Pre-Independence Accra. Drawn by Mark Hauser.

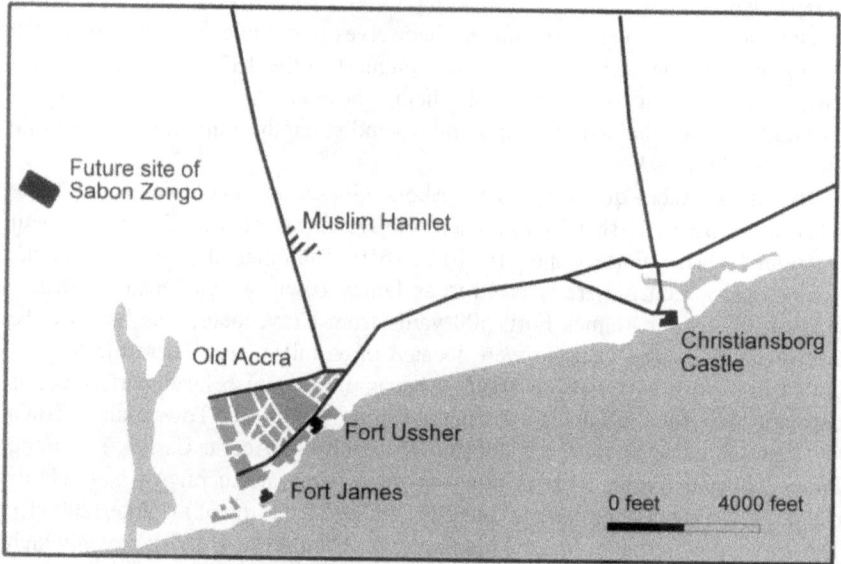

other imports" (Parker 2000:29). Asante imperialism enabled them to control the economic system in which they participated. Trade in Accra flourished, and new forms of wealth deriving from the commercialization led to increasing socio-economic inequality.

Along with the switch away from the slave trade to "legitimate" trade, there was a rise of traders, many of whom were women, of Ga artisans and an emergence of literate African and Euro-African elites. The latter served as brokers between the various Europeans and the Africans. According to Parker (2000), it was Accra's function as a place for exchange, transaction, and power that was basic to the city's urban identity.

EUROPEAN DOMINION

Ga activity notwithstanding, Accra's growth was stimulated by the Europeans, the first of whom were the Portuguese who built a small fort at Accra in 1482. They were attracted by gold. They were followed over the next 100-plus years by the English (arrival 1553), Dutch (1595), Swedes (1640), and Danes (1640s). Coincident with the European arrivals, there were great migrations to the area of new African populations. As the Ga gained political and economic ground, they developed strong contacts with other African ethnic groups, which included intermarrying with them (Robertson 1984). The various Africans established territorial rights and hierarchies and competed over trading links with the Europeans. At the same time, the European powers were vying amongst themselves for trading hegemony. European trade was based in the Europeans' forts and continued into the nineteenth century.

The forts became centers of economic and political power, often stronger than the traditional capitals. Growth of European influence on the Gold Coast corresponded with the increasing number of European powers involved. The forts to the east and west of Accra carried on the export trade in gold and slaves. The profits of slave-trading introduced the greatest European competition, and most of the castles were built in the 1600s to accommodate the slave trade. However, "legitimate trade" in palm oil and kernels, spices, ivory, gold dust, and copra continued throughout the period with Accra as a primary entrepot.

European trade competition led eventually to Britain's economic and political supremacy in the Gold Coast resulting from slaving contests with other European nations, especially the Dutch, and not without disruptive effects on local peoples. The European powers aligned themselves with different ethnic groups: the Dutch supported Asante and the British supported Fante, while both of these African powers were interested in maximizing profits from trade and maintaining security for their people. The Asante provoked a war with the Fante in 1806 and came face to face with the British—the first time an African state was challenging a European power successfully in 1823. Not until 1831 was a treaty signed, settling relations between the British and coastal peoples on the one hand and the Asante on the other. The Asante, unlike the Fante, had always resisted British intervention. It was Asante expansionism that had driven the Fante and other peoples to commit themselves to British protection. Their determination to drive out the British inspired the Asante to invade the Fante domain of Cape Coast-Elmina in 1873–1874. During most of the nineteenth century, the Asante successfully held off the British, using negotiation and military force. However, in 1895, the British invaded Kumase and arrested the Asantehene, and in 1900 finally subdued the Asante in the Yaa Asantewa War.

Once the British established their imperial interests in the Gold Coast, they separated it from Sierra Leone as a distinct colony and made Cape Coast the capital. As Brand (1973) observes, the critical event that favored Accra's future was the decision of the British to transfer their administrative headquarters from Cape Coast to Accra in 1877. The choice of Accra was based on several criteria: Accra was perceived to be superior to Cape Coast because it was cleaner, militarily it was more stable, because it was under the protection of King of Asante and thus would escape the hostilities and disturbances that afflicted Cape Coast, and commercially it was already a flourishing commercial town. Moreover, it was close to Aburi, the "Whiteman's health resort" (Brand 1973:27; Konadu-Agyemang 2001:62).

Missionaries preceded and accompanied the colonial administrators to Ghana. The forts established along the coast had chaplains, whose concern was "not with the conversion of African peoples, but with the spiritual welfare of the European and Eur-African enclaves" (Isichei 1995:59). Africa's first Anglican missionary went to the Gold Coast in 1752. One of the local Fante he converted, Philip Quaque, created a school in the late eighteenth century; this led to a Christian study group that generated the Methodist Church in 1831. Four Basel (Presbyterian) missionaries came in 1828. In 1893 the Roman Catholics arrived and in 1905 the Anglicans (Acquah 1958). Seven more Christian groups followed during the first half of the twentieth century. Christian churches which were African in origin and membership also were established, the earliest, in 1888, the National Baptist Church. Many were revivalistic, embracing faith healing and prophecy (Isichei 1995).

An important result of colonialism has been the imbalance in the urban economic base. "Accra and other coastal entrepots were developed as warehouses rather than factories" (Brand 1972:285). Indeed, until 1874, Accra remained a trading town, although no identifiable business cluster was in evidence in 1873 (Brand 1973:32). Rather, businesses and traders had set up shop along Otoo Street, later renamed High Street. Some of Ghana's largest foreign companies established their headquarters in Accra during the colonial period. These included Cadbury, Standard and Charter, Barclay's, and Coca Cola. In fact, 20 percent of the foreign companies still active were established between 1900 and 1982 (Grant 2001).

With the British transfer of the capital from Cape Coast, Accra also became the administrative headquarters, which stimulated further commercial activity. With the improvement of port facilities and construction of a jetty and breakwater in 1906, Accra grew rapidly (Planning 1992:43). An "economic revolution" hit Accra due to the cocoa boom and the consequent port activity (Arn 1996). Cocoa was first introduced to the Gold Coast by a Ga man, Tetteh Quashie, in the late nineteenth century, and quickly spread.

British control of land and political power was not merely symbolic. By 1900, as we have already seen, they had defeated the highly-organized Asante. But even before 1900, they reduced the power of the Ga, for example, sending the Ga Manche into exile for disobedience (Robertson 1984:28).

SPATIAL AND SOCIAL ENGINEERING

Colonial domination meant control of the means of production; in West Africa this included British ownership of land (Kaniki 1985:384). "In theory all lands in the conquered areas of British West Africa . . . or lands ceded to the British Crown . . . were owned by the Crown" (Kaniki 1985:390). While British efforts to establish direct control over land in the Gold Coast failed,[3] largely due to well-organized oppostition in Acra and Cape Coast, their control was apparent in the spatial delineation of their administration and the space they accorded local peoples. The British used space as a means to their political ends by appropriating and redefining ownership, especially on the Gold Coast.

In the Gold Coast, the development of modern gold mining increased land values and brought in considerable wealth to the affected villages. The Government Lands Bills of 1894–1897 attempted "to control excessive alienation and facilitate approved expatriate enterprise" (Kimble 1963:21). The laws also instigated much indigenous opposition, from the chiefs and the people because they altered "natural rights of absolute ownership into that of mere holders and settlers . . . the [1897] Bill would destroy the control exercised by headmen over villages and families" (Kimble 1963:345). Ultimately, due to African opposition, the Bill was withdrawn, and in the Colony and Asante specifically, the British left untouched traditional systems of landownership (Harvey 1966:81).

The British did succeed, however, in developing their West African space—dividing it, building it up and building on it, and increasing its value. They constructed infrastructure—roads, railroads, harbors, and telegraph lines (Hart 1982:44f.); while this facilitated the export of raw materials and products of interest to the British, it was not sufficient to the country's future needs and set the scene for neocolonial dependency. Emerging processes of urbanization and colonial domination became "the expression of this social dynamic at the level of space," functioning to administer and fix political sovereignty and exploit the colony's resources (Castells 1979:44). From 1877, the growth of Accra accelerated. Investment capital was channeled to Accra, the volume of trade increased, and by 1889, Accra possessed the largest number of private bonded warehouses along the Gold Coast (Konadu-Agyemang 2001:64).

"The interwar period also saw the first major changes in transportation which helped make Accra the major Gold Coast port" (Robertson 1984:33). The Accra-Kumase railroad was completed in 1923. Municipal bus service replaced mule transport in 1927.

From 1910 to 1942 Accra was the largest port in the Gold Coast for the export of cocoa, and it was also the largest center for the import of foreign goods from 1918 to 1936. Thus, it was the major center of surface transportation in the Gold Coast in the interwar years. (Robertson 1984:33)

Other major changes included the provision of European-style hospitals, with Korle Bu opening in 1923. The Administration engaged in campaigns to deal with sanitary conditions. Between the two world wars, significant improvements raised the standards of health care and daily life. While World War II was the impetus for huge numbers of immigrants, it was during the 1950s that the city boomed, with a great deal of building taking place, and all subsidized by cocoa (Robertson 1984).

Like colonial cities throughout the world, Accra is a product of cultural interaction between two or more systems of culturally-specific values, technology resulting in the separation of home and work, and the development of new institutions, methods, technologies, and roles to deal with the change in knowledge and organization. Missionaries preceded and accompanied the British administrators. They established schools and preached sermons that carried the lessons of the West. These lessons were often antithetical to those taught by the traditional sages but reinforced the codes of dress and conduct carried by the British colonists, codes often based upon the Bible. The missionaries beseeched their students and congregants to abandon polygyny and the extended family in favor of monogamy and nuclear family living. The spread of Christianity was aided by the value placed on Western education, improvements in communication and the missionary activity of Fante and Akwapim traders (Isichei 1995).

Criteria reflecting occupation and education replaced customary conceptions of social status and self-respect such as that accorded age and lineage (Pellow 1978:772). Access to mobility through Western education and new roles threatened authority based on ascriptive criteria. British criteria of privilege were internalized by those Gold Coasters desirous of making their way in the comparatively open society. Educated Africans, many of them converts to British norms and values, became a new elite and mediated between the Europeans and the African masses.

Colonial impact on an indigenous people's social and physical space is most evident in the colonial city, where urban districts reproduced the cities of the home country, affecting a standardized colonial plan. The colonial city consisted of two or three major parts: the indigenous often precolonial, settlement; the oft-termed "modern," "western," or "European" sector, which King refers to as the "colonial urban settlement," and in some colonial territories, a "stranger" sector, occupied by migrants (King 1976:33).[4] In West Africa, the colonial city was intended for a principally African population and served as a nodal point within the export-based colonial spatial economy (Mabogunje 1970:346). The social organization of the colonial city reflected the spatial organization of the colonial society, a "pastiche of zoned functions, land uses and populations" (Blair 1971:229), with six typical zones—five controlled by Europeans, one encompassing the old city and stranger community.

While the colonial government interfered with local systems of governance and also impacted on space and its allocation, they failed to disrupt the indigenous systems of land ownership (Larbi 1996). In the Gold Coast (and Ghana), the stool or skin representing the collective authority of the community is the custodian of the collectivity's land; the occupant of the stool or skin "is a trustee holding the land for and on behalf of the community, tribe, or family" (Ollennu 1962:6). Thus, if a person or group of people, whether African or the colonial government, wanted to acquire a piece of land, they had to do so through the local chief or family head. If the colonial government wanted land to develop, they had to acquire the land "compulsorily" and pay compensation. Two main types of land tenure resulted: customary and state.[5]

NEIGHBORHOODS, HOUSE FORM, AND CULTURE

The physical settings of the home and the home itself are essential to enabling peoples' behaviors, values, and positions in the family (Birdwell-Pheasant and

Lawrence-Zuniga 1999). The built form encodes and expresses power relations within the home and between homes of different people or members of different populations. These settings, the actual structures and layouts of the house as well as its situation in a neighborhood, represent an imprint of culture. They help to produce and reproduce behavior.

This is evident in Accra, which exemplifies the spatial imprint of European imperialism on the urban landscape and its system of organization, with regional inequalities complemented by socio-spatial inequalities of density, modernization, and residential exclusion in the capital city (Brand 1972). Social differentiation is expressed through mechanisms of differential associations and spatial isolation. Privileged individuals participate in exclusive membership groups of a political, social or economic nature. Similarly, space has become a resource; privileged individuals could occupy the parts of the urban space most valued by the society-at-large. The kind of house people live in has become a symbol of status (Konadu-Agyemang 2001:72). The contrasting structures of nuclear versus extended family, of master and servant, are expressed in spatial layout. Concepts of proper sleeping arrangements, of privacy, of separating adults and children, are spelled out in domestic space (Birdwell-Pheasant and Lawrence-Zuniga 1999).

When Henry Stanley came to Accra in 1873, he found the houses of Africans (primarily Ga) and the handful of Europeans jammed in together in the James Town/Ussher Town area.

The huts of the natives have been established everywhere, without regard to order or to any symmetrical arrangement. The consequence is that the streets are uniformly narrow, crooked, and oppressive. (quoted in Acquah 1958:27)

In contrast, the house of the principal European merchant of the town rose three stories above the gray thatched roof huts.

After the British transferred their headquarters to Accra in 1877, the Administration formed the Accra Municipal Council to oversee Accra's development with respect to water, lighting, sanitation, street maintenance, and market and slaughterhouse facilities (Larbi 1996). While the British could have planned, directed, and controlled the development of Accra, in fact they concentrated land-use planning in the areas occupied by Europeans (Larbi 1996).

At the turn of the century, when the British were well-ensconced, the Asante diminished and the stranger community flourishing, the city of Accra consisted of the so-called Central area, in the shadow of the three forts, with its concentration on trade and the Administration's settlement in Christiansborg (Osu) three miles away (Lisowska 1984). While separate neighborhoods did not initially separate the indigenous people from the Europeans, their house styles and the homes' amenities varied considerably. De facto segregation developed: "social differentiation became an unwritten part of the city's constitution allowing people unequal access to the resources and rewards of the environment"

(Konadu-Agyemang 2001:73). Both neighborhoods and housing evolved. Land tenure types included Ga stool/shrine lands, colonial and post-colonial government/public lands, extended family lands, and finally individual lands (Asabere 1981:388). Class differentiation produced social exclusivity and has been associated with rather distinct kinds of housing in distinct kinds of neighborhoods—indigenous, colonial, estate, elite residential, and mixed urban adaptations.

Thus, as Accra expanded, neighborhoods similar to the old Ga towns, with distinct locations and names and housing types, grew up. Differences among the indigenous people[6] were used by the British to construct notions of "tribe" and were reified by segregation. The British cordoned off other sections for various ethnic groups among the Africans, reinforcing the social and spatial compartmentalization of the town (Brand 1972).[7] For example, in 1893 the British relocated the Hausa police force (see Chapter 3) to a newly-created Cantonments just north of the city,[8] a military enclave typical of British establishment throughout their Empire. At that point another Muslim community, which came to be known as Tudu, sprang up one-half mile north of Ussher Town (see Figure 2).

When the Muslim community first took root in Accra, it was concentrated in Central Accra. Ga leaders allowed the Muslims to live first among them and then in their own *zongo* on land nearby. It was there that the migrants also worked and built their mosque. And it was there that the old Muslim headmen (of the various ethnic groups) held sway, acting as patrons to their countrymen by aiding them and giving them succor, as the newcomers sought to adjust to a new place. The census of 1891 lists Accra's population at 19,999 of whom 15,948 or 80 percent were described as "pagan," 2,434 or 12 percent as Christians (the latter including 68 non-Africans), and 1,617, or eight percent, as Muslims.

The house form most commonly built by the African populations throughout Accra has been the compound or courtyard house. Here as everywhere, social composition and physical form are mutually constituted, based on social and cultural values and expressed in the people's daily routines and exchanges. In essence, the compound form consists of rooms on three or all four sides of an open atrium. In hot countries, it performs a climatically important role: thick walls prevent too much heating from the sun on the courtyard and cool air from the surrounding rooms is drawn into the atrium (Oliver 1987).

This house form is widespread, historically and geographically. While often associated with Islam and Arab culture, in fact the origin and development of the courtyard house predate Islam in Arabia as well as the introduction of Islam in Nigeria and Morocco (Schwerdtfeger 1982). It was present in Mesopotamia in the seventh millennium in the Chaldean city of Ur in 2000 B.C.; in Kahun, Egypt, 5,000 years ago (Schwerdtfeger 1982; Oliver 1987). Variations on its ancient plan are present as far east as India in cities developed under Moghul influence (such as Haridwar, Jaipur, and Ahmedabad), in the Mediterranean in Greece and Rome, in Hispanic Latin America (Rapoport 1969; Oliver 1987), and in China (Boyd 1962; Knapp 1989).

Throughout Africa the common version is the compound (with its enclosed yard). Most contain round dwellings, when conjoined create the compound: northern Ghanaian villages of Dagomba, Konkomba, and Tallensi (Prussin 1969), Northern Nigerian Hausa villages (Smith 1965). Among the forest-belt Asante in southern Ghana (Rutter 1971), Accra's indigenous Ga (Field 1940) and among Muslims or those influenced by Islam, in sub-Saharan Africa as in North Africa and the Middle East, the geometrization of buildings and court-yards is common (Prussin 1986). "The original architectural norm in Accra was a round house made of swish and topped by a conical roof" (Parker 2000:25); by the 1850s, most of the houses in Accra were rectangular. In contrast, Accra's elite during that period apparently built multi-storey residences of stone, but still following the courtyard style (Parker 2000:25). Such courtyard types provide privacy to the inside rooms when there is only one entrance; the courtyard with four buildings in a square, joined at one corner, and with one entrance, common among the Asante, it also makes the buildings secure and easily defensible (Denyer 1978:164).

The compound house satisfies basic family requirements: a place for each member to sleep, a place to cook, places to store food, places to pen animals such as chickens, goats, and sheep, a place to eat and socialize (Denyer 1978:21). It is everywhere congenial to the form of economic activity and to its social organization (King 1984). In all compounds, demarcated spaces are often multi-functional.

Such African housing created a suitable environment for the development of community living, testifying to the definite place the individual occupied within the group (Kulturmann 1963). In the typical Akan (southern Ghana) house, the individual rooms are on average 12 feet by 12 feet, serve as bedrooms, are rarely in use during the day, and open onto an internal courtyard where daily interaction among residents occurs.

This courtyard is the living area of the house; it is there that arbitrations occur, cooking is done, children play, stories are told, and family celebrations and funerals are held (Architecture 1978:458). This is no less true in the city of Accra at large, no matter the genealogical relationship of residents to one another. Rooms are used primarily for sleeping—in part due to crowding, in part due to weather (Pellow 1991b). The compound space is an outdoor room, and it is the room within the compound with primacy. For in Accra, like other West African cities, the courtyard has been documented as "the spatial arena in which social interaction and inter-household co-operation are typically nurtured" (Korboe 1992:1160)—and it is this communal lifestyle with which the poor and more traditional tend to be associated. This housing is family housing, and in it the compound yard is ubiquitous. The well-to-do and more Westernized, on the other hand, "have a more nuclear lifestyle and—choice permitting—opt for uni-nuclear, villa-style accommodation" (Korboe 1992:1160).

The communal lifestyle, of course, is directly tied to the extended family, which in turn is facilitated spatially by the "family house." Among the Ga,

Accra's earliest and longest settled inhabitants, the house symbolizes the
builder's social identity; thus it is the most socially significant piece of property:
it leads to the builder's establishment of a new lineage and serves as "a mnemonic for his success in furthering the expansion of the community" (Parker
2000:27). It is the setting for the enactment of social activities. "[P]hysical
structures serve as visible reminders of fixed points in an otherwise amorphous
cognatic descent system" (Kilson 1974:31).

While the housing units in the Central Accra Ga traditional area vary from
one room to a compound house, most do follow the compound style; the houses
are mainly the old family houses and generally very deteriorated. Both men and
women build houses in Ga society with a similar structural layout: rooms opening onto a roofless courtyard. But the use of space differs, because Central Accra
Ga men live not with their wives but with "brothers" and sons (of the same
agnatic group) and women live with their daughters and granddaughters (of
different patrilineages) (Field 1940:3–4).

A house built by a man is divided into two adjoining sections: one for men (*hiiashia*),
one for women (*yeiashia*); the house built by a woman consists only of a woman's section
(*yeiashia*). . . . While a number of women and children may share a room, each man
occupies a single room. These spatial differences have implication for the structuring of
the dwelling groups within houses built by men and women. (Kilson 1974:30)

The compound yard is the common living room. The women's compound,
which contains about four times as many adults to each room as the men's, is
where most family life goes on and is the scene of all the domestic tasks—
cooking and clothes washing. There are advantages and disadvantages for both
sexes, as described by Field sixty years ago:

The Ga admits that his system gives him little control over his wife and that when she
has the connivance of her mother she can deceive her husband grossly. . . . On the other
hand, the Ga man is alive to the advantages of a system which allows him to have all
the dignity of a married man and a father without renouncing the joys of the bachelors'
mess and without surrounding himself with the domestic turmoil of the nursery and
kitchen. (Field 1940:7–8)

It is the family house that in much of urban West Africa has enabled the
survival of many of the poor, who may live there rent-free. In Central Accra as
in Sabon Zongo and elsewhere (Pellow 1991b), this family house-form has been
easily adapted to accommodate tenants (see Chapter 7). And in both places,
along with preserving the "spirit" of the lineage that the house represents, the
poor living in those houses, many of which are now ramshackle if not dangerous,
resist razing them. And while many of the buildings were built during the colonial period, "the character of the area in its entity is historic urban African"
(Bremer 2000:8), and that is why the district and its buildings deserve to be
preserved.

It is significant, King asserts (1976:37), that in the colonial city, physical space between the colonial settlement and the indigenous city "is organized according to mid- and late nineteenth century scientific and especially medical theories which, in brief, assume a causal connection between aerial distance and bacterial infection."[9] Prior to the administrative move to Accra, there was no evidence of spatial segregation by race or class, the few Europeans in Accra living among the Africans in James Town and Ussher Town. Subsequently, this changed and in Accra, this *cordon sanitaire* was provided by the

former location of the former race course site, which provided a buffer between Ridge Residential Area (formerly European Residential Area) and Osu to the east. To the west, the land stretching north from Accra Polytechnic to the Holy Spirit Cathedral, covering an area of 20.84 hectares, was acquired for a building-free zone. To the north an area of 118.35 hectares was acquired for dairy farming. The purpose of these acquisitions was to separate the European Residential Area from the African settlements at Adabraka and La. (Larbi 1996:197 n.8)

In the 1890s, the government had changed the practice of Europeans living among the Africans because building and health regulations were barely enforced in non-European areas. The latter were deemed unsanitary and unhealthy due to malaria, especially once the male administrators were joined by their wives. The principle of "health segregation," used in Sierra Leone, was the proposed solution.[10] In the 1890s, the British built up Victoriaborg, between Accra and Osu, as a European residential enclave, "constituting the first physical addition to the Dutch and English Accra originally sketch-mapped in 1826" (Arn 1996:435). In the shadow of Christiansborg castle, Victoriaborg had large lawns and gardens and luxurious single family bungalows for civil servants. "The bungalows were wooden structures, erected on concrete pillars; they had much window and floor space and proved a great improvement on town dwellings" (Acquah 1958:23). They were spacious and lofty with surrounding verandahs to deal with the hot and steamy climate. Not only did these houses communicate social status and position, but they also revealed cultural expectations, for example of climate control, states of health, nuclear family living, and privacy for domestic activities (King 1984:209).

Similar housing was subsequently also provided to Europeans working for expatriate firms. As in other colonial cities in Africa, the wealthy class of Africans were prevented from living there, being forced to reside in the African parts of town, until the promulgation of the Devonshire White Paper of 1923, which officially ended this kind of segregation in West Africa (Brand 1973:44). Over the following years, the residential elite came to include well-to-do Africans, who could afford the pricier housing in the formerly European suburbs. Moreover, as Leys (1975) noted for Kenya, indigenous people interested in organizing and facilitating the new economic activities became the mediating

elite, and in Accra, upon independence, they moved into the physical and leadership spaces vacated by the British.

They also began to copy European housing, in both form and materials. The
alternative to a bungalow on raised piers was a two-story structure with the
living rooms upstairs and the downstairs an arcade, to be used for storage or
office space (King 1984:211f.). This style of house was built downtown, where
the British merchants carried on their business. Not only did the house forms
change, the building materials did as well. European missionaries introduced
iron roofs in Ibadan, Nigeria, in the mid-1800s, and in the next 50 years they
replaced the thatch so common to native construction. In Accra, because of rust
caused by the sea air, iron was replaced by asbestos. These roofing materials
have been adapted by vernacular builders for room additions or entire huts. Iron
and asbestos are also not particularly suited to the heat of the tropics.

In 1908, after the bubonic plague hit Accra, Governor J.P. Roger initiated a
three-year program of town planning, renewal, and clearance. The plans, which
reveal British cultural norms and the imposition of European standards, were
not necessarily responsive to local needs, of either a cultural or spatial sort, and
had a variety of consequences for town sites and the buildings erected. As King
has observed, housing standards, such as those of a colonial administration, have
to do with forms of culture, of ways of life, social priorities and the distribution
of wealth (King 1984). Thus the British razed crowded and badly constructed
huts and shanties in the congested Pagan Road area, which, like the houses
throughout the old settlement of Accra, were built of swish (red earth with water)
and had grass roofs. They instituted zoning regulations. One of the early sites
planned was Adabraka, established on April 24, 1910. It was intended to accommodate Ga people from Ussher Town, as well as "two Hausa tribes viz.:
the Fulanis and the Yorubas [sic]."[11] Two plot sizes were designed: large ones,
160' × 82', and smaller ones, 58'6" × 60'. The latter were conceived for the
Hausa and Fulani, "in order to limit the number of buildings on a plot and
successfully cope with the tendency of the Hausas to overcrowding."[12] The Ga
were reluctant to relocate, in part because some were fishermen who wanted to
be close to the sea. But the Sanitary Engineer, commenting on the success of
the relocation project, also believed that their behavior reflected class distinctions: "It can be seen from the type of houses now being erected that those who
do go are of a better class, who appreciate the advantages of a healthy well laid-
out township."[13] There were urban renewal plans in 1923 and 1925 as well, and
additions made to the already-planned sections were uniform rectangular blocks.
The houses were built within walled properties, many of them two-storied, but
all with a courtyard.

Governor Roger's plan included codes stipulating that all new buildings had
to be stone or concrete. Early constructions in the old sections of town, primarily
wooden structures, were torn down in favor of "better" ones—in 1923 alone,
more than 100 grass-roofed huts were razed in the old Pagan Road area. In the
1920s, the British delineated the neighborhood of Korle Gonno about one mile

west of James Town, on the other side of Korle Lagoon and by the sea. This so-called "model" settlement was built to provide good housing to those relocated. But this area deteriorated as people erected corrugated iron hovels (Brand 1973:142, 144).

As observed earlier for the well-to-do Ga in the nineteenth century, the African elites in the early twentieth century took over the two-storey structure of the Europeans and built it in the new town sites, like Adabraka. The change by Africans to Western house forms occurred in a couple of different contexts which included Africans adopting European lifestyles. For instance, elite norms included separate sleeping room for parents and children. The British imposed building standards; European firms or the Public Works Department provided housing to their employees (King 1984:216). Very low density patterns originated in Victoriaborg and extended northeast. Most of the low-density housing in Accra was planned and financed by the government for expatriate civil servants or rented to European businesses to house their employees. Ever since, the elite has occupied spatially segregated communities: colonial society developed Ridge and later Cantonments. Airport Residential Estates, developed in 1943, is a more recent elite tract. Adabraka became a central residential area, and as the demand for land in Accra increased, between 1947 and 1951, the cost of an acre of land in Adabraka increased by 350 percent (Quarcoopome 1993:18).

After the earthquake on June 22, 1939, the Ghana government began plans to build housing estates to rehouse the victims. The lands chosen for the housing, which were stool lands, were officially and properly acquired by the state from the local chiefs. The first, constructed in 1949 in Accra, also helped relieve the housing shortage (Blankson 1988). The estates were located at Korle Gonno, Christiansborg, and South Labadi (Ga settlements), and the three proximate areas of Kaneshie, Abossey Okai, and Sabon Zongo.

The housing estate is the product of public sector building modeled after the bungalow: each dwelling, divided into separate rooms, housed a family. The declared government policy in Accra was to provide affordable housing for low-income workers, and while only twenty to thirty percent were developed as rental units, it appears that many of the owners were subletting them to the poor. Three major categories of houses were built: 1) row houses, with one or two room units and a verandah, sharing kitchen, bath and toilet among four or five rows of housing; 2) one- to three-room semidetached houses; and 3) fully detached houses. The latter two have separate kitchens, toilets and baths. Residents had two major complaints: the bedroom in type two was eleven feet by eleven feet, the ventilation insufficient for the number of people sleeping in it; the bedrooms in type one were too narrow. In addition, there was either no living room or it was too small. A majority of the residents (who were not owners) made changes. Spatial changes included converting verandahs into living rooms, bedrooms, storerooms. Extensions took all sorts of forms like erecting walls and constructing rooms. "In a society where marriage is an important social institution, the bearing of children a cherished ideal, and the extended family system a critical component of the social structure, the construction of army-type barrack-like single rooms is culturally unacceptable" (Blankson 1988:61). Moreover, tenants also erected makeshift structures which ranged from open sheds to buildings made of packing cases or aluminum. These ad hoc additions show direct carry-over from the more traditional compound in their uses for productive informal sector activities: as chicken coops, shop kiosks, bakeries, poultry farming, soap manufacture, and corn milling. In some cases, residents added more than five rooms, dwarfing the original house.

Between 1952 and 1953, 168 houses were built not only in Accra, but also in the cities of Kumase and Sekondi-Takoradi. Each house actually constituted several dwelling units. By 1970, Kaneshie had 1,109 houses, East Christiansborg 203 houses, and South Labadi 413 houses. In Blankson's sample study (Blankson 1988), "the estates are ethnically and occupationally heterogeneous and the landlords reasonably literate. The presence of the large number of tenants on the estates shows that the original houses were bought by people who could have afforded to build their own houses . . . [who] were being subsidized by the government to make a profit at the expense of the truly needy" (Blankson 1988: 63).

Since World War II, the commercial area in the center of Accra has reflected considerable and rapid development. "Previously buildings in this area consisted at the most of two stories, the ground floor being used for shops, and the first floor for offices or flats. Since the war there has been an appearance of large, multi-storied, substantial buildings used for department and wholesale stores, and offices" (Pogucki 1954:19).

The creation of Ring Road in the 1950s permanently separated mixed but mainly southern areas like Asylum Down from areas of northern migrants to the north of the Ring Road. During that decade, one could point to two types of residential areas in Accra—so-called superior (e.g., Adabraka) and popular (e.g., Korle Gonno). The buildings in the former "are mostly large and modern detached dwelling-houses," the whole building or flats for rent, whereas in the latter, there are "one-storeyed, small dwelling-house" primarily with leases of single rooms (Pogucki 1954:21).

In 1958, a Master Plan of Accra was developed, which divided the city into exclusive zones: commercial, light industrial, heavy industrial, educational, civic and cultural, high-class residential, middle-class residential, low-class residential, and recreational (Asabere 1981). Given the prevalence of favoritism and backdoor connections, the zoning of new homes and businesses has not always followed the letter of the law.

In Accra, as in many African countries, upon Independence a number of changes were instituted, such as the growth of the civil service and centralization of politics, that made the city attractive to migrants. Another pull factor for Accra was the availability of small and intermediate enterprise employment

(45%); one-third of all manufacturing was also concentrated in Accra (Rakodi 1997a:36).

Clearly, economics has been an important factor in the city's growth in population. This is evidenced in migration to this new business and administrative center from different areas of the Gold Coast and neighboring countries. The increasing number of migrants to Accra in the second decade of the twentieth century indicates the economic vitality of the city. The importance of the cocoa boom was such that "commerce replaced government as the primary element in the urban economic base" (Brand 1973:104). But the city's growth is also due to the extension of the city's administrative boundaries. For example, by 1943, Korle Gonno, Mamprobi, Sabon Zongo and its neighbors Abossey Okai and Kaneshi, and Labadi by the sea had been incorporated. Within 10 years, another six suburbs (the *zongo* Nima, coastal Teshie and Nungua, Achimota of the famous secondary school, the university's Legon area, and Medina) were also added.

After Independence, Accra grew considerably and its planning and development followed the colonial pattern. "Though all the barriers of segregation were removed, the fundamental principles, laws and procedures of planning remained the same" (Larbi 1996:198). Accra's growth necessitated expansion of commercial and residential space. Newly planned residential areas encroached on indigenous ones. Between 1960 and 1970, the rate of Accra's urban growth slowed down, although the city received about 70 percent of Ghana's increase in urban population (Lisowska 1984).

After 1960, with the expansion of the airport and a direct road to Central Accra, housing was developed in Victoriaborg and Cantonments (Lisowska 1984:119). Great extensions also took place on the Government residential area, north of Nima village, which came to be called Airport Residential Area. Driving through Airport Residential Estates, as is true for a number of the other suburbs like Roman Ridge, Dzjorwolu, Tesano, one is struck by the gated character of the suburb. Each house is grand in size and appointments and bounded by an even grander wall. There are well-kept gardens and none of the food animals, like chickens and goats, which one finds throughout the city's urban and peri-urban neighborhoods. Pedestrians are absent and the only people who are regularly present are the watchmen in front of each gate.

The village of Nima's expansion was due to its situation between a military base and a European residential area. Incorporated into the municipality in 1951, it had already attracted those who worked in the two adjacent neighborhoods (cooks, stewards, laborers, and prostitutes). It also attracted migrants. Many soldiers in the Gold Coast military were notably of Muslim and/or northern Ghanaian extraction, and after the War many settled in Nima, expanding the population. The cocoa boom and new economic programs in the 1950s boosted the economy and brought in others. Nima presents an extraordinary contrast to the quiet and ghostly appearance of Airport Residential. It is densely populated, much of its housing sub-standard, bathroom and toilet needs often satisfied through public facilities. The community is vibrant and alive, overflowing with pedestrian and vehicular traffic, traders and businessmen, women and children.

The areas that have most needed planning (like James Town and many of the *zongos*) have been neglected and residential areas have been fragmented into "a classification into first-class, second-class, third-class and slums" (Larbi 1996: 213) which reflects the wealth of residents. In contradistinction to the majority of the city, which is predominantly Christian, Western in orientation and outward-looking, the Muslim communities are insular and inward-looking and represent a type of ghettoization that occurred both by accident and by design and produced the third-class or slum-class *zongo*. The *zongo* in Ghana has marginal zoning insofar as it has been unregulated by the municipality. This reflects the separateness and powerlessness of the component populations, who are treated as culturally different from the southern Ghanaians and who therefore lose out in the distribution of power. The contrast between the elegant Airport Residential suburb and the nearby *zongo* Nima provides a case in point.

In fact, according to Peil (1979:124), "segregated housing and employment are the exception in Ghana. The *zongos* . . . still exist, but their population today is usually a mixture of aliens and northern Ghanaians of long residence who are traders or laborers." The population in the *zongos*, also from other West African countries, constitutes a group with the lowest social status. Their communities in Accra have been established on the periphery of the settled areas or beyond. To some extent, these communities segregated themselves, but their exclusion was also sustained in large measure by the proclivities of the indigenous groups for central residential locations. There is also no doubt that colonial influence left its mark on the differentiation of residential land use (Brand 1973:47).

The spatial shifting of the Muslim constituency has echoed that of the population at large, harmonizing with the expansion and fractionation of Accra's physical parameters and the diversification of the city's inhabitants. Today there are at least 11 recognized *zongos* in Accra: besides Sabon Zongo there is Accra Central, Nima, Newtown (Lagostown), Adabraka, Alhamdu, Abeka, Darkoma, Shukura, and Madina. Each has its *zongo* chiefs, its mosques and imams, but all recognize Accra's central mosque and chief imam as their spiritual center.

HOUSING TODAY

Looking at neighborhoods and housing has been helpful in three ways. Firstly, we see generally the varying local socio-spatial contexts for interaction among residents and neighbors and outsiders. Secondly, we can better comprehend the interconnection of culture and its attendant social relations with the material culture that they produce and use and in turn through which they are anchored. Thirdly, it lays the groundwork to better understand what is distinct about Sabon Zongo, in terms of the community and the housing its people have produced,

Figure 3
House in Suburban Labone Estates. Photo Courtesy of the Author.

the how and where of the encoding of cultural rules and norms, which guide peoples' activities and behaviors and which are reinforced and reproduced through the repetition of those daily activities in which people participate.

In Accra today, given the differences in ethnic background, cultural beliefs and practices, and socio-economic status, there is a range of house types that conform to certain neighborhoods and accommodate certain life-styles: 1) the single story compound house, found mainly in the indigenous, non-indigenous and middle income areas; it accounts for about 52 percent of the housing stock (Planning 1992); 2) the multi-story tenement, similar to the compound house, although built up with the rooms arranged differently around the compound yard. Today, "one- and two-story compound houses eventually containing as many as 80 rooms accommodate three-quarters of households in Accra, of which 65 per cent live rent free" (Rakodi 1997b:379); 3) the bungalow, containing a single household, for senior civil servants and business executives; 4) the semi-detached house, similar to the bungalow and found in middle income areas; 5) flats, for single households, in government estates and corporate housing; 6) barracks, for members of military, police, prisons, fire services, and institutional employees (Planning 1992:88). And then there is also the so-called "other ac-commodation," what I would call type No. 7, the make-shift shelters of the poor.

Thus, at one extreme are huts made of metal sheeting, with dirt floors, lacking water, light, and ventilation. At the other extreme are the palatial homes of well-to-do professional Africans, following the pattern of an English mansion with grand gardens and all modern amenities (see Figure 3). In between is a variety of swish, wood, concrete, stone, metal, varying in size and quality, density of buildings and people, plots of land (Acquah 1958). The former and the middling type are both typically found in Sabon Zongo. In Accra generally, the most common wall construction material used in building houses today is sandcrete and landcrete (in a ratio of 2:1). Wood is not common because of fire risk and termites. Mud or mud straw, common in rural areas, is found in Accra's migrant areas (Planning 1992:89). As one gets to the periphery of the city, the single family imposing mansion is common in the suburban areas, the shabby and sub-standard house in the marginal, often migrant, areas.

The social development of Accra over the past 300 years is tied to the political and economic incursions and interactions of foreign colonial powers, indigenous peoples and migrants from elsewhere in Africa. Colonialism has had a mixed legacy: many benefits derived from the city's status as capital. Making Accra the colony's headquarters led to the migration of people to Accra and the growth of the city's population, the physical infrastructure was improved, education and health services were brought in. But Accra is now saddled with a multiplicity of problems, most conspicuously a shortage in housing, poverty, transportation problems, an atrophied infrastructure, a deteriorating environment and the social stratification of the city (Konadu-Agyemang 2001:73). It appears that there has been an inability of urbanization in Accra to produce desirable changes that would trickle down to the population-at-large.

Social elements are encoded in the spatial growth and layout of the city, of the types of communities that simply happened or were planned, the populations associated with them, and the housing constructed. The mutuality of the two dimensions, the social and the spatial, have reinforced one another and together relate the tale of one city and its many constituent parts.

NOTES

1. Some sources estimate the population at three million as of January 1996 (Assembly 1996:26).

2. Dakubu distinguishes between the two terms: multilingual refers to a state, town, community, or other social-geographic unit in which several languages are used, while polyglot refers to the individual who speaks several languages (Dakubu 1997:22).

3. Prevention of wholesale alienation of land was due to its not being very rich in minerals, and to failure to institute plantations (Kaniki 1985).

4. It is clear from the literature that the migrants may have come to Ghana (the Gold Coast) not only as recruits (for example, in the military) but for idiosyncratic entrepreneurial reasons.

5. See Larbi (1994, 1996) for a detailed examination.

6. For example, the Hausas continually violated Ga traditions by killing crocodiles and cutting down mangrove trees by the Sakumo River. Then the Ga would complain

to the British ("A Report of Ga Chief Tackie's Complaints," January 27, 1893, SNA 1086, NAG).

7. See Campbell (1994) for the "traditional" city town of Koforidua.

8. Since Independence, this has become one of Accra's elite suburbs.

9. For example, when New Delhi was being planned as the capital of India, some British officials had suggested that it be placed in the hills of Simla, the hot-weather capital, in part because it would be remote from the indigenous people (Irving 1981). This is not only true in India; Spitzer (1974) documents the British creation of a hill station in Freetown, Sierra Leone, as a means of health segregation—to protect the Europeans from an unsalubrious climate and malaria-carrying mosquitoes by housing them in their own enclave above Freetown.

10. In fact, the health premises of Freetown's Hill Station were proved erroneous, serving only to segregate the races (King 1984:203).

11. Secretary for Native Affairs 1348/12: Sanitary Engineer L.C.S. Wellacotts remarks; December 4, 1912. NAG (National Archives of Ghana).

12. Ibid.

13. Ibid.

3

STRANGERS, STRUGGLES, AND THE CREATION OF SABON ZONGO

Malam Bako came here not as a soldier but as a teacher. When his father Malam Nenu was succeeded by Malam Garuba as Imam in Accra, Bako became Garuba's assistant. Malam Garuba was charged with adultery and in January 1900 Sir F. Hodgson the Governor removed him from office. But two years later, when an inquiry found Malam Garuba to be innocent, Sir Matthew Nathan reinstated him. Yet, the Acting SNA decided that Malam Garuba should not officiate in the mosque. There was all sorts of jockeying for positions within the Muslim/Hausa community, and a number of factions took shape. One of them followed Garuba and Bako, who "then built a mosque in what is now known as Malam Bako's zongo [in Central Accra] and the schism was complete." Malam Garuba died shortly thereafter and "the mantle of Malam Gariba [sic] fell on Malam Bako" (ADM 11/1502; Case No. 1331/07).

Malam Bako was not only a teacher and a religious functionary; he was also a fine politician. He gained the support of important men, like Fulata Bornu, the neutral figure brought in from Cape Coast to serve as Chief Imam when Accra's Muslims were quarrelling. "The Hausa became many. At that time, Malam Bako was their head" (Munka'ila, Chief of the Blind, 5/31/1995). He was a patron for his people, and when fights within the Muslim community became too intense, he approached the local Ga chief for a piece of land for his followers.

In addition to being a teacher, an imam, a patron and a good politician, Malam Bako was also the ideal patriarch. He was a good Hausa man, who in the course of his adulthood, married nine women. In line with orthodox Hausa Muslim principles, he tried to institute the rule of seclusion—married women were not supposed to be "roaming about." He also sired 37 children, thereby guaranteeing the continuity of his line.

After Malam Bako had established his new community, he continued to live downtown at Zongo Lane for several years. But he regularly came to check on things at Sabon Zongo. He would ride up from Central Accra on a horse, with Sha'aibu Bako, his eldest grandson, sitting in front of him. Malam Bako would dress him all in red and observers would shout, "Hey *Mai Ja Riga!*" [hey you wearing red]. Sha'aibu was turbaned chief of Sabon Zongo in 1981; he died in March 2001.

For hundreds of years, West Africans had moved from one area to another. They came as "strangers" and often created stranger communities. This chapter traces the beginnings of one such community, Malam Bako's "new zongo"— the first *zongo* in Accra designed for a group of people by a leader of that very group. They domesticated what had been a "wild" space making it into their place, a site where the roles and relationships of the Hausa pioneers could be constituted along with the domestic and public physical structures that also anchored them. Sabon Zongo's establishment was enabled by a combination of factors: the fights for leadership within Accra's downtown Muslim enclave, the Hausa sense of superiority, Malam Bako's "wealth in people" (playing patron to many clients) and the British concern with sanitation.

MUSLIM MIGRANTS IN ACCRA

The diasporic communities in West Africa derived their political rights from local African authorities, whose rules they were expected to obey (Skinner 1963). Such communities were observed in the early cities of the Western Sudan, such as Gao and Timbuktu. "The foreign Africans or strangers in the African polities and societies of the pre-Colonial period were primarily merchants and their families, engaged in both local and foreign trade" (Skinner 1963:308), and they lived in enclaves under the control of their own headmen. These traders linked West African societies economically. They also introduced new elements. A particularly important introduction has been Islam.

"Wherever trade went, there was a Muslim trader" (Dretke 1968:10). These early commercial travelers were probably of Dyula (Mande) origin, and whether they first came to the Gold Coast to trade with the Portuguese (Adamu 1978: 134) or in fact preceded these merchants (Wilks, cited in Dretke 1968:13), we know that they were already present in the late fifteenth century.

As early as the eighteenth century, Muslims resided in the southern Ghanaian city Kumase where they held prominent advisory positions in the Asantehene's court and were protected by the Asante ruler. By the mid-eighteenth century, under the impetus of the vast West African kola trade, "a series of trade settlements connected Asante with the Hausa cities" (Lovejoy 1973:i). Following Usman dan Fodio's *jihad* in 1804, kola became the substitute for stimulants banned by Muslim leaders, resulting in a major movement of Muslim traders into Dagomba and Eastern Gonja where they could buy the nuts (Reynolds 1974 and Wilks 1971:62). This in turn stimulated the development of a trade route to the northeast from Kumase, where a Muslim community was already established by 1817 (Dretke 1968).

The present Kumase *zongo*, however, can be traced back only to the late nineteenth century (Schildkrout 1970a; Schildkrout 1978), having developed from the multi-ethnic settlement of Muslim traders—Hausa, Yoruba, and Mossi—and of the Northern Territories (Ghana) migrants—Frafra, Grusi, Kuasasi, and others (Schildkrout 1978:78). The collapse of Salaga as a major trading center in the northeast in the latter part of the nineteenth century had great consequences for Accra, as many Muslim traders relocated to that coastal city.

Concurrent with this southward trade migration was the creation of a Muslim community of liberated African slaves. Originally purchased by the Dutch and taken to Java as soldiers, they were returned as pensioners to Elmina and formed the settlement of Java Hill (Adamu 1978:135), where their presence attracted other Muslims from up-country (Crooks 1923:414).

Colonialism and modernization facilitated travel and exposure to new modes of behavior and brought social, political, and economic change. The growing intensity of intercommunication in the colonial period led to greater contacts with strangers. Roads, railroads, and shipping stimulated mobility. Cosmopolitan towns like Kumase in Asante attracted travelers. The number of migrants increased considerably, as colonial governments built-up urban centers. However, the relationship of the stranger to local leaders changed because the latter no longer carried the same kind of authority as they now answered to European administrators.

People also migrated in response to a colonial call. Muslim soldiers were recruited by the British from both northern and southern Nigeria (e.g., Hausa and Yoruba, respectively) to serve in southern Ghana in the Gold Coast Hausa Constabulary (GCHC). The British established the GCHC in 1870 as an arm of British defense and security,[1] and two years later the first group of Hausa police, numbering 100, were brought from Lagos to garrison the Castle at Cape Coast, still the administrative capital of the Gold Coast Colony. By 1880, when the Colony's boundary was extended eastwards, the GCHC had posts in Denu and Aflao (towns near the eastern border with Togo). The constabulary force was engaged in the native Ga areas of Accra. By 1889, it was operating in Salaga Market, the main market of Accra.[2] The GCHC was called upon to deal with a variety of disturbances. On one occasion, the James Town (Ga) people used the Ussher Town (Ga) people's ritual bell. When a fight broke out among them, the "Captain of the Hausas" was called.[3]

Before the turn of the twentieth century, the Muslims developed a "stranger" collectivity in the old Ga section of town. It was composed of Yoruba, Hausa, Nupe, Fulani, Wangara, and others.[4] Alliances of the Muslim strangers were situationally defined and ever shifting.[5] The pre-eminent ethnic groups were the Hausa and the Yoruba. While the latter were the more numerous (Dretke 1968), many of them were Christian, the earliest migrating from Abeokuta in Nigeria. Accra's first Muslim chief was in fact a Yoruba from Ilorin, Nigeria, Ibrahima Braimah. He had established himself as a cattle dealer in the 1880s and became known as Braimah Butcher. He built his family house at Horse Road, the current location of Accra's main post office. A great conciliator, he died in 1915: "To his Yoruba brethren he was a 'major Domo' the proverbial household chief, while to the wider Muslim community he was an ardent organiser of the muslim [sic] chiefs."[6]

Even though the Yoruba population in Accra was larger than the Hausa and Braimah the Yoruba had been "crowned" the Muslim chief, the Hausa achieved dominance in the zongo. After 1874, Accra had become a magnet for Hausa due to four factors: the establishment of the GCHC, the lifting of the Asante ban on northern traders travelling to the coast, the break-up of Salaga as a major market, and the recruitment of Hausa to fight the Asante (Adamu 1978:166).

It has been observed that many of the men enlisted or recruited into the so-called Hausa forces were not Hausa, "as even today any man from the North [Nigeria and Ghana] is often called a Hausa" (cited in Dakubu 1997:135). For example, Native Officer Harri Zenuwah, who had enlisted in Glovers Hausas in 1858, was a Kanuri from Bornu.[7] Dan Bornu, his brother, was an officer who also came to the Gold Coast from Nigeria to fight for the British against the Asante. According to Dan Bornu's son Malam Sharbatu, it was the persuasiveness of the colonial government that led his father to enlist (Malam Rubutu Sharbatu 3/6/1982). The Hausa and Yorubas were both also used in the "Houssa [sic] police force" in Accra as early as the 1880s to keep the peace among the different Ga groups.[8]

Many have felt the Hausa perceived themselves to be superior to all other Muslim ethnic groups (Geoffrey 1982).[9] They had a disproportionate influence on the others in religion and learning, economic affairs, roles and offices, dress and language. Musing about why Hausa became the lingua franca, given the small fraction of Hausa in the population, Dakubu (1997) found evidence that it was used in the colonial military: British officers in Nigeria were encouraged to learn Hausa, and after 1886, "when Lagos Colony was separated from the Gold Coast, they were examined in it" (Dakubu 1997:136).

Thus, the Hausa speaker with whom the Akan-, Ga-, or Ewe-speaking Gold Coaster was most likely to come into contact was not the first-language speaker, let alone the man educated in the Hausa literary tradition, but the soldier or policeman (frequently perceived as alien) who spoke a vehicular variety.... The greatest concentration of numbers was in Accra almost from the beginning since the headquarters of the Gold Coast Constabulary were moved from Cape Coast to Accra in 1888, but the "Hausa" forces were used to enforce the colonial presence throughout the country. They were frequently pitted against local people. (Dakubu 1997:137)

In the religious arena, the Hausa were revered and appointed as imams. Since 1891 there have been 12 chief imams in Accra; nine have been Hausa, three Fulani (Odoom 1971). The major Arabic teachers have been Hausa. Along the coast, Hausa settlements became outposts of Islamic culture and savannah-forest trade. While the settlements were not limited to trade, the commercial network sustained the Hausa West African communities and over the years united them with Hausaland (Cohen 1969; Works 1976).

In the sphere of economics (trade) beginning in the sixteenth century, the Hausa have contributed to the development of West Africa (Adamu 1978). Trade, especially in kola and cattle, was an important source of wealth in Accra, as elsewhere in the Hausa diaspora (Cohen 1965), and thus a basis for patronage. Many Hausa migrants brought wives and families. Rather than integrate with the growing cosmopolitan community of Accra, the Hausa stayed within the strangers' domain and worked as individual entrepreneurs.

Malam Idris Bako Nenu is remembered as the first Hausa to settle in Accra according to various members of the Bako family (see also Odoom 1971; Adamu 1978:166).[10] Arriving from Katsina in the mid-nineteenth century to teach, he and his wife and foster son lived among the Ga at Lighthouse in old Accra's Ussher Town, nearby to Braimah Butcher. On his way to becoming the first Hausa *mai gida* (patron), Nenu needed a piece of property so that he could take in and help settlers and transients alike.

In Accra, the Ga or a specific Ga stool were (and are) the owners of all lands. According to the Gold Coast native laws, "a person of a different tribal origin is regarded as a stranger" (Pogucki 1954:31). Strangers could not aspire to true land ownership, that is, ownership of stool land. However, Ga native policy towards the Muslims in general and the Hausa in particular was welcoming, "knowing the worth and value of strangers."[11] Like others of African origin, they could "be given the opportunity of obtaining land by gift or grant upon payment of a prestation" (Pogucki 1954:32).

Thus, the early Muslims who came to Accra fell into a patron-client relationship with the Ga, as they were beholden to the Ga to allow them to conduct their affairs, to observe their rituals, to settle their disputes, to select and honor their leaders. However, Ga land allotments to non-Ga were subject to British approval. Moreover, because the Gold Coast was a colony of Britain and these African foreigners had come with no prior rights, their behavior was also moderated by the European administrators.

Malam Nenu created the nucleus of a Hausa settlement by formally approaching the local Ga Manche and in 1881 secured a piece of land at nearby Swalaba. There he lived and kept cattle. As *mai gida*, he also apportioned living space to his followers, who lived nearby to other members of the early Muslim collectivity at Okanshie and Horse Road.[12] This area came to be known as Zongo Malam in his honor, and with the passing of time, Zongo Lane. Once it was identified as a Muslim area, no non-Muslim was supposed to live there. At Zongo Malam, the residents built not only a wall; "they made it like Kano," the medieval Hausa city in Northern Nigeria, with a gate which was regularly locked against outsiders.[13] They also built the main mosque where all of them prayed *en masse*.

In 1891, Malam Nenu became Chief Imam, serving until his death two years later when he was succeeded by Malam Garuba. Malam Bako, Nenu's son, also migrated from Nigeria. He became Garuba's assistant (Case No. 1331/07, 29 May 1909, ADM 11/1502, NAG).[14] In 1899, after Nenu's death, Malam Bako inherited his land and his role of patron.

The Muslim community grew. Neighborhoods within developed. A spot below the central bus station is still called Cow Lane by many Hausa in Accra. Owning cows was a sign of wealth. At Cow Lane, Chief Braimah raised his cows. Malam Nenu also had cows in Accra (down the road at Swalaba). The slaughterhouse was in back of Ussher Fort.

In 1908, the Muslim population was estimated at 1,500 by the Yoruba leader Braimah and at 3,000 huts by a prominent Hausa man, Alhaji Muhammad Ali.[15] The Muslims had a socio-religious unity that carried greater salience for them than their hometown or ethnic origins: they looked and dressed alike and lived near each other. They spoke little of the local language, communicating among themselves in Hausa. They married off their daughters to one another. They sent their children to the same Koranic school (*makaranta*) at Nenu's house.

The students were Hausa, Yoruba (Braimah's children), and Muslim Ga. More of their classroom studies were in *makaranta* than now, because fewer (especially the Hausa) attended Western schools. Few of the students were girls. Malam Gambo was one of Malam Bako's sons who maintained the family *makaranta*. He recalled that in those early days of his youth, girls did not go to *makaranta* because "girls were considered grown earlier than boys" (5/4/1982). It also was not important for girls, because they married early, at about age 13, and when they married, they were not supposed to work. Indeed, according to Malam Hamisu, another son of Malam Bako, the elders felt that when the woman knows more than the husband, she will try to overcome him (6/4/1982). But some husbands did teach their wives at home.

The Muslim community in Accra had been described as "foreign," inward-looking and largely immigrant in character. Both the ethnographer/filmmaker Jean Rouch and British jurist J.N.D. Anderson concluded that in the Gold Coast, "the Muslim elements in the Colony and Ashanti are largely limited to immigrants from the north or from outside the territory" (cited in Dretke 1968:78). The Hausa and Fulani arrived fully Islamized in contrast to the Yoruba, Zabrama, Wangara, and others. However, the majority of these other migrants adopted Islam and the religion became a new adhesive, often supplanting the tribal factor from which they were displaced (Levitzion 1969; Grindal 1973).

MUSLIM LEADERSHIP IN ACCRA

The British used the phrase "Mohammedan Community" to refer to all of the Muslim strangers, and they worked alongside the Ga chiefs in allocating land

and other benefits potentially useful as sources of power. In Accra, the British did not prescribe a specific policy to deal with this collectivity.[16] As circumstances warranted, they dealt accordingly. In general, however, they regarded these newcomers as a unity in counterpoint to the local Ga.

"From the beginning, first [Kadri English], and Chief Braimah, and Chief Bako, and [Tanimu Dan Gimba, the *sarkin yaki*, captain of war] all moved together" (Mohammad Ra'abiyu, *Sarkin Yaki*, 2/27/1982). Yoruba and Hausa shared the same *sarkin yaki*, symbolic of the fact that these men would never go to war against one another.[17] They formed a large and apparently unassimilable group (Peil 1971:20ff.). During those early days, all Muslims were like one people. "They moved strictly according to Muslim law. All helped one another. Thus, if a group of four families shared a compound, all would eat together. Or if the wall of one of the houses collapsed, the others would naturally help him rebuild it. Formerly, if an area was Muslim, no non-Muslim was allowed to live there" (Alhaji Faruk, Secretary to Council of Muslim Chiefs, 3/23/1982).

The British acknowledged the foreign-ness of the Muslims, as distinct from the others who were "really the original inhabitants and therefore have the prior claim to consideration,"[18] and they administered them as a group apart. Initially this meant designating one man to represent the "aliens." As the Secretary for Native Affairs noted for the benefit of the District Commission: "The practices of the Government in dealing with Mohammedan communities throughout the Colony is that the local Political Officer addresses all communications for such communities to one Headman."[19] And since the latter was viewed as the caretaker of the land, it was also the invariable practice "to invite the views of the owner of the land [the Ga Manche] upon which such a community resides as to the suitability of a candidate for Headman."[20]

After the death in 1902 of Tackie Tawiah, the Ga chief, Muslim leadership became problematic as disunity reigned. Tackie Tawiah had selected Alhaji Ibrahima "Butcher" Braimah,[21] the Yoruba headman in Accra, as Muslim headman. But the Ga chief died before he could have Braimah installed[22] and the acting governor rejected him as headman. Moreover, emphasizing the limited authority of local powers, the acting governor reminded Braimah that the Ga Manche needed the sanction of the colonial government to make him a chief.

Religious tensions brewed among the Muslims, so the British brought in a neutral figure from Cape Coast, Fulata Borunu. Garuba and Bako were annoyed and created their own following. After Garuba's death, Bako became the leader of the faction, while Fulata headed up a separate one.

In 1907 Malam Bako decided to relocate his followers. A variety of factors may have influenced his decision. The early Hausa community multiplied, and he reasoned that his people had outgrown the space at Zongo Malam and Horse Road.[23] The British had granted the request of a Hausa faction to recognize N.O. Ali as headman of the Hausa (although he suddenly died) (Figure 4). Then in 1908, plague hit Central Accra.

The disease affected all quarters with the exception of those living in "good

Figure 4
Captain Glover's Hausas, with Native Officer Ali to the Right of Captain Glover.
Courtesy of Alhazai Alhassan and Huseini Sulley.

native houses" (e.g., those that belonged to lawyers).[24] As a result, Governor J.P. Rodger commissioned the first urban renewal plan in the Gold Coast—"the renewal of the unordered congestion of African huts, houses and shanties in Jamestown and Ussher Town" (Brand 1973:81). The British evicted the residents at Bako's *zongo* so that it could be rebuilt (December 1, 1909, ADM 11/1/32, SNA 21/09, NAG). And in accordance with principles of preindustrial locations, the lower the status group, the further it relocated from central Accra (Brand 1973).

Leaders came forward to pioneer new areas and they met with the British, whose administrative policy designated specific areas (*zongos*) for the "strangers," "so that all the Muhammedans can have a place to live together."[25] While the British supported Bako's plan for a new *zongo*, they saw it as a heterogeneous stranger enclave rather than for the Hausa alone,[26] as was the case in Ibadan's Sabo Gari.[27] In 1909, while Malam Bako was engaged in engineering a move for his family and followers, the aging Fulata Boronu decided to resign and return to Cape Coast. He recommended his former antagonist Bako as his successor. This appointment was defended by Braimah, Harri Zenua (a Kanuri elder), and Bako's people. Braimah was again nominated as chief as N.O. Ali had died. The majority of people supported him, including Bako and his followers.[28] The Bako support swayed the British.[29] In July 1909, Bako and Braimah thus became, respectively, the Muslims' head Imam and head chief. The British viewed this as a way of uniting the community's two strongmen. The government was also sanctioning Braimah's role as a patron, since he helped maintain the mosque and poorer Muslims.

The death of Braimah on May 1, 1915, was the catalyst for ethnic disturbances in the Muslim community. These revolved around the issue of the leadership of the Muslims as a whole, and the attempt to bring together secular and religious rule in the person of Malam Bako, already Accra's chief Imam. The Hausa were in favor, the Yoruba against, and the Hausa persuaded the Fulani to join their side in the fight. When the acrimony climaxed with fighting in the central mosque, the government ordered the building closed on September 3, 1915, and Bako's imamship ended (Dretke 1968).

Some Hausa people at Zongo Lane supported Kadri English, not Malam Bako as Hausa leader. Kadri English was a Hausa merchant who came to Accra because of the kola trade. When he first arrived from Nigeria, he lodged with Malam Nenu. Malam Nenu and Malam Bako were just teachers, while Kadri English became a wealthy man. According to Chief Amida Braimah,

Kola used to be our fathers' business. And they had a truck. And the Ga people used to work for us. They were the carriers (even though the Ga say that the Hausa and Yoruba were the carriers). So they used to shout "kaya kaya-o, kaya kaya-o." They would carry the kolas and at that time to the German ships, and then they would transport it to Nigeria. [Kadri English] liked Elder Dempster, the English ship line. So [he] would say, "hey, I don't like them-o; take it to English-y. I don't like German." Then they called him Kadri English (2/2/1982).

The kaya-kaya lodged with Kadri English, which contributed to his growing success (Alhaji Faruk 3/30/1982). Kadri's money allowed him to be his own man. And when Hausa came from Nigeria, "Kadri would let his wife cook plenty of food. When these people come, Kadri would give them food. But Malam Nenu can't, he doesn't have the money. So these Hausas who come, they used to go to Kadri with their goods. Kadri 'caught them' with the food" (Chief Ali Kadri English 2/11/1982). And Kadri English's patronage translated into leadership at Zongo Lane in Central Accra.

By 1910, Malam Bako had already launched his plan for the new Hausa settlement which served the British plan of social and spatial compartmentalization. As its founder, Malam Bako had proprietary rights and he named his portion Sabon Zongo, "new *zongo*."[30]

THE HAUSA MOLD

When he created his new community, Malam Bako incorporated intertwined elements of Islam and Hausa custom and practice. These included an electorally-based chieftaincy and titled offices. Since the fourteenth century, the Hausa have been organized into seven homeland states, the Hausa *bakwai* (Smith 1965; Smith 1978; Smith 1997). The states are organized centrally: each contains a hierarchy of offices that are competed for by important men. "Hausa government proceeds through a system of titled offices known as *sarautu* (sing. *sarauta*). The boundaries of Hausa government coincide with the boundaries of this *sarauta* system" (Smith 1961:91). There is an interplay of kinship and office in the noble lineages that have maintained political prominence over generations; so for example, in most states, descent lines are ranked, depending upon their political success (Smith 1965:133).

While Hausa may live in hamlets, towns or cities, it is urban residence that has carried the greatest prestige and urban residence has also been associated with the adoption of Islam. Each Hausa state has a primary city (*birni*, pl. *birane*), that is a center of political power and closely tied to the emergence of that state (Smith 1976). Well before the capital cities, there were large settlements each in the form of a town (sing. *gari*). Each had a political authority, the chief of the town (*sarkin gari*), which was kinship-based. The change from the town (*gari*) to the city (*birni*) was unique for three reasons (Smith 1976): 1) it was clearly an urban settlement "with a population comprising many groups of diverse origins lacking kinship relations one with another" (Smith 1976: 181); 2) it was fortified; and 3) it had a new type of political power, vested in an authoritative *sarki* (chief). The power of this chief depended on

the degree to which he could command the service (*barance*) of supporters of his authority; this degree in turn being dependent on the wealth of the *sarki* which could be used for rewarding his supporters, and on the needs of potential supporters. (Smith 1976: 183)

Social stratification, and its element of clientage, has been a basic Hausa marker for hundreds of years, as expressed in occupational ranking. Like the titles that attach to traditional offices in the capital city, occupational groups are also allocated titles. Thus, the occupational units (butchers, blacksmiths, etc.) have each had an officially-appointed chief who oversees the membership (Smith 1965).

Hausa distinguish between hereditary occupations (*gargagiya*, ascribed) and new occupations (*shigege*, achieved). Inherited occupations "indicate an occupational order in which most men follow in their fathers' footsteps and in which mobility is quite low" (Smith 1959:248). They are more prestigious, insofar as they perpetuate values and the same definition of social stability. "Occupational classification is the most important factor in the evaluation of social status" (Besmer 1983:31). Occupational groups are also ranked, and by custom, people are relatively indifferent to strictly economic differentials; for example, officials, Koranic teachers, and well-to-do merchants are at the top. Butchers are among the wealthiest members of society yet occupy the lowest social category, along with the lowly praise-singers (*maroka*, sing. *maroki/marokiya*). The latter are

Figure 5
Salli Mai Gunduwa, a Sabon Zongo *Maroki*. Courtesy of the Author.

men and women who actually proclaim another's name to honor him or her (Pellow 1997; Smith 1957; Furniss 1995). They are normally attached to prominent title holders or wealthy people, as their clients (see p. 134). Indeed, the *maroka* are a clear representation of the prominence of patron-client relations in Hausa society; actually, they are beggars, who by proclaiming a patron's qualities can expect to be cared for in return (Figure 5).

Writing about Daura, the first Hausa state, M.G. Smith observed that local clientage demarcated its boundaries (Smith 1978). One can more generally say the same for certain types of exchange, also characteristic of Hausa social organization. Ceremonial gift exchange commonly occurs at kinship ceremonies, such as weddings or baby outdoorings, and at the Muslim festivals marking the end of Ramadan and the beginning of the *hajj*. Commercial exchange is of two kinds: within the community and between communities. The latter, constituted by transactions in cash crops, meat, and imports, ties the community with others. The former, which involves crafts and various services, bounds and is bounded by the community.

Another institution of social relations that bounds Hausa society is agnatic descent. Patrilineages are the primary units of social organization (Smith 1978). The lineage segment matters, insofar as members have collective interests, for example in their compounds and other sorts of corporate property. Terminology reflects seniority, another way of reinforcing the importance of rank and station. The Hausa are polygynous, the Muslim man allowed up to four wives simultaneously. Residence after marriage is normally virilocal, and where room permits, patrilocal. A co-wife is referred to as *kishiya*, jealous one or rival, from the Hausa term *kishi* or jealousy. As in all other areas of relational life, co-wives are ranked, the most senior known as the *uwar gida*, mother of the household. While it is a cultural norm for adults to be married, the marital relationship is extremely brittle and the rate of divorce high.

Marriages are classified socially according to the mode of arrangement and degree of wife seclusion (Smith 1965). Cross-cousins, matrilateral or patrilateral, are addressed and described as *abokan wasa* (joking relations), in keeping with cross-cousin marriage as the preferential type. There is also *auren sadaka* ("charity" marriage, when the bride is married to a Koranic teacher without payment of bridewealth), *auren so* (marriage of desire) and *auren bare* (marriage of non-kin, of strangers). Smith's data from 1950 Zaria, another Hausa state, indicated that one-quarter of rural marriages were between kin (Smith 1965:147).

Auren kulle, marriage of seclusion, is sanctioned by religious teachings and values, but it has been more understandable in economic terms: undertaken by the man with economic wherewithal who has been able to provide entirely for his wife and could afford to forgo her earning power. Of course, social prestige would accrue to the husband whose wife is secluded, and by extension, to the secluded woman as well. And while this prestige may be phrased in religious terms, it has clearly been understood in economic terms. However, in northern Nigeria today, with the greater adherence to *shari'a* law, the norm of seclusion is so well-established "that it is primarily its absence which attracts attention, bringing shame upon the offending wife and her husband" (Pittin 1984:474).

Seclusion is a means of enforcing the division between men and women and the ranking of them relative to one another. Certainly "adulthood means separation, even avoidance, between male and female" (Pittin 1996:34). In effect, men and women occupy two different worlds. They observe a strict sexually-defined division of labor. They celebrate rites of passage and festivals separately. Hausa custom and Muslim law not only conceptualize women as a group apart, but classify them as legal, political, and religious minors and the economic wards of men (Yeld 1966; Smith 1978; Schildkrout 1986; Callaway 1987).

Heterosexual contact is circumscribed by rules and regulations, both social and spatial, based upon a code of modesty derived from the Koran. Wife seclusion thus symbolizes cultural attitudes toward women.[31]

As we see, the ranking of people is crucial to Hausa social organization. Genealogy as well as patron-client relations are key, underlying who has power and status, who might pursue which occupation, who might marry whom. Through daily ritual, political exchange, people delineate the bounds of operational society.

THE EARLY COMMUNITY: LAND AND LEADERSHIP

Although it lies only two miles northwest of Zongo Lane, Sabon Zongo was at first a town apart, outside Accra's city limits (see Figure 1). Like his father Malam Nenu at Zongo Malam, Malam Bako was awarded custodial rights by the "stool" that owned the Sabon Zongo land. For the Ga distinguish between permitting a stranger to *use* land and actually selling it to him.[32] Thus the custodial grantee, the Bako family, could divide and distribute the land given them by the Ga and rule over it (English 1982; Bako 1982; Braimah 1982).[33]

Some Hausa chose not to come, remaining with Alhaji Kadri English, the kola trader from Kano who had become a *mai gida* for visiting Hausa traders in central Accra. Like other successful *masu gida* who could organize demonstrations and advance their election to headmanship, Kadri English succeeded in positioning himself to become the Accra Central Hausa chief once Malam Bako had left (Bako 1982; English 1982).

Although Malam Bako remained at Zongo Lane for some years,[34] he demarcated living space at Sabon Zongo and allocated it to his followers. When first surveyed, the acreage was sub-divided into thirty-two parcels, varying somewhat in size and greatly in the number and dimensions of compounds (see Figure 6). About a 100 people settled at Bako's new *zongo*,[35] and by 1912 the residents had built about 165 compounds.

These "new *zongo*" dwellers were no longer forced to live among, pray, and trade with the embattled members of Accra's ethnically diverse downtown Muslim community. Sabon Zongo's distance from Accra Central facilitated the founder's express desire to avoid "any contradiction in our religion which is Islam."[36] The residents built their own mosques; the first, Malam Bako's Mosque, was constructed adjacent to the palace.

Malam Bako was both a religious and secular leader. He continued as chief imam for the Accra community (until the closing of the central Mosque in 1915), while he served as headman in Sabon Zongo, answering to the authority of the British and the Ga.[37] For example, the British Colonial Secretary allocated to the Muslims a section of the Christian cemetery and free burial, regularly writing to the chief to remind him that they had to dig the graves according to regulations, keep their section neat by weeding and the paths tidy and clean.[38]

As was true for the headman of Kumase *zongo* (Schildkrout 1970a:373), Malam Bako's judicial powers were confined to his own people and limited in scope. For example, he did not have the power to make arrests. He also owed his tenure in office to the good humor of his followers. As the son of N.O. Ali wrote to Secretary for Native Affairs W.J.A. Jones in 1930, "Our status [as Muslim chiefs in Accra] is only determined by the Subjects who agree to serve us and [we] have practically no effective or absolute control over them if they resent to be our subjects. . . . Our position is only as you know Sir, to conserve peace among our subjects and to guide and protect them in cases of difficulty."[39]

As headman, Malam Bako acted the classic role of *mai gida* to his followers,

Figure 6
Malam Bako's Land: Official Survey Map ca. 1915. Adapted by Mark Hauser from a 1948 Tracing. Courtesy of the Chambers of Aknfo-Addo Prempeh & Co.

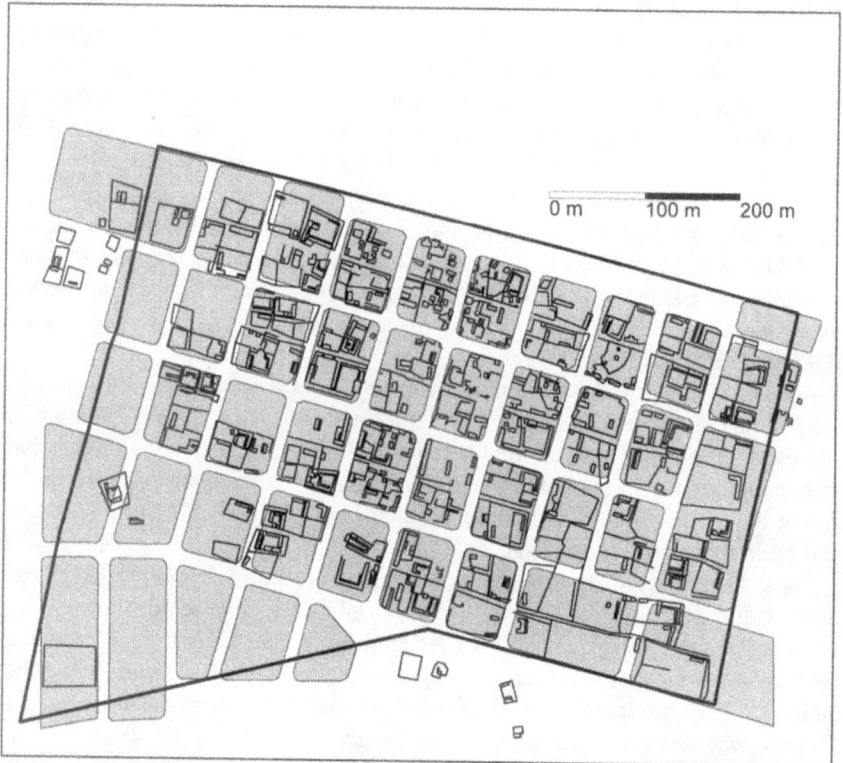

who were his clients: he looked after those who were ailing and without family, buried the dead, and arbitrated disputes. He also recruited workers for government-initiated tasks—maintaining the main road that bordered the community,[40] informing reservists of the Gold Coast Regiment to report to the district commissioner,[41] and recruiting others to serve in the regiment.[42]

Never formally recognized as a Hausa chief, Malam Bako succeeded in establishing the chieftaincy in his family line. And he re-created typical offices of Hausa authority, such as a *sarkin makafi* (chief of the blind), *sarkin fawa* (chief of the butchers) and *sarkin aski* (chief of the barbers). Such chiefs, who oversaw their constituents and advocated for them, were ultimately responsible to Malam Bako. When there was any misunderstanding within any one of these groups, they would go to their chief. And if the chief saw that the case couldn't be settled, he would bring it to Sarkin Bako. Several of the titled groups were also allocated space within Sabon Zongo, each of which cohered as named neighborhoods or areas within neighborhoods.

According to Munka'ela Mohammadu, the fourth chief of the blind, there is an origin myth for how there came to be a chief, a specific quarter and even a mosque, for the blind (5/31/1995):

The reason for *makafi* [the blind] to be here is not because a plan came from Nigeria to beg. Rather, in Nigeria, near Chad there is a place for *makafi* called *Lokoja*. There were so many blind there they had a chief. The blind from Ghana and Nigeria would go there. At that time, Hausa traded kola; they would gather on Fridays, the blind would pray for the traders, and the traders would give them something. Daudu Lawal and Idrissu, Malam Bako's oldest sons, took kola to Lokoja. When they went there, the people welcomed them and on Friday prayed for them and the two of them gave them something.

There was a man from Sokoto in Lokoja called Sarkin Samari [*samari* are 20 and 30 year olds] and he was blind, tough and tall. After prayers, Malam Bako asked to talk to Sarkin Samari. What's your name? Idrissu (like Malam Bako's first son). What tribe? Bogobiri. Malam Bako asked him to swear he'd come with three or four blind to the community in Accra. He told them he was chief of Hausa in zongo. It was the tradition for a chief to gain power, to be considered powerful, to have more people—and especially the disabled. It makes you as a chief more god-fearing, as you can live with imperfection.

Sarkin Samari agreed to within seven days. He got seven boys to accompany him, who agreed to stay with him wherever he went. They traveled by land to Lagos; stayed 6 months in Lagos; stopped in Ajiyase (near Cotonou, in Benin) and stayed with the blind community there. They used canoes to cross rivers.

People in Accra (the Ga) had never seen blind people like them, seeing seven begging. They took them to Malam Bako's house at Zongo Lane. They brought them to sit in the *zaure* [entryway] and gave them food. They were given houses to live in at Zongo Lane [Malam Bako had not left Zongo Lane yet].

The *makafi* were the first to live at his house in his zaure at Sabon Zongo before Malam Bako moved there.

Like the blind, the barbers in Hausa society also had their chief. From the early days in Sabon Zongo until the present, the work of the barber (*aski*) has gone beyond cutting the men's hair and shaving them. In addition, he performs as a "doctor." This has included cutting tribal marks (currently done rarely) and pulling out the uvula at the baby's outdooring (seven days after birth) or later if it is too big (*hakin wuya*). The "barber" has also circumcised boys between the ages of four to seven. In his day, Malam Bako would call together all boys in the zongo of that age group and, according to Chief Sha'aibu Bako and Salama, he followed the tradition of the Emir of Kano in having them all cut at the same time (5/8/1982). And the barber has treated pains, like headaches, or blood clots by putting an animal horn on the spot, sucking in, cutting the place, sucking in again: "and the black blood will come out, and then water— and the water is the fever in you" (*Sarkin aski*, Ibrahim Bababar 5/30/82). While all of the barbers have not resided in the same quarter, each has had his designated "shop" where he carries out some of his occupational tasks.[43]

Early on in his headmanship, Malam Bako appointed Wansa Damaley as his chief barber. Using that role as a jumping off point, Damaley contested Malam

Bako's headship of Sabon Zongo. He solemnized marriages, granted divorces, had drums beaten and horns blown on his behalf. The talking drums would announce: "This is the Senior chief . . . here is a chief, here is a chief."[44]

The problem, of course, was that legitimacy was and is tied to rights to land and only the Ga had an ascribed right to the land. Thus, each man sought to "prove" his right through outside support. According to his grandson Adamu Damaley, Wansa was given the space (and the legitimacy to rule) Sabon Zongo in 1918 by Kadri English, the Zongo Lane patron and Hausa chief. However, it was not Kadri English's right to declare him leader. The British colonial government and the majority of the Ga stools recognized Malam Bako as leader of the community, and Bako dismissed Wansa as chief barber for "bad conduct." The Bako line was given "the proprietary rights . . . in Sabon Zongo lands as Founders of the Hausa settlement thereon."[45]

But the Damaley challenge would not go away, inherited as it was through successive generations.[46] Each of the three Damaley's who contested a Bako leader had the following of the classic *mai gida*. As one of his detractors observed, Damaley bought people.[47] And as one of his primary supporters observed, while Malam Bako had land, Damaley had people. Damaley accepted all strangers, Bako only his own family.[48]

The strangers who came would stay with Damaley . . . When the strangers came, Bako said he didn't have space, so they should go to Damaley's place. All those Hausa who came from outside came to Damaley—he was like a *mai gida*, the Hausa mai gida . . . Damaley suggested that the strangers/guests shouldn't be part of the communal labor, because they come and go. He'd been hosting the strangers and he said that they shouldn't have to work. But the Bako family said it should include everybody. So Damaley said to Idrissu, as he stood for people to follow him as chief, he too Damaley could stand for people to follow him as chief. So Kadri English said, I will help you Damaley, so you can be chief of Sabon Zongo.[49]

Years later, as the Damaley claim on the Sabon Zongo chieftaincy wore on, Wansa's grandson Adamu Damaley had as patrons both Ali Kadri English, the grandson of the first Kadri English, and Alhaji Maicancan, a wealthy Hausa trader and a modern *mai gida*.

The Bako-Damaley struggle had more than just a social dimension; it also played out spatially on the up/down axis. The two early socio-spatially distinct areas were and are Kan Tudu, "on top," and Gangare, "below." As current resident Papa Carlos observed, "it was a misunderstanding between down and up" (5/26/1996). According to Damaley supporter Alhaji Idi, "Damaley said that if the Kan Tudu people would stop the fighting, the Gangare people would too. But if they wouldn't stop, they too wouldn't stop" (2/26/1995). In other words, it was Kan Tudu, the old core, against Gangare (also known as Zabrama), near the Oblogo Road boundary. The Kan Tudu people sided with Bako because they lived there. The Gangare people sided with Damaley because that is where he lived and he helped everyone in his neighborhood—even, said one supporter, those from Bako's side; "he doesn't discriminate."

Malam Bako was losing his eyesight and in 1933, stepped down from the headmanship. Idrissu, his eldest son, was formally recognized as first chief of Sabon Zongo by the colonial government, the Ga and the other stranger chiefs after he was turbaned in July 1933. Malam Bako died on January 16, 1938.

Idrissu was a malam, though he had also travelled with his father to Nigeria to trade kola (Baba Mai Doki 5/31/1995). Like his father (and other early Muslim leaders in Accra), Idrissu Bako faced problems within the *zongo* community regarding his leadership. The British had reinforced Sabon Zongo's spatial and political separateness, the right of the James Town Ga to acclaim its headman, and of a Bako family member to be that headman, with all of the office's responsibilities, pomp, and circumstances. However, the Hausa headman's authority was also circumscribed by the colonial government. The District Commissioner reminded the Sabon Zongo headman in a letter dated May 27, 1940 that "you with your Elders are at liberty at any time to endeavour to Settle disputes and quarrels by arbitration. . . . I must however point out that you have no legal right or other power to enforce any finding of such arbitration neither can you charge fees nor can you inflict fines" (No. 879/36/33).

As a *zongo* chief, Idrissu's importance was tied to the functions he performed for his people, either directly or indirectly. The Hausa in Accra had contributed in the arena of public administration. *Zongo* leadership positions (*sarauta*) were borrowed from Hausa state tradition, but the structure in its constituent units and their articulation and functions, was quite different. Because the Hausa and other Muslims in Accra and Kumase were strangers, there was, for example, no endowment of fiefs as a condition of eligibility and tenure.

Like the other Hausa chiefs in Accra (as well as non-Hausa like Kanuri who were influenced by Hausa form), Idrissu established various offices characteristic of Hausa chieftaincy, such as *ciroma* and *galadima*. Both of these positions went to members of the Bako family.[50] *Ciroma* was a title given to a son of the paramount chief and the *galadima* was an important pre-Fulani position reserved for son or brother of the emir (Schildkrout 1978:92). In pre-colonial Zazzau, one of the Hausa states in Northern Nigeria, it was rare for the sons of one mother to succeed to the chieftaincy. With the British came changes in rules, form, and direction; for example, they dropped the rule that only sons of kings could succeed to office (Smith 1960).

In seeking the principles of Hausa succession to the chiefship, M.G. Smith interprets the Kano Chronicle[51] to say that "the office, being hereditary in an agnatic group, would pass collaterally and lineally at different times" (Smith 1997:118). In other words, sometimes the son succeeded his father, sometimes it was the chief's brother.

The *galadima* should be a brother of the chief but the son of a different mother than the chief. During Idrissu's reign, this could have been his half-brother Hamisu.[52] And while Idrissu never turbaned a *galadima*, Hamisu acted the part; the son of his full brother Lawal, Sha'aibu (chief between 1981–2001) was his *ciroma*.

Another important position is that of *Sarkin Fada*, the chief's major domo who also speaks for the chief. Normally, when a stranger comes to the chief, he must first see *Sarkin Fada*, who alerts the chief. Yet, it was Hamisu, in his role as *galadima*, who not only lead the chief on occasions like Id il Fitr or when the Ga Manche (Ababio) called but who even spoke for Idrissu. This was a rational adaptation of roles, given abilities and locale: Hamisu spoke better Ga than *Sarkin Fada* or anyone in the Bako family and much of the chief's duties took him outside the bounds of Sabon Zongo into the world of the Ga. Moreover, according to Idrissu's son Baba Mai Doki, Idrissu was a serious man. "You say, go here go there? No [he was] always in the *zaure* reading Koran" (Baba Mai Doki 5/31/1995). Thus, he needed an able officer who could go out into the world in his place.

In Sabon Zongo, the positions of *madawaki, maaji, sarkin fada* were and still are chosen from other families, though only Hausa, because (according to Alhaji Hamisu) Idrissu wanted the *zongo* people to unite. Clearly at that time, "*zongo* people" translated as Hausa but who were not related to the Bakos.

Idrissu also had a *magajiyan bori*, a female head of the *bori* spirit possession troupe. Sha'aibu Bako, the current chief, remembers Idrissu's *magajiya*. "At the time that we were small boys, the *magajiya* was somebody—how! You know this big tree around the corner? When we were small boys, the *bori* people would jump off that tree and land on their legs. *Bori* at that time was no small thing" (3/23/1982).

Idrissu Bako died January 10, 1969, supposedly ninety-five years old, having been chief for thirty-six years. If Alhaji Hamisu, the family head in the 1980s, was correct and succession in this diaspora community is in fact the same as in the Hausa homeland (since, he said, "our parents come from Nigeria") after Idrissu's death the chieftaincy should have gone to another one of Malam Bako's sons by a different wife, or to a brother. Indeed, if a son, it should have been Hamisu, because his mother Hadisatu had been Malam Bako's second wife (from whom he was divorced) and Hamisu her eldest son. But, Hamisu felt he was too old. In fact, he observed, all in his generation were too old. For example, the next choice would have been Alhaji Harona, son of wife number three, So Mutane, but he had already died while on *haji*. The next eligible would have been Yusufu, son of Abeche, wife number four, but he was dead as well. So instead, the chief was chosen from the next generation down: after Idrissu's death, the son of his brother Lawal, Lebo Bako, a tailor, was installed as chief.

Lebo Bako was installed as Sarkin Zongo on December 28, 1970 and formally recognized by the Ga Manche three months later. Lebo set up his version of Hausa officialdom. Its foundation also derives from the prototypical Hausa chieftaincies of Northern Nigeria,[53] but like the contemporary Daura, some titles lapsed and others were innovations. The titled offices fall under the rubric of *fadawa*, courtiers; some are hereditary, others free. All are intermediary to the chief.

Under Lebo, Inussa (son of Lebo's father's brother Hamisu) became *galadima*, while Sha'aibu (Lebo's brother), continued as *ciroma*. Three years after assuming the headmanship, Lebo became ill and Sha'aibu took over his duties. Lebo died in 1981, and Sha'aibu was formally installed as *sarkin zongo*, while Inussa remained as *galadima* and Inussa's younger brother Yehaya became *ciroma*.

Table 3.1
Chief's Office-Holders

Ciroma	equivalent of *yerima*, official under the chief, usually son of chief
Galadima	senior councillor
Ubandoma	goes out to inform people of chief's arrival
Sarkin Fada	majordomo and messenger to the chief; speaks for chief
Madawaki	*Sarkin Dawaki*, in charge of horses
Salama	porter; visitors to chief must see him first
Kilishi	official who sees to spreading of chief's rug
Maaji	treasurer
Majidadi	"expresses chief's happiness"
Magajin gari	a member of the titled administrative staff
Waziri	deputy (vizier)
Alkali	judge
Magajiya	"queen mother," though never mother of reigning chief
Magajiyan bori	"queen mother" of the *bori* cult

In Sabon Zongo, the hereditary posts were assigned as follows: *salama* to Malam Bako's brother Sha'aibu's son, Sani Sallama; *kilishi* to Malam Bako's brother Adamu's son's son, Issa Odonkaw; *waziri* to Malam Bako's senior sister's son's son, Abubakar Baban Tani; *ubandoma* to Malam Bako's son Haruna's son, Yushau; *galadima* to Malam Bako's son Hamisu's son, Inussa; *magajin gari* to Malam Bako's brother's son, Mohammed Nabawko; *ciroma* to Malam Bako's son Lawal's son, Sha'aibu. The free posts, which include *sarkin fada, madawaki, maaji, alkali, magajiya*, and *magajiyan bori*, go to local eligibles. *Sarkin fada* was in fact passed on to the son of Idrissu's *sarkin fada*; the others have varied, depending upon the task. *Alkali*, for example, demands reasoned judgement, and a clever malam would be selected (though politics are not absent). The position of *magajiyan bori* has been occupied by three different women in the last 20 years. When asked about *magajiyan bori*, Chief Sha'aibu has steadfastly maintained that anyone who reads the Koran knows that *bori* is "not true," even as he himself has had two *magajiyan bori*. He chose the first, because his predecessor Lebo had one and then she died. After she died, Lebo died. Sha'aibu was turbaned as chief, and the *bori* people came and said that they wanted a certain woman, Bahi, to be their *magajiyan bori*. The chief, he said, could not reject the post, because "it is custom." Every Hausa chief has to have his *magajiyan bori* (Sha'aibu Bako 3/23/1982).

Lebo continued the Hausa tradition of appointing sub-chieftaincies, adding *sarkin kutare* (chief of the lepers) to blind, butchers, and barbers. As Chief Bako and Sallama explained to me (4/17/1982), given fears of contagion, Malam Bako had given lepers a place to live, a compound, in an area that came to be called leper's quarter (*ungowan kutare*). As related by the current *sarkin kutare*, a chief of *kutare* was elected because the leper people needed one. One day, one leper died here. He had things in his room. The lepers went to Chief Lebo and told him and Lebo said they must elect a chief so that there will be some to take care of all matters that come up (as a patron would do). Then if there are further problems, he can send to the Chief of Sabon Zongo (Garuba Suleimana, *Sarkin Kutare* 5/16/1982).

With the exception of *majidade* and *magajiyan bori*, all of Lebo's court continued to serve under his successor Sha'aibu. This has also been true among the *fadawa* of the Accra Central Hausa chieftaincy. When their chief dies, the officers retain their posts. It is only when an officer dies that a new one is chosen. "Our chieftaincy is not like politics: if you are in [governmental] office, when they sack the government, then they will sack you" (Alhaji Idi, Zongo Lane, 2/10/1982). Thus, Chief Ali Kadri English, head of the Hausa in Central Accra, has his father's officers.

Today, the four most visible of the Sabon Zongo chief's *fadawa* are *Sarkin Fada, Madawaki, Majidade* and *Magiyan Bori*, all of whom accompany the chief to mosque on the Id celebration, ride with him in the parade that snakes back through the streets of Sabon Zongo, and then surround him when he sits in state at the end of the day.

Over the years, the internal leadership of Sabon Zongo's Bako family has followed a patrimonial, not a chiefly, line. From Malam Bako, it went to Idrissu (his son with his first wife Amina); from Idrissu to Lawal (son of Malam Bako and Amina), to Hamisu (son of Malam Bako and his second wife Hadisatu), to Gambo (son of Malam Bako and his fourth wife Abece) and to Isaaka (nickname Dan Baba, son of Malam Bako and his eighth wife Inda, and the last remaining son of Malam Bako).

THE EARLY COMMUNITY: THE POPULATION AND ITS CHARACTER

While Sabon Zongo elders characterize the community's early population as Hausa, it may not have been exclusively so, because the British collapsed strangers into one category and housed them together. Moreover, like Hausa diaspora communities elsewhere in West Africa, Sabon Zongo exhibited cultural unity and ethnic flexibility (Works 1976). This is concretely portrayed on a map drawn early into the establishment of the community, which indicates the names of the allotted plots. After reading through the names on the mapped plots, Chief Sha'aibu Bako and his elders could estimate the ethnic variability of houseowners as minimal, the Hausa alone constituting almost 85 percent, with the related Northern Nigerian, Muslim Fulani added in, 87 percent, and with the Nigerian (and probably Muslim) Yoruba, Nupe, and Kanuri, 92 percent (Table 3.2).[54] Each of the thirty-two parcels contained at least one property (Figure 6). Seventeen out of thirty-two parcels had no non-Hausa property-owners; another ten each contained only one non-Hausa owner. With the exception of the Ga farmer who did not leave, the non-Hausa owners were in effect northerners. Ethnically mixed houseownership was confined to four sections, adjacent to one another at the far northern edge.

Table 3.2
Ethnic Composition of House Owners

Hausa	175
Fulani	7
Yoruba	8
Wangara	5
Mossi	4
Kanuri	1
Nupe	1
Zabrama	2
Ga	1
Benin	1
Zugu	1
Unknown	3
	209

In the 1930s, some twenty years after its founding, the majority of Sabon Zongo was still Hausa and most spoke the Hausa language. The current *Sarkin Fada* recalls that when he was a boy, the immediate neighborhood was Hausa, with the exception of a few Zabrama and Adar tenants. Moreover, most people owned their own homes, which became family homes, inhabited by groups of extended kin. In 1933, Malam Bako stated that there were "600 persons in this zongo and about 160 Rate payers" (taxpayers or property owners).[55] Each property was listed under the family head.

Kinship and descent continued to be important, since pedigree carried rewards like rights to family housing (see Chapters 7 and 8). They also figured into marriage. The Hausa preferred form of cousin marriage was frequent, according

to Malam Bako's son Malam Gambo, because parents saw this as a good way
to perpetuate the family and generally children acquiesced (5/4/1982).

An easy way to enlarge the family was for a man to marry multiple wives
and procreate. As Muslims, the Hausa men could be married to as many as four
women at a time. Over his adult lifetime, Malam Bako was married to nine
women, of whom he divorced two. His wives bore him thirty-seven children.
His son Idrissu married four women, one of whom he divorced, and had fourteen
children. Idrissu's brother Malam Hamisu married four women, who bore him
eight children (see the Bako family genealogy, Chapter 5).

Along with polygyny, some of today's Sabon Zongo elders remember wife
seclusion among early Hausa residents. In reminiscing about his childhood, Malam Gambo recalled that the only non-family who could enter his father's compound were females. He remembered male visitors sitting in the *zaure*. It was
his feeling that during his childhood, wives and mothers did not just go out;
they sent maidservants on errands. "Even if you did not have money, you could
do *kulle*. You can do *kulle* if you know you can look after the girl" (5/4/1982).

Malam Gambo remembered that when his father saw a woman selling on the
street, he would call in her husband and chastise him. If they did not accept his
judgement, Gambo says, Malam Bako would send them to the British (5/4/
1982). The British were, in fact, asked to deal with related issues. In 1925,
Kadri English wrote to the District Commissioner (DC) asking his assistance in
eliminating Hausa prostitution in Accra. He reminded the DC that chastity
among Muslim women is essential and that no Muslim woman should be without a husband. Yet, "good Hausa women who were living good lives in Northern
Nigeria change for the worst on arrival in the Gold Coast Colony in which evil
influences are somewhat paramount. . . . At present the women are daily divorc-
ing their husbands without cause in order to carry on immoral practices and the
result is sickness and untimely death."[56]

In fact, among Sabon Zongo's early Hausa residents, seclusion was not so
much a norm as an ideal. The first generation of Sabon Zongo men practiced a
kind of temporary confinement of their wives. According to Malam Hamisu (4/
9/1982), in the early days of Sabon Zongo, women worked from the house. And
like the secluded Hausa women in Kano today, they used their children to sell
their products outside. But none of the elders today can think of more than two
men who practised *auren kulle*—Malam Bako, and possibly only with his senior
wife Amina, and Ali Ango, a descendant of the Garuba family (M. Barko 9/25/
2001). What was normative was that women display the proper appearance of
kunya, of modesty, and not "go roaming about." Gambo and Hamisu's recol-
lections were probably colored by their father's attempt to instill *kulle* as a norm
in Sabon Zongo. Yet, Alhaji Baba Mai Doki, the son of Malam Bako's son
Idrissu, remembers only Malam Bako's senior wife Amina being in *kulle*.

Thus, Sabon Zongo's married Hausa women had some mobility. As in

Northern Nigeria today, they negotiated with their husbands or managed to con-
test control (see Pittin 1996), in order to attend life-cycle celebrations with other
women. On other occasions, they visited family members after dark. Travelling
in the company of other women or children and wearing a prayer shawl over
the head, they maintained their modesty as moved with a shield of protection,
which communicated to men that they should keep their distance.

Schooling at that time, according to Malam Hamisu, occurred in Koranic
school (*makaranta*). There one learned the Koran, language, *hadith* (traditions
of the Prophet), *horewa* (discipline), and *nahawu* (grammar). When Malam
Gambo, Malam Hamisu's brother and successor in the family Koranic school,
was growing up, more boys than girls attended. "At first, girls didn't go to
makaranta"—the husbands taught them at home. Some had girls working in the
house. In those early days of Sabon Zongo, girls also did not read Koran at
their weddings, since most had not yet studied. Malam Bako wanted his boy
children to attend school, because he believed one cannot achieve anything in
these modern times without schooling; but he felt it was not important for girls,
because once they marry, they are not supposed to work outside of the home.

Baba Mai Doki is one of the community elders and a son of Chief Idrissu
Bako. Idrissu would not allow him to attend Western school for fear that he
would leave Islam or traditional Hausa society. "My mother put me into school
at Cow Lane, me and Ali [his brother], before my father disagreed. He told his
brother Lawal, to go bring me from Accra and send me to Arabic school. [To
learn English] he said he disagreed" (5/21/1995).

Bab Alaj is a successful Hausa architect/engineer, who years ago moved to
the suburbs. When he was sent for Western education, "My time, I was alone"
(5/12/1995). In Accra, those Muslims/Nigerians who sent their children to
school were the Shadows who were Nupe and the Braimahs who were Yoruba;
the Kadri English family was the Hausa exception to the rule of sending their
children to *makaranta* only. "Most Hausa believed you were 'carefree' [irre-
sponsible] if you went to school—you didn't want your children educated outside of Islam" (Bab Alaj 5/21/1995).

Sule Bako, Chief Sha'aibu Bako's son, points out that Hausa people would
have key positions in industry, government, health, had they been educated in
Western schools, but their fathers feared that if they went to such schools, they
would become Christians. And the Hausa were the most observant of the Mus-
lims, Hausa practices being the model for the other Muslim groups. Lawal and
Hamisu, two of Idrissu's brothers, maintained friendships with some Christian
boys who went on in school. Lawal could read English better than his son
Sha'aibu, later the chief, having learned from his friends (Sule Bako 6/7/1995).
Within Malam Bako's family, only three individuals—Haruna Bako (son of
Idrissu), his son Sa'idu and Chief Sha'aibu's son Sule Bako—were sent to
Western school. It was Sha'aibu, Sule's father, who was responsible. "My father

was called by Chief Idrissu—if Haruna should go astray, if he should abandon Islam, all the sin will be borne by my father" (Sule Bako 6/14/1996).

In fact, before Independence, the so-called secular schools were actually mission schools. If one went to Catholic school, he was expected to become Catholic, if to Presbyterian school, to become Presbyterian, and so on. Sule Bako attended Presby Primary. Every Monday he was caned for not attending Sunday church. He knew a Presbyterian boy who often did not attend church on Sunday and finally quit school because he was tired of being caned (Sule Bako 6/7/ 1995).

In those early days, according to Hamisu (4/9/1982), the women may have been in seclusion, but like the Hausa women in Kano today, they were able to work from the house. Using their children to sell their products outside, they made k'afa and gari (maize flour) and tawada (ink).

The Hausa men worked primarily as traders in cows, sheep, goats, or kola nuts; they also dealt in kwali (antimony, used by men, women, and children to line the eyes), kanuwa (potash, used in foods), and they worked as retailers. The Hausa would bring needles, kwali, kanuwa and cloth from Nigeria. In Salaga Market in northern Ghana, this would be exchanged for kola, transported from Ghana's forest zone by the Asante. In Accra, at Timber Market, the traders dealt in kola. There were carriers (kaya-kaya) who put two to three hundred nuts into a basket and carried it. At that time, Kadri English was the head of the kola traders.

Others worked as Koranic teachers, tailors, butchers, traditional doctors/barbers, and maroka (praise-singers); among the Hausa, as in Hausaland, these occupations were ranked. There were also beggars, which included lepers, handicapped and the blind.

Some became innovators. Because Alhaji Baba Mai Doki, the son of Chief Idrissu Bako, was not allowed to attend school, he got a job working at the post office in the telephones. But he also rode horses (hence his name, Baba the horseman)—his father had a horse he rode at the Id il Fitr parade. Riding Idrissu's horse through the Korle Bu Hospital grounds to the beach, Baba met a physician Dr. Ribeiro, who also enjoyed horseback riding. Dr. Ribeiro taught him all about riding and taking care of horses.

Baba was a small man. He had the perfect body and riding abilities to become a jockey. He started racing before Independence (1957) and raced for about 19 years: during one three-year period, he rode in Accra and Kumase; then to Nigeria and Lagos, Ibadan, Abeokuta, Zaria, back to Lagos; and then home. When he stopped racing, he began training horses for racing. When he was about twenty-five years old, he got to know a woman from the Danish Embassy who enjoyed horseback riding. She wanted to take him to Denmark for a visit and perhaps to study veterinary medicine. Idrissu refused to let him go and seized his passport, presumably for the same reason he pulled him out of school. When Idrissu died, they found the passport among his things. Baba Mai Doki is a highly respected elder in the community; he is a good Muslim; he defends custom. But he also achieved in ways quite different from those around him.

TIES WITH ACCRA

After Malam Bako set up his new community and relocated there, he did not cut off contact with the Accra Muslims: he had been a member of the Building Committee of the Main Mosque (along with Chief Braimah, Harri Zenuwa, Father Shardow and Malam Enguma) and he was still the Chief Imam. He continued "to move" with the first Braimah and after his death, the second Braimah, and Kadri English. In the 1980s, the collectivity included the latest Chief Braimah (Yoruba), Chief Ali Mada (Grunshie), Chief Jimala (Wangara), and Chief B.B. Shardow (Nupe), while Ali Kadri English and Sha'aibu Bako each went off on his own.

During the Gold Coast days, there was also a lot of communication between Idrissu and the Ga. At the regional level, Idrissu was an important leader (Sule Bako 6/24/1996). Even in the 1940s, 30 years after the community had been established, the chairman of the Accra Rehousing Committee wrote several letters to the Sabon Zongo chief (addressed to Malam Bako, although it was now Idrissu who was chief) complaining "that goats and sheep persist in destroying plants and shrubs in the Zongo Estate" and asking that the owners be persuaded to keep them penned.[57] And in 1964, "Chief Malam Bako [sic], Chief of Sabon Zongo" was contacted by the James Town Stool Lands Registry, observing the erection of wood and iron sheet structures and demanding they be demolished.[58]

Sabon Zongo was very much a part of Accra as far as British regulations for the city were concerned. For example, when Idrissu was chief, he heard from the President of the Accra Town Council who was concerned that house numbers were not visible on many houses, due perhaps to wear and tear or as he suggested, to periodic cleaning. And he quoted the law as follows: "The owner and occupier of every house or building which has been numbered as aforesaid shall at their own expense keep the numbers exposed to public view, and shall not allow them to become obliterated or illegible. Every person contravening this section shall be liable to a fine of five shillings, and to a further fine of one shilling for each day during which the offence continues after conviction."[59]

People did not move to Sabon Zongo never to leave: men worked in Accra, they prayed at the main mosque on Fridays and on holidays. Men and women visited family living in Central Accra and other *zongos*. They celebrated life-cycle events of family and friends outside of their enclave.

By the same token, Sabon Zongo was physically a place apart. In the next chapter, we will consider the physical distinctiveness that continues to characterize it even today.

NOTES

1. According to Select Committee discussions in 1865, the colonial government felt it would be useful to employ "the natives of one country in another . . . Houssas [*sic*] from Lagos, for instance, might be distributed all over the Gold Coast."

2. SNA 1086. 24 January 1889, NAG.

3. SNA 1086. Letter to Hon. Col. Sec'y from Brandford-Griffith, Governor, 9 November 1884, NAG.

4. Documents regarding the composition of the Islamic population at the turn of the century are generally vague about ethnic affiliations and often not reliable when they are specific. For example, many migrants classified as Hausa "were not members of the same ethnic group and many of them took Hausa ethnicity only while away from their homes" (Adamu 1978:15). This included recruits to the GCHC. Two of the better-known officers, Harri Zenua and his brother Danbornu, were Kanuri from Bornu (Interview with Chief Amida Braimah, 18 January 1982).

5. Much of the early material is based upon Dretke's (1968) account of the growth of Accra's Muslim community.

6. M.T. Braimah, undated obituary.

7. Obituary. Government Gazette No. 50, 14 August 1920. P. 1023.

8. Disturbance at Accra between James Town and Ussher Town people. Letter to Hon. Col. Sec'y from Brandford-Griffith, Gov. 11 September 1884. SNA 1086, NAG.

9. Junius Geoffrey is former Secretary of the Ghana Muslim Mission.

10. Adamu may have consulted British records for this information, which throws into suspicion what is meant by Hausa. Is it simply a general term for "Muslim stranger"? I use the term as my informants presented it: their "forefather" who came from Katsina, one of the Hausa *Bakwai*.

11. Tackie Obile, Ga Manche, to DC, Accra, 15 September 1904; ADM 11/1502, SNA 900, NAG.

12. Interview with Amida Braimah, 18 January 1982, and B.B. Shardow, Chief of Nupe, 28 January 1982.

13. Interview with Amida Braimah, 2 February 1982.

14. Odoom (1971) has Abu Bakr next in line.

15. ADM 11/1502, 9 June 1908.

16. As was true for Kumase (Schildkrout 1970a).

17. Interview with Mohammad Ra'abiyu (also known as Baba Agba Goldsmith), *sarkin yaki*, 27 February 1982.

18. SNA 1331/07, 20 November 1908, NAG.

19. ADM 11/1446 and SNA 35/1926, 9 November 1926, NAG.

20. In later years, this was expanded to the selection of tribal heads for the constituent ethnic groups as their members increased. Cited by Junius Geoffrey, former Secretary, Ghana Muslim Mission, in an interview June 21, 1982, regarding the 1930 Fulani chieftaincy fight.

21. Ibrahima Braimah was a cattle dealer. His middle name apparently refers to his occupation, which, among the Hausa, is ranked at the bottom of the occupational ladder.

22. As Ga Manche, and thus owner of the land, he had the right to accept or reject a candidate for chieftaincy over any resident stranger tribal group (memo, November 28, 1902, SNA file 2288/01, NAG).

23. Malam Bako recounted this episode in a letter to the district commissioner dated July 10, 1933. I obtained a copy from Chief Sha'aibu Bako.

24. SNA Case 65/07, ADM 11/9, Notes of Proceedings at an Interview granted by His Excellency the Governor to the Manche of Accra on Saturday the 3rd of August, 1907 at 3 P.M., NAG.

25. ADM 11/1502, July 9, 1908, NAG.

26. Correspondence from 1907 reveals that the British were involved in negotiations to survey a *zongo* outside of town, which was the section of land that became Sabon Zongo (letter to Y. Ex., 10/24/1907, ADM 11/1502, NAG).

27. In 1916, Sabo Gari, Ibadan's *zongo*, was created by the British as a Hausa "village." All Hausa in Ibadan were ordered to move there, and Hausa exclusiveness was formally institutionalized (Cohen 1969).

28. N.O. Ali's eldest son Mama Ali was also nominated by Malam Abubakar and his "Fulani" followers.

29. Letter to the acting governor, June 16, 1909, SNA 1331/07, NAG.

30. Chief Lebbo Baako v. Alhaji Adamu Damanley [*sic*] and Anor., December 23, 1981.

31. As it is stated in the Koran, Sura IV:34,

Men are the protectors and maintainers of women,
Because God has given the one more [strength] than the other . . ." (Koran 1975:190).

And furthermore, their modesty must be guarded, as in Sura XXIV:31,

. . . say to the believing women
That they should lower
Their gaze and guard*
Their modesty; that they
Should not display their
Beauty and ornaments** except
What (must ordinarily) appear
Thereof; that they should
Draw their veils over
Their bosoms and not display
Their beauty except
To their husbands, their fathers,
Their husbands' fathers, their sons,
Their husbands' sons,
Their brothers or their brothers' sons,
Or their sisters' sons,
Or their women, or the slaves
Who, their right hands
Possess, or male servants
Free of physical needs,
Or small children who
Have no sense of the shame
Of sex . . . (Koran 1975:904f.).

32. See Tetteh Kwahu *versus* Kpakpo Brown & others, 16 February 1910.

33. Kimble (1963:18) notes that customary law provided for a permanent grant of land to a whole group of strangers who wished to settle; it did not need to be renewed upon the chief's death.

34. The Zongo Lane address was on the return address on various pieces of correspondence he had with the SNA as late as 1921 (e.g., ADM 11/1502; SNA Board 133; 5 June 1921, NAG); however, his great grandson Sule Bako believes that the address may have been an oversight. It is more likely that he moved to Sabon Zongo when the main mosque was closed by the British in 1915.

35. Malam Bako's testimony, *Hammond v. Ababio*, April 12, 1912, 61.

36. See letter cited in note 26.

37. In 1917, Malam Bako wrote as "High Priest" (Chief Imam) to the District Commissioner to request "a piece or parcel of land for the purpose of using same as Cemetary for burying the deads [*sic*] of my people at the above place [The Hausa Settlement, Oblogo Road] where I am present [*sic*] settled" (August 24, 1917).

38. E.g. letter from Medical Officer of Health to "Sarikin Zongo Malam Edrisu & Ors" [*sic*], No. 6/4.C/1941, 1/3/1941, NAG.

39. Letter of 5 May 1930, ADM 11/1446, NAG.

40. *Hammond v. Ababio*, April 25, 1912, 75.

41. Letter from the District Commissioner's office, Victoriaborg, April 18, 1939. I obtained a copy from Chief Sha'aibu Bako.

42. Letter from the district commissioner, Victoriaborg, to Hausa Chief, Sabon Zongo, July 17, 1940. No. 1329/263/1939. I obtained a copy from Chief Sha'aibu Bako.

43. Circumcision of a group of boys or removing the uvula at the time of the outdooring would be done wherever the event is occurring.

44. Abudu Razarku testimony, appeal proceedings *Idirisu Bako v. Wansa Damaley*, November 4, 1933.

45. *Chief Lebbo Bako v. Alhaji Adamu Damanley* [*sic*] and Anor., December 23, 1981.

46. Pellow 1991, 1999 discuss the case in detail.

47. Interview with Sarkin Fada, 7 May 1982.

48. Interview with Bako B.K., 7 May 1982.

49. Interview with Alhaji Idi, Sabon Zongo Lane, 26 February 1995.

50. For example, B.B. Shardow, Chief of the Nupe, observed that his chieftaincy carried the same officers as the Hausa. These included a *galadima* (who was family), a *sarkin fada*, and councillor (both Shardows), and a *magajiya* for the women (January 28, 1982). Sha'aibu Mai'yaki who had been the Hausa chief in Nima since 1954, maintains a *galadima, sarkin fada, waziri* and *dogari* ("policeman") (January 28, 1982). Abayazidu Zenuah, son of Officer Harri Zenuah, is the chief of the Kanuri community in Accra, and he too has a *fadawa*, as well as *galadima, sarkin fada, magajiya gari*, and *waziri*. The Kanuri have two chiefly houses, and the chiefship alternates between the two (February 5, 1982).

51. The Kano Chronicle is a document which records the reigns of forty-two Habe kings in the Hausa state of Kano between the end of the tenth and the beginning of the nineteenth century, and 5 Fulani emirs to the late nineteenth century.

52. According to the chief advisor to Chief Bawa Kadri English, father of the current Hausa chief of Central Accra, the term "brother" is used loosely. For example, Chief Ali Kadri English's *galadima* is his father's brother's son (Alhaji Idi February 10, 1982).

53. See M.G. Smith (1978:77–142) for a comprehensive delineation of Hausa categories of office.

54. I derived the breakdown in Table 3.1 from the survey map, which actually lists the names of the owners on each compound delineated. The copy I acquired was traced

on August 25, 1945. I do not know when the original was drawn, but according to the chief and his elders, the listing is an early one, from Malam Bako's time.

55. See letter cited in note 23.

56. Letter from Chief Kadri English to D.C., 5/13/1925, ADM 11/922, Case No. 25/1925, NAG.

57. No. 145/M.F./40, 9/13/1941; No. 196/M.F./40, 2/2/1942, NAG.

58. Secretary, James Town Stool Lands Registry, 2/3/1964,

59. No. 1C71/51/1921; 3/22/1937, NAG.

4

SABON ZONGO: ENVIRONMENTAL DELIMITATIONS

Boundedness can be manifest in the community landscape, as I have noted for early Victoriaborg or Jamestown. In the 1950s, when Alhassan and Huseini Sulley (great great grandsons of Malam Garuba) were growing up in Sabon Zongo, there was little built up between their community and the Lighthouse area of Jamestown due east at the sea. At night they could hear the sea rough and rumbling. Even in the 1960s, there was no electricity in Sabon Zongo. The twins would walk a half mile or so to Town Council Line to study under the street lights (Alhassan and Huseini Sulley 6/18/00). In those days, there were lots and lots of trees. It was a pretty and shady community (Alhassan Sulley 7/1/1996); however, as the trees died, they were not replaced. Bushes or flowers are now absent; they would be eaten by the sheep and goats wandering the streets. Among the Hausa and many of the other groups who migrated into Sabon Zongo, keeping animals is desirable and many are left to roam. People say that the sheep must be penned, because otherwise they will wander off. Goats, on the other hand, are wander freely. And they eat any and all greenery. Until the 1980s, those "with capacity" kept cattle in pens alongside residences. The Municipality no longer allows cows to be raised within the city limits (though one does see them being grazed in open spaces), but sheep, goats and poultry are legal.

Thus, unlike the lovely suburban areas of Accra, or even Sabon Zongo's neighbor Larte Biokarshie, with their elegant homes and manicured grounds, there is a distinctly rural feel to Sabon Zongo, in terms of sights, sounds and smells.

Sabon Zongo is shabby. This reflects the early ecological effects of European influence, which in turn fostered a pattern of neglect by municipal authorities, traditional leaders, and private houseowners in the years that followed (Pellow 1999). Sabon Zongo has urgent infrastructural needs—for gutters, roads, toilets.

Fundamental to this study is how space and the built environment are created by and create social relations. As will become evident in Chapter 7, a unique element in this community is the involution of the courtyard in the compound houses, due to peculiarities of kinship, inheritance, and building practices. The safety and availability of the streets is significant, because of the loss of the shared "commons" in each bounded compound property. Activities that would traditionally take place in the compound yard of needs are extended out into the street. It is the street that becomes the "common space" and for a larger and less connected group of people than the residents of a house. The joyful outdooring held for a new baby, the dance festivities of a wedding, the somber sitting of mourners after a death—all take place in the street. The user behavior of participants is in the vein of what I call public privacy, "each allowing the others to carry out daily activities in the open space but as if they were not visible" (Pellow 1991b:203). I explicate this concept in my analysis of the way strangers share compound space (see Chapter 8), but we also see it in the way groups of people share use of the street, for activities that are really semi-public—in the public eye for those who are invited and participated in by those who are not (see Chapter 6).

Sabon Zongo is one of the town sites that was aided by Governor J.P. Roger's three-year urban planning initiative following the epidemic of the plague in Accra in 1908. It was settled by strangers, which in Ghana means they came without prior rights to land, because all land was owned by either stools (in the south) or skins (in the north). Land is of fundamental importance in Ghana, because it enables various kinds of legitimacy: it provides the means to setting up enterprises, creating relationships, engaging in exchanges, indeed providing a place for a family to live. Malam Bako and his descendants would have had no issue with Damaley and his descendants had the rights to land been, for example, ascribed and thus unambiguous.

Rights to land also play into social rights, or at least perceptions of said, of who belongs and who does not. Thus, the physical lines of demarcation are crucial to social understandings, identities, and roles and rights.

Sabon Zongo was physically distinct when it was established and continues to be so. Even from the turn-off at Ring Road, one can see the profile of two of its mosques: Zana, built on the side of Oblogo Road, and Abokin Ango, pale yellow with distinctively blue ornamentation and an electrified muezzin, a block in from the main road but towering above the built landscape. These may stand out physically, and Abokin Ango may be quite audible because of its public address system, but this seventy-five acre community in fact has thirty mosques (see Figure 7), reflecting Sabon Zongo's Muslim character. Two of the mosques are roofless and several others are incorporated within residential compounds.

Exemplars of an important element in this community's built environment,

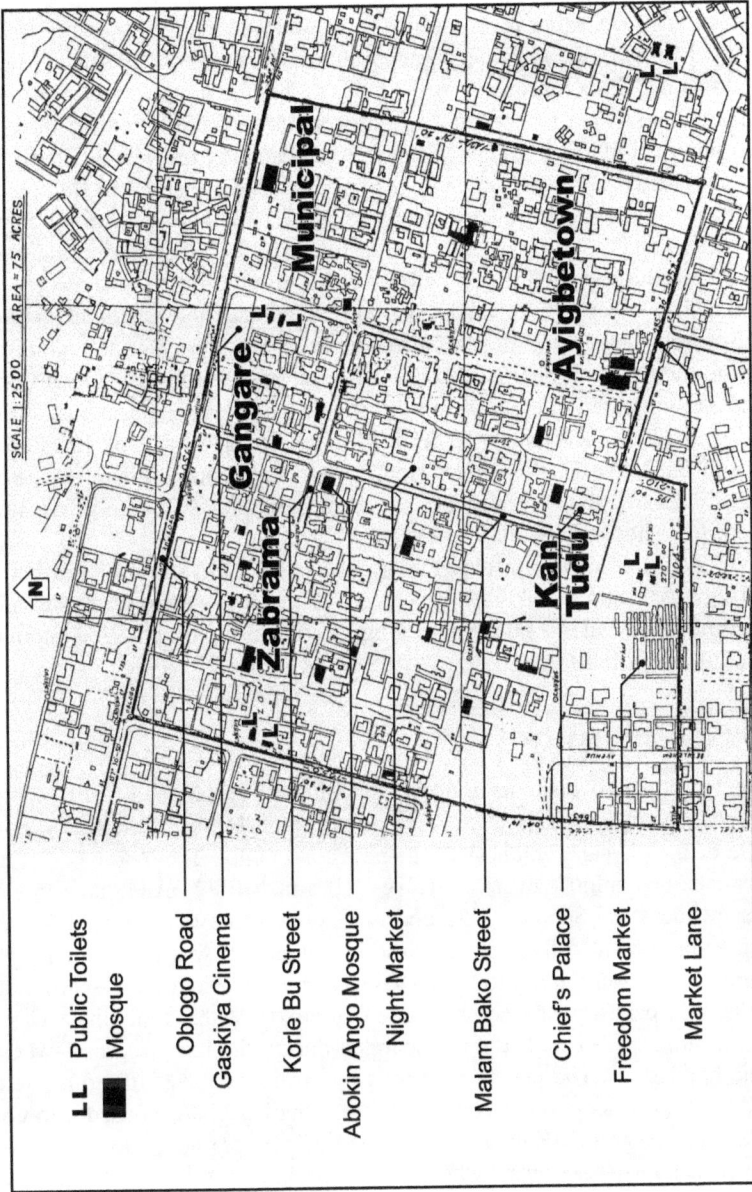

Figure 7 Aerial Map of Sabon Zongo, with Unguwa Divisions and Public Toilets

the names of the mosques record a history of social exchange: of owners of the land, local patrons, identifiable populations of worshippers. *Masalaci* Malam Bako, Malam Bako's mosque, was the first one built and it was built next door to Malam Bako's palace. Abokin Ango Mosque is named after one of the early settlers who had married Amina (Azumi), granddaughter of Malam Garuba and of Malam Nenu's brother. Damaley's Mosque, named after Malam Bako's first Chief Barber who sired a line of chiefly hopefuls, was built near to his house; one of the Damaley boosters, Bako B.K., lived in the same quarter and had a mosque built there as well. Ethnic groups built mosques: in Ayigbetown, as the commuity has expanded, they built *Masalaci* Gao-Gao and *Masalaci* Timbuktoo, both frequented by Malians. Other identifiable groups, like the blind, had a mosque built in their quarter. *Masalaci* Idrissu (also known as "Sabon Gida," new house) is named after Idrissu Bako. As Malam Bako's eldest son, Idrissu owned land all over Sabon Zongo. That Idrissu's Mosque was built just in front of his son Baba Mai Doki's stables signals interesting connections with the city at large: Baba houses and trains the horses of ex-patriates (a number of whom are from the Middle East) that race at Accra's track.

Sabon Zongo is now also clearly part of the built modern urban landscape with a movie theatre (Gaskiya Cinema), video theatres, and several communication offices for making calls and sending faxes. And it has changed internally in identifiably spatial terms.

A BOUNDED COMMUNITY

Initially, eighty-seven years ago, the impediments of the natural environment telescoped the separateness of Sabon Zongo. Some Hausa chose not to come because of the physical wildness of the new community. The Yoruba chief told of "animals, bad animals even . . . wolves" (Braimah 1982). And one of the old women residents of Sabon Zongo concurs: At the time of Malam Bako, you needed to be a man to live here because of animals. It was a place apart. "At that time, if you were going to Sabon Zongo, you came to a river—they called it Korle. You paid a penny before you could cross. At that time, there was no street" (Braimah 1982). "The ferry operated during the rainy season—when it became flooded. . . . The people paid tolls by means of foodstuffs to the ferryman. . . . It was an important ferry for the surrounding villagers used it to go to the market at Nkpono" (Emmanuel Kpakpoe Allotey 5/30/62, 143).

The community was "bush" where Ga people farmed the land. "I had casada [cassava] and Okroi [okra] farms . . . I left my farm when the Hausas were put in; they caused my removal. Their sheep spoiled my okro" (Odenke, Mantse D.P. Hammond of Asere v. Mantse Kojo Ababio IV and Chief Malam Bako, 3/14/1912). Another Ga man had planted "casada [cassava], mango, cashew, plenty palm trees and other smaller fruit trees and pine apple and other things before Malam Bako came. . . . They have felled some of the trees the farm is now in the middle of their houses" (Charles Addy, Mantse D.P. Hammond of

Asere v. Mantse Kojo Ababio IV and Chief Malam Bako, 3/13/1912). Most relinquished their farms and were relocated. Malam Bako kept cattle. In court testimony, Idrissu Bako recalled growing cassava and corn on the farms that the Hausa made when they moved to Sabon Zongo (7/6/1962 Tr.L. Suit No. 22/1948, 156). Chief Idrissu stabled horses. His son Baba Mai Doki kept cattle until the 1980s, when it was no longer legal to do so within the city limits.

By the 1950s, the community was still considered far from Accra. The colonial government had engineered the city's internal spatial differentiation into enclaves and neighborhoods. Their socio-economic inequalities were exacerbated by time and the municipality's (dis)interest. Sabon Zongo's "foreign-looking" population made it easier for the municipality to ignore it. Poverty worsened. In the 1970s, Sabon Zongo was described as one of the "highly traditional tracts" and a "low status migrant sink" (Brand 1972:296, 292). This characterization still holds true; in fact Structural Adjustment has not been good to either the community or its residents, and many non-zongolese still consider it spatially and socially peripheral to the city.

But in fact, Sabon Zongo has been part of the city of Accra since 1943. It is also very much a part of the urban landscape: it is edged by main roads that are traveled by commuters into Accra from other urban and suburban areas. City public transportation vehicles and taxis make pick-ups within and alongside the community. Many of its residents go to work elsewhere in Accra, and there are businesses in Sabon Zongo patronized by people from elsewhere in Accra.

As observed by an architect who works for TSC (Technical Service Centre), Sabon Zongo functions like a village: people know each other and their property and genealogical connections to the past continue to be influential; they have a traditional chief as the community head; the community is commercially alive, and it is unusual even for a *zongo* insofar as it is the oldest of the *zongo* spin-offs from Zongo Lane in Central Accra and the only one with a proper site plan (Elliot Barbour-Sackey 6/17/1996).

While residents do not all agree on the physical boundaries of this community, they do know that the community has grown. According to a Bako family member who has also run for political office, Sabon Zongo has expanded considerably in his lifetime. "Formerly, Zongo is just a small community, a small area. But now Zongo has expanded. To the Mortuary Road, Oblogo Road, Link Road, Market Road. Then we have Zongo Estates, at Town Council Line. Zongo has expanded" (Mohammed Bako 6/6/1995).

In calculating Sabon Zongo's delimitation in strictly physical terms, we might look to an old city like Kano, or even Accra's downtown *zongo* in the early days of the century; both were walled. Sabon Zongo, however, like most of Accra's neighborhoods, has not been so delineated. Looking at the 2001 aerial map of Accra (which has the same configurations as the 1969 Lands Commission survey map), the boundaries of Sabon Zongo are ambiguous: 1) the community ends at St. Thomas Street (as the northern edge), not at Zongo Junction (Link Road)[1]; 2) it does not contain the entirety of Freedom Market—it cuts off one of the stalls; 3) it does not include the eastern edge of Larte Biokarshie (just immediately adjacent to the south, at Freedom Market); 4) it does not go all the way to Mortuary Road, the continuation of Ring Road (probably because it was not finished on the survey map; and 5) it does not include part of Blacksmith (the northwest edge, beyond the market).

According to some "local knowledge," the cut-off between Sabon Zongo and the adjacent areas (Larte Biokarshie and Town Council Line) is represented by the house numbers: Sabon Zongo is B___/2, whereas Larte Biokarshie is A___/2. In fact, the house right after the two-story building across from Freedom Market, is A/2, whereas the houses even further north are B/2. Larte Biokarshie, like Sabon Zongo, is part of Nmemete.

Local opinion on the northern street boundary varies. A Hausa man living on St. Thomas Street near the lane that leads to the western-most set of Sabon Zongo's public toilets refers to St. Thomas Street as the end of Sabon Zongo: "We're in Sabon Zongo." Also on St. Thomas but near the corner of Oblogo Road live the members of an extended Ga family compound, who disagree with him. They say that they live at Zongo Junction, not Sabon Zongo. Their patriarch, Alhaji Babah-Alargi, who built the house and who lives in one of Accra's suburbs, is a Hausa who had left Islam and returned to it after his children were grown. His deceased wife and mother of his children, was Ga, and his descendants living in this house not only identify as Ga but are also practising Christians.

Babah Alargi is a London-trained engineer and architect who provides a significant local perspective on the development of the western periphery of Sabon Zongo. In 1950, he obtained the proper document for the piece of land his father, a Hausa, left him on St. Thomas off of Oblogo. In 1952, Babah Alargi developed the single story part of the house—two bedrooms, living room, dining room, kitchen, bathroom, garage—and he moved in late that year. In 1963, he built a two-story building perpendicular to the first structure and moved into that.

In the early 1960s, there were virtually no buildings on the roads bounding Sabon Zongo. On all of Oblogo Road, between the current location of the Gaskiya Cinema (at Ancobra Street) and Link Road there were no structures. At the western-most boundary, down the street from the current location of one set of public toilets, in addition to Babah Alargi's first structure there was a house owned by a Wangara man. Across Oblogo Road in Zongon Tuta (land that was owned by Chief Alhaji Kadri English in Central Accra), some houses had been built (Babah Alargi 5/12/1995).

At Babah Alargi's western end, and on into Sabon Zongo, the infrastructure has been notably absent or inferior: the streets and their layout, the gutters, electricity and water, health care, schools, telecommunication. In 1950s Accra, infrastructure was generally minimal. Although Oblogo Road and Link Road were a primary route to Korle Bu Hospital, they were not paved and there was no public transportation after 6 P.M.

On St. Thomas and into Sabon Zongo, there was neither electricity nor piped water. In that decade, Babah Alargi had water and electricity brought in "long distance" to his house. He also put in a septic tank. While some of his efforts were for his personal convenience, Babah Alargi also played the role of the patron. In 1960, he had his road (St. Thomas) tarred up to Ojo School, the primary school that many Sabon Zongo children still attend.

Forty years later, after much of Accra has enjoyed infrastructural improvement, we might delineate Sabon Zongo by virtue of its infrastructural neglect. Patronage matters, because with connections, changes like better roads can be instituted. But patronage also matters because patrons gain in status. One of the well-educated residents believes that because of jealousy, some people prefer to allow the neglect to continue because if the community is visibly improved, the Bako family will benefit or get the credit. And there are also more personal jealousies, but that again reflects on the individual's social prestige. This same person decided to deal with the filth in front of his house by constructing a gutter. The house owner across the gutter was against it, as if it was unnecessary and just a way for the man to show off. The neighbor's objection, he thinks, was based on ignorance and activated by jealousy.

Sabon Zongo is a planned site, based on a grid (see Figure 6). But, codes are not enforced. Throughout the community, many of the roads have lost their alignment and are impassable for vehicular traffic. This is due in part to the construction of buildings right in the path of a sited road by paying off a city official. Korle Bu Street, for example, at its western edge is obstructed by houses and the public toilet. Before gutters could be laid on Malam Bako Street and the road paved in the late 1990s, the walls on a number of houses that protruded into the road literally had to be demolished.

Most of the "streets" in Sabon Zongo are narrow, unpaved winding lanes, similar to the alleys of the downtown *zongo* area. Most lack proper gutters. During the rainy season, there is considerable mud. The *Gangare* section near Oblogo Road is colloquially known as *unguwan laka* (the mud quarter) because of the problem. Even Ancobra Street, a main (albeit barely two-lane) internal north-south road with public transportation stops, can be impassable during the rains because it is unpaved and becomes rutted and slick.

Generally when residents complain about Sabon Zongo's infrastructure, the first things they refer to are the Streets and gutters. One day during the rainy season, some passenger tro-tros[2] got stuck in the mud and ruts on Ancobra St. by Idrissu's Mosque. In the absence of a better solution, a community elder who keeps sheep and goats in a pen by the mosque had the decaying peels of casava, yams and plantains (brought to him by neighbors for his animals to eat) put on the road as filler. Alhaji Adamu, one of Sabon Zongo's few financially successful residents, negatively characterizes the community, in large part because of the streets: *"Zongo bai [sic] da kyau, saboda titi"* (Zongo is not good because of the streets, 6/9/1996).

Just as connections can benefit an individual at the expense of the community-at-large, patronage or connections can help. In the mid-1990s, the main north-south road that runs by Malam Bako's old house was destroyed by erosion. As on Ancobra, people had been filling in the holes with food parings and the like. Chief Sha'aibu went to see the City Engineer. The city came with ten trucks of gravel. Contact between the chief, the Assemblyman and the Accra Authority (the City Engineer) made the difference.

Three streets were fully paved and "guttered" in 1999 as part of an urban development plan. They are Market Road, which runs through Sabon Zongo at its southern end; Malam Bako Street at the core of the old community, running from Oblogo Road up past Chief Sha'aibu Bako's house and ending at Malam Bako's palace; and a chunk of Korle Bu Street (one block south of Oblogo Road running east-west). Why those roads? All three connect with city arteries: Market Street with the Mortuary extension of Ring Road at the east and Link Road at the west, Malam Bako Street from Oblogo Road to Market Street (and, of course, right past Chief Sha'aibu's house; Malam Bako Street is also the pivotal core of Sabon Zongo), and Korle Bu also joining with Mortuary Road.

The streets large and small have names that appear on maps but which residents either do not know or do not use. In parts of Ayigbetown, local knowledge alone enables pedestrians to "follow" the road as it lacks any delineation and houses are not aligned. As elsewhere in Accra if not all of urban Ghana, locationality is given in terms of commonly-recognized landmarks—for example, a tree, a house of a particular form or color or resident, a community institution such as a mosque or the corner barber.

Other elements of infrastructure include electricity and water. There was no electricity in Sabon Zongo during World War II. While Babah Alargi was able to connect his house in the 1950s, according to Malam Tahiro, electricity came to Sabon Zongo *"guda guda"* (little by little, house by house) when General Afrifa became head of state, that is, after the coup that deposed Nkrumah in 1966. There are still no street lights. Night traders illuminate their stalls or tables with small kerosene lanterns crafted from recycled tin cans. Water was piped into Abossey Okai, across Oblogo Road, before Sabon Zongo, and *zongo* residents would carry it in buckets (Baba Mai Doki 6/13/1996). Water now is readily accessible, which is of particular ritual significance to the predominantly Muslim population. There are still compounds without a pipe and individuals with water pipes capitalize on their fortune by selling water by the bucket to those in need. Thus the sight of boys and girls and men and women carrying buckets of water on their heads is common. The real problem with water is related to soil erosion. Sabon Zongo is sited on a slope, with the market and *Kan Tudu* at the top; few of the streets are paved and there is little vegetation to anchor the ground. As a result, there has been considerable erosion. With erosion, water pipes are exposed and eventually break, and homes and businesses lose their water connection.

Water falls within the purview of the AMA and Sabon Zongo lies within the jurisdiction of the Ablekuma Sub-District of the AMA, which also includes

Korle Gonno, Maimaita, Dansoman, Abossey Okai, and Odonkor. This decentralization aims "to increase the potential productive role of local government in raising resources, providing services, expanding rural-urban linkages, stimulating private investment, and implementing national development policies" (Mousset-Jones 1999:37). It gives the assemblies greater independence, their revenue to come not just from central grants but also local taxes. The AMA's major sources of income are business licenses and fees and property taxes. In Sabon Zongo, the houseowners pay tax to the city and the city is supposed to provide municipal services in return. These would include water, electricity, garbage pick-up, bus service, and a primary school. The local market, Freedom Market, also falls within their purview as part of the city's market structure. As in the rest of Accra, the AMA is also responsible for maintenance of public toilets, waste management, and schools.

"The existing toilet facilities in Accra, both private and public, include pan (or bucket) latrines, pit latrines, septic tank latrines, KVIPs,[3] and WCs with or without connection to the central sewage system" (Obirih-Opareh 2001:16). Accra had initiated a three phase plan to deal with sewage. Phase 1, begun in the 1960s but not completed, included the Ga area: Bukom/Central Accra, as well as Ministries, Kingsway, and Korle Bu Hospital. The sewage main was laid but the constituent areas were never connected to it. Individual householders were expected to link their houses to it, but the plan was not carried out. For one thing, most individuals could not afford it. But it was also problematic that, due to military take-overs, governments came and went. The sewage lines for Phase 2 (Airport Residential Estates and Roman Ridge) and Phase 3 (Kaneshie) were never created, so anyone wanting flush toilets has had to install individual septic tanks. This has not been problematic in the elite suburbs of Phase 2, where people can afford to do so.

According to AMA ordinance, every home in Accra should have toilet facilities. Since the central sewage system in Accra covers only a small area, for the private household there is considerable cost and logistical difficulty in emptying the liquid waste. Public toilets are therefore more than a simple convenience. A HUDA (Housing and Urban Development Associates) study cited by Tipple (1999) reports 77.5 percent of houses with a toilet. Yet, in Tipple's study "only 30.8 percent of [Accra's] households have the use of flush toilets. Almost as many rely on removable buckets for domestic sanitation. Less than 20% have functioning indoor plumbing" (Tipple 1999:256).[4] Furthermore, a study by Obirih-Opareh (2001:16) reports that 25 percent of Accra dwellers use public toilets (there were about 127 in all of Accra), with a fee, and 10 percent do not have access to toilet facilities.

Even given this low percentage, the situation in Sabon Zongo is worse. Individual septic tanks are necessary to accommodate flush toilets. In theory, septic systems could be brought in. But there are problems. The engineer, Babah Alargi, estimated in 1995 that to build a WC and roof would cost upwards of

₵500,000 (in September 1995, $415). Given the poverty, "how can they afford
it?" (5/12/1995). Another problem is logistical: the main core of Sabon Zongo
is so densely settled, there is little room to sink individual septic tanks.

It was the PNDC (Provisional National Defense Council), the revolutionary
government that came in under Flight Lt. Jerry Rawlings December 31, 1981,
that mobilized people in Accra to clean the public toilets and their environs.
And it was at that time that user-fees were introduced for public toilets in Ghana.
As with water, the AMA decentralized liquid waste management, sub-
contracting out management of public toilets in the early 1990s and finally
allowing privatization of this "gold mine" in the later 1990s (Obirih-Opareh
2001).

In Sabon Zongo, there are four sets (male and female) of public toilets, overseen by the AMA within the Ablekuma sub-metropolitan assembly.[5] They are
very public, not very clean, inadequate for the number of people, and may be
several blocks away from where one lives. They are located in *Unguwan* Zabrama at the western boundary on St. Thomas Street down the road from Ojo
Primary School; on the north, just behind Gaskiya Cinema; on the south, at
Freedom Market; and on the eastern edge of Ayigbetown (see Figure 7). For
Sabon Zongo, some of the tax comes from the toilets. In 1995, there was a
charge of 30 cedis, to "relieve oneself all over Ghana," with an extra 10 cedi
charge for toilet paper. This would work out to about 360,000 cedis/month for
one set of toilets, 1.48 million cedis for all four. The money is deposited monthly
at the Ablekuma Sub-District office. In 2000, the price was up to 100 cedis. A
private concern opened a new set of toilets next to the old ones at Gaskiya;
cleaner and more modern, the cost was 200 cedis per visit. Thirty percent of
the money is supposed to be ploughed back into the community for development. Indeed, it is possible that the roads are being renovated from the proceeds
of the toilets (Alhaji Foster Faruk 5/30/1996).

The AMA is also responsible for solid waste management. At Sabon Zongo,
they installed four huge (8 cubic meters) containers each next to a set of public
toilets: at Freedom Market, Gaskiya Cinema, and Ayigbetown. They were picking up solid waste maybe once a week, more likely once in two weeks. According to Elliot Barbour-Sackey, an architect with Technical Services Centre
(6/17/1996), the Waste Management department could not service all of the
containers. There is a real problem with garbage/trash collection all over the
city. In Nima, for example, as a result of a World Bank project, 18 containers
were installed; yet, even at the onset, the AMA could service only five (Barbour-
Sackey 6/17/1996).

Because the Sabon Zongo waste had not been collected frequently enough,
the massive containers were overflowing with trash and garbage. For this reason,
or perhaps due to inertia, many residents did not even bother to deposit their
refuse. One said to me, "the rain is our AMA" as it washes away refuse. But
as with the mud, so with the refuse, the rain brings it down the hill: ". . . one
block up they send down their garbage" (M. Barko 6/4/1996). I ask how they

know where it is coming from: "everyone has their own garbage." For example, when grass is washed down the hill, they know it belongs to those who keep sheep; similarly, the husks that float by are the rubbish of the corn sellers.

The AMA has tried to work with individual compounds on waste removal. According to Sule Bako, the former chief's son (2/13/1995), in the mid-1980s the AMA introduced a fee of ₵600/year for disposal of solid waste; it was additional to property tax and it was to be paid by landlords. The landlords refused to pay because in a house with tenants, the collection of fees is difficult and landlords would not pay such a fee out of their own pocket only. Because the landlords failed to pay, the AMA came up with a new strategy, i.e., pay as you dump. But this also failed: no receipt was issued, therefore the Ablekuma office of AMA could be given anything or nothing.

The problems with maintaining the street gutters are not specific to Sabon Zongo but are common all over the city. For economic reasons, too few laborers are hired to attend to gutters, so that system has also failed. It was phased out and every house was made responsible for its respective front gutter. This too failed as a policy. And, people may ask, why clean out the gutter if there is no refuse pick-up?

In 1999, because the AMA simply could not cope city-wide, they decided to find a private organization with experience in waste management. They brought in Country and City Waste (CCW), a Canadian company, and it made a difference all over the city, even Sabon Zongo. There are now large waste containers in more locations and CCW trucks come regularly to empty them. The question, of course, will be how to shift the cost onto the citizenry. The AMA is working out how the households will be taxed.

Ghana's telecommunications system is one of the least developed in Africa. In 1994 there were about 50,000 telephones in the entire country, the telephone service concentrated in Accra. Even there, only government offices, large commercial firms and well-to-do houses had service (Berry 1995:184). In 1996, there were four telephone lines in all of Sabon Zongo, and none of them worked. Ghana Telecom Company, Ltd. subsumes Sabon Zongo within Larte Biokarshie, which has old, weak, underground cables that need replacement. In the last few years, overhead wires have been introduced. In addition, there is the alternative for individuals in Sabon Zongo of the WLL (pronounced "wheel"), the Wireless Local Loop. This was designed for Dansoman, where there is no underground network of lines. Anyone who requests WLL will get it easily—as long as he/she can afford the initial payment of ₵500,000 cedis (the cost as of 1997 when the equivalency was about $1 = 2,242 cedis). For poor people, this is a big "as long as." Westel, a private company, is a competitor to Ghana Telecom. Service is prepaid and unless the power is out, there is less trouble with making phone connections. Unfortunately, they cannot as yet operate throughout the Sabon Zongo area.

According to Alhaji Foster Faruk (Assistant Manager of Human Resources Management Department with Ghana Telecom who has lived in Sabon Zongo since about 1972), there have been plans to put in telephone lines. NKF (from Holland) had signed a contract to rehabilitate telephone lines, expand lines where there are none, and modernize to eliminate faults (5/30/1996). He expected telephone poles and lines in Sabon Zongo by the end of 1996. In fact, by the end of 1999, the only working telephone lines had been brought in earlier in the year from Abossey Okai by a private individual who opened a new communication center. Yet, Ghana Telecom was wiring all of Sabon Zongo (putting up poles) in 1999. By summer 2000, there were 12 communication centers. Only five use regular lines; another five use the WLL.

As we have seen, Sabon Zongo is a neglected area: it does not have good roads. It also does not have easily legible house numbers. This makes it difficult to survey and install phone lines. Foster Faruk observed that you cannot have phones where areas are not well-developed. Indeed, even Foster, as an area manager, is privileged to have a phone and fax, yet he has neither. "The phone people would come, but the roads are bad and the person says 'The roads are another person's job; we can't do the lines till the roads are done'. . . . Because he [the phone line man] can't trace the house, he will go back" (Alhaji Foster Faruk 5/30/1996). Foster Faruk is a Fanti (southern Ghanaian), who became interested in Islam when in school, married a Zabrama woman, and settled in Sabon Zongo. Looking around, he observed how government upon government have neglected "them": "they call them the Hausa people—that they live in unhygienic conditions—not knowing they have neglected them" (Alhaji Foster Faruk 5/30/1996).

SPATIAL SUBDIVISIONS: *UNGUWA*

Fernandez (1977) has observed that in some cultures, meanings, and values attach to directions in the natural and the built environment (see also Moore 1986:54; Bourdieu 1979). They may be tied to cosmology, myths of origin, myths of migration, and so on. This spatialization of culture is marked through language, dress, and activity. We see it in Hausa linguistic endings that distinguish between going (in) and coming (in). We see it in the distinctions made between in(side) and out(side), who is in, i.e., a member of a group, and who is not, and thus who may enter or join or who may not. Direction or orientation may be associated with social groups, like lineages or clans. Directionality or spatial orientations, like social engagements, may change over time.

When Sabon Zongo was established, the pioneers built domestic space, as well as public areas, like mosques and markets. These places became associated with particular people or groups and gained pedigrees. Their social practices and spatial/temporal practices (the use of public and domestic spaces over time) have been linked through their production of their social and spatial environment. Their locations map out relations along socio-spatial axes. Over the years, many of these practices have been modified, as places and the people occupying or using them have changed.

Sabon Zongo is divided into quarters (see Figure 7) that are informal and not clearly demarcated. They encompass distinct social and physical differences and they are known to all.

Unguwa	*Sub-unguwa*
Kan Tudu →	Tripoli, Ojo
Gangare	
Zabrama	
Municipal →	*Makafi*
Ayigbetown →	Stable, *Katifa*, Sunshine

The *unguwa* categorization is consistent with several interlinking socio-spatial delineations that carry meaning for the residents: up/down (*Kan Tudu/Gangare*); core/margin; landlord/lodger; male/female. These axes are tied into webs of exchange and solidarity.

Kan Tudu is the neighborhood at the top of the slope and literally means on top of a hill. *Gangare*, at the bottom of the slope near Bus Stop (a named location), means downhill. It includes Dan Malley's side, that is Korle Bu Street to the west of where Malam Bako Street comes in. *Kan Tudu* is the old core where Malam Bako built his palace and where the Bako family members lived. It is the most densely populated with the oldest structures. There is a bit of an ascent coming from Oblogo, hence the name ("atop the hill"). Night Market field is on Malam Bako Street. A worn path follows its southern edge, picking up the lane from the west that ends at Malam Bako Street, the corner of Sha'aibu Bako's house. The lane continues on through Ayigbetown, in some spots obstructed by a building. The field is eroded, and until the road was properly paved and guttered in 1999, a well-placed cinder block functioned as a step down from the gutter.

Gangare has some old compounds, like Sarkin Fada's (see Figure 8), but the Bako family did not live down there and today it is bordered by Oblogo Road. *Kan Tudu* is associated with the Bakos, *Gangare* with non-Bakos (this was Damaley's area). The landlord/lodger dyad ties into the spatial demarcation, insofar as the Bakos were the original landlords, and lived at the top; renters are not Bako family members and initially were more likely to be housed peripheral to the old core. *Unguwan* Zabrama abuts on both *Kan Tudu* and *Gangare*. There are also old houses there, like Yaro's and Al'wali's, both discussed in Chapter 7. Walking south towards Market Road, there is less building and more open space. At the northern end is Municipal, marked by the Zana Mosque just off of Oblogo; this area is generally less densely settled, although it does include the blind quarter (*Makafi*), which is a maze of oddly shaped and sized dwellings. Many of the structures are one-room affairs with a door but only a few have a window—a simple piece of wood on two hinges. Electricity is

Figure 8
Outside *Sarkin Fada*'s (Kariki Family) Compound in *Gangare*. Courtesy of
Bossman Murrey.

brought into the rooms by bootlegging it on wires from outside. "Houses" are locked from outside by padlock.

There is also the Ayigbetown:*Kan Tudu*/*Gangare* split. Ayigbetown was built later and for a "foreign" (non-Hausa) population. "That's where formerly every Ewe went to stay. Whenever there was Ewe in Zongo, yes go there, you will find Ewe man. That's why they call it Ayigbetown" (Mohammed Bako 6/6/ 1996). The layout there is quite different from *Kan Tudu* and Zabrama: some of the north-south roads are quite wide, many east-west roads have not been cut through at all, many houses are well-spaced. "That one is undeveloped land"— where the development is now going on. As compared to the core of Sabon Zongo, there is so little congestion. Around *Kataki*, for example, there are wide open spaces. *Kataki* Mosque, like Stable, is unroofed. It sits down the road from the three-story building known as Yoruba House (after the owner), an apartment house that has residents living there, despite the fact that it is literally falling down. In front of one of the sample compounds in Ayigbetown (Figure 46), Alhaji Adamu Yahaya rents out showers (₵40 for a spigot shower, ₵20 to fill bucket) and has also built a new "guest house." He has laid a proper cement gutter for about 10 meters. It is in Ayigbetown particularly that most houses are not walled and lack the typical exterior compound demarcation. There are a number of single family bungalows in Ayigbetown, as well as houses with indoor plumbing. And in the Sunshine area, the housing is very different from the rest of *zongo*. Much of it is newer, more substantial, some is quite large, and much of it is single family houses with properly-built enclosing walls.

The area known as Sunshine, Toyota, or Municipal lies between Oblogo and Korle Bu, from just east of *Makafi* at Abia Road to the eastern-most boundary (Bartholomew or Ring/Mortuary Road). Actually, the AMA tax maps for the Sunshine area are in two block units—from Abia to Wood, and then from Wood to Ring Road. Sunshine is named for the Sunshine Hotel (in 2001, ₵35,000 cedis a night for a single, ₵40,000 for a double)[6] and Toyota Park. Across the street from Timbuktoo Mosque is *Gidan Laka* (a mud house owned by a Hausa man). New gutters have been laid in the last two years on Korle Bu Street from Sunshine to Tula House (the lane down to Zana). The gutter is double width and depth, and Korle Bu is also wider here than further west.

The boundaries between these quarters are not exact and individual percep- tions of where one ends and another begins come into play. The real significance of boundaries is how they are perceived. Talking with members of a Kwahu (Akan), non-Muslim family who live opposite Timbuktoo Mosque on Korle Bu Road, one 13-year-old girl distinguishes the area as "Zongo Ayigbetown." Thus, she says she lives in (Sabon) Zongo. Her 16-year-old brother, distinguishes (Sabon) Zongo, Ayigbetown and Sunshine, and he says they live in Sunshine— presumably because he has different social interests and interactions (6/8/1996). A descendant of one of the original though non-Bako families who lives in Zabrama excludes Ayigbetown from Sabon Zongo, because of "mixed race." In *Kan Tudu*, he goes on, it is not one race as such but one dialect. In Ayigbetown, they are not. Moreover, they don't follow the chief and there are few Muslims (Papa Carlos 5/26/1996).

Many Wangara live in that group's original section (*Unguwan Wangarawa*) created by Malam Bako and where their chief, when they had one, resided.[7] There is also a house for a Chamba chief, who, when alive, met there with his people and heard disputes. The Ewe live near their chief's house in what is known as Ayigbetown (Ewetown). The Mossi chief's house is in the Mossi area.

Ever since Malam Bako turbaned a chief of the blind (*sarkin makafi*), they have had a quarter in the community. According to the *Sarkin Makafi* Munka'ela, when Malam Bako came to what is now *Makafi*, he brought his sons Idrissu and Lawal Daudu. It was all bush. He had Lawal throw a stone to map out Sabon Zongo. First east, then west, north, south. *Unguwan Makafi* was the first section to be created. They began to build there. Malam Bako gave it to the blind in perpetuity. The blind person's children inherit from them (5/31/ 1995). *Makafi* also houses several members of the local *bori* troupe[8] and some of the local drummers.

In addition to the blind, other specialized populations have also been mapped onto the community's landscape. *Kutare* (lepers) were also allocated an area, clearly justified as long as there were any actively contagious lepers. They still live in a compound called *Unguwan Kutare*, within the larger quarter of Ayig-betown. Their chief (*Sarkin Kutare*) lives at Malam Harona's house at *Katifa* in Ayigbetown. Both the blind people and the lepers also maintain their own mosques (*Masalaci Makafi* and *Masalaci Kutare*) each within their respective quarter, although open to anyone who chooses to attend. The handicapped pop-ulation, *guragu*, are scattered throughout Sabon Zongo. The first *sarkin guragu* of Sabon Zongo, Harona Abdullahi, was appointed in 1989 by Chief Sha'aibu Bako. Abdullahi lives in the blind quarter. But the group's meeting place is at the *guragu* imam's house *Gidan Beriberi* (Kanuri House) in Ayigbetown (Imam Alhaji Idrissu 8/16/1997). Thus, these three specialized populations are all cen-tered in Ayigbetown, Sabon Zongo's newest and most diverse area.

The growth of Sabon Zongo has led to other divisions as well: one area in Ayigbetown is called *Ungowan Katifa* (mattress area), due to the occupational specialty engaged in there; another, also in Ayigbetown, is known as Stable, where they used to keep horses. In fact, the roofless mosque nearby is also known as Stable. Piles of old wood and a huge pile of scrap metal are regular fixtures in a scrap area, near Timbuktoo, in the area called Unguwan Malam Tula (named for a local politician).

At the community's core are several centripetal socio-spatial structures: the chieftaincy and its palace, the overarching Abokin Ango mosque (see Figure 9), the Night Market, the street scene of traders. What is interesting is the amount of concurrence in opinion as to what the heart of Sabon Zongo is, where the center lies. "The night market. That's the center of Sabon Zongo. Every political party can come, do a rally, at the night market. Maybe you've seen the wres-tling—they go there" (Mohammed Bako 6/6/1996). Alhaji Musa Alhassan, the chief's *majidade*, agrees: the center (*tsakiya*) is *Makwala*, the night market, across the street from the house of the *zongo* chief. And a member of one of the original but non-Bako families says the center is *Kan Tudu*, as associated with the Bako's generally, more specifically the palace of Malam Bako (where he believes the chief should be living) and the night market (Papa Carlos 5/26/ 1996). The core is bounded by Ancobra to the east, Freedom Market to the south, Alhaji Avenue in Zabrama to the west.

The Night Market field is a multi-functional space where at different times of the day and night, and sometimes even simultaneously, different populations engage in different activities: barefoot young boys play football, older shoed youths play football, Nigeriens hold wrestling matches during the dry season on Sundays, ritual observances like dancing on Id il Fitr are held at the end of Ramadan, Arabic schools perform plays on the anniversary of the birth of the Prophet, political rallies are staged, and at night traders sell prepared food.

The closer to the center one lives, the more central one's position. Or so the perception goes. But Babah Alargi, the engineer/architect, wonders aloud, why you see "proper" buildings in Ayigbetown or near Zongo Junction but not in the center of *zongo*? He goes on: people are able to buy land and put up buildings

Figure 9
Overview of Sabon Zongo, with the Landmark Abokin Ango Mosque. Courtesy of the Author.

outside of the nucleus. "When I'm comparing the 1950s and the people I know in the *zongo* [the core], I don't see the changes" (5/12/1995).

"In Accra . . . the overall constraints on availability of stool land have led to shortages of [stool] subsidized plots, queues, and litigation" (Rakodi 1997b:381). And according to Alex Quainoo, a lawyer in Accra who specializes in land law, Sabon Zongo has the highest land litigation in the city of Accra, a city where law suits over rights to land represent the most common kind of legal wrangling.

The Bako family is the major landholder in Sabon Zongo, insofar as the land was granted directly to Malam Bako. But numerous cases, often involving rights to land within the community, have been argued at all levels of the court system. Going back to 1912, after the Ga James Town stool (made up Alata, Akumaje, and Sempe) agreed to begift land to Malam Bako that became Sabon Zongo, Sempe reneged. The case was argued in London (Manche Hammond v. Manche Kojo Ababio IV) and decided in favor of the Bako grant (Pellow 1999). But because the legitimacy of the land claim implicated the legitimacy of the right to chieftaincy, and members of the Damaley family have contested that right, the case has been re-visited over and over. Indeed, the question, to which of the James Town sections does Sabon Zongo's land actually belong, went to superior court as recently as 1990 (Civil Appeal No. 110/89).

In 1975, Usman Bako, a son of Malam Bako by his fourth wife Abece, initiated a case against a resident whom Usman said acquired a piece of land from him to build a small two-room house in 1966. The defendant had married into the Bako family, and according to the plaintiff (the Bako family), the defendant was to start paying rent once he had recovered his cost of building the house (*Malam Gambo Baako v. Abdulai Toure*, Civil Appeal No. 112/91, 1/28/1993). The defendant, who has refused to pay rent or remove his structure, claims that he bought his land from the Abloh Mills family. The court decision denied his claim, noting "it is crystal clear that the land in dispute falls within the Sabon Zongo lands granted to the late Malam Bako in 1909" (88).

Problems with land are also brought to the chief's court. For example, in 1982, some residents came to Chief Sha'aibu Bako for a judgement: two men had planted corn behind a woman's property. She asked them not to, because she said thieves hide in the corn and then "thief" her house. But they did it anyway. One of the men was then cutting down corn from her property without asking her permission. *Sarkin fada* said the chief saved the day by making the following resolution: "Let them leave the corn for now. When it is ripe, they will harvest it. Then they won't plant more. That way, now that there's a 'green revolution' going on [this was several months after Rawlings' December 31 coup d'etat], no one will be accused of counter-revolutionary activity for cutting it down now. It just won't be replanted" (5/16/1982).

The issue in Sabon Zongo is at heart not complicated: the strangers came without prior rights to the land. But because land matters, there are daily problems over encroachments within the community.

MARKET AND STREET TRADE

In Accra, there are four levels of markets: 1) the central markets such as Makola, Agbogbloshie, Kaneshie, and Mallam Atta; 2) neighborhood markets such as Adabraka, Osu, Kwashieman, Salaga and Nima; 3) night markets as at Bukom, Osu and Kwame Nkrumah Circle; and 4) specialist markets at the Timber Market, and slaughter house and the fish markets, such as Salaga Market (Mousset-Jones 1999:33, fn 48). Sabon Zongo has two spatially-defined markets: Freedom Market, which is a neighborhood market, and the Night Market.

Freedom Market has a formal site, with stalls, is overseen by the AMA, and each trader pays a monthly rent. It bounds the southern edge of the community, across Market Street, is open daily and trade runs the gamut from body products and services such as hair plaiting to all sorts of food stuffs. It was Letitia Tetteh, long-standing Queenmother of all of the market women of Accra (2/26/1995), who founded the market in 1959. Pre-1957, some women had already created a small market at Bus Stop on Oblogo Road to sell cassava and such so they wouldn't have to go to Accra. The market was very close to the road and there were often accidents here and there. It was also very small—from Bus Stop not even to Gaskiya Cinema. Aside from those selling charcoal, there were only about 35 women. Letitia Tetteh was living in Accra before she bought the land to build a house just over the line from Sabon Zongo in Larte Biokarshie. When she moved, she realized that they had to build a better market here; at that time, the buses charged two-pence to go to Accra.

Because the land in the area belonged to the James Town Ga, Letitia came and begged the Ga James Town sub-chief, Nii Lateh Kobinah, for a piece of vacant land. "Because the women have to find something to eat, they have to earn their own living, because of that he let them come to this place and build their market here" (Letitia Tetteh 2/26/1995). Once they established the new market, it expanded. It was Kwame Nkrumah, the first president of Ghana, who built the market for them. And the greetings at that time were always "freedom." And so when the market was built, they named it Freedom Market. At that time, all this area around the market and Larte Biokarshie was bush. After building this market, she went on, many people bought land here in Larte Biokarshie and came to settle.

When they first built the market, many lorries came. Women also bought their meat here at the market. The butchers here were the suppliers for the rest of Accra—this is where most of the butchers were. Some of the market women were from Abossey Okai (across Oblogo Road), and others lived in Sabon Zongo's *Kan Tudu*. Some were Hausa women. Letitia and her assistant Sarah Quay say that over the years, there has been a big change. The market is now falling apart—the roofs literally falling in. The women with stalls lobbied the city (the AMA) to help fix it up. As one of the traders said, as this is a *kauye* (village), the market should be smaller than one of the main markets in Accra. But it should also be in better shape. The local Member of Parliament brought in a contractor who began work on this market. The contractor and the market women contributed money to the project, but it was not enough, and the renovation was halted.

One problem was that the plans had no place for "fire service," a kind of first aid office should a fire break out as happened in Makola Number 1 Market in Central Accra. As with so many urban building projects, public and private, a partially-completed structure stands. The new construction, with concrete foundations, is laid out in parallel lines, running north-south toward Market Street. The original market stalls are situated behind, running east-west. Organized by products sold, in 1995 there were ninety-nine occupied stalls.

The Night Market is held in an open space in *Kan Tudu*, which as observed earlier, is multifunctional both simultaneously and sequentially. Sha'aibu Bako's audience room faces the space. Garuba family members own the Night Market lot; traders there pay rent, which is divided up among the family. The Night Market began when Idrissu Bako was chief (Tahiro 5/29/96). The traders dealt primarily in meat (they were butchers), *kenkey* (the local Ga corn staple), *tuwo* (the Hausa staple). Until the late 1960s, the food traders were only Ga and Hausa. Now they are joined by many others, including Asante and Fante.

In the early days, the colonial police patrolled the city because of thieves; they came around Sabon Zongo from Korle Bu Hospital at 9 P.M., so the Night Market closed up by 8 P.M. During Nkrumah's time, the police continued patrolling but came through later, after 10 P.M. (Tahiro 5/29/96). Now, the Night Market is active from about 6 P.M.–11 P.M., the normal time span for the evening meal and before bedtime snacks. It is held nightly, the women trading in prepared foods. There are tables and benches so that customers can sit and eat.

The site is perceived by many as the center of Sabon Zongo, not because of the market per se, although the market is one of the social institutions that give it meaning. Rather, it is the cumulative effect of the variety of core social activities and institutions that give it meaning, and because its spatial location is at the core of the original community, across the road from the home of the last chief.

In addition to these two formal spatially-defined markets, there is the street selling which, to the unseasoned eye, appears spontaneous but is systematic and ordered. Customers have "local knowledge" as to who is where when they are not visible from the street. From the Night Market proper east about two blocks along a lane to one of the remaining large shade trees, and down Malam Bako street to Abokin Ango Mosque, the same traders occupy the same spots nightly. From Gaskiya Cinema, at the corner of Oblogo Road up the block to Makafi Mosque, there is more of the nightly trade in prepared food. As at the Night Market, on Oblogo in front of the cinema there are tables and benches. Night-time also brings out specialized evening foodstuffs: the *cicinga* (kebabs), *balangu* (grilled side of lamb), sweet tea, omelets.

During the daylight hours as well, appointed traders sell at appointed times in appointed places. Prepared food sellers of morning fare begin work with the first rays of the sun. Some sell from within their compound, some from a shelter of sorts, others at a spot on the street (the absence of traffic and sidewalks make setting up a table or temporary stall quite simple), still others sell from their heads as they traverse the community. Other traders sell noontime food and still others, late afternoon or evening meals. The prepared food sellers are highly localized: leaving aside the Night Market proper and the Gaskiya, they are concentrated in *Unguwan Zabrama/Gangare* and *Kan Tudu/Makwala*. In the evening, they are also to the east and west of the Night Market and west of Gaskia.

In the morning, prepared foods include *koko* (porridge), *masa* (a fried cake made from corn), *wake* (beans and rice), *pinkaso* (wheaten cake fried in oil); *banku* (a starch made from fermented corn, typical of Ga and Ewe cuisine) is sold in two spots nearby to Ayigbetown, where there are more southern Ghanaians resident. In the evening, the clumping is similar, but even more concentrated: snacks like fried yam and *kelewele* (a fried Ghanaian treat of spicey ripe plantain), specialties like *cicinga* and *balangu*, omelets, *tuwo*, the omnipresent Ga *kenkey*, and tea (with bread).

The foods available in Sabon Zongo are significant to community definition: a Hausa woman from Darkuman (a new Muslim area north of Kaneshie) believes that only in Sabon Zongo do people (Hausa) not cook, and this is because unlike Zongo Lane or any of the other Muslim areas, anything sold in Northern Nigeria is sold on the street. On any day, you can get virtually any Hausa food (Hajiya 6/4/1995). But the Hausa residents, like others who have been living in Accra, also regularly eat local foods, like *kenkey*, that are found all over Accra.

Like the four sets of public toilets, the food selling is more than simply convenient; for many it is a necessity. Just as the majority has no toilet facilities within their compounds, so many families do not have the financial wherewithal to cook meals at home. Ghana's Structural Adjustment Program has made life for the poor considerably more difficult. To prepare a meal of *tuwo* and a simple soup, one needs charcoal, meat, vegetables, and so on. Without reckoning in one's labor time, the cost of these ingredients is more even than the cost of purchasing the already-cooked dish for several members of the family.

Throughout the day and evening, raw ingredients are also for sale throughout Sabon Zongo; at small shops or stands one can buy rice and milled cassava, as well as provisions and perishables.

CONVENIENCE VS. EXPECTATIONS AND ATTACHMENTS

The real significance of boundaries is who is perceived as being on the inside or the outside, given positive or negative associations. Also important and a corollary to the foregoing is how limits play out socially—who interacts with whom, who avoids whom. Location and pedigree are intertwined, at least in the minds of many. This has helped to define Sabon Zongo as a community to its residents.

A Hausa man from one of the other *zongos* observed to me, "[Sabon] Zongo people are more interested in spirituality" than the environment. Whether this is true or not, the negatives of Sabon Zongo's environment do appear to be counterbalanced by a variety of positives of a spatial or material sort. The structures erected and the building materials employed are discernibly different from the rest of the city. For the Muslim majority, the community has a Muslim tenor that is expressed in cultural material terms through a multiplicity and diversity of mosques. The Abokin Ango mosque (see Figure 9) stands out and helps proclaim the community's identity. As with all of the other mosques, it has a following, including men from the immediate neighborhood, relatives of the respective imam, or friends from around the community. The compound structures, which I detail in Chapter 7, are distinctive, in part due to economics, in part to cultural norms, in part to the activities anchored there. The availability of Hausa prepared foods, which far exceeds that of any of the other *zongos*, is a point of pride not to mention a plus for traditionalists. Specialties like *balangu* are attractions for non-residents.

Sabon Zongo is like a village in the city. Because it has unpaved and badly rutted roads, there is very little motorized traffic. There are two north-south streets that cut through from Oblogo Road to Market Street: Malam Bako and Ancobra. The latter is also a public transportation route; however, it is narrow and unpaved, and in the rainy season very difficult to navigate. The only interior east-west street for car travel is Korle Bu, but cars cannot exit either at the Zongo Junction edge, where a house and one set of public toilets encroach onto the road, or the Mortuary Road end (the continuation of Ring Road), where the road has no outlet. What this means is that with a few exceptions, the streets can be safely used as extensions of the compound yard: children can play in the road, and they do so in all forms of undress, just as they would in the house. The street is the backdrop for their games. There are toy seasons—for example, in February children fly home-made kites; in later months, they bring out the cars and trucks they make out of tin Nestle cans, running down the road pulling them by string. Women sell in the street. There are few sidewalk areas, especially in the areas of Sabon Zongo where food selling is most common. While some women actually sit under or inside some sort of minimal structure, many also simply set up shop on a table or next to the fruit basket or the cooking fire, depending upon the food being sold. Animals that are kept inside the compound or in small outside pens can be allowed to wander. Not only is there little worry of their being hurt; there is also little concern of theft, another indication of small-town or village life.

The public and domestic built environments encompass and express genealogy and memories as well as new ideas and routines that are produced and play out on a daily basis through social and material exchange. It is social activity and exchange that particularly constitute the positives of Sabon Zongo living, and these are explicated in the next two chapters.

NOTES

1. This is according to informants interviewed in 1982 and again in the mid-1990s.

2. Tro-tros are a form of public transportation. At first they were lorries, wide trucks, with benches across for passengers. Now they are more often small vans. The name derives from the initial cost, thruppence or "tro-tro."

3. A KVIP (Kumase Ventilated Improved Pit Latrine) is simply a pit latrine provided with a vent (flue) that channels the odors out of the space. It is usually built with two pits. One is used and when it fills up, the seat is changed to the other pit. (The design provides for a seat and cover, as opposed to the squat version of old.) Most models are designed such that the effluents of the filled-up pit can be harmlessly removed after a number of years, (that is while the other pit is being used). Filling one pit can take years (maybe ten), depending on occupancy.

4. The AMA rule for one toilet in every home is observed nowhere in the city.

5. Ablekuma is the largest district in Accra because of re-districting and there is a total of only forty public toilets throughout Ablekuma sub-district.

6. The dollar equivalency of the Ghanaian cedi in September 2001 was $1 = ₵6928.

7. The main Wangara chief, Jimala, lived in Accra Central.

8. *Bori* is a spirit possession cult, common among the Hausa, Zabrama, and Fulani in Northern Nigeria and Niger (Besmer 1983; Masquelier 2001; Onwuejeogwu 1969).

5

TIES THAT BIND

One day in August 1997, the women in Baba Mai Doki's compound were talking about one Hawa who had fallen and hurt herself. I asked whether she was crazy—they said no, just old. None of her children lives in Sabon Zongo and the discussion centered on locating one daughter whom they thought lives at Ashiamah, though no one seemed sure. Hajiya Tani said she would go the next day to find the daughter. Meanwhile, Hawa's neighbor Arziki, came to the compound to speak to Baba Mai Doki. Apparently, Hawa had at one time lived in one of Baba's rental rooms but for free. For some reason she got mad and moved out to her current room, where she was paying ₵30,000 per month. Arziki was concerned. She came to speak to Baba, both because he had been Hawa's patron and because Arziki trusted him. But she also said Hawa hadn't spoken to her in two months. The story was re-told among the various women several times. Finally, the compound head walked down to Hawa's room. She was as thin as a rail. Her eyes were closed. He felt her pulse. Her chest rose and fell with her breathing. After questioning others nearby, he determined that her fall was due to faintness. Once she was fed, she recovered.

The boundaries of Sabon Zongo that most interest me are cultural. They constitute a *zongo*-ness, which is produced and re-produced there in time and space. This coherence is born of social relationships, knit into social networks, played out in cycles of observances and activities, which are associated with the community, produced by and anchored in the material environment.

Sabon Zongo perfectly exemplifies the northern community delineated in Peil's schematic overview of Ghanaian society (1979). The "northern" community is Muslim and composed of a range of so-called stranger groups (from neighboring countries) and northern Ghanaian ethnic groups such as Dagomba and Frafra. It is bounded by a social and a spatial component: socially members are bounded and bonded by language (Hausa), cultural orientation (clothing, food, Islam, insularity), and education (a Koranic school system); spatially, they have a regional identity and live in residential enclaves (*zongos*) (Pellow 1987).

This scheme is integral to the appearance and workings of Sabon Zongo. Sabon Zongo is continuous with the urban system of Accra in space and time, in its incorporation into the municipality's responsibilities, in the comings and goings of residents, of their social, economic, political and religious engagements. But it also embodies many of the characteristics of a village, in its character and the institutions that have evolved over the last nine decades. Malam Bako created Sabon Zongo as a place for his Hausa followers, and from the beginning, the community (i.e., landlords and their families) was bounded by four dimensions of belonging: 1) the intertwining genealogies and corporate ties of kinship; 2) the bonding created by Hausa ethnicity, although ethnicity no longer carries the earlier exclusive claim; 3) the affiliative identity of Islam; and 4) the formal bond of patron-client.

This chapter has two basic thrusts: that these four dimensions are implicated in how one's relation to the history of the *zongo* affects one's social identity within the *zongo*, and that while the community is no longer only Hausa (it never really was), Muslim, and/or kin-based, these dimensions continue to dominate perceptions (if not reality) and lie at the heart of Sabon Zongo's social boundaries.

KINSHIP

It is still kinship that provides rights to corporate family property, that is, the family house. For those on the edge of survival, rights to family housing mean free lodging. It is also kinship that helps in child-care and in paying debts. And rights to property also translate into rights to participate in community policy decisions. According to an educated tenant, whose attempts at community involvement have been frustrated, "some people claim their fathers founded Sabon Zongo and you're not related to the Bako family, so you're nobody."

Throughout Africa, "the most continuously significant ascriptive structures" have been those based on kinship (Chazan 1999:79). This is no less true in Sabon Zongo. Indeed, it is genealogy that largely explains the inner workings of Sabon Zongo: who is married to whom, who owns property, whose house is where, what kind and the degree of involvement persons have in community politics. In thinking about the organization of Sabon Zongo, Malam Sule, son of Musa Abokin Ango, observed to me, *duka kudundune* (everyone is intertwined, literally crumpled or curled up). And this is due to the genealogical ties of descent and marriage. Everyone trades on genealogy and everyone keeps

Figure 10
Nenu-Bako Family Genealogy.

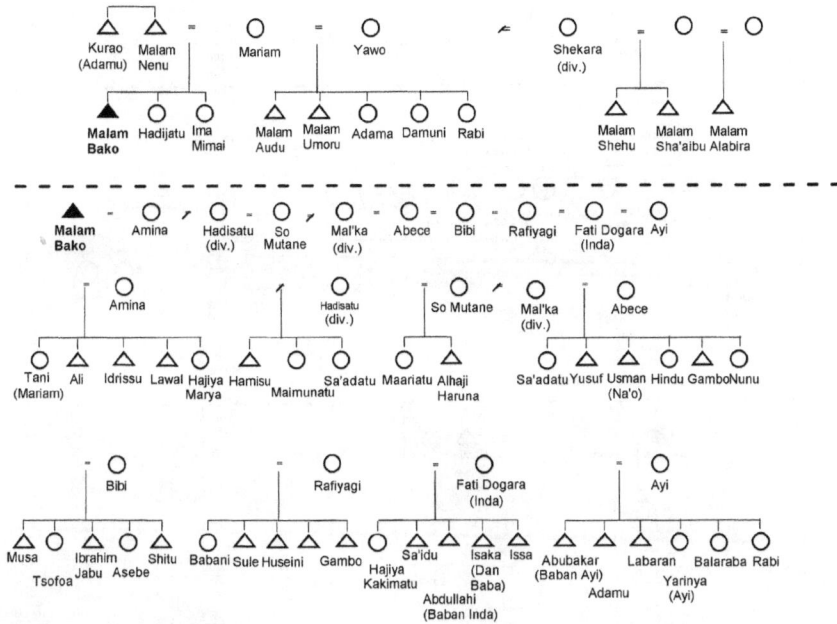

Kurao (Adamu) — Malam Nenu = Mariam = Yawo — Shekara (div.)

Malam Bako — Hadijatu — Ima Mimai — Malam Audu — Malam Umoru — Adama — Damuni — Rabi — Malam Shehu — Malam Sha'aibu — Alabira

Malam Bako — Amina — Hadisatu (div.) — So Mutane — Mal'ka (div.) — Abece — Bibi — Rafiyagi — Fati Dogara (Inda) — Ayi

Amina — Hadisatu (div.) — So Mutane — Mal'ka (div.) — Abece

Tani (Mariam) — Ali — Idrissu — Lawal — Hajiya Marya — Hamisu Maimunatu — Sa'adatu — Maariatu — Alhaji Haruna — Sa'adatu — Yusuf — Usman (Na'o) — Hindu — GamboNunu

Bibi — Rafiyagi — Fati Dogara (Inda) — Ayi

Musa Tsofoa — Ibrahim Jabu — Shitu Asebe — Babani — Sule — Huseini — Gambo — Sa'idu Hajiya Kakimatu Abdullahi (Baban Inda) — Isaka (Dan Baba) — Issa — Abubakar (Baban Ayi) Adamu — Labaran — Balaraba Yarinya — Rabi (Ayi)

track of genealogy. That everyone remembers is indicative of the importance of oral history (Sulley twins 6/18/00).

Four "big families" are key to Sabon Zongo's social and spatial organization and their descendants are the primary landlords in Sabon Zongo. The first, and the main root of Sabon Zongo, was Malam Nenu (father of Malam Bako) and two of his wives, Mariam and Yao. Malam Bako, the son of Mallam Nenu and Mariam, obtained and allocated the Sabon Zongo space to family and followers (see Figure 10).

"Then outsiders also came in by way of marriage, into this interwoven family" (Sule Bako 6/14/1996). These outsiders and followers included, secondly, the offspring of Garuba (Figure 11). Garuba succeeded Malam Nenu as Imam for Accra Muslims and built the first mosque in Central Accra. Malam Bako was his assistant.[1] Garuba, like Nenu, was already deceased before the move occurred from Accra Central to Sabon Zongo. But each of Garuba's children got a piece of land in Sabon Zongo. His son Salisu brought forth one branch of the family; Alhaji Hamza, patriarch at *Gidan Baƙi* (Compound #13), is his son. Another son, Badamase, had a daughter Azumi (Amina) who married Musa Abokin Ango, also a follower of Malam Bako and an important community member. A third son Malam Hassan produced a son Inanu, who married his father's half-brother's daughter Aisha (through prescriptive cousin marriage).

Figure 11
Malam Garuba Family Genealogy.

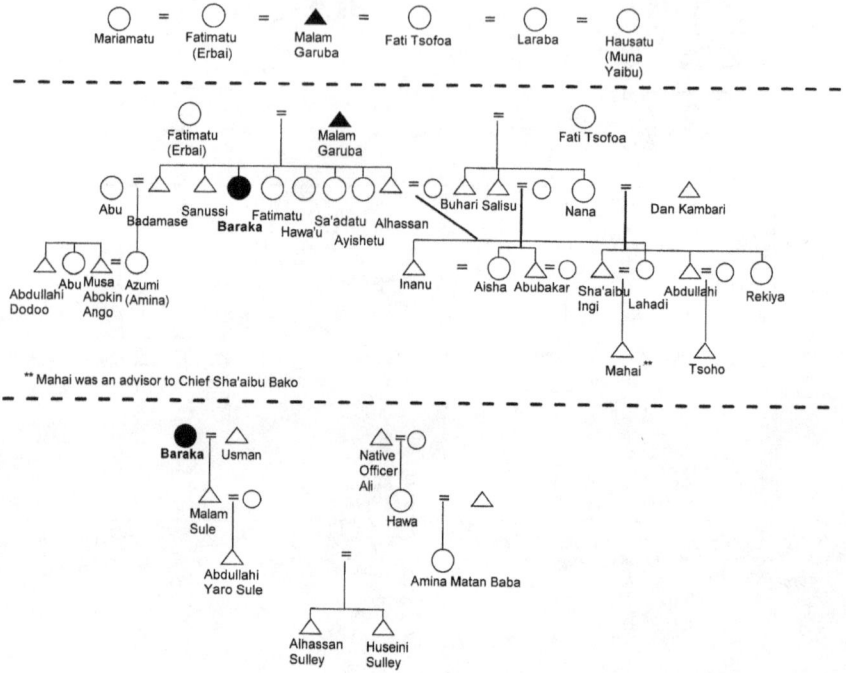

** Mahai was an advisor to Chief Sha'aibu Bako

Inanu was very powerful during the heyday of CPP (Convention People's Party, the party of Ghana's first president Kwame Nkrumah) politics, and as an old man, he continues to be revered.

The Garuba/Abokin Ango alliance is spelled out spatially, in property owned, which includes Sabon Zongo's landmark yellow and blue mosque, named for Abokin Ango. Alhaji Yaro, one of the landlords interviewed for this project, was the elder member of the Abokin Ango family until his death in 1997. Garuba's great grandson Abdullahi Yaro Sule married Hajiya Amina Matan Baba, the granddaughter of Accra Central's Native Officer Ali (briefly the head of Accra Central's Muslim community at the turn of the twentieth century). Her husband pre-deceased her and she became the effective household head until her death in late 1998.

Garuba family members all know that Baraka was the eldest daughter of Malam Garuba and Malam Sule was Baraka's only son, Garuba's eldest grandson. This gave his son Abdullahi Yaro Sulley a certain cachet. The latter's marriage to the granddaughter of Native Officer Ali has given his sons that much more clout (Figure 11). And these ties play out on the ground. Malam Garuba may not have been related to the Bakos, but his descendants in Sabon Zongo inherited rights to compounds in *Kan Tudu*, the old core and some mar-

Figure 12
Musa Kariki Family Genealogy.

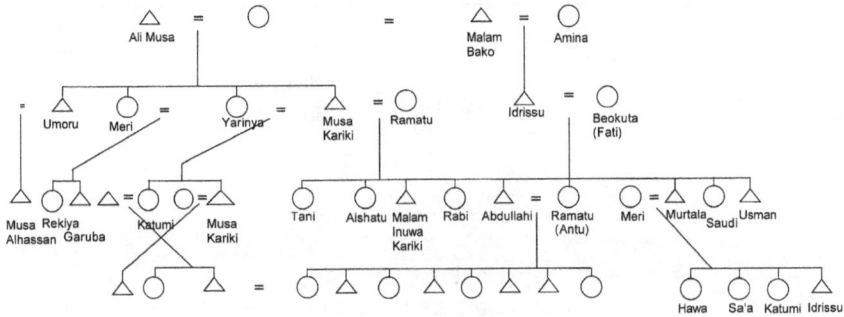

ried into the Bako family (see Figure 14). In addition, the five daughters of his wife Fatimatu ("Erbai") were apportioned the piece of land that became the Night Market. The salience of corporate family ownership has kept that piece of land from being sold.[2]

A third socially-important landlord family is Kariki (Figure 12). Ali Musa Kariki moved from Kano to Salaga in northern Ghana to Kete Krachi in the Volta Region, where his son Musa Kariki was born. The name Kariki is a corruption of (Kete) Krachi. The Kariki family was one of the first to move to Sabon Zongo. "When they moved to Sabon Zongo, they built their houses one by one. At that time, people didn't go out after evening prayer because of the wild animals—*kura* [hyena], *zaki* [lions], snakes" (Abdullahi Kariki 6/13/96). Musa Kariki was Chief Idrissu's *Sarkin Fada*. His son Abdullahi Kariki has been Chief Sha'aibu Bako's *Sarkin Fada*. Musa Kariki was the older brother of Umoru, father of Alhaji Musa Alhassan, Sha'aibu's *Maji Dade*.

The fourth of the families is Damaley (Figure 13).[3] The Damaley family has been important for political reasons. As recounted in Chapter 3, Wansa Damaley was appointed chief barber by Bako, became a *mai gida* and ultimately contested the Sabon Zongo chieftaincy by behaving like a chief and engaging followers. Wansa moved to Sabon Zongo from Mangoase, in Ashanti. At first he lived in *Kan Tudu*, down the road from the current chief's house. When the barber Ubangijin Butulu died, Malam Bako gave Wansa his house. This was located in *Gangare*, also known as *Unguwan Zabrama*, while the Bakos lived in *Kan Tudu*. The political differences of the two men (and their followers) were often articulated in spatial (geographical) terms.

Other socially and politically important families have included that of Dan Kambari, a friend of Malam Bako's father Malam Nenu, whose offspring are intertwined with the Garuba and Nenu/Bako families.

From the community's earliest days, not only did outsiders marry in but members of all of these families have cemented their alliances through marriage between their members. Abu, the daughter of Malam Nenu's brother Kurao

Figure 13
Wansa Damaley Family Genealogy.

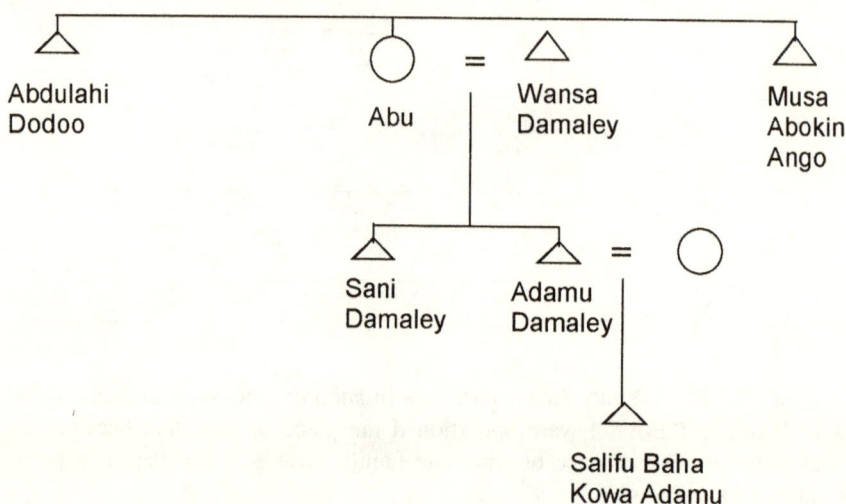

(Adamu), created the connection with Garuba's family by marrying his son Badamase. Malam Garuba's son Salisu married Meri (daughter of Shekara, former wife of Malam Nenu). Wansa Damaley married Musa Abokin Ango's sister Abu. Alhaji Huudu (son of Lawal) married Halimatu (Shekara's daughter's daughter). Mohamadu Al'wali came from *Kano* to *Zongo Nenu* (Central Accra). He married Malam Bako's daughter Hajiya Maria and was given land; his son Tanko Al'wali married Malam Bako's daughter's daughter (Yarinya's daughter Saratu). Tanko's sister Sakinatu was married to Yahaya Adamu; after they divorced, he married one of Malam Bako's sister's daughter, Hawa Mai Danbu. Their son, Alhaji Adamu, married the last-born of Malam Bako's son Haruna. Sarkin Fada (son of Musa Kariki) married Ramatu (daughter of Idrissu). Such marriages between houses within the community have solidified family connections (see Figure 14).

These so-called first families have been important in terms of agnatic descent and lineage affiliation, the accompanying property and leadership (the chieftaincy and its offices). The *zongo* chieftaincy follows the Hausa line of agnatic descent, with all of the traditional court offices, and the Bako family maintains the trappings of leadership. The Bakos have cemented intrafamilial bonds through cousin marriage (what the Hausa call *auren gida*, marriage of the house): Hamisu (son of Malam Bako) married Ayishetu (daughter of Malam Bako's sister); Hamisu's daughter Rekiya was the first wife of Sha'aibu Bako (son of Lawal, Hamisu's brother); Hamisu's son married Hamisu's sister's daughter; Sha'aibu's present wife Saratu's father's father (Audu) and Sha'aibu's father's father (Malam Bako) were brothers; Sule Bako (son of Sha'aibu, son

Figure 14
Interconnections of the Four Families.

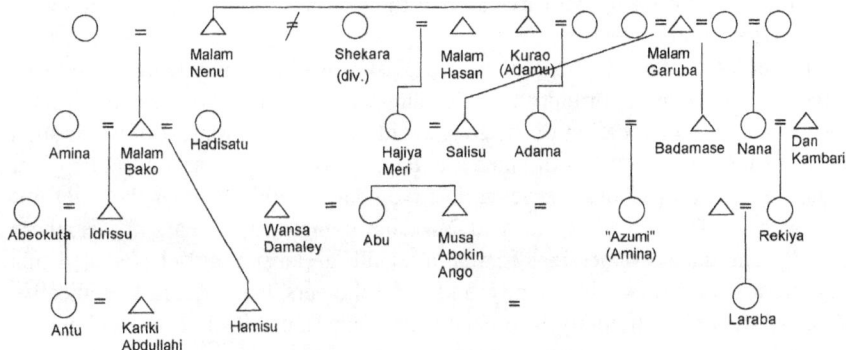

of Lawal) married Hadiza (daughter of Lebo, son of Idrissu) (see Figures 22 and 53).

ETHNICITY

When we speak of ethnicity, we refer to "a subjective perception of common origins, historical memories, ties, and aspirations" (Chazan 1999:108). Ethnic groups are used by their members to achieve particular interests, whether social, political, or economic, and ethnicity carries implications for how to behave in particular relationships (Grillo 1974; Salamone 1975). In Africa, ethnic groups may be fluid (which is to say, lack a fixed, primordial consciousness); they may not be either cohesive or homogeneous (enabling the emergence of various interests and identities); and they often exhibit intragroup splits (Chazan 1999: 109f.). Ethnicity, like other social categories, is played out in areas of hierarchy, dominance and territory (Pellow 1996).

What about the salience of ethnicity in Sabon Zongo? Does ethnicity as such matter more than other facets of identity? I don't think so. Ethnicity is acknowledged by neighbors. And neighbors know each other's ethnicity. But when one refers to someone through his or her ethnicity, it is used as a label (positive or negative) and as a way of identifying the individual (like skin color). When I was talking to Shadow, a housing agent in Sabon Zongo, he referred on one occasion to the new house of a particular Alhaji, "the Yoruba," on another to a room that a Kotokoli lived in for 30 years (3/15/1995). When the landlord of a tenanted compound was explaining how quickly vacant rooms are grabbed up, he told me the story of "some Kwahu woman [who] died sometime ago in one of the 'stables' " (Baba Mai Doki). In both cases, the label was matter-of-fact, in place of an unknown name.

From the backgrounds of the women who sell at Freedom Market (see Chapter 6), we see that Sabon Zongo is a stranger area not just for Muslims/Hausa, but for anyone who is not from Accra.[4] Housing agent Shadow observed to me that "Sabon Zongo is known as a Muslim area, but those who come from the interior, from the bush, can't live among the Ga, because the Ga look down on them. Here nobody does" (3/15/1995).

Hausa-ness in Sabon Zongo is diluted. Distance from hometowns in Northern Nigeria, with little opportunity to visit, inter-ethnic mixing, and marriage within the *zongo*, and the location of the *zongo* within the larger context of a Christian outward-looking, Western-oriented society, have led to acculturation. Yet Hausa-ness, being Hausa, carries a positive charge. While neither the chief nor any of his elders have been to their Nigerian hometown in years if ever, there is still a mythical connection. It was, after all, a Hausa man who created this community to remove his family and his followers from Accra's ethnically-diverse Muslim community in order to maintain Hausa institutions without interference from other stranger groups.

In Accra, like Kumase, the "northern" Muslim enclave has always reflected a conspicuously Hausa influence. The Hausa immigrants have been leaders in the northern community. Their language is the *lingua franca* of the northerners, and this is true in Sabon Zongo as well. Even at the national meetings of the Ghana Muslim Representative Council (GMRC), English and Hausa are used (Ibrahim S. Darpoh, Sec'y, Ghana Muslim Rep Council, 6/8/1993). Over the years, throughout Accra and in Kumase as well, the Hausa have held leadership roles over other strangers, as *zongo* chiefs and chief *imam* (Schildkrout 1970; Pellow 1985); the headman or chief of Sabon Zongo has followed the Bako family line and thus has always been Hausa. Hausa men have had a near monopoly on butchering throughout the urban markets in southern Ghana (Peil 1979). At Freedom Market, there are about ten butchers, all of whom are Hausa and live in Sabon Zongo. In Sabon Zongo, late afternoon and evening, *cicinga* and *balangu* are sold by Hausa men.

Hausa men's sartorial tradition, including *riga* (gown), loose pants and head covering, has been embraced by the "northerners" in Accra. Sabon Zongo boasts many traditional tailors, those who sew the outfits and others who do specialty embroidery. Any style worn in Kano or elsewhere in the Hausa homeland can be made here. The patrons in the community also host itinerant traders from Northern Nigeria, who bring men's attire to sell. The women are less distinctively garbed as a group, although they do wear outfits common in other Muslim areas of West Africa: some wear a loose flowing bubu (common in Mali and Senegal), some Yoruba cloth (cotton lace edging the boatneck blouse and mid-length skirt). All of the Muslim women usually wear a diaphanous prayer veil draped lightly around their shoulders. Both men and women who have made the hadj often sport a gold tooth.

Actually, throughout much of West Africa, Islamic and Hausa culture are thought of as a single body of tradition. The two have been intertwined for so long, that many basic tenets of Hausa society are Islamic. For example, in Sabon Zongo, as elsewhere in Accra, Kumase, and southern Nigeria, the Muslim children all attend Koranic school. The *malamai* (teachers) are primarily Hausa, thus the children's early schooling carries a Hausa imprint: "cultural indoctrination always [begins] at the *malam's* feet" (Adamu 1978:174). In fact, due to their orthodoxy and skill in fashioning charms, the itinerant Hausa *malamai* have had a generally unifying influence on Muslim settlements such as Accra. Hausa also serves as the *lingua franca* of Islamic scholarship and proselytism. In questions of religion, the Hausa (then as now) perceived themselves to be superior to all other Muslim ethnic groups, reckoning religion (Islam) and ethnicity (Hausa-ness) to be inseparable. Even today, the Imam of Ghana's armed forces is a Hausa, though few soldiers are. The chief Imam of Kumase and of Accra, and the founders and important members of most Muslim voluntary associations, are mostly Hausa.

Hausa influence may in part result from their notable stability. Unlike the Zabrama, for example, from the very start the Hausa brought along wives and families (Rouch 1956; Acquah 1958), thus situating themselves to lead the community. Forty-five years ago, 40 percent of the Hausa community were women (Rouch 1956); fifteen years later, the same was true (Hill 1970). In 1948, 35 percent of the Hausa residents in Accra had been born there (Acquah 1958:39). As long-term residents in the southern *zongos*, the Hausa have served as hosts to more recent migrants and northern traders (Hill 1966; Peil 1979).

Under certain circumstances in the early twentieth century, the exclusive identity of ethnicity (not necessarily detectable by the indigenous people or by the British, for that matter) was more salient than the inclusive religion (Islam) of the "aliens" in Accra. For example, in 1930, the Muslim leaders lobbied the British administration on behalf of the Fulani who lacked a headman:

We Mohammedan Chiefs in Accra came or hailed from different nationalities . . . We speak as you know, Sir, different languages, and although we own one religion in common yet our tenets, habits, principles, and customs are different from one and other.[5]

Even today, at times of stress, traditional ethnic biases come out. The chief of Sabon Zongo (a Hausa) was stalking off to complain about Chief Braimah (a Yoruba), whom he felt had insulted him. The Hausa, as I've already observed, consider themselves superior to the other Muslim groups, including the Yoruba, for example in terms of traditional customs, religious orthodoxy and education. Rather than simply vilify his chiefly colleague in ethnic terms, he couched his denunciation in Hausa status terms: "Hey, chieftaincy is not a small matter. Braimah can't play with it. And who is he, anyway? He's just the son of a butcher. His father cut the throats of sheep. I'll show him!" (Sha'aibu Bako 4/27/1982). Old prejudices die hard: butchers may earn a lot of money, but their social status is still low.

In the past, four ethnic groups have had chiefs in Sabon Zongo so that their interests could be represented or their problems adjudicated by one of their own: the Mossi, Wangara, Chamba, and the non-Muslim Ewe. The last Wangara leader, Malam Maman Ibrahim, was the son of the first Wangara chief in Sabon Zongo, selected by Idrissu Bako to succeed to the post. In the on-going Bako-Damaley chieftaincy dispute, Maman Ibrahim supported Sha'aibu, because Malam Bako chose his father as Wangara chief and gave him a house: "If someone gives you your place, you can't then take that person as your enemy. If anyone in Sabon Zongo tells you Malam Bako didn't give him his house, he is telling lies" (Ibrahim 1982). Unlike the Wangara chief, however, who clearly stated that cases beyond his power went to Bako, the Chamba chief equivocated on the Sabon Zongo chieftaincy dispute. Malam Halidou said he forwarded cases to "the Hausa chief," meaning Bako and Damaley, both of whom he recognized (Dedji 1982).[6] There is currently neither an Ewe or Mossi chief.

The only significant ethnic chieftaincy to be maintained in Sabon Zongo is that of the Hausa, and whoever occupies that position is also recognized as the chief of the community in its entirety. In the Accra *zongo* Nima, the situation is reversed: there are many individual ethnic chiefs but no overall *zongo* chief. Thus in Sabon Zongo, when a Ga man and woman had a boundary dispute with a Hausa neighbor, because there is no Ga leader, the two came to Chief Sha'aibu for a judgement.

We know that ethnicity can become inclusive. While ethnicity has boundaries, they are permeable (Barth 1969). Schildkrout (1978) has shown for the northern Muslims in Kumase and I for those in Accra (Pellow 1985) that ethnic group definition is often situational. Indeed, Salamone (1975:410) demonstrates for the Gungawa-Hausa in Northwestern Nigeria that an ethnic group can share a culture with other ethnic groups or be part of a social system that incorporates other ethnic groups; thus, one could "become" Hausa in particular situations, acquiring this ethnic identity if it is useful.[7] For example, by dressing Hausa, speaking Hausa, hanging out with Hausa, observing Hausa customs, one may be treated as a Hausa—whether this means being included in the wedding rituals of lathering a bride with henna or hearing her read the Koran. Taking on social Hausaness might have no particular consequences or it might result in the intangible of increased status or tangible of political or economic opportunity. Individuals everywhere must navigate a variety of social situations, choosing their behavior accordingly—indeed, changing their behavior depending upon the social situation, the relationships implicated and their underlying values. Analogously, in the complex urban environment, where there is a plurality of ethnic groups and membership in one may be regarded as more useful than one's own, a migrant may sometimes "become" the member of an ethnic group for instrumental reasons. There is a self-defining quality to ethnic membership: one identifies oneself and is identified by others as belonging to a group. "Ethnic identities function as categories of inclusion/exclusion and interaction" (Barth 1969:132).

Despite Sabon Zongo's strong Hausa/kinship beginnings, there is considerable ethnic admixture in neighborhoods. There are only two named "tribal" areas—Ayigbetown and Unguwan Zabrama—and both are now very mixed. There is no particular Akan or Ga area per se. Akan are scattered throughout Sabon Zongo. Though there may be ethnic groupings within compounds: one person comes, another room becomes vacant and he tells a friend. Each Akan group seems to congregate in a particular church but outside the *zongo*, as there are no churches within the community (Sule Bako 2/13/1995).

There is also considerable ethnic (and religious) mixing in houses. I surveyed compounds that encompassed as many as ten different ethnicities, including in the mix those from southern and Northern Ghana, southern and Northern Nigeria, Hausa from Nigeria and from Niger. But as the majority of original landlords were Hausa, family houses in the community continue to be Hausa-owned. If one is Hausa, one is more likely to be from one of the settler families. It is primarily Hausa who are the landlords. Within Sabon Zongo, non-Hausa ethnic identity does not carry a negative, but to be Hausa is a positive. And according to one popular guy, most people in Sabon Zongo have been "Hausaized," therefore, he claims, there are few real Hausa!

THE CORNER MOSQUE

Over the years, while the respective Muslim groups have sustained their customs, the "northern" identity has often overridden the different ethnic loyalties. The significance of Islam in the community is evidenced by the profusion of mosques—the thirtieth, *Masalaci* Kariki, was established in the year 2000. Islam helps to provide and reinforce the sense of community, "rendering a degree of permanence and order to the constantly fluctuating, pan-tribal realities of *zongo* life" (Grindal 1973:345). The simple act of people (primarily men) coming together to pray is routinized in a particular time-space (see Giddens 1984). It both produces and reproduces elements of social life.

Just as "Hausa-ness" is diluted in this coastal community, so too is Islam. Sabon Zongo's version of Islam is less orthodox than one finds in Northern Nigeria. The strictures against the mixing of men and women are relaxed. The prohibition of non-family men entering the compound does not exist. In addition, Sabon Zongo is also home to recent southern converts to Islam, such as the Ga and Fante, who intermingle their practice of the religion with elements from their own ethnic traditions. Moreover, non-Muslim southern Ghanaians also live there.

Nevertheless, Islam is a centripetal force for community identification and continuity in Sabon Zongo. Churches and mosques are both found elsewhere in Accra, but as Ojo (1968) noted for Yorubaland, in this *zongo* one finds only mosques. For the non-Muslims in Sabon Zongo, most of whom live as tenants in mixed (Muslim and Christian) compounds, Islam does not appear to be problematic. In fact, many of those non-Muslims I spoke with used the word "peace" or "harmony" in describing their living situations. And while they do not participate in Muslim worship, they can be drawn into publicly observed religious festivals and events. There is the *Salla* (Id il Fitr) celebration at the end of

Ramadan that takes over the community's streets and lanes, or a wedding or birth outdooring, that begin in a compound, whether family or not, and for lack of space spill out into the road.

For the Muslims, living in a primarily Muslim community is very significant. Islamic institutions express the collective solidarity of the northern community, while also "involving such members in a complex network of rights and obligations with fellow Muslims" (Grindal 1973:345). They live insular lives, maintaining an inward-looking posture, distancing themselves from the Western orientation of the "southerners."

While Muslims may be mistrustful of the political and administrative system in Accra (Grindal 1973:344), they have also displayed their commitment to living there by taking an interest in politics and making a difference. During the 1979 elections, many "strangers," all citizens of Ghana, voted as a bloc to eliminate Victor Owusu from the race, because he was previously associated with the Progress Party that had promulgated the Aliens' Compliance Ordinance.[8]

The inhabitants of Sabon Zongo are not just an aggregation of diverse individuals. There is the sense of an overarching morality and Islam is an important element. Being able to attend daily prayers in a mosque near to one's house is a fundamental indicator of convenience for many residents. Praying together daily at the mosque is a source of solidarity. I asked one man why it was necessary for him to go to mosque every morning at 5 A.M.; why not just pray at home? "Here we have group morality: if they don't see you at mosque, they start to wonder if you pray. If they start to wonder, you develop a bad reputation. This is another reason to live within a Muslim community—the mosque is close by, one can go there easily (not just Friday) and no one will talk about you" (M. Barko 5/28/1995). This, of course, does not apply to women, although some mosques do have a separate area for women and there are women who attend.

The mosque is also a node on the information network. "If you go live [away from the *zongo*], people take it like you want to go out from Muslim society. There are no mosques around there. And then if anything happens, you don't hear it quick. Things will happen, and then they will just pass before you hear it. [Within the *zongo* it is] easy for you to hear, because you are with the people and then people still regard you as being with them" (Hamidu 1982).

Everyday during Ramadan, *Masalaci* Bako B.K., a small pink mosque on Korle Bu Street, has preaching from 3:30–5:30 P.M. Imams and *malamai* known for their speaking abilities and interpretive style give Koranic commentaries. A canopy is stretched across the street and there are benches and chairs; only men participate directly, though some women do come to listen, sitting on the periphery, on the other side of the gutter across the street. For the retired men, this is a particular convenience; a few others arrive in taxis.

Actually, observing the monthlong fast and then celebrating its completion are far easier for those living within the community than for others who reside in non-Muslim areas. During Ramadan, the food scene changes dramatically.

The usual foodsellers are not out on the street during the daylight hours. By 5 A.M., those fasting have begun their day. Many women cannot get up early enough to make a meal to be eaten before dawn. Thus, well before dawn, prepared food sellers are out on the street, selling to those who will be fasting. Similarly, after sundown, foodsellers have available fruit and the porridge desired for breaking the daily fast.

While there are Akan and Ga residents in Sabon Zongo who have converted to Islam, most of the community's Muslims are "northerners." While the northerners have always sustained their respective customs, in many situations the "northern" identity (largely imprinted by religion) has overridden the different ethnic loyalties. As a group, the northerners in southern Ghana have made little effort to fit in with the local population. Even before the British planned *zongos* for them, the Muslims had created their own in the old Ga section of town. Rather than refer disputes to local Gold Coast chiefs, they established their own Muslim Native Court.[9] They avoided intermarriage with non-Muslims unless the latter were willing to convert.

Even today, the Hausa criterion of endogamy is religion (Islam) not ethnicity, thus they are free to marry across all ethnic lines (Peil 1979) while privileging religion. And some southerners who have converted to Islam to marry Hausa have become absorbed into the northern/Hausa group, in effect have "become" Hausa. Moreover, many Hausa, both within and outside of Sabon Zongo, downplay the significance of ethnicity as compared to religion. Indeed, over the years there have been several cross-Accra traditional associations that are Islam-based but ethnically-mixed—for example, *zumunci* (for women) and *zumunta* (for men). Both were mutual aid societies, both inactive since the mid-1980s. Bako B.K., the chairman of Sabon Zongo's branch of *zumunta*, indicated that the membership while mainly Hausa, also included Zabrama, Kotokoli, Chamba, and a couple of Akan and Ga. While attended by men, the chairman said it was open to unmarried women. *Zumunci*, also an Accra-wide association, had many members in Sabon Zongo. Its ethnic admixture was neither a unifying nor a dividing factor, overridden as it was by the binding nature of a northern ethos (Pellow 1987).

Today in Sabon Zongo there are many internal cross-cutting associations. While all of them are Muslim, some do accept as members non-Muslims (Muhsin and Rukaya Barko 4/18/1995). I discuss associational life in Chapter 6.

PATRONS AND CLIENTS

As in Hausa society generally, patron-client relations have been crucial both socially and structurally in the *zongos* of Accra (Pellow 1985, 1997, 1999). *Barance* or clientage is one institution of social relations that has distinguished Hausa society from others with whom it has been linked (Smith 1978). Clientage "is a relation between two individuals, groups, or social units of different status, for example, suzerain and vassal, principal and agent, lord and courter, teacher and pupil, the object of which is the reciprocal and mutual promotion of one another's welfare and interest by mutual loyalty and good faith (*amana*) within a competitive context" (Smith 1997:38). In fact, throughout Hausaland, one could say that "in all cases, clientship links individuals of unequal status, fortune, and political position or prospect" (Smith 1965:135).

As a principle of social organization, *barance* underlies other forms of exchange. In Muslim Hausa enclaves—Sabon Zongo, Zongo Lane, Kumase (Hill 1966), Sabo Gari in Ibadan (Cohen 1969) and Mushin in Lagos's migrant (settler) villages (Barnes 1986)—the *mai gida* has been an internal source of authority, a man who cares for and is championed by his people, his clients. Defined as a landlord or settled stranger (Cohen 1965), the *mai gida* has accommodated long-distance stranger-traders and assisted them (Hill 1966). In Mushin, the strangers could establish permanent ties by assuming a territorial identity, purchasing or leasing plots of land, and moving into the position of patrons. Land and housing became sources of power (Barnes 1986:48ff.).

Like Malam Nenu, Malam Bako and Kadri English, a Hausa man could establish himself as a *mai gida* in Accra, as elsewhere, by providing for those in need. His reputation as a patron would be dependent not just on his wealth but on his generosity—taking homeless or visiting stranger in and housing, feeding and helping him adjust to life in this new city. If a man died on the street and had no nearby kin, the *mai gida* would see that he had a proper burial (Pellow 1985). The patron-client relation is one of unequals, the patron superior in status, the client perpetuating the fact and advertising it through dependence upon and support for the patron. Since the chief in Sabon Zongo, for example, has never had a structurally sound position, like the patron *par excellence*, he has supported and has in turn been sustained by the exogenous authorities of the colonial and indigenous structures: pre-colonial chiefs, the British during the colonial era, and the post-colonial Ghana government.

Throughout the Hausa "diaspora," "the chief *mai gida* . . . if he is Hausa, is likely . . . to be chief of the Hausa stranger-community" (Hill 1966:365), yet anyone with power and influence could vie for leadership and the position of patron. A man could establish himself by providing others with lodging. This primarily meant enacting the traditional role of the *mai gida*. Such a man not only needed to have money but also had to be generous with it. For example, during the colonial period in Accra there was a man called Alhaji Sha'aibu who was a wealthy trader in kola, cattle, and palm oil. But, because he was stingy, they nicknamed him Sha'aibu Maikudinera, Sha'aibu the man with money (i.e., who did not spend it); thus, he could not rally people around him.[10] By way of contrast, there were other early settlers (who were not necessarily Hausa but who engaged in the same system of *barance*), such as Braimah Butcher (Yoruba) and Shardow (Nupe), who built themselves up in their respective businesses and then were able and willing to take in the homeless of visiting Yoruba and Nupe, respectively—to house, feed, and help them adjust to life in Accra.[11]

The choice of a secular leader lay with the people. No "alien" had prior right:

there was no royal family connection among the immigrants, no lineal privilege. They came, after all, as merchants and malams. But they also functioned as soldiers, and a new source of legitimacy for chiefly office which dovetailed with that of *mai gida* was the prominence attained by military types and through the agency of the British. Native Officer Ali, for example, was acclaimed as head of one Hausa section, but fell short of the popular consensus that the Colonial Office desired before confirming his appointment. Officer Harri Zenuah, on the other hand, was sought out by his fellow Kanuri for advice. This led to his investiture as a royal and the chieftaincy came to alternate between his house and that of his brother Danbornu, also a military recruit.[12]

In the eyes of the people, the eligibility of a man to be their secular leader was determined by his ability to unite and take care of them. Many Hausa became patrons—providing food and lodging and general care to those away from kin, receiving their clientage in return. Kadri English, the Central Accra Hausa chief in the early 1900s, is a good example of one who parlayed this power into a *zongo* headmanship.

Kadri to the left, Malam Bako to the right. At the time he lived at Zongo Lane, Malam Bako was their [the Hausas] head. Kadri English wanted to stay with Malam Bako. There was a misunderstanding, because everyone wanted to be leader. They made Malam Bako *imam* since Kadri English's money talked; but Malam Bako didn't want the position. (Sarkin Makafi 5/31/1995)

So Bako relocated his followers, leaving Kadri English as the head of the down-town Hausa community.

The complexities of patronage in Accra Central have roiled Sabon Zongo's leadership ever since. When Malam Bako's chief barber Damaley assumed the symbols and rituals of a chief, in a sense he was following Kadri's lead; he was certainly encouraged by Kadri English and Kadri could put his money behind him. Damaley had become a *mai gida* and it was this position that enabled his claims to power, because he could play the part of patron to various resident clients. His behavior showed how patronage mimicked the benefits and obligations of kinship while contesting the primacy of kinship.

Like Malam Bako, Damaley also heard cases—disputes, divorces and so on. If there was a dispute between a follower of Bako and a follower of Damaley, each would meet with his own chief. One day, according to one Damaley supporter, a Nigerian man and wife in Damaley's house had a fight. He resolved it. "Someone told Bako, so Malam Bako said he can't be *Sarkin Aski* [chief barber] anymore" (Idi 2/26/1995).

By the 1980s, according to another of the Damaley defenders, "those who like (Adamu) Damaley surpass Bako, because he helped people and has [more supporters than] Bako" (Bako B.K. 5/7/1982). Whether the latest Damaley had the right to be chief or not, he was important because he was backed by a wealthy Hausa man in Accra, Alhaji Maicancan. In 1979, Maicancan arranged

for Korle Bu police to accompany Damaley as "chief" at the Id parade to celebrate the end of Ramadan. Before the December 31, 1981 coup in Ghana,
Maicancan was chairman of the Mosque Committee (for the building of the new
mosque), Advisor to the Council of Muslim Chiefs (he became an advisor to
the Council around 1976) and Chairman of the Cattle Dealers' Association.
According to some, this showed that Alhaji Maicancan wanted to be head of
the Hausas in Accra.

The Hausa chiefs were among those who sat on the Council of Muslim Chiefs,
which included initially Braimah (Yoruba), Jimala (Wangara), Ali Grunshie
(Grunshie), Bawa Kadri English (Central Accra Hausa), Shardow (Nupe), Bako
(Sabon Zongo), Dagomba, and Chakwashi (Togo/Ghana). Over time, with the
deaths of the original members, the membership altered. Maicancan wanted
Damaley to sit on the Council of Muslim Chiefs, which would help cement both
men's status. Maicancan was already an "advisor" to the Council, having been
appointed by Braimah after Kadri English's death. Maicancan did not attend,
but he wielded influence. And as long as Damaley was accepted on the Council
of Chiefs, Maicancan gave money. This was particularly important since the
Muslim chieftaincies do not have revenue. Thus, Damaley had contacts, certainly with Maicancan, and that translated into *money*, the stock in trade of the
mai gida.

Maicancan and Damaley could both "buy" people; they could underwrite
good works. The people they were caring for were not just Hausas, as the
community had long been ethnically heterogeneous. Thus, when Damaley or
Maicancan had some paving done (because the chief had no clout and the Municipality was not responsive), they were not just benefiting their own families
or ethnic group or fellow Muslims. Anyone living in the area profited. The
boundaries of patronage had widened as the community's population did.

When Adamu Damaley died in 1982, an enormous funeral was held in Sabon
Zongo. And just as Kadri English had supported Wansa Damaley in his quest
to be chief, his grandson Ali Kadri English was in charge of the funeral.

Women can be patrons too among the Hausa, because women are ranked
among themselves. Smith (1959), Yeld (1966), and Mack (1991) have written
about the relations of patronage established between women of different ages
and rank in Hausaland. Thus while women as a class may be conceived of as
subordinate to men as a class, there are women who are regarded as high-status
(Mack 1991), while there are men (like butchers) who are regarded as low-status.
Since the traditional occupational ranking is less significant in Sabon Zongo, one
can say that there are women with money and men without, and the women with
money to burn may act as patrons to men without money. For example, in Sabon
Zongo the Muslim women behave as patrons to the praise-singers, the *maroka*
(Pellow 1997). The *maroka* are basically beggars, men and women who attend all
life-cycle events; it is the men who actually proclaim someone's name in order to
honor him/her and in exchange, they are remunerated. It is the women who actually hold parties with singing, dancing and eating, that go on for hours.

At outdoorings and weddings, the *maroka* act as emcees, overseeing donations to those being feted. The *maroka* clearly look to the women as patrons, as a main source of their financial support.

In this urban village, clearly not everyone experiences the same kind or degree of place attachment. Commitments to the place and the people who live there vary. There are those whose lives are completely tied up in Sabon Zongo, its institutions and people. There are others who work elsewhere, who have friends elsewhere, but whose family is here. For yet others, it is simply a place to sleep. The differences between Hausa and non-Hausa, northerner and southerner, Muslim and Christian, landlord and lodger, may translate into differential feelings about Sabon Zongo. Those whose pedigree is mapped onto the house where they live have a different commitment to Sabon Zongo than do new arrivals. Renters or Christians may be there simply because that is where they found a room. The interactions and exchanges that help define the community vary in degree and kind.

At the same time, there are structures and institutions that undergird Sabon Zongo. Some, for example, the chieftaincy and Islam, are formal; others, like the patron-client bond, are less so. Socially-produced and spatialized, they are re-enacted and reproduced daily. They have created this particular place, while also evolving through this place and being anchored in it. They have helped mold the tenor of the community and have impacted the lives of people who live there.

NOTES

1. In the archival accounts from the first decade of the twentieth century, Malam Bako is referred to as the nephew of Garuba. I have never heard anyone in Sabon Zongo refer to the Garuba family as blood relatives of the Nenu/Bako group. And I have no details of the genealogical tie. Dan Baba (Malam Bako's last surviving "child") thinks that the British may have assumed the family tie because Garuba and Nenu were very close (14 June 2000).

2. Years ago, Malam Sa'a, the Imam of Takoradi, wanted to buy it. Malam Sule (Baraka's son) felt it should not be alienated from the family property, and his ruling became precedent setting. In 1971 the doctor who cared for Hajiya Amina Matan Baba (Malam Sule's daughter-in-law) wanted to open a clinic on the land. The elders in the Garuba family cited Malam Sa'a's case from forty years earlier to reaffirm the decision not to alienate the land.

3. I am quite sure that members of the Bako family would not agree with the inclusion of Damaley, given Damaley's contestation of the Bako myth of origin and the ongoing legal battles they have had with him and his descendants; structurally, however, he has been important, at least as a patron.

4. Although there are also some Ga whose residence in Sabon Zongo pre-dates the community's establishment, as well as other Ga who have moved there in more recent years.

5. ADM 11/1446, June 15, 1930.

6. Malam Halidou Atcha Dedji was the Chamba chief in 1982.

7. "Situational ethnicity" as I use it derives from J.C. Mitchell's writings on "situational change" in urban Africa and "the situational approach" in urban African studies (1966:44, 48).

8. The Aliens Compliance Order of November 18, 1969, was enacted by the Busia government to nationalize businesses and provide more occupational slots for "Ghanaians" (defined as anyone whose mother was born in Ghana). The Order resulted in the deportation of an estimated one million people—Africans, many of them Nigerians, Europeans, Lebanese, and Indians.

9. ADM 11/1502; December 3, 1914, NAG.

10. Interview with Chief Amida Braimah, January 28, 1982.

11. Interview with Alhaji Idi, former advisor to Hausa Chief Bawa Kadri English, February 10, 1982.

12. Interview with Abayazidu Zenua, Chief of Kanuri, February 17, 1982.

6

EVERYDAY LIFE

Children can be found everywhere. They make toys, such as kites, windmills and drums, which they play with outside. The toys are seasonal, depending in part upon the weather. My favorites are the tin cars and "articulator trucks," which are made from tins for Milo (the chocolate drink) or tomato paste. They are sometimes painted, with cut outs from flip-flops as wheels. The players attach strings and lead them through the lanes in their play. There are also some foosball games scattered about—one sits on the edge of the Night Market field and another is on a lane in Ayigbetown—which the larger boys play.

Since the roads do not accommodate fast or dangerous vehicular traffic, the children are as likely to be playing in the street as inside a compound. There are always small children playing in the dirt or in the brackish water flowing through the decayed gutters. The little ones playing outside in front of their compounds are often in various forms of undress, as if they were playing in the privacy of their own homes. Like the animals, they are welcome anywhere. And like the animals, they evince no fear. Everyone in the neighborhood knows the children, or the grandchildren, of nearby residents.

Sabon Zongo is an amalgam of traditions, an urban community. As in other West African cities, ethnicity still matters. In Sabon Zongo, however, ethnicity is not the defining feature of life. Here, extracted patterns from the cultural lifeways of numerous "stranger" groups have been melded together to create a new urban culture. Like city dwellers everywhere, the residents must learn how to negotiate the city. For many, Sabon Zongo is a point of orientation to the urban system. As in other cities, this developing cultural neighborhood identity is informed by the urban institutional structure. But there is also something about this particular space that has transformed it into a place of great positive significance to those who choose to live there, despite its material deterioration.

Just as Sabon Zongo has evolved a spatial identity over the last eight decades, so has it evolved a social identity. A close account of the power of social networks helps explain peoples' attachment to the community (Bestor 1986). Connections are forged with the community more generally as residents participate in public exchange through community-wide institutions, such as the chieftaincy, court or market. These create social boundaries, networks and exchanges, as they cross-cut the community daily. They take place in, even as they create, meaningful spaces, some of which are artifactual, like compounds and mosques, some of which are conceptual, like the Night Market field. These connections are enacted by individuals whose actions are infused with meaning. They are anchored in socio-physical structures (community places and social institutions) which then help to reproduce those connections by enabling the generation and reproduction of meanings and action, of social strategy and behavior.[1] Ties are created between individuals, as friends and neighbors, as participants in patron-client relationships, and through activities such as commercial transactions.

This urban locale has its own urban culture, constitutive of and expressed in the socio-spatial order. The residents share symbols, shops, languages, foods, festivals, rituals, family, and kinship (Rapoport 1980a:72–73). For some, the social boundaries of community involve the degree of closeness to Sabon Zongo's "first families" and the myths of origin. For others, community institutions produce and encapsulate the exchanges that tie them to one another, that are anchored in community spaces and in the built environment. Sabon Zongo is intermediate between one's dwelling and Accra the city. To some extent, living in this community with which one has more identification (however minimal) than the larger, unknown city, eases residents into "metropolitan knowledge," the meanings shared by city dwellers (Rapoport 1980a; Rotenberg 1993).

Sabon Zongo is distinct, due in part to its genealogical basis, its Muslim tenor, its physical character, and the behaviors and activities produced and anchored there. The organization of social exchange in everyday life today is insular: institutions such as leadership, marriage, *esusu* are inward-looking. But Sabon Zongo is also very much a part of the urban landscape, in social and spatial terms. As already illustrated, it lies within the city's limits and it falls within the purview of the AMA for a variety of infrastructural concerns. To participate in or use institutions such as schools (secular), banks, the post office, main market, even work, its residents must go elsewhere in Accra. There is no post office in Sabon Zongo; the closest is in Kaneshie or Abossey Okai and both have few boxes to rent.[2] Not only is there no bank; there is also no forex (foreign exchange) bureau. There is the *esusu* man, who makes the rounds of the compounds regularly, collecting money from passbook holders, recording the amounts, and keeping it for them.

In Chapter 4, I discussed the significance of place; in Chapter 5, I discussed the significance of pedigree. In this chapter, I explore various domains of exchange or transactions that take place in Sabon Zongo. As already indicated, these spatial and social dimensions are mutually constitutive. Like people everywhere, the residents of Sabon Zongo are socialized into roles and ways of behaving. And like people everywhere, this socialization occurs in particular places and through the practices of daily life. Practices and exchange have helped shape, and are shaped by, Sabon Zongo, and have socialized the residents of Sabon Zongo, as zongo-ites and as urbanites as well.

PARTICIPANTS IN DAILY EXCHANGE

Sabon Zongo began as an immigrant community. While its population has changed and become more varied, it is still very much an immigrant community. Created as a refuge for outsiders, it became a home to them and their descendants. According to the 1948 census, "the Hausa then constituted the largest single non-Gold Coast ethnic community in the city, at 3.4% of the total population" (Dakubu 1997:130). Of these, 41 percent were women, more than in most migrant groups, and 35 percent of this ethnic group was born in Accra.

Increasing numbers of ethnically diverse renters began moving into rented rooms in Sabon Zongo after World War II, in the 1950s, when there was a flurry of modernization in Accra as part of the ambitious program of Kwame Nkrumah's First Republic.

The 1970 population census of Sabon Zongo (which includes Lartebiokarshie and Town Council Line), lists 24,245 residents. In 1996, there were 14,000 registered voters. According to provisional figures from the 2000 Population Census, the population is 17,838. The Urban Preparatory Study (Ghana 1992) estimates the population density at 330.19 per hectare. And according to the tax rolls, there are 360 residential structures in Sabon Zongo.

In fact, the population may very well be closer to 25,000, as I have estimated elsewhere (Pellow 1999:297). There are the uncounted, like the Chadian families who landed in Sabon Zongo after fleeing civil conflict in their own country; several of them squatted in a vacant storefront, visible to all passersby. When I wondered aloud how many families were camping out, my assistant said, "Just count the number of mosquito nets!" There is also a continual flow of long-term "temporary" residents, such as Tuareg men from Niger, who come to Accra on commercial jaunts, or the Fulani women who walk throughout the country, carrying medicine in bundles on their heads.

Whatever the numbers, in 1979 "Hausa people still constituted the largest community in Sabon Zongo" (Moser cited in Dakubu 1997:130). My sense is that this is still true, even though in my census of 714 adults living in nineteen compounds, only 279 (or 39 percent) are Hausa. Certainly they continue to have an overarching influence. Many of the Muslims identify themselves as Hausa, perhaps due to the perception of Sabon Zongo as a Hausa community but probably also because of that ethnic group's flexible boundaries and continued importance as a model of orthodoxy.

The many non-Hausa who have swelled the ranks include Kanuri, Zabrama, Wangara, Fulani, Busanga, Chamba, and Kotokoli from neighboring African countries, Chadians, the northern Ghanaian Frafra, Wala, Sisala, Dagarti, and Mossi, and Ga and various Akan sub-groups from southern Ghana. Most, but by no means all, of the residents are practicing Muslims; all of the Hausa are Muslims while virtually none of the northern or southern Ghanaians I interviewed are Muslims: only three of the 163 Akan and only three of the twenty-four Frafra so self-identified. Given the general perception of non-zongo dwellers that Sabon Zongo is a community of northerners, it is quite striking that southern Ghanaian Akan (most of whom are tenants) compose as much as 23 percent of my sample (see Table 6.1), and of those, the Kwahu constitute 53 percent.

Table 6.1
Ethnic Background of Adult Residents in 19 Compounds

Ethnicity		Number	Percent
Hausa		279	39
Akan		163	23
	Akan/"twi"	20	
	Kwahu	87	12 (53% of Akan)
	Asante	17	
	Akwapim	14	
	Akim	2	
	Fante	23	
Ewe		73	10
Zabrama		47	7
Frafra		24	3.3
Kotokoli		21	2.9
Chadian		19	
Kusasi		15	
Wangara		13	
Sisala		11	
Busanga		9	
Ga		10	
Yoruba		10	
Dagomba		5	

Ethnicity	Number	Percent
Gao	3	
Dagarti	2	
Chamba	2	
Mossi	2	
Adar	1	
Fulani	1	
Dagbani	1	
Mamprussi	1	
Barga (Benin)	1	
Ibo	1	
Upper West	?	
TOTAL	714	

In Accra, the greatest increase in the number of people from various parts of Ghana between 1960 and 1970 "took place in Abossey Okai (from 33% to 49%), Sabon Zongo, and Kaneshie" (Lisowska 1984:121). Abossey Okai lies right across Oblogo Road from Sabon Zongo and Kaneshie is about one mile to the north and west. During that same decade, the distribution of foreign Africans did not change much, continuing to be concentrated in Sabon Zongo, Nima and Newtown (Lisowska 1984:121).

The seeming non-Ghanaian appearance of Sabon Zongo residents, in dress, religion, and cultural orientation generally, is intriguing because according to the 1970 population census, of the total Sabon Zongo area, 76 percent was born in Ghana and only 6 percent in Nigeria (Ghana Government 1978:194, Table 9). Those identifying themselves as foreign nationals numbered 5,742, of whom 1,401 or 24 percent were Nigerian. And of those 24 percent, 45 percent stated they were born in Ghana (Ghana Government 1978:374, Table 23).[3]

The main languages spoken are Hausa, Ga, and Twi, with Hausa clearly the *lingua franca*. But in fact residents speak an extraordinary range of languages, including Fulani, Yoruba, Kanuri, Zabrama, Wangara, Buzu, Kotokoli, Mossi, Ewe, Sisala, Dagomba, and Dagarti. Many of the older-generation northerners are not fluent in English. The multilingualism and polyglotism so characteristic of Accra as a whole is clearly true of Sabon Zongo; the primary languages and/ or *lingua franca* spoken are simply different than in the rest of the city.

North of Ring Road (the area that includes Sabon Zongo), to the extent that one can say that there is an internally cohering network, the northern migrants are bound together by the use of Hausa. This contrasts with Central Accra, where Hausa is not a second language in general use except in specific locations in connection with certain types of trade (Dakubu 1997:66). I have already proposed that in Sabon Zongo, ethnicity is less salient than genealogy in particular and zongo-ness in general. Dakubu's linguistic findings in Accra at large may be evidence of the same phenomenon: "to its speakers [Hausa] may index a kind of northern identity but precisely *not* northern ethnicity, if 'ethnicity' implies conservative acceptance of a bundle of inherited attributes that include political status, symbolic culture, and language" (Dakubu 1997:96). But Hausa language use does "index northern otherness in the eyes of southern Ghanaians" (Dakubu 1997:68).

Residents in Kan Tudu are still primarily Hausa. The spatialization of the landlord/lodger distinction is less true in Sabon Zongo, as more and more compounds are renting out rooms to non-family and some family-owned compounds are rented in their entirety. Similarly, the Bako/non-Bako affiliation no longer holds, as individuals unrelated to the first families are able to buy into compounds or buy a piece of land and build in non-congested areas like Ayigbetown and the Market Street edge.

But the reality is that compounds are still overwhelmingly owned by descendants of the original Hausa families, very few non-northerners have bought into the community, and those who have tend to own residential properties on the edges of Sabon Zongo (Oblogo Road, Market Street, and the west and east periphery). Northerners (clearly Muslims and often Hausa) are the primary residential property owners listed even for Ayigbetown, the quarter in Sabon Zongo that is the least built-up and where land is most likely to be available.

At the easternmost end of Ayigbetown (and Sabon Zongo), a tax block that extends north-south from Korle Bu all the way to Market Street and east-west between Bartholomew and Wood, only two owners out of thirty-three listed in the property tax rolls might be southerners, a woman by the name of Mama Thompson and a man by the name of Lamptey. Hausa, Yoruba, and other northern owners are scattered throughout the adjacent sub-area of Municipal (also known locally as Toyota, because of the car repair businesses there). In the AMA tax area that would be the Ayigbetown sub-area of Sunshine, 30 owners are listed. The names include seventeen who are definitely southern Ghanaians (Ga and Akan). Most live in the area east of Bartholomew (included by the AMA but not by core *zongo* dwellers as Sabon Zongo, and certainly not part of the original tract). But there are also at least four Ga and Akan house owners in the block east of Abia—including the Nortey's (at Abia and Korle Bu). Theirs has been a family house since before the arrival of Malam Bako and his followers. At the other end of Sabon Zongo, from St. Thomas up to Link Road (the west-side parallel to the Bartholomew-Ring Road segment), all eight home owners are southern Ghanaians. Along Oblogo Road, where there are primarily businesses, most are southerners. And along Market Road, from Hide Link to Alhaji Street, five out of eleven of the property owners are southern Ghanaian, and four of them own property near the Market Street edge.

Thus, over time Sabon Zongo has reproduced its social identity while also producing change. Residents' daily routines, built into Sabon Zongo's system of social and physical elements, have similarly been routinized even as they have altered with the change in residents. Community spaces are fluid, flexible, and multifunctional, and activities are adapted to fit where space is available. The street activities are characteristic of the respective sub-areas. As delineated in Chapter 4, these areas represent geographically reconstituted social meanings and differ physically: the width of the streets, the density and type of housing, their distance from the center. But they also embody distinct social differences that tie in with the spatiality and physical differences. These include the particular population that lives in an area (as distinguished by such features as physical disability such as blindness); their genealogical relationship to original inhabitants and the generation of residence and thus location; and the occupation/s or work practiced there.

The three main neighborhood divisions *Kan Tudu*, *Gangare*, and Ayigbetown have significant social delineations. Walking to *Kan Tudu* from Oblogo Road, Malam Bako's palace sits at the top end of Malam Bako Street, from which he could metaphorically "look down" on his subjects. Two blocks down the road, Sha'aibu Bako, his grandson and heir to the chieftaincy, often sat in the doorway to his audience hall, watching the street scene, in particular the activities at the Night Market field across the street. The market side is known as *makwalla*, since it is an informal as well as formal gathering place. There is little hawking on Malam Bako Street proper but there are small shops and on the far side of Night Market field there are women selling fruit, bread and other food stuffs during the day.

RELATIONS BETWEEN THE SEXES

While Islam and Hausa-ness color the northerners' world view and behavior in general and male-female behavior in particular, these have been diluted or altered by the incorporation of different ethnicities and their attendant customs and ideas as well as the constraints imposed by city living. For many West African men, having more than one wife is desirable; it is a sign of social and financial success. This is no less true for Muslims. The four wife limit is hardly restrictive; given the exigencies of housing and school fees for children, it is the rare man in Sabon Zongo who exercises the right to marry four women. Actually, having even two wives has become far less common. Chief Sha'aibu Bako has not had two wives simultaneously in many years. Sarkin Fada, his linguist, had two wives, one of whom died in the mid-1990s. Kilishi has had two wives. Alhaji Alhassan, Sha'aibu's *majidade*, has the full complement of four. Yet, Alhaji Huudu and Baba Mai Doki, both grandsons of Malam Bako, both community elders, both childless, have not taken more than one wife simultaneously.[4] Going down one generation, polygyny is rarer. None of Sha'aibu's children has multiple wives (or co-wives). His son Sule, a potential successor, has only had one wife. Two other potential successors, Yahaya and Inussa Bako, the sons of Hamisu Bako, have only one wife each.

It is instructive to look at Sabon Zongo more broadly. Out of all nineteen sampled compounds, twelve men have been supporting two wives, one has three.

Two of the men are currently deceased, their wives continuing to share the residence. Four of the thirteen are not Hausa; one is Zabrama, one Kotokoli, and two are southern Ghanaian (Kwahu and Ewe). Five of the men were the houseowners (all Hausa). Only one of the thirteen is of the younger generation, and his family so objected to his taking a second wife (he is not properly employed and his first wife is well-liked by all in his family house, where they live) that no one attended the wedding.

While male-female distinctions are still ideologically marked among Sabon Zongo's Hausa, the restrictions on male-female interaction in Sabon Zongo are also considerably diluted, often vestigial at best. This again results in part from the economics of life today, in part from distance from hometown customs, in part from living among non-Hausa.

The rules of seclusion do not exist anywhere in Sabon Zongo. "Because people come together from [different] areas," Malam Hamisu mused. Some are Zabrama, Hausa, Mossi, Buzanga, and others. They marry each other. Buzanga and Zabrama don't do seclusion, so if your tribe doesn't do seclusion and I come and marry you, I'll never put you in seclusion" (4/9/1982).

Chief Sha'aibu understands the change through a change in up-bringing. "Here in Ghana, it's very hard to have *kulle*, because we were not brought up with *kulle*. . . . It was our great grandfathers who wanted to make the *kulle*. But gradually. . . . The up and coming generations weren't brought up in *kulle*. And at the same time some of them cannot do the *kulle*, because it is difficult to live in *kulle* in Ghana. [Then], when you had even a penny you could buy things, you would be satisfied with that one penny. Now, because of money, men want their wives to go and sell and get money" (5/11/1982).

Thus, the arguments against seclusion involved various elements of culture change: socialization and familiarity, finances, differing customs. The Yoruba and northern Ghanaians, for example, practice Islam but do not observe wife seclusion. Moreover, as is delineated in Chapter 7, it is difficult to do *kulle* if there are tenants (read: strangers) in the house.

Shortly after my conversation with the chief, a Hausa malam who taught in one of Sabon Zongo's Koranic schools took me to his home. He lived across the road in Abossey Okai, where he kept his two wives in seclusion. The house had two rooms (one for each wife and her children) and a small courtyard. To ensure his wives' concealment from the gaze of unrelated men, he built a high fence around the house. There was no toilet. To relieve themselves, they would put on a veil and go to the toilet near the school a block away. Both are from Hausa Muslim families (the senior's mother is a Muslim Ga). When growing up, neither of the two women knew anyone in *kulle*, even while the senior wife had only a few non-Muslim friends and all of her co-wife's friends were Muslim Hausa. They knew of the custom from malams "who preach the way a Muslim woman should live . . . that at the time of our Prophet Mohammed, the wives are not allowed to go just as the men are going. They wanted them to live at home, to care for the children. They don't want any man to see their faces.

When going out, they should cover their faces so that other men cannot see their faces" (Rukaya Abdurahaman 5/24/1982).

Before marrying, the husband-to-be informed each that she would be in *kulle*, teaching her how he wanted her to live. When each of them married him, she accepted *kulle*,

even though our friends always make fun of us, saying we are fools, sitting down here day after day. We don't see the way they are living. But everything is under God. So when they come and see us sitting here. . . . It's not that we don't want to go out. Of course if we are allowed we will go. But we don't know what we are going to get outside. We get everything we want here. And it is called will, the Prophet's will and God's will. The way a Muslim should live. . . . So even when they come [our friends], we preach them that even if your husband does not *kulle*, the way you are living, the way you address yourself is up to you—cover your face. But some of them do not cover their face. The veil is always under the arm. So they make fun of us, the way we are living. This is modern Ghana and we are living in the past, and so on. (Rukaya Abdurahaman 5/24/1982)

In Nigeria, it is a Hausa custom for women to give birth at home, with a traditional birth attendant. Only the husband can make the decision to send the woman to a hospital. In Accra, it is normative to go to the hospital or a midwife's clinic to deliver. When the senior wife of the aforementioned malam was about to deliver her first child, he did not want her to go to the hospital. It was when she began to hemorrhage that he backed down and sent her to the hospital. Other Hausa men regarded this malam's behavior toward his wives as cruel. According to their culture-based reasoning, seclusion is not the custom in Ghana and a man certainly should not do seclusion if he cannot provide properly for the wives. At the malam's there was barely room in the tiny compound yard for the household's activities, the cooking and the children's play, let alone the enormous ram tethered on a rope. The two women justified their seclusion through religion. Others, Hausa men as well as women, found it bizarre, not in keeping with the local Muslim ethos.

While the Sabon Zongo Hausa may not observe seclusion, men and women do operate in separate social networks and celebrate ceremonies and rituals such as baby outdoorings and weddings separately. For example, at the baby outdooring (*suna*) on the seventh day after birth, the full extent of the men's observance is for the father and his male kin and friends to go to the mosque for 5 A.M. prayers, where the father has the imam announce the child's name. The women, on the other hand, hold a *biki*, a celebration, with music and dancing and eating, that might go on the entire day. Weddings are a three-day affair, and like the *suna*, involve the men and women separately.

At some occasions, men and women are within eyesight of one another. For example, when Alhaji Bebe's daughters had a double wedding, on Sunday morning August 3, 1997 the brides did the reading of the Koran in their father's compound yard. There were perhaps 250 men from Sabon Zongo and all over Accra. The women—family and friends—draped themselves over the verandah at the rear to listen and observe. They were technically not present, because they were outside of the circle of participants. But they were obviously there and could be seen by all. As at other times and other such celebrations, the separation is symbolic at most.

Some Muslims, like the Yoruba, do not practice sexual segregation at all. Yet, when the event is for all Muslims, public or semi-public, the symbolic separation is observed. These sexually-specific spatial arrangements are common. During Ramadan in 1995 (2/25), there was a political rally at Bako B.K.'s Mosque. It was overwhelmingly attended by men, while about fifteen women sat at the periphery on the other side of the street behind the gutter. As the MP Alhaji Ila said, "it is our custom." When the community self-help group, the Sabon Zongo Youth Association was functioning in the early 1980s, the male members would meet in the *zaure* of Malam Bako's palace. The women always sat outside, leaning in through the windows whenever a topic of interest to them arose. As the secretary of the Association explained to me, "This is our custom, the Muslim custom, which bars women from mixing with men any time we have a meeting. That's why they sit outside."[5] Of course, Christians do not observe the separation at their events. But if they attend Muslim Hausa occasions, they follow the rule of sexual separation.

Most interesting is the very public parade on *Salla*, the day of festivities celebrating the end of Ramadan. The Muslim women are dressed up in new clothing, those who belong to organizations wearing the same textile pattern and dress style. And they claim the streets. All vestige of *kunya* (modesty) is gone, as they walk and dance through the streets of Sabon Zongo, wiggling their hips and behaving in a flirtatious manner. The only men mixed in with the dancing women are the musicians and youths. It is reminiscent of life-cycle observances: the men's participation is religious and sedate, the women's secular and ostentatious.

As a consequence of all this admixture of peoples and customs, the hierarchical relations between men and women are potentially much more complicated. Women can and do come into contact with men other than their husbands (from whom they surely derive some of their status) or relatives (presumably of the same kinship status).

SCHOOLING

All Muslim Sabon Zongo parents send their children to *makaranta*, Koranic or Arabic school. They begin to attend the moment they start to talk, by two or three years of age. They attend five days weekly, Monday through Wednesday, Saturday and Sunday. Once they are old enough to enroll in Western school, they attend *makaranta* on Saturday and Sunday only. Thus the weekday *makaranta* is composed mainly of very small children and those who do not attend regular school. The system of teaching is by rote recitation, and walking by any one of the *makaranta*, typically you hear the children reciting while the teacher wanders among them, smacking slackers or those distracted by passersby with a pointer. There are many stories of teachers engaging in corporal punishment, but there are also limits to what is permissible. One of the community elders was outraged when a Liberian child he was caring for, whose family was scattered by that country's civil war, came home covered with welts from the malam's stick. The guardian saw no excuse for that kind of a beating and warned the teacher that he would take action should this ever happen again. (The community is tightly knit enough that negative gossip could ruin the teacher's reputation and his business.)

There are currently eight operational *makaranta* in Sabon Zongo. They are teaching approximately 1,100 children; the other children are sent to *makaranta* elsewhere in Accra. With the exception of one, which is not functioning well at the moment because it has lost its teachers, all are melting pots of ethnicities. In the approximate numbers obtained, 60 percent of the children attending *makaranta* in Sabon Zongo are Hausa. The balance includes not only Kotokoli, Zabrama, Fulani, Yoruba, and Busanga—generally considered to have Muslim affiliation—but also small numbers of the southern Ghanaian Ga, Akan, and Ewe (Muslim converts). In the past, those girls who were sent to Koranic school received a minimal course of study, even though one of the most influential teachers, Malam Gambo, always felt girls should attend *makaranta*, because it helps them in their prayers. With the dilution of custom, in fact all Muslim girls are given some Koranic schooling.

Three of the eight Koranic schools in Sabon Zongo now offer a combined English/Arabic curriculum, in addition to the regular Western primary-plus schooling that children receive in secular schools. In fact, the first Arabic/Western school established in the GoldCoast/Ghana was the Larte Biokarshie Primary School, on the southwestern edge of Sabon Zongo. It was started in 1956 by Nkrumah out of appreciation for Hausa support in his political campaigns. Since all of the children do attend Western school, the *makaranta* today are responsible for basic Koranic training. The individual who studies Koran and language, *hadith*, grammar—the norm in the past for basic knowledge—now becomes a big *malam*.

Under the current educational system, children begin primary school at age six and go from P1 to P6. Primary is supposed to be taught in English, but in fact many schools use the local language for the first three or so years. At Ojo, the primary school on the edge of Sabon Zongo, they use Ga. It is only in the primary schools in Sabon Zongo that the curriculum combines secular and Arabic.

Youths attend Junior Secondary School for three years. Sabon Zongo students can go to Town Council Line (which is the most convenient), Salvation (near the Mamprobi Post Office), Abossey Okai (across Oblogo Road), or Ayololo (near Central Accra). Most go to Town Council Line and Salvation, largely because sports are very competitive and the two play football, volley ball, ping pong, track and field, in the same league. Senior Secondary School is three years, vocational or academic, and those youth who attend go to schools elsewhere in Accra (or depending upon finances, to boarding schools elsewhere in the country).

Even in 1970, the level of education was low in Sabon Zongo—over 30 percent in Nima and Sabon Zongo, the largest communities of the foreign Africans, had not attended Western schools (Lisowska 1984). Yet, the highest increase in the number of skilled workers took place in both areas (Lisowska 1984:126). And despite the growing spatial concentration of foreign Africans, there is evidence of an increase in their social and professional differentiation (Lisowska 1984:128).

Malam Hamisu saw far more girls going to school in the 1980s than in the early days of Sabon Zongo. "Now," he observed, "everything has changed—they go to Western school and *makaranta*, and some girls finish" (6/4/1982). But fewer girls than boys are sent for *Western* schooling beyond the primary grades; thus, even if they are free to work, assuming opportunities exist, they lack job skills for work in the modern sector. The persistence of northern traditionalism underscores the marginality of the community.

So, Sule Bako (the university-educated son of Chief Sha'aibu) observes, there are people who do not see the importance of Western school, though they are anxious to send their children to *makaranta*, "which is the same idea our forefathers had." Those parents who see the light may have had contact with Western educated people through work.

I know my father sent us to school, because he was a messenger and he realized we should be educated—he sent his cousin and his son. But the majority don't see the need for it. They send them four or five years to *makaranta*, and then they abandon them, to fend for themselves. Maybe it is Islam that is having the effect, that no matter the material world, in the end you die. Schooling means you are looking for a job, for the material world. But if those people are phased out—the young people don't have any proper training, even in Islam—when they come to realize the real situation of survival, and they can see the difference between them and the educated—maybe that will make the change . . . [some members of the older generation] take things for granted. After all— in the end you die. Some in the Arab world where Islam is dominant, they are *serious* about education, far more than here in Africa, in the Muslim community. The Muslim community in Ghana has not been influenced by modern education. So we have a lot of young people in *zongo* here who are not properly educated. Not trained in any vocation. They just roam about. They're a problem to the society. (Sule Bako 6/14/1996)

OCCUPATIONS

The monopolization of certain occupations not only sets Sabon Zongo off from much of the rest of the city; it even differentiates between the quarters within the community. Among the adult population, many of whom have had minimal secular education, professional expertise is low. As indicated 30 years ago, there has been severe unemployment among men, and there are fewer women than in the wider society in the wage-earning labor force (Brand 1972: 288). Many still follow roles barely changed from the early days of Sabon Zongo. Moreover, following the ethnic stereotypes, carpenters are overwhelmingly Ewe, charcoal sellers Sisala or Grunshie, corn sellers in the market Zabrama, butchers and Koranic teachers Hausa.

Today, certain customary occupations, like the chieftaincy and its offices, continue to carry prestige. According to the insider stereotype, the men in "downhill" *Gangare* are tailors and mechanics, while all the men in *Kan Tudu* are Koranic teachers. And according to Malam Hamisu, the elder of the Bako family in the early 1980s, to be a malam is the most important among all occupations. "Even if you want to be chief, you have to be a learned man. . . . You can buy respect and importance, but as for malam, you can never buy him. Even if you say you are more than the malam, you may need something and have to come to the malam." (Malam Hamisu 5/28/1982).[6] To some extent, the continuity in occupations across generations is the result of the apprenticeship system that draws on kinship and clientship.

But in fact, even for the Hausa, the occupational range today is considerably broader. Again Malam Hamisu: "Today what the people are learning is what the white man is doing—learning mechanics, engineering, electronics, and so forth. What was formerly learned was more respected than today, because that is the knowledge man has to acquire and there is no knowledge other than that" (6/4/1982). Among the 302 men of mixed ethnicities I sampled, 19 percent are tailors, 30 percent are in commerce, 17 percent are in transport (as drivers or repairmen). Commercial enterprises span mobile traders in watches and used cloth to wholesalers and large-scale merchants. While traditional service roles for illiterates, like tanning work (*majaimah*) is still practised (the tannery area is nearby), others such as carrier ("kaya-kaya"), watchman and messenger, have been transposed to the modern sector, in government and private business. Until they retired, Chief Sha'aibu Bako was a messenger at the Public Works Department and Baba Inda (a son of Mallam Bako) was a messenger at the Supreme Court. Literate men are also white collar workers and businessmen—all indications of slowly penetrating change as the social insularity of the community has eased.

For Sabon Zongo women, the changes have been greater than for the men. The married Hausa women are far more mobile than they were in Malam Bako's day. Like most of the other Sabon Zongo women and women everywhere in Accra, women are highly active in the economic sphere, and as in the rest of the city, their major occupation is market trading, street hawking, selling on the street, and selling from their doorways. Moreover, much of what they sell is food—raw ingredients or prepared dishes.

In 1995, there were ninety-nine stalls at Sabon Zongo's Freedom Market.[7] While the stalls at old Makola in Central Accra cost about ¢200/day, and at

Kaneshie the price on the ground floor where produce is sold was ₵50/day and the two upper floors ₵25–90/day, at Freedom Market the traders paid ₵150/day to the municipality (Mousset-Jones 1999).[8]

The first of the stalls, at the back of the market, houses the butchers. Ten Sabon Zongo Hausa men sell fresh meat and uncooked kebobs, a number the Queenmother considers insufficient. The other ninety-eight stalls carry a variety of foods or ingredients for cooking. There are starches, the basis of the generally one-dish meals: at twenty of the booths, women sell yams, plantain, cassava, cocoyam, rice, and sometimes leaves as well. There is starch-based flour or dough, made from cassava and maize, it is sold at ten stalls. Accra is fish country, given its location and the traditional industry of the local Ga; thirteen booths at Freedom Market carry dried fish, plus one where the fish is fresh. (The fresh fish is best purchased downtown at Salaga Market or several miles east in Teshie.) Very little fresh meat is sold: one trader carries pigs feet, two beef. The fact that pork is sold immediately tells us that there is a local buying population that is not Muslim. Four women sell fresh eggs, often accompanied by other foodstuffs such as tinned meats and tomatoes. Vegetables, including greens to be cooked and tinned tomatoes, are carried by twenty-one traders. And five sell various sorts of cooking oil (vegetable, coconut, palm). The balance sell herbs and spices, other ingredients for particular dishes, and only one person sells palm nuts, a core ingredient in southern Ghanaian cooking. Most of the food traders sell combinations of foods, for example, rice, tinned beef and fish, oil, spices, sugar, soap; or fresh meat, okra, garden eggs, onions, ground nut paste, and salt. Two Yoruba traders are one-of-a-kind at this market, one selling *kayan Yorubawa* (Yoruba "things," such as black pepper, ginger and cowries), the other plaiting hair and doing "weave on."

The Queenmother's records include names and photos of all of the sellers. If they want to sell in the market, they come to her and she asks, what kind of thing do you want to sell? And they tell her and then the person must come to Sarah Quaye, her assistant, and give her two pictures. The Queenmother maintains a separate section entitled Zongo, which lists not so much Zongo women as Zongo Hausa women.

None of the Hausa Sabon Zongo women are selling there now: Letitia the Queenmother believes that this is because of the market, that if only the market would expand, they would come back. The buying population is sparse. "If the market were like the new market on the road to Accra [Agbogbloshie] with lorries bringing things, coming and going. . . . There are many people who have interest to come here, but because of the look of the market, they are not buying things here like they once were" (Letitia Tetteh 2/26/1995).

Certainly other traders have not been deterred by the deteriorated state of the market. Many of the women I talked to in the market live in Sabon Zongo, they just are not Hausa. There are between eighty-nine and 100 market traders there on a daily basis: 35 percent are Sabon Zongo dwellers; 38 percent are Ga, 26 percent Ewe, the balance primarily Akan—all from southern Ghana. The vast majority are Christian.

In fact, what many Hausa women engage in is what the Yoruba call *jojoma* (always, i.e., everyday): they give something to the market women to sell. "Credit" women pay for the items gradually, so those who leave them to be sold must come everyday to collect payments from the traders selling for them. So these women are registered but they do not sit in a stall—they give their things to someone else to sell. *Jojoma* traders sell cloth, petty goods, jewelry. In the nineteen compound samples, eighteen out of 174 traders do jojoma; 24 percent of the other traders sell their goods in the house or very nearby outside. In other words, one-third of the traders do not sit out in what is construed as the public space. More than half of the traders deal in food, 36 percent in cooked food. The non-traders are predominantly seamstresses.

It seems entirely reasonable that the Hausa women do not sit and sell at the market. Women may be out in public, but to use the public space as an avenue to get somewhere is seen as less exposure than to actually sit where one can be stared at. Many of the Hausa women sell "*a baƙin ƙofa*," at the opening of their house, "because of *kunya*" (modesty)—to maintain their modesty by staying out of the public eye, even as they participate in public commerce. "You will never find a Hausa woman selling in the market—only in her doorway—because of *kunya*" (Rukaya Abdurahaman 2/3/1995). This is similar to VerEcke's (1993) finding for Fulbe (Fulani) women living among the Hausa in East Central Nigeria, who do not sell in the market because of *semteende* (shyness, reserve).

The Sabon Zongo Hausa women who sell food in the street tend to sell near their own or their mother's house. Somehow, this is less public than being in the official market. Moreover, they tend to sell prepared foods, while the traders in the market proper do not. Three women who sell on Korle Bu Street in Zabrama quarter live near Ojo School. But their mother lives down the street in Zabrama, which is why they sell here. The granddaughter of one of the local old ladies lives with her husband in Ayigbetown. But the younger woman is an apprentice sewer in the kiosk to the side of her grandmother's house and is in the house daily. A daughter who lives on the edge of Ayigbetown with husband and children comes daily to her mother's to sell the *taliya* she makes and to fry snacks. Other women who live in the area travel to Shukura (another newer *zongo*) to sell at their mothers' houses.

In fact, *Unguwan* Zabrama, like *Kan Tudu*, is a hotbed of food activity throughout the day and night. This translates into lots of street life, as evidenced by the discarded plastic and paper prepared-food wrappers that cover the streets and clog the channels for water run-off (proper gutters are non-existent). During the day, there are about fourteen food sellers on Korle Bu Street, in the heart of Zabrama. They decide what to sell and where depending upon the market for their product and also their ties to the immediate area. The one male trader I interviewed sells firewood, which makes sense because of the many cooked food sellers who use wood rather than charcoal for commercial cooking. His wife sells raw rice, which is used in or eaten with many of the cooked foods sold on the block.

One also cannot ignore the social aspect of it—a kind of mingling of business with pleasure. When people and cultures travel and mix, messages change, as do the habitats of meaning—the cultures and the spaces (Hannerz 1996). The parameters, contents, and contexts of exchange alter. The foods available in Sabon Zongo are a defining parameter of the community. The women choose to sell foods or ingredients that are desirable in general to the locals and that in particular mesh with others foods being sold. The foods of Accra, like *kenkey*, and southern Ghana's *fufu* or *banku*, mix with those of the Hausa. On any day, and only in this Accra community, can one find virtually any Hausa food and at the time of day that it would be eaten in Northern Nigeria. Starting at dawn, there are women out selling *kosai, masa, wake, pinkaso,* and *wagash* (fried cheese). At midday, a couple of women sell *fura* from inside their compounds. In the afternoon and evening, women sell different types of *tuwo* with soup, such as *taushe, kuka* (from the baobab tree), and *kubewa* (okra). Nighttime brings out specialized evening foodstuffs: the *cicinga* and *balangu*, both sold by men. *Masa* is the most popular item eaten on ritual occasions, thus is also available on Thursday evening for the Friday sabbath.

Musing about the food scene in Sabon Zongo, a Hausa woman from Dark- uman (a newer Muslim area beyond Kaneshie) observed: "The life of Sabon Zongo people is not good. How they bring food out and eat. There is selling food outside in any area, but here it is too much. In the morning, in the after- noon, in the midnight—at anytime, one can buy food. A child buys, his mother buys, his father buys. Three times in one day—buy food, buy food, buy food. [Sabon Zongo is very different from other *zongos* in Accra] not because of so much food here. Every *zongo*, food 'dey dey' [is there]. *Kenkey* is there, rice there, *wake* is there. But in the night when you go, you won't get some. Ev- erbody cooks in his house. But here—every food you want since from morning to 12 o'clock, you will get" (Hajiya Rabi 6/9/1996). She and her husband agreed that a girl brought up in Sabon Zongo would thus not know how to cook, an important criterion for Hausa marriage.

But it is only certain areas of Sabon Zongo where food is so available. Walk- ing through Ayigbetown after 8 P.M. on a random night, one sees next to no street life, and as cause or consequence, virtually no food selling either. As a result, the roads are much cleaner than in *Kan Tudu* and Zabrama: far fewer people on the street, eating or drinking and tossing their refuse. From Katifa east to Sunshine Hotel and from Market Street north to Korle Bu Street, about one-quarter the size of the balance of the community, there is only a handful of traders: five tea sellers, two rice sellers, a couple of kenkey sellers, one banku seller, a couple selling fruit, several selling bread, and a few "chop bars" (native restaurants). Many Ewe sell at the Night Market in *Kan Tudu*.

In recent years, some property owners have discovered a new source of in-

Figure 15
Renting Showers. Courtesy of Bossman Murrey.

come by offering two new services, toilets and showers, and the fact that these are profitable speaks to the community's level of development. As we saw in Chapter 4, Sabon Zongo's infrastructure is barely adequate at the community level, in terms of roads, gutters, postal, and health agencies. There are also basic deficiencies in many compounds, such as piped water and toilet facilities. Water is especially necessary in Sabon Zongo, given the large Muslim population and their five-times-daily ablutions before prayer. But in fact, throughout Accra, bathing twice daily is the norm for both adults and children. At the community level, water is quite available in Sabon Zongo; and there have always been compounds that do have a water pipe and sell water to those in need.

The commercialization of shower and toilet facilities creates a new kind of exchange among residents, among users and suppliers. In 1996, there were twenty-nine sets of showers throughout Sabon Zongo, except in Municipal and *Gangare*/Kariki (see Figure 15). Each contained as few as two shower rooms (two of them) and as many as eight (two of them):

	Showers/Rooms	*Toilets*
Gangare/Al'wali	24/6	
Zabrama	28/7	
Kan Tudu	31/8	1
Ayigbetown	35/8	1

The shower room in most compounds is a small separate structure, with four walls, a wooden door and no roof. Rather than a drain, it has a small gutter that terminates outside, feeding into a large street-side gutter if there is one, or just into the road if not. The shower room is used for urination, and every Muslim household has a plastic teapot filled with water that is used like a bidet to clean up afterward and to dilute the waste water. Showers are typically taken by filling a bucket, kneeling and doing a sponge bath. There are shower rooms with showerheads, but they are "owned" by those with seniority.

The rental showers open out on the street or lane. They are differentiated and priced according to whether the service offered is in a bucket or through a showerhead, the latter more expensive as the amount of water is not fixed.

The toilet situation is different. At Sabon Zongo, of the nineteen compounds sampled, eleven have no toilet facilities. Of the eight that do, only one has a WC—which was installed in the last year. Two have KVIPs—at Chief Sha'aibu's and "Small London"—and they are for family only. The balance are bucket latrines.

KVIPs were installed in the World Bank-financed project in Nima-Mamobi (another *zongo*). According to an architect who worked on the project, they installed a very large one with twenty-two compartments, eleven for males and females. Unfortunately, the use and maintenance were wrong.

What happened was that a lot of people want to use these facilities—people from outside the community. So it should have taken a year to fill and took three months and even less. So then the concept of KVIP here didn't function. So they had to be dislodged quite often. (Elliot Barbour-Sackey, Technical Services Corporation, 6/17/1996)

The KVIPs have functioned well when used only as domestic toilets, though the commercialization of "private" compound KVIP toilets has been successful in Sabon Zongo. When Sule Bako built his house (sample compound #5), he included a room inside for a toilet. He did not have the money for a WC at the time, so he left the room empty. In the compound yard, he installed three KVIPs, which his wife and other household members could use but which non-family could also use for a fee. In 1999, he replaced the rental KVIPs with three WCs and installed a WC in his house.

Showers are also rented out; however, unlike the toilets, they are extricated from the compound yard and erected at the streetside, upsetting the public/private gradation of spaces. While the compound yard is not exactly private (see Chapter 8 for a social analysis of domestic space and its transformation), user protocol makes it completely open to residents only; others must be invited or granted permission to enter. Thus, showering in the compound amounts to showering in one's home. The door to the compound, whether real or conceptual, represents a transition from public to not-public. On the other hand, taking a shower on the street, one is behind a door, of course, but not insulated from people on the street. Some customers arrive wrapped in a towel or a piece of cloth—clothing appropriate to the home but, for adults, not the street. Yet, ensconcing the shower as a business makes it permissible.

People throughout Ghanaian society are far more accustomed to, indeed in need of, telephones than was the case even a decade ago. They need them to contact businesses. They need them to talk to family members who have relocated away from Accra or even from Ghana. The lack of telephone lines and thus phones in the home, in Sabon Zongo as elsewhere in Accra, has been the impetus for the creation of communication centers. These businesses at minimum have telephones, which patrons can use for a fee. Old ladies, whose children are working overseas—Hamburg, Germany, and Bronx, New York, both have sizable West African communities—who have never been in a private car let alone an airplane, who speak local vernaculars, pay for one or two minutes, enough to hear about the birth of a grandchild or to inform of a relative's death. Word processing and desktop publishing have also entered the realm of communication centers. Some have taken the place of the faithful typists who sit outside the main post offices, prepared to write out personal and official letters dictated to them by the illiterate. Announcements of births, outdoorings, funerals—all can be easily and cheaply printed.

Over the past several years, Accra has developed what might be called a kiosk economy—small-scale businesses that sell goods or provide services, that are set up with a minimum of capital, in "temporary" quarters by the side of the road. In Sabon Zongo, there has been an explosion of kiosks. In addition to serving as provision shops, pharmacies, tailorshops and hairdressing salons, they also house video game businesses and communication centers.

INSTITUTIONAL GOVERNANCE

Like Jane Jacobs's idiomatic characterization of American cities of the past, in Sabon Zongo neighbors are "the eyes of the street" (Jacobs 1961). They look out for one another, as compared to residents in the upscale Airport Residential Estates, who shut themselves behind high walls. Does Sabon Zongo have institutions specific to safety? Is there an overarching *morality* as I have suggested? Does the chieftaincy or social boundaries have anything to do with the community's apparent collective security?

Malam Bako did establish formal institutions to oversee and adjudicate community members' interaction with one another and their participation in the community and these are still in force. In effect, the *zongo* has a pyramidal structure of chiefs and linkages between them: the Sabon Zongo chief is at the top, under him are the sub-chiefs and under them are community elders. In disputes between residents of differing ethnicity, if the aggrieved have a chief, they go to him first, only coming to the Sabon Zongo chief as a court of last resort. If the fight is between ethnics without resident chiefs, the Sabon Zongo deals with it himself. The traditional Hausa sub-chiefs of barbers, butchers, blind, and lepers oversee their constituents. When resolution of a problem is difficult, the subchief brings it to the Sabon Zongo chief.

The petty traders have one woman appointed as head, the *maroka* have an elder as do the carpenters. If there is a dispute within the group, the disputants go to the group's elder; if he/she cannot settle the problem, they bring the case to the Sabon Zongo chief. By the same token, if the Chief wants the kola traders, etc., to engage in some activity, he will call in their elder who then transmits the message.

Undergirding the whole system is the institution of the patron-client bond, of trusting in the help, wisdom, resources, of one's superior. One level of authority consists of community elders, like Baba Mai Doki, son of former Chief Idrissu Bako. Old and young, community residents come to Idrissu's Mosque, where he sits everyday, to ask his advice on a whole range of issues. As Sarkin Fada had pointed out to the *fadawa* some years ago, community institutions underline the importance of respect for elders. "The chief is there, the elders are there— one must behave properly" (Sarkin Fada 6/5/1982).

Like the chiefs who preceded him, Chief Sha'aibu Bako's power was in part dependent upon outside authorities; today, these include the local Member of Parliament and the Assemblyman (Alhaji Musa 5/28/1996). Also like those before him, Chief Sha'aibu had both a formal and an informal role in the community. He authorized marriages (which the imam performs), granted divorces and judged disputes. Most of Chief Sha'aibu's cases involved property disputes and domestic problems, including paternity suits. His *fadawa* would advise him, the *alkali* consulting the Koran for aid in coming to a just resolution. On April 23, 1982, late in the afternoon, I was sitting inside the chief's house with him; members of his *fadawa* were outside. A woman had come to complain that her daughter's husband rejected the child who had been born the day before. About ten minutes later, Kilishi came back, ranting and raving, because the father of the child, or anyway the husband of the woman who gave birth, refused to come. The chief grumbled: "Hausa chieftaincy is finished. Small boy, he doesn't come." Finally the husband arrived. The chief sat inside listening while the man pleaded his case to the *fadawa*. In giving his judgement, Bako also underlined his power as chief. While he clearly did not have the power to force the man to come, this did not stop the mother-in-law from asking for the chief's help.

In addition to domestic problems, the chief also hears cases involving work issues. For example, one day *Waziri* brought Ibrahim, a mattress maker, to appear before the chief. Ibrahim had given another man, Musa, money to bring grass to make a mattress. A third man, Braimah, also a mattress maker, told Musa not to bring the grass. He said that when anyone brings Ibrahim grass, Ibrahim fights with him. So Musa stopped bringing the grass. Three months went by—no grass, no money. Ibrahim, did not live in Sabon Zongo, he lived in Tudu in Accra, but because Musa and Braimah did, and were under Bako's authority, he came to give Chief Bako money to make a summons.

The *fadawa* no longer meet regularly, because they work at jobs, many outside of Sabon Zongo. So if someone comes with a case and there's no *sarkin fada* or *waziri*, Chief Sha'aibu would hear cases alone. Then if he thought it necessary, he would send Salama to call the *fadawa* together (Sarkin Fada 6/4/1993). Another time when I was at the chief's late in the afternoon (3/10/1995), a woman came for advice about a property dispute. Her sister had sold her own portion in the family house. But this woman was fighting for the sister to have a portion! The chief said, "You have your portion, you have nothing to fight for." The woman said, "What's on paper is not what's in reality." There was no case to decide.

The chief clearly serves a more informal role as well. Chief Sha'aibu did not live in the palace, the grand compound built and occupied by Malam Bako and Idrissu after him. His house is down the road from the palace, on the main north south street, opposite the Night Market grounds where there is considerable activity. His entrance hall is flanked by shops. Chief Sha'aibu retired from his work as a "businessman" (messenger) years ago. In the late afternoon/early evening, he would sit in his swivel armchair in the doorway, watching the street scene. Joined by individual advisors who may be free and by male friends who drop in to spend time with him, he was available to advise his constituents. As it happens, like his father's brother Alhaji Hamisu, Sha'aibu was also recognized as a "healer": people suffering from aches and pains from various joint problems come to him.

To choose new officers, the chief sits with his *fadawa, manyan gari* (elders), and his secretary. First they write down the positions to be filled. Then for each one, they nominate one or two people. Then everyone votes. Yet it is unclear how instrumentally important the chieftaincy and the affairs of the chieftaincy are, when people do not show up for a meeting to appoint officers to vacant posts.

When Malam Bako was the Sabon Zongo headman, he had authority over several other Muslim/Hausa communities, also part of the same Ga stool. One was a village about five miles west of Zongo Lane, where Malam Bako appointed the first chief.[9] Residents of those communities paid tribute to him: at Salla, bringing him firewood and food, as well as cassava, kola, yam, then during the Ga Homowo festival, sending some of the food to the Jamestown chief. The Sabon Zongo chief was also supposed to redistribute some of the food to the *manyan gari*. Now, according to members of Sha'aibu's court, these subject communities are taking the position that they are not under anybody. They haven't brought firewood and food since before Idrissu, the first chief, was installed.

Like the other Muslim chiefs, the Sabon Zongo chief has no stool land, no authority to make arrests and no revenue. None of them have clout, because none of them is in the National House of Chiefs. They do not have paramount status but are similar to village chiefs (Alhaji Faruk 4/26/1982). But there is a symbolic importance to the Sabon Zongo chieftaincy, acknowledged by Sha'aibu's nickname *zaki* (lion). The chief is important to his subjects, because of his wise counsel. He is always informed of occasions, of rites of passage in the community. He is presented with Hacks cough drops prior to a wedding,[10] and he leads his people during festivals, including the annual *Salla* procession at the end of Ramadan.

An institution often associated with the chief, as well as with all male and female patrons and the community as a whole, is that of the praise-singer.[11] Praise-singing, *roko*, is a traditional form of Hausa oratory, which involves proclaiming another's name to honor her or him (Smith 1957; Furniss 1995). It expresses social and cultural values, enjoins the maintenance of those values, and supports certain types of relations that hold between those values. Through the songs, an individual articulates and defines social status. The praise-singers, *maroka*, have the license of public spokesmen and clearly engage in a form of customary exchange, that of clientage: they are clients who support (or undermine) their patrons through vocal distribution of praise and shame. As such, they are agents of public opinion, and for that they are remunerated. The praise-singer both interacts with members of society and also helps to connect them to one another, through providing information or bringing them together around another person or persons.

The occasions for *roko* in Accra's *zongo* culture are the same as in Northern Nigeria, although acculturation has added occasions and modified roles. There are three types of *roko*: the first commonly heard in Sabon Zongo is done with the talking drum. It may be simple praise-singing, for example, of the chief—*zaki, zaki, ba mai mulki kamanka* ("O lion, there is no ruler like you"). When the chief is going to an event within the community, the *maroki* precedes him, singing his praises. Following a wedding I attended from the chief's family, his courtier Kilishi preceded him, acting the part of *maroki* and shouting: "Walk gently, Zongo is for the chief. This is the chief of Sabon Zongo coming." When the chief is sitting "in state," receiving his subjects for example at the conclusion of the Salla parade, several *maroka* are present, singing praises. The praise-singer also proclaims the arrival of other "big men" to the chief and to the community-at-large.

The second type of *roko* is performed by *mai gunduwa* (a man playing a two-sided covered drum with a stick), who sings praises while drumming. He often fulfills the role of town crier, wandering through the community communicating news and announcing events like the Sunday wrestling matches. The traditional Nigerien Hausa wrestling at Sabon Zongo takes place on Sunday afternoons on night market field during the dry season.[12] The drummers play the talking drums. The cadence of the drums changes. Paid by the people attending, the musicians begin drumming to announce the wrestling around 3 P.M. on Sunday, the day of the match. Thus if one is not in Sabon Zongo, he will not know ahead of time. Male children wrestle as a warm-up act. The spectators are primarily Zabrama and other Nigeriens. It is a men's affair, with no women present. Some men come from other *zongos* in Accra. A lot of money changes hands, as the big men gamble. The *maroki* proclaims names and sums and winners.

When a wedding is to take place, the *maroki* announces it to the men. In the past, when there was a naming, he was given kola nut, now he is given Hacks. They are distributed along with the announcement of when the naming will take place.

The *maroki* makes other sorts of announcements. One afternoon, a woman came to Chief Sha'aibu, because a four-year-old child in her compound followed her and got lost, and she didn't know where he was. But if the child were really lost, the community would hear about it on the drum: Salli Mai Gunduwa would walk through *zongo*, sent by the chief, crying out that a child named such and such, age such and such, was lost. This is also done for a goat or sheep. The *maroki* may also be summoned by the chief to communicate something to a particular person.

The third type of *roko* is performed at life-cycle events—the naming ceremony for a new baby, a wedding, a funeral. The *maroki* is present at men's events, both *maroki* and *marokiya* are present at the women's celebrations. But at the latter, the *maroki* is the master of ceremonies, encouraging contributions and announcing them to the crowd. The *marokiya*, on the other hand, does not proclaim—she ululates.

Praise-singing has also been adapted to contemporary Sabon Zongo activities. For example, in 1996 (6/16), there was an NPP (New Patriotic Party) political rally at Gaskiya Cinema on a Sunday afternoon. There were various luminaries there from the party. There were also several Hausa drummers, including Salli Mai Gundawa, because there was money circulating and as *maroka* they aided its redistribution. They also helped introduce attendees to one another. Their activity represented the syncretism of a traditional Hausa institution with party politics.

CAMARADERIE

Men and women both have extensive social lives, of a formal and informal nature. Formal ties are evidenced by associational membership. Over the years, Muslim-based organizations have come and gone. Both community-specific and city-wide in their participants, Hausa is the language used in all of them. The men's have been open to women, but, like the mosques that also have a women's section, there are conditions for membership and in any case, few women join. The women's are sex-specific and their associations that are current in Sabon Zongo (*minti* = meeting) are both Sabon Zongo-wide and neighborhood (*unguwa*)-based. All are mutual aid societies, and meetings are usually held for life-cycle events. In fact, whether they belong to an association or not, the Muslim women are socially very active around life-cycle events.

At the *Salla* celebration, members of each group often dress in the same kind of cloth and walk/dance together in the community parade behind an association flag. These women's groups are age-graded: Sweet *Aminchi* (trusting, trustworthiness) is for girls and young unmarried women. Their banner reads:

Wait and see, never jealous.
Sea never dry as *aminchi* never end

When they march, they do not wear head scarves, symbolic of their unmarried status. Expensive Ladies are older than *Aminchi* but still young. Their banner reads:

Forward ever, backward never
Motto:
Good name is better than riches
All things are possible
Yaran [children who are] Expensive

Personality is for those too old to be in *Aminchi*, and some are married, some not; Happiness—for newly married women

Yaran [children of] Happiness
Enemies are worried, we thank God

Young sixteen—married but not too long; Challenger—thirty-years-plus; Wonderful; Commander; Turmi (mortar): first formed for women about thirty, the membership are now in their forties and a thirty-year-old cannot join; at a baby outdooring or wedding, this group brings a mortar and pestle (female and male) and sings risque songs; *Shin fi da Fuska* (spread your face, the old ladies); *Sha Hudu; En Ashirin* (old yet you feel like a twenty-year-old). Groups are forming all the time. The *Salla* parade in 1995 also included Understanding Ladies ("Understanding is our word"), Secret Millionaires ("*Iko allah* [with God's power]; motto: The Best Among the Standard"—these are young-ish marrieds), and New Edition Fun Club ("Appearance is not the man but the knowledge"). There was also a group called Foreign Ladies:

Tsui Tse Gbawmaw Gbo [Ga: quick tempered person dies]
Motto:
We reap what we sow

While the groups are age-graded to start, they stay together indefinitely. Only for *Aminchi* (or other young never-marrieds) does membership have to change.

The men belong to a variety of associations as well. Some that are inactive include the *Zumunta* Club (Hausa: clan feeling, friendship), the Sabon Zongo Youth Association, the Ghana Muslim Youth Research (with offices at Ramaniya Mosque/School) and the Islamic Youth Club, a social club. *Zumunta* was active in the 1970s and 1980s and according to its constitution, its aim was "to unite—to be one body." Its chairman and creator was Bako B.K., its national headquarters were in Sabon Zongo. It was Muslim-based with an ethnically-mixed membership that included Hausa, Zabrama, Kotokoli, Chamba, and a couple of Akan and Ga. The membership was open to men and unmarried women. They did not allow married women, "because if you have a husband, you can't come to a meeting—you will be busy and don't want men to become vexed and the Islamic religion doesn't allow married women to come out" (Bako B.K. 5/7/1982). A self-help club, the members contributed money to help one another out for birth outdoorings and marriages (though not for funerals).

Zumunta was analogous to a variety of Accra-wide women's associations that were active at that time, including *Zumunci* (see Pellow 1987), as well as the current women's associations. A new men's group solidified in 1996, when a group within *Unguwan* Zabrama who had belonged to a card *cum* social club decided to change their group into a mutual assistance organization (similar to the women's clubs). They inaugurated it as The Gentleman Club, at that point inviting others to join. They changed the name to Gentility Club when women joined. The monthly dues were 1,000 cedis/month. They engage in communal labor and assist one another when sick, marrying, giving birth. One man received 11,000 cedis at the time of his marriage and then again when his wife gave birth. They meet the last Sunday every month and the twenty-five members include six women (four Kotokoli, one Sisala, and one Yoruba). At first they used the women just for cooking, but the women objected and were made regular members. But not just anyone can join: "someone with understanding, who is not a troublemaker" (Papa Carlos 5/26/1996).

Community development organizations are forming all the time. The now-defunct Sabon Zongo Youth Association is a classic example of the type. It was organized by the youth with the younger generation in mind; later on, they invited the elders once they won their confidence. At that point, the Chief began coming to all of the meetings. Its aims were to raise funds to develop the area, to organize the youth and

to help them acquire education, good, sound Western education. Because from time immemorial, we have been undergoing our Arabic education, and in fact when they finish this kind of education, they become dependent upon the other. So we have found it necessary to help our area brothers to acquire the Western education such that they can fix themselves in the society. (Issifu Farouk, secretary of SZYA, 5/30/1982)

They also tried to raise funds for the development of Sabon Zongo.

Right now when we look at our streets and gutters, they are not in good condition. The set-up of our government is such that what they are trying to follow now is something that we ourselves should have before any other thing. If we started, we took the initiative, then the Government can see our effort and then they can rush in to help us. (Issifu Farouk, secretary of SZYA, 5/30/1982)

Moreover, as with the mutual benefit associations, if someone is marrying,

we rally round and everybody donates what he has, then we raise a certain fund and give
it to him. If it is outdooring, we follow the same suit. If it is a yearly ceremony, like
the Ramadan festival, after fasting, we just rally round the people, we make donations,
and we buy cloth and other things. (Issifu Farouk, secretary of SZYA, 5/30/1982)

When I asked about SZYA ten years later, one of the important members of
the community shrugged his shoulders and said, "Those societies have been
born and died." In the mid-1990s, a group of men organized The Sabon Zongo
Youth Association for Development, a new society with the same aims and
almost the same name as SZYA. Meeting the first and last Sunday of every
month, they discuss "how we can develop our area in Sabon Zongo, especially
the streets. The streets and the gutters and after we have done that, we will try
to get lights on every point (Mohammed Bako 6/6/1996). After meetings and
extensive discussions, they contact their MP (Member of Parliament). They send
letters to the AMA. "Because in Ghana now, you have to help yourselves before
the government will help you. That's why we say we are going to do it ourselves. For so many years, *zongo* is just like how you see *zongo*" (Mohammed
Bako 6/6/1996).

Other associational work goes on, including various kinds of community-
organized labor.[13] The political party NPP has a non-political arm that is active
in Sabon Zongo. It provides assistance to individual members similar to the
mutual benefit associations. But it has also organized work in some quarters in
the community. This has included cleaning out the gutters and roads and removing garbage in Unguwan Zabrama (4/23/1995, 4/30/1995). Similarly, the
Malam Bako Youth Assocation (of younger people) and Kariki Youth Association (of elders) meet for celebrations and every two weeks clean gutters and
streets.

Some of the informal socializing of men, and primarily Muslim men, in Sabon
Zongo has a formal aspect to it, insofar as it has become institutionalized in
time and place. The men gather to play cards (Figure 16), Ludu, checkers, to
talk, to hang out, even to nap. The most common gathering places include the
mosques. Most, like Abokin Ango, Damaley and Idrissu, always have a coterie
of men sitting and lying around, talking and sleeping throughout the day; there
is one man at Damaley, for instance, who is said to go home only at night to
sleep; Idrissu is situated in such a way that it catches breezes, and there are
men who sit and talk till sleepy, then spread out on the floor and nap there in
the afternoon. At Abokin Ango, the men arrange themselves against the
outside wall, which is right on the main drag and facilitates encounters with
passers-by.

The corner barber (*aski*) is another favorite gathering place for men. Going
to the barber is a Hausa tradition, to have the face and/or head shaved. The
popularity of barbers is signified by their institutionalized chief. In Sabon Zongo,
one of the barbers has created a "shop" on the corner kitty-cornered from Makafi
Mosque. He has a radio with music, and as at the local mosques, men spend

Figure 16
The Daily Afternoon Card Game in *Gangare*. Courtesy of the Author.

time with one another there. Late in the afternoon, Fulani traders bring fresh milk and yogurt to sell.

In *Gangare*, on the street in front of Sarkin Fada's compound, every afternoon at about 4 P.M., a group of older men gathers to play cards. The regulars include a local malam and a GBC (Ghana Broadcasting Corporation) broadcaster. On Fridays, the faithful are resplendent in their gowns and hats; other afternoons, one is often wearing a striped baseball cap, jersey, and slacks. Some of the men live in adjacent compounds, others live elsewhere in Sabon Zongo. One collects for a nearby set of showers. They sit on benches playing "Spa" and conversing. Some, who are members of a political opposition party, hotly debate local political issues. The players and on-lookers are joined daily by a man who makes and serves green tea in tiny cups to any takers. Non-partakers laughingly claim that the tea will prevent sleep for three days. The group often strings a canopy across the lane to block the sun.

Another male gathering spot is the *lungu* (alley) next to the carpenter's, to play cards. Everyone plays "spa" all over Accra.[14] Cards are a passion and Sabon Zongo is divided into teams—by *unguwa*—started in the early 1990s. Anybody can join the teams. Carpenters—*Unguwan Zabrama*; Audu Bako Stars—*Kan Tudu* (these guys play this for fun, but they are also gamblers); Dynamic Dynamite—Stable; Chairman's Stars—*Makafi; Gindin Itace* (buttocks of the tree)—*Katifa*. The last did not come to the championship play off as a team, rather some of them joined Chairman's Stars. They normally play late afternoons/evenings, with Sundays for matches. At *Gangare*, the guys play the game, though not in teams.

In 1995 (5/28), I watched a championship match, held on the *lungu* in the blind quarter, under a rented awning. It was organized by the Chairman (of Chairman's Stars), which is why it was held in *Makafi*. They played from 10:30 A.M. to 1 P.M., then there was a break for prayers. The Chairman brought in minerals and food, which were served after 1 o'clock prayers. They played again from 2–3 P.M., then broke for prayers; and from 3:30–6 P.M. During the first block of time, the Carpenters played the Audu Bako Stars, the Carpenters winning, and the Dynamic Dynamite played the Chairman's Stars, DD winning. From 2–3 P.M. and 3:30–6 P.M., the Carpenters played DD while Audu Bako Stars and Chairman's Stars played off for 3rd and 4th place. The Carpenters won. During the first years, the teams just played one another, then they began trying to create a league, so that the Sabon Zongo winner could play, e.g., Osu. The Chairman was looking for sponsors, like PTC (Pioneer Tobacco Company).

Other male gathering places include a so-called "gambling house," the outside verandah of a compound on Korle Bu at the far end of *Unguwan* Zabrama, where there are always Nigeriens throwing dice. "Siicopaa" is a clubhouse in *Kan Tudu*, which is actually a wooden lean-to. A local group of male members hangs out; they are about twenty to thirty-two years of age and some of them are married. It is said that they are mixed up with drug sellers and users, that they go to Siicopaa to smoke "wee" (marijuana), do cocaine and speed, drink alcohol; alternatively, that they go to Ojo to smoke wee. They all have work in Sabon Zongo—some are mechanics, some electricians. At *Salla*, like the women in clubs, they wear the same t-shirts and march behind a flag.

The public venue of men's particular friendships also hearkens back to the early days of Sabon Zongo, when the women were less visible and men were out and about. It is very common to see men sitting around outside of one person's compound like an extension of the *zaure*. They are like the men at the mosques or at *Gangare* in front of *Sarkin Fada*'s—sometimes on a mat, sometimes on a bench. And then there are the nights when there is a televised football (soccer) game and sometimes when there is a televised play. Several men with televisions bring their sets outside; I've seen it at the corner across from Abokin Ango mosque where as many as thirty men and boys, some friends, others just spectators, stand and watch together. In 1997, the video game craze hit Sabon Zongo. There were two locations: one on Korle Bu Street near *Makafi*, one in Tripoli/Ayegbetown. One or two guys would play while others sat and watched.

In Sabon Zongo, as elsewhere in Accra, children's labor is also used by poor families who live on the edge of survival. They particularly help out their mothers who prepare food to sell, either in the cooking or in the selling. Areas such as James Town (the fishing port), Kwame Nkrumah Circle (a convergence point for passenger vehicles) or Makola Market (the center of commercial activity and location of the central lorry station) have a real problem with "street children," "those children who spend all or a significant part of their time in the streets"

(Van Ham, Blavo, and Opoku 1991:10). These are children of school age, primarily in early adolescence, "who roam the street, market places, lorry parks, beaches, video centres, and recreational grounds during school hours" (Van Ham, Blavo, and Opoku 1991:11). The Ghana National Commission on Children (GNCC) found that the lower the educational level and occupational status of parents, the more likely that the children would engage in deviant behavior (at a minimum, staying away from school, at a maximum, criminal activities). One of the conclusions reached in the survey of street children is that neglect by family is a crucial factor.

Sabon Zongo, while a similarly deprived area, does not suffer from the problem of street children. This is not to say there are no "bad kids," certainly there are children who are truants from school. Yet the phenomenon of "children of the street," children who have chosen to leave their families, and abandoned children, those without home or family, does not appear to exist. The kin-based core of the community, the interconnectivity or *kudundune* described by residents, may be strong enough, may carry enough of a moral imperative, that social coherence persists. Residents perceive the *zongo* as safe. (I might add that I do as well.)

PUBLIC ENGAGEMENTS

Life-cycle rituals, particularly among the Muslims and following the Hausa model, have helped forge links in the community. Since in most cases there is no compound space for the partying accompanying such events as baby outdoorings, weddings and funerals, women "appropriate" the street outside. For it is women who celebrate, who hold the *biki*, the traditional festivities where they sing and dance and eat. Because the celebration is in the street, it brings in the whole community. It takes place in the eyes of men, though no male guests attend and men do not watch. The only adult men who come are the "hired help," the musicians, *maroka*, and perhaps an imam to say a prayer.

There are several stages to all of these events. For example, a Hausa wedding spans an entire weekend. During the day on Friday, the bride is painted with a paste of *lalle*, henna (see Figure 17). At the joint wedding of Alhaji Bebe's daughters the weekend of August 1, 1997, the two brides, about eight of their girlfriends, and two *al'wanka* (the woman who does the ablution of the bride) crowded into a small room at the rear of the father's compound at noon. Each *al'wanka* applied the *lalle* to one of the brides (*sa lalle*): first the hands, palms up, painted, wrapped in plastic (*k'unshi*), the plastic tied with cord. Then the feet were covered with *lalle* just above the ankle and on the bottom, also wrapped, the plastic tied with a cord. Finally the *lalle* was rubbed on the body (*tuda*). In the course of the session, which took a few hours, children from the compound came in, pushing and shouting. The girlfriends fed the brides, who could not use their hands for the two or three hours that the henna was left on.

The painting of the henna is important, as it is a visual symbol of marriage.

Figure 17
**Applying Henna to the Bride, in the Company of her Female Friends. Courtesy of
the Author.**

I was told about a Hausa girl in Sabon Zongo who insisted on staying with her
boyfriend, without benefit of marriage, despite the objections of her parents. The
family solved the problem by grabbing her, putting her in a room, putting henna
on her and carrying her to the boy's room, in effect performing an "express
marriage" (Muhsin Barko 6/4/1996).

On Friday night, there is music and dancing for the bride-to-be, the women
celebrating out in public. The only men ever present are the musicians, modern
and traditional, and the *maroka*. At most weddings today, a video production
company films the event, and the videographer is a man. When two daughters
in the Salisu family were marrying in April 1995, from about 7:30 until 10 P.M.
there were three types for three different groups: 1) *sha'adi*, recorded pop music,
for the brides and their unmarried girlfriends. The dancing was very subdued,
a kind of gentle swaying. The brides showed no pleasure—they are supposed
to look unhappy at the prospect of leaving their parents. While they danced,
their friends dashed them gifts of money in coins and bills; 2) *Fa'ila*, electrified
contemporary Muslim music, with live drumming and singing; for married

women in their twenties and thirties. They and the musicians were under a canopy that stretched across the street; and 3) *Gargajiya*, traditional drumming for the older women. One or two of the local drummers played and the women danced. All three types went on simultaneously, the first two abutting one another in the street, the third just inside an adjacent compound.

The wedding proper always takes place on Sunday. Early in the morning at her father's house, the bride is washed with water that is red from *lalle* and spiked with lavender (*tulare*). Men are scarce. The formality of the day in Sabon Zongo is for the bride to read the first page of the Koran, "proof" of her Muslim credentials, to invited men. Depending upon the number of guests and the families involved, this may take place at the groom's family's house, at the bride's (as was the case for Alhaji Bebe's daughters), in the chief's *zaure* (when there was a wedding in his family), or in a mosque. While the women may listen in, they do so from the margins—on the edge of the courtyard, outside the windows, and so forth. At Alhaji Bebe's, there was praise-singing at about 9:30–10 A.M. as the men arrived. The street filled with women under a canopy, the compound filled with men, some women on the edges.

The Imam gives a blessing, and the men's part is finished. At a wedding in Chief Sha'aibu's family in 1982, Accra's Chief Imam was present and blessed the two brides, his words repeated by the *maroki*: regarding Bride One: Umoru has taken a wife to marry her. He has given ₵1000 for the bride. Prayers. The *maroki* punctuating each phrase with *amin* (amen) and *alhamdu lillahi* (God be praised). Regarding Bride Two: Hamisu has given Belau to Abubakar. Abubakar has given ₵500.

And the Chief Imam intoned: "You shall follow the teachings of Islam, not forget it. The groom should not allow his wife to do what is not in the Koran, but she should do the right thing." And he preached: "No men should go and talk to some woman on the road when she is not his wife; women should not wear lavender, because when a man is passing, the smell will attract him. Those who do not have a husband, may Almighty God give them a husband. Those who do not have a wife, may Almighty God give them a wife." Various men gave money, via the *maroki*, to the Imam to pray for them and and he did so. So ended the men's involvement in the wedding.

On the Sunday afternoon of the wedding, there is a repeat of the music and dancing from Friday night: *sha'adi* for unmarrieds, *fa'ila* for young marrieds, *gargajiya* for the elders. The bride appears in her finery, walking to the bridegroom's behind drummers who proclaim her arrival. At the Salisu wedding, the two brides walked under the canopy stretched across the street. A Ga group sang, women friends dancing with gifts of stacked cooking ware on their heads. The older women dancing to the drumming had their prayer veils tied around their hips. The music and dancing continued into the evening.

Salla, the celebration at the end of Ramadan, is a Muslim-specific affair, but like the festivities surrounding the weddings, the entire community is transformed by the noise, music, parades and general celebratory ambience. In the morning, the Muslims from all over Accra gather at Black Star Square for prayers and speeches. The city streets are clogged with the merrymakers, all dressed in their newest finery. For the 1:15 P.M. prayer, the Sabon Zongo men go to the main mosque, conveniently located less than a mile away on Ring Road.

The Sabon Zongo festivities really begin when the chief and his entourage leave the main mosque. In his younger days, the chief would ride a horse; as an old man, he rode in a pick-up truck. At the 1995 celebration, the chief sat in back in his arm chair under an umbrella held by an umbrella carrier and was accompanied by Sarkin Fada and Maaji Dade. All three men were turbaned. The chief's truck was preceded by men on horses and a "Salla-mobile," a rental horse-drawn cart with pictures of Santa Claus and jingle bells painted on the sides. Tabaraka, the *magajiyan bori* (head of the *bori* spirit possession cult) rode in the cart with two of the other *bori* women. Tabaraka was turbaned and the two women were wearing the *bori* cowry shell headdress and white strapless cloth. Three talking drums and various smaller drums walked alongside one of the *maroka* (who sang the praises of local men and women as the parade passed them). A *marokiya* rode with the *bori* women, periodically ululating. There were young boys riding along on bicycles.

The parade route followed Ring Road to Oblogo, turned on Oblogo, passed the Zana Mosque, and turned into Sabon Zongo at Gaskia Cinema, west on the first street (Korle Bu) up to Malam Bako Street and up to *Gidan* Malam Bako. Once the chief arrived at his grandfather's palace, he sat there in state on the verandah of the *zaure*, surrounded by his three courtiers, eldest son Sule, the *bori* women, *maroka*, drummers, and visitors from Niger.

Following the chief's entourage through the streets of Sabon Zongo was a truck full of men singing Muslim music. There were Dixieland-like bands and, as mentioned earlier in this chapter in the discussion of gender, the parade featured dancing groups of Sabon Zongo women. The groups were the women's associations. They followed one by one, with musicians and a flag in front announcing their name. The women dropped their expected demeanor of modesty, in dress and behavior, and almost like actors playing a role, they took over the public domain ostentatiously. They engaged with one another and those lining the route. None of the women in the parade wore a prayer veil; the married women wore fancy head scarves, the same textile pattern as their dresses. As at the women's *biki*, the only men marching alongside them through the streets were playing the role of musician or praise-singer.

Once the parade enters its Sabon Zongo phase, which is when the women join in, few of the spectators are Muslim males. But even some of the men act out: they claim the Night Market field, dancing and doing extreme pelvic thrusts to the beat of the drummers. Here, the spectators are men. Thus the social engagements of the sexes within Sabon Zongo, for those influenced by Hausa custom and for Muslims generally, are symbolically separate.

The cross-community organizations and institutions in Sabon Zongo are Muslim. The public and semi-public celebrations are Muslim-based. The place anchors are Muslim. Christians do not have an institutional anchor in the community. There are no specifically Christian places or hierarchy. Christian family events are observed, but they do not encompass the entire community in the same way that the Hausa/Muslim events do.

AN URBAN NICHE

Sabon Zongo is not a walled community, sealed off from the rest of the city. Residents participate in the more general urban system in two ways: their community is part of the city, thus they pay taxes to Accra, they receive municipal services from the municipality, they enjoy Accra Assembly and Parliamentary representation, and they provide goods and services that attract people from elsewhere in Accra and its environs. Moreover, the multiplicity of ethnic and linguistic backgrounds and multi-ethnic tenancy characteristic of Accra in general, produced by the city's pull and the consequent migration, is true for Sabon Zongo as well, although the specifics of that heterogeneity are different from much of the city. Second, they also go elsewhere in Accra to work, attend religious functions, visit friends and family, and engage in other recreational activities.

The residents of Sabon Zongo are more integrated with Accra's other Muslim/Hausa communities, especially that of Accra Central, than in the days of Malam Bako, when there was only Accra Central. There are currently ten Muslim areas in the Accra district: Sabon Zongo, Accra Central, Nima, Newtown (Lagostown), Adabraka, Alhamdu, Abeka, Darkoma, Shukura, and Madina, each with a Muslim headman. On Fridays, most of the men go to the main Accra mosque, walking distance from Sabon Zongo since it was constructed in 1982.

Chief Sha'aibu Bako, chief of Sabon Zongo till his death in 2001, had strong political ties to the other Muslim chiefs and automatically belonged to the Council of Muslim Chiefs. He also had strong ties to a select group of chiefs, descendants of the "first families of Islam" in Accra, and unlike his grandfather, involved himself in parochial Muslim affairs external to Sabon Zongo.

As in times past, the chief also serves as a link between the government and the community. If Sabon Zongo needs certain services, the chief makes the request, for instance, to have better roads laid or new gutters dug. To expedite his "green revolution" in the early 1980s, Rawlings notified Sha'aibu, as one of the chiefs, to get his people involved. During that time, in a meeting of the Sha'aibu's *fadawa* (5/15/1982), the Chairman talked of Sabon Zongo's poor correspondence with the outside world, especially contacts with the press, and the need to do better.

In the mid-1990s, Alhaji Ila, a descendant of the Bako family, was an MP who represented five wards within Ablekuma (one of Accra's six sub-districts), including Sabon Zongo. He explained to me the differences and responsibilities that distinguished Council/Parliament in relation to the local community as follows: Sabon Zongo's assemblyman is a member of Ablekuma. With eighteen members, it is the largest in Accra. The Assembly member should organize the community. Joseph Ayikwei Amah, a Ga and the former Assemblyman for Nmenmeete Electoral Area, who lives in Larte Biokarshie across the Market Road from Ayigbetown, agreed with Ila. He saw his job as making the environment clean by organizing communal labor and going to the authorities about the roads, and so forth, as part of Accra's decentralization (4/18/1995).

Whenever the State wanted to relay information to Sabon Zongo, it was the MP who would be contacted and he would then go to the community. Ila said he would tell the chief and the "elders," his translation of elders being National Democratic Council (NDC party) men (2/25/1995). Whenever the Assembly members have a problem, in the new decentralized system, they bring it to the MPs, who are lawmakers and politicians. The last day of commentaries during Ramadan 1995 became the occasion for a political rally at one of the local mosques, the MP Ila speaking.

When elected politicians are also kin, some residents conflate the obligations of kinship with those of politics, the inside with the outside. During the 1996 election campaign, residents who subscribed to the main political party, NDC, debated with those following the main opposition party NPP, the performance of the MP who was running for re-election. The argument went something like this: "So who are you going to vote for?" "Alhaji X." "But Alhaji X didn't clean up the environment," and the response, "It is true (*gaskiya ne*)." "And Alhaji X didn't have gutters put in," and the response, "It is true (*gaskiya ne*)." "And Alhaji X didn't have the State pave the roads," and the response, "It is true (*gaskiya ne*). But he is family!"

Children and youths must go outside the community for Western schooling. Virtually anyone working in the modern sector is employed elsewhere in Accra, but even tailors/embroiderers and traders work in businesses and markets and on street corners outside of Sabon Zongo. And outsiders come in to do business, in some cases for services available everywhere like car repair, in many cases for specialized purchases or services. One of the more curious is race horse training. To this day, Baba Mai Doki, son of Idrissu Bako, is renowned throughout Accra as a race horse trainer; he boards and trains horses for Ghanaians and expatriate Europeans around Accra, and he is highly-respected at Accra's Race Course.

There is no bank in Sabon Zongo, but even if there were, it is not clear that people would use it. In Accra generally, individuals do not use banks. Rather, they prefer ambulatory bankers, the *esusu*, who operate throughout Accra and come compound-to-compound to collect and record the residents' deposits. The *esusu* is used for convenience: if you want more than ₵200,000 (this when the dollar was worth ₵1,500), the bank either will not loan it or will not have it and will tell you to return. One of the few university-educated residents has been dealing with the same *esusu* man for more than ten years. He never goes to any bank. "You know," he says, "the World Bank has come to recognize this kind of work, so they're going to organize them in such a way to bring them up to a certain level, so that people will appreciate it more and have trust in it . . . any amount I need, any project, I tell him and I get it. With the bank and collateral, it's not easy. Even a basic loan like this. They want to make sure you pay back. . . . But the *esusu* man—yes, because you pay them. You see I can't go to the bank for even 100,000 cedis and they'll give it to me. When I was teaching at the school, my salary was going to the bank, but I couldn't get a loan."

NOTES

1. Rapoport (1980:68) speaks of the facilitating environment and its cues.

2. There is no mail delivery anywhere in Accra. Each post office rents out boxes. Individuals either use the post office box of their employer or rent one themselves.

3. The 1970 census was taken shortly after the enactment of the Aliens' Expulsion Act (1969), and it is impossible to know to what extent fear of deportation affected the truthfulness of the responses regarding nationality and place of birth.

4. Baba Mai Doki has two children, a girl and a boy, through two external relationships. I have been told that because he has no children with a wife, he dotes upon his son, who will be his heir and carry on his line.

5. Issifu Faruk, May 30, 1982.

6. According to Chief Ali Kadri English, this emphasis and ability among the Bakos on Koranic learning has always distinguished them from Hausa leaders in the other Accra *zongos* (June 2000).

7. All of the information on Freedom Market came from Letitia Tetteh, Queenmother of Sabon Zongo's Freedom Market and Sarah Quaye, her assistant, whom I interviewed on February 26, 1995 at Letitia's home in Larte Biokarshie.

8. In 1999, the dollar equivalency was about $1 = ₵3775.

9. It has been referred to as Toonga (Moro 1982; ADM 11/1502; SNA 2288/01), which corresponds to what others call Jonkobli. In his statement as the defendants' lawyer, Mills makes reference to "Jogobli" as a Hausa village (*Mantse D.P. Hammond of Asere, Ussher Town as Mantse of Asere v. Mantse Kojo Ababio IV and Chief Malam Bako*, June 7, 1910); Daniel Armatey Sampah, in his testimony, refers to Jonkobli as one of the villages founded on the disputed land (Supreme Court, Ghana, on appeal from the High Court, Lands Section—Accra; Tr. L. Suit No. 22/1948; Tr. L. Suit No. 25/1948; Tr. L. Suit No. 30/1953; 18 May 1962).

10. Now that kola nuts cost ₵100/each, candy is substituted. For some reason, the preferred candy is Hacks (pronounced "haas"), the medicinal cough drop. A bag of Hacks costs ₵3000.

11. See Pellow 1997 for an analysis of praise-singing in Sabon Zongo.

12. Many Nigerians are seasonal migrants. They come "in convoy" for a few months to make money.

13. NGOs and The World Bank have used the presence of such groups and community-initiated projects as a measure of community coherence, as included in the Final Report of the Urban Environmental Sanitation Project, produced by the Government of Ghana (Ghana 1995:55).

14. In the standard game: the ace is the highest, excluding the ace of spades, and 7 is the lowest, excluding 1–6. The spade = *spa*, club = *kule* [kulay], heart = *yet*, and diamond = *kanlo*.

7

ANTHILL ARCHITECTURE: THE INVOLUTED COMPOUND

I'm living with my family. And then we are used to our traditional aspects, including our culture, like marriage, outdooring, funeral. And then what we call the entire connection (*dagantaka*) with each other.

[But] I have to renovate the house, especially our rooms. We have to get a bathroom, we have to get a toilet. Most of the houses [in *zongo*] have no toilet. And you have to get a very big hall [living room]. Mostly in *zongo* you get a single room, one family—almost about 5 people—in one room. It's not good. So if I were to develop my house, that's what I would do.

I have a plot here, behind Ila's storied building, with wooden structures on it. That's why I'm trying to get something better—if I get money, then I will develop. I want to move here, because I want to get what we call our own self-contained, which would include sitting room, a bathroom, a toilet, other rooms for the children. You will do everything inside—nobody will see what you are doing—you have your kitchen (Alhaji Mohammed Bako 6/6/96).

If Alhaji Adamu were to build his Sabon Zongo house now, he says he would follow a different design because he now has different ideas. For example, he would want a bigger hall (sitting room) and only one bedroom; a bigger kitchen—now they must cook rice outside because there isn't room to make all the food inside; a w.c.—previously there was no way for a lorry to come in to lay a septic tank, but now they can do it outside and connect it to a pipe.

Housing is an integral part of culture. People everywhere design and build housing that suits their form of domestic organization. In Sabon Zongo, as in the

rest of Accra and indeed much of Africa, the typical housing form is the courtyard or compound house, and in Sabon Zongo it is the single story type.

This chapter has two missions: to examine the social and spatial principles
built into Sabon Zongo housing and to chart the significance of the compound,
its reproduction, and change. These I do by examining nineteen compounds in
the various neighborhoods of Sabon Zongo. As artifacts, these compounds are
physical representations of peoples' lifestyles. They not only embody social life;
they have helped constitute social life. Each has a history, and each in itself or
as one of many represents the progressive nature of the community's culture
and its change. For the nineteen compounds surveyed, sixteen of the landlords
are Hausa, one is half Yoruba/Hausa, one is half Wangara/Hausa (related to the
Bako's on his mother's side) and one is Kanuri.

EVOLVING FORMS

The original houses built in Sabon Zongo are vestiges of urban northern
Nigerian Hausa style, cultural templates of domestic spatial design carried by
the early settlers here and elsewhere in the Hausa diaspora (see Figure 18).
While there may be considerable variation between Hausa compounds, "they
follow a basic pattern, elaborations of which merely indicate differences of
wealth and status of the household head, or structure of the domestic group"
(Smith 1981 [1954]:28). Hausa vernacular architecture incorporates principles
of Hausa social and spatial organization. Walled on the outside, with a gradation
of space from public on the outside to private on the inside, the house of Malam
Bako's day expresses the gendering of space—the importance of sequestering
women. The result of increased concern with visual privacy was evidenced in
Hausa architecture by high compound walls pierced only by doors to the *zaure*
(entrance hall). The *zaure* leads into the compound, *gida* (which actually means
house). "The door openings become visual foci, and all interaction becomes
concentrated around these points in space. The doorways are staggered, pre-
venting any direct view into the entrance way" (Prussin 1986:212).

The house layout has evolved from a Hausa template to a synthetic one,
incorporating themes of Hausa, southern Ghanaian and urban Accra models.
The courtyard is crucial in all, its rationale in large part tied to climate and
social life. Here in the tropics, where rooms are small and hot, the courtyard is
where the life of the house goes on. Cooking, eating, bathing, chatting—people
spend their time outside of their rooms in the compound yard.

Customary southern Ghanaian design, as exemplified by the Akan Asante
prototype, entails an open, square, interior courtyard, bounded by four rectangular building units (Prussin 1986:236). This courtyard is designated as *gyase*,
which literally means "below or beneath the hearth" (Prussin 1986:236). Similarly, among the coastal Fante (another Akan sub-group), the customary spatial
configuration of the house includes a four-cornered interior courtyard: "The
houses [are] grouped together in four, six, or eight units, leaving a four-cornered

courtyard which [is] used for cooking, washing, and other housework" (Prussin 1986:237).

But contrary to both southern Ghanaian and Northern Nigerian plans, many of Sabon Zongo's houses today do not reproduce the atrium form. Owners and residents in many of the original family houses have run out of space: they cannot afford to add floors above by building up, they have little room to build out, given their proximity to lanes or roads, and they do not want to move away. This has resulted in what I call the involuted compound. The integrity of the central all-purpose yard has been lost as owners have built *in* to create more rooms. They have built rooms within spaces that are built within the rooms, often creating an intricate pattern of interior lanes around rooms.

Is involution of the courtyard bound to happen no matter what? What about other changes in layout—are they less predictable outgrowths of particular historical circumstances, for example, family cycles, rather than demographic shifts? When Hajiya Hasana's daughter got married, she built a wall to separate her apartment from the rented rooms in the compound; in another compound, a married couple had another child and decided to add a room; Baba Mai Doki rebuilt one of the stables as a room for visiting traders from Northern Nigeria— are these not all examples of individual cycles rather than either a historical or social structural change? At Gongadi's compound (Figure 46), Alhaji Abu has purchased one chunk of space on the west end of the compound and has architectural drawings for a self-contained apartment; is this strand of variation due to differences of class and status or historical progression to a new form? When we consider the disappearance of seclusion, does the issue come down to the social change in gender relations, to a change in polygyny, or perhaps to the immigration of strangers?

BOUNDARIES, MATERIALS, AND FACILITIES

The map of Malam Bako's land (Figure 6) clearly delineates the boundaries of the thirty-two plots of land, each about one-quarter block square, where the compound houses were built. The original compounds in Sabon Zongo still stand, the building materials crumbling. According to the Urban II Preparatory Study on Accra residential and market areas, "housing in the Sabon Zongo area reflects the original status of the settlement. . . . Plot boundaries are ill defined. Majority of houses are mud houses which are falling into dilapidation. . . . Houses are poorly ventilated" (Government of Ghana 1992:43). In the interior of Sabon Zongo, that is the old core of the community, deterioration reigns, whereas along the commercial periphery housing seems more kempt and better appointed. This perception is reinforced by the survey of compounds and enclosed sleeping structures discussed later in this chapter. Even Ghanaian architects I showed the drawings were amazed: "How do people breathe?" they asked.

The building materials (for example, see Figure 27) vary widely from add on to add on. According to the Urban Preparatory Study, cement block or burnt bricks constitute 65 percent, mud and wattle and wood of varying kinds constitute 10 percent each. The balance are materials such as asbestos and zinc. All of the structures from the early days are still at least in part mud and wattle. As the drawings of the 19 sample compounds make clear, where the mud wattle is crumbling it has been repaired with plaster or replaced by cement blocks. Those built in the last 30 years are primarily cement block (landcrete); indeed, the houses built by Ilyashu Salisu, Hajiya Hasana, Gongadi, Alhajai Sule Bako, Bebe, and Adamu, are cement only. Baba Mai Doki's rental property (Figure 43) is entirely wood, with the exception of the mosque and concrete renovations of three of the rooms. Residents build new structures and also add to original structures (individual walls, whole rooms, roofs) in a variety of materials, some new, some scavenged. Modes of adaptability are as infinite as one's imagination and access to resources, whether money (less likely) or scrap (more likely). Most of the building adaptations, in any case, are makeshift. What matters to these "people builders" is the basic function of shelter.

The roofing of the compounds was originally straw. It was replaced by metal because of fear of fire. Now because of the corroding effect of the sea, the roofs here as in the rest of Accra are primarily corrugated asbestos and aluminum. The roofs have a temporary feel, as they are held in place by stones, broken furniture, extra stools, or other household oddments.

But even the owners of such simple or decaying houses in Sabon Zongo, like house owners of all kinds throughout the Accra area, must pay property taxes to the AMA. The AMA classifies residential structures, and thus calculates a property rate, in Accra according to two criteria: 1) area facilities: roads, water, electricity, layout (e.g., whether there is road access to park a car in front of the house), 2) building: size and facilities within the building.

Accra's residential structures fall into three classes: Class 1, the well-to-do suburban houses; Class 2, urban, generally well-built housing; and Class 3, urban, generally inferior structures. According to a civil servant in the AMA's Valuation Section, the houses in Sabon Zongo fall primarily within Class 3 but some fall within Class 2 (Mr. Asiemah, AMA Head Office, 3/7/1995).

According to AMA records, Sabon Zongo has 352 taxable residential listings, 267 mixed residential and commercial. Looking at residential property in the city at large puts Sabon Zongo's property ratable values into context. The highest taxable residential property in Accra is in Airport Residential Estates; including gardens and a pool, it was valued in 1995 at ₵29,000,000 (in 1995, $1 = ₵1,360). The highest taxable residential property in Sabon Zongo (never successfully located), was valued at ₵14,576,000. The lowest in Sabon Zongo is valued at ₵13,000. Situated in the core of the old part of *zongo*, it has enough space (about 3,550 square feet) and rooms to accommodate fourteen households, eleven of them tenant households. But it is worn, has no water spigot inside the compound, and residents must walk outside of the compound to reach the shower room.

The AMA uses a house numbering system for its property tax rolls.[1] The house numbering is very confusing for a variety of reasons. Because of the maze-like character of the old *Kan Tudu* area, the numbers do not follow; some people paint over their house number; in 1994, the AMA changed the house number system and some people continued to use their old number, some their new one; and some people own several properties and give them all the same number to avoid paying full taxes.

There are all sorts of difficulties in collecting this source of income, compounded by the AMA's own management difficulties and slow valuation of properties in the city (Mousset-Jones 1999:38). For example, while the AMA property tax maps were re-checked in 1987, they are inaccurate: they omit structures that were built years ago, they lack householder names, and there was no attempt to draw the property according to its actual shape. A source at the University of Ghana in the Archaeology Department had a friend who worked in the Survey Department at the Government Lands Department. The latter reported that people in the Survey Department "run away" when asked to come to work on Sabon Zongo maps because the structures are so complicated (Murrey 4/16/1995).

The status of facilities analyzed for the Urban Preparatory Study included shower rooms (generally standing cubicles in which one bathes from a bucket), kitchens (open air, on a verandah or coal pot in the compound yard), toilets (public latrines, though some houses have KVIP and some have pan toilets), and water taps (compounds with water have a standing pipe) (Ministry of Works and Housing 1992).

In Sabon Zongo, when a compound's water pipe is outside of the property, it is kept locked and only those with rights to draw water have a key. Because the compound yard is a semi-public space, with strangers wandering in and out, some landlords lock inside spigots as well. The occasional compound shower room has running water; more often, residents take bucket baths.

There is electricity in all nineteen of the sampled compounds. Most compounds pay as a whole—either the landlord (as at Alhaji Baba Mai Doki's), a caretaker or a tenant (as at Mumuni's) is in charge of collecting from each resident and paying the bill. The problem here, as with waste disposal fees, is if one person does not pay and no one else wants to pay for her/him, an electrician is sent and service to the entire compound is cut. As soon as the bill is paid, the Corporation reconnects service. There are also rooms in compounds that are not wired for electricity. Tenants in such a situation may "steal" electricity by bringing an illegal connection into the room from the line servicing the compound.

The Enumerator's *Manual of the Ghana 1960 Population Census* defines a house or compound in Ghana as "a self-contained building unit. It is a structurally separate and independent place of abode. The essential features are separateness and independence. An enclosure may be considered separate if it is surrounded by walls, fences, etc" (Caldwell 1967:63).

The compounds in Sabon Zongo are separate and independent. Many are known by a popular name, often not of the owner but of some resident or characteristic. For example, Al'wali's house (Figure 27) is named *Gidan* Dan Maraiya, because Dan Maraiya who lived there was very popular. Up the street, there is a house known as *Gidan* Muda (Muda's house), although Muda was only a tenant there and has since died. House #7 (Figure 31) next door to Muda's is known as *Gidan Makaranta* ("house of a Koranic school"), because the family has had a Koranic school there for years. And *Masalaci* Idrissu (Idrissu's mosque) is in fact known as *Masalaci Sabon Gida* ("new house mosque").

People do know where one property ends and another begins, even when physical demarcation has gone to ruin. Such spatial dissolution and transformation have occurred in Sabon Zongo compounds and they may have social implications. These include: 1) compound boundaries. The original houses have an outside wall, but in many cases stores or rooms have been embedded in place of walls in beehive-like fashion, and, contrary to the norm in Ghana, newer houses have been built without such a wall; 2) compound yard. The family house originally had an interior court, but over time, in many houses this has been absorbed as rooms were built-in, leading to involution and a maze of interior lanes; and 3) the *zaure* or entryway. This constituent element in Hausa domestic architecture has either been reinterpreted as a social space or eliminated.

Residents, even tenants, regularly add-on rooms from the outside, as in Alhaji Yaro's compound (Figure 29) where the house eats into the proximate lanes. As the Ministry of Housing has noted, "in the back alleys access to most houses is through paths which cut across neighbours' yards" (Ministry of Works and Housing 1992:43). Compounds have also expanded in such a way that "setback between houses is inadequate" (Ministry of Works and Housing 1992:43). When I spoke with Alhaji Baba Mai Doki, owner of House #14, he acknowledged that much of the house on the mosque/animal pen side is built where a road is supposed to be. He knows, and the tenants know, that if a road is finally built, that part of the house will be torn down. Others, like Alhaji Yahaya (Figure 54) built a new house right in the path of a planned road. Yahaya has violated building regulations, as did the tenants at Alhaji Yaro's house. But, he really wanted to build his own house in Sabon Zongo, available property was tight, and given the State or municipality's neglect of the community, he has no reason to believe that a road is going to be cut anytime soon. Moreover, regulations are not enforced.

Like most indigenous Ghanaian or Nigerian structures, the original houses (see, for example, Figures 19, 25, and 27) and some of the newer ones (Figures 41, 50, 52), were built with walled perimeters. Many also have businesses built into the encircling wall (Figures 21, 31, 52, 54). In 1999, Sarkin Fada incorporated a mosque at the front of his house (Figure 37). The eastern side of a nearby house served as a "semi-mosque" and people referred to it as "*bi ta da kallo*" which literally means "follow her with your eyes" due to its open space, i.e., one could see and be seen when one is in the mosque. Sometimes you can "meet" some devotee's eye gazing at you when passing on the street. In some cases, like the western side of Figure 31, a store was turned into a chamber and hall.

But many compounds are not bounded, contrary to northern Nigerian and southern Ghanaian principles. Number 14 (Figure 43), built for tenants only and incorporating a set of stables for horses, lacks any peripheral marking whatsoever. Number 17 (Figure 46) has spawned a line of free-standing rooms in front of the original structure and an enclosed set of rooms bordering the southern side. And the windows from the neighboring compound look in on *Gidan Baki* (Figure 35), as the wall between is not a boundary but part of the house.

Except for the newest compounds, the vernacular nature of much of the building (room and porch add ons) means the structures are composed of a varying assortment of materials. They are also not uniformly shaped, which is obvious in the 1969 survey map, the 2001 aerial GIS photo and the nineteen individual plans. *Unguwan Makafi*, the blind quarter, exemplifies the irregularities of construction. Along its back lane, behind the mosque, all of the walls are a mixture of wood and rusting scrap zinc. Even kiosks have been adapted as housing: one about 2m by 1 3/4m, is a combination of wood and zinc and is just big enough to lie down in with one's knees bent. It is propped up on one corner by a truck hubcap with a rock in it, and a piece of cement under the front corner. Yet further along in the quarter is a compound with a cement wall topped with broken glass burglar-proofing.[2] In addition to the blind people, a number of the local *bori* adepts and drummers live in the area—most living hand to mouth existences.

In the Hausa vernacular, the *zaure* is by custom the men's space, but only at Malam Bako's palace is it used in the customary manner—for meetings with the chief or sleeping space for long-distance visitors (most frequently Tuareg and other traders from Niger). In many compounds, the space has been appropriated by the women of the house—for their work activities, visits with friends, or ritual occasions. Many others lack the signatory area altogether.

MODELS TO FOLLOW: GENDERED SPACE

The Hausa compound, *gida*, is customarily inhabited by agnatically-related kin. It may house two different units: the individual family (*iyali*), composed of a man, his wife/wives, his children, and possibly his mother; and the household, consisting of all persons who eat from the same pot, live in the same part of the compound, and contribute to the household budget. The compound head, the *mai gida*, is clearly distinguished from the heads of other households living in the compound "by his capacity to take independent action, which may include the building of new rooms or the accommodation of other family members" (Schwerdtfeger 1982:34).

The urban compound is a rectangular enclosure (see Figure 18). Hausa town architecture is striking in its distinctiveness: unlike that of the countryside, which

Figure 18
Hausa Ideal House. Adapted by Mark Hauser from Sa'ad, 1981.

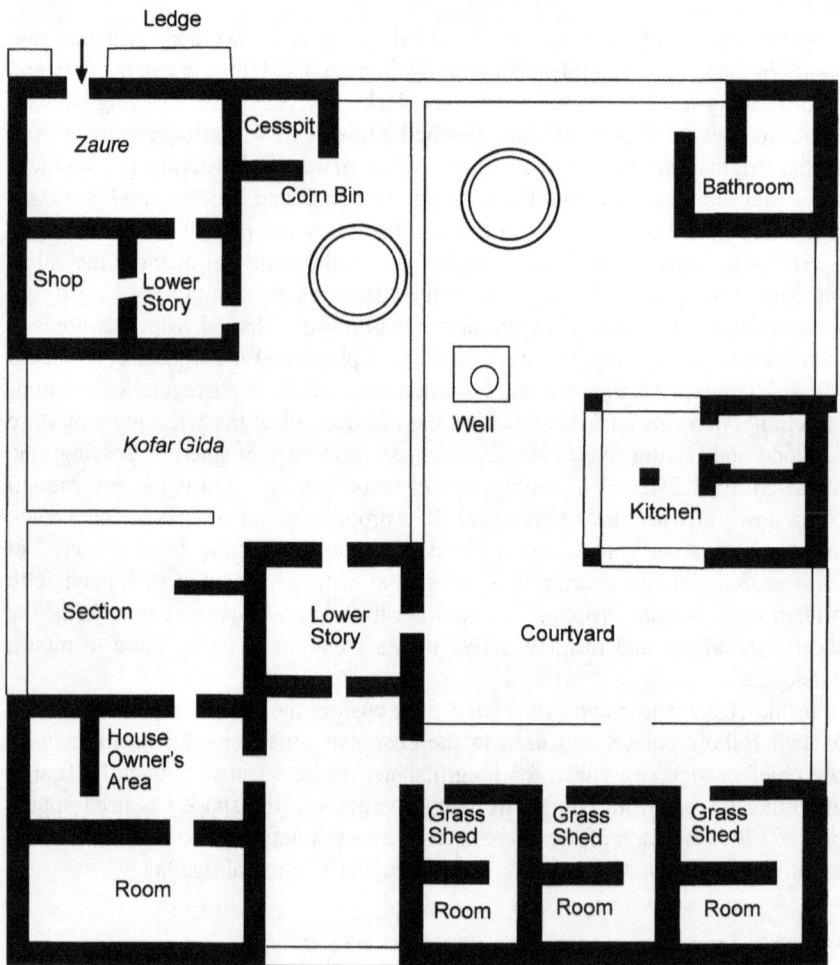

is round with grass walls, "house and boundary walls and roofs in the towns [are] built of mud . . . the basic house walls [are] often made of mud"(Denyer 1978:35). It is typically divided into a forecourt (*k̃ofar gida*) and the central courtyard (*cikin gida*, literally the interior of the house). "The public and private areas of the house are clearly defined and are respected by the public" (Schwerdtfeger 1982:299). The *zaure* is the domain of the male compound head and the only way to enter the compound. In the *zaure* "he entertains his visitors and friends, takes his meals and, if possible, pursues his occupation such as weaving, tailoring, embroidery, or teaching the Koran" (Schwerdtfeger 1982: 28). Male visitors may also sleep here. Poor compounds may lack a *zaure*, instead having a *ƙofa*, a doorway or recessed entrance (Smith 1965). Over time, the only original architectural elements that remain intact in the Hausa compound are the perimeter wall and *zaure*.

"Important to an understanding of the form of the Hausa dwelling is the influence of Islam" (Moughtin 1985:59), which has resulted in the division of homes into separate spaces for males and females (see Figure 18). The sleeping rooms for the various family members—householder, young men, wives—are huts grouped within the compound yard according to sex, generation, relationship, allowing for such domestic activities as cooking and eating.

The *zaure* leads into the forecourt (*ƙofar gida*), where male youths from the household or male guests sleep in huts. "The forecourt functions as an intermediate zone between the outside world and the centre of the compound" (Schwerdtfeger 1982:29).

From this forecourt, one transits through the *shigifa*, a transitional zone, to enter the women's quarters, the *cikin gida*. The heart of the home, the *cikin gida* is a core open space, with sleeping rooms in or off of it. As is the case cross-culturally, the house is women's spatial domain; it is here that they are most strongly connected, which helps explain their role differentiation from men. Illich reminds us that gender shapes bodies as they shape space and are in turn shaped by its arrangements (1983:118–119). We see how women's physical placement provides support for gender ideology and energizes the cultural definition of female roles, as they are grounded in and create structures such as kitchens.

There is a hierarchy among the wives, the most senior known as the *uwar gida* (mother of the house). A compound must include at least one private room for each wife, and the majority of compounds includes a separate room, or set of rooms, or indeed a whole section of the house, for the compound head (Pittin 1996:182). "[I]t is an important rule that each wife should have her own hut in which she keeps her possessions, and in which her young children sleep" (Smith 1981 [1954]:23; cf. Moughtin 1964, Schwerdtfeger 1982). In average urban households, each wife has one or two rooms. "The husband in a polygamous marriage may or may not have a separate sleeping-hut of his own, opposite those of his wives" (Smith 1981 [1954]:23).

The *cikin gida* is the arena for family life where women play a central role. Not required to work in public venues, Hausa women are responsible for overseeing the compound. Their position and mobility vary according to the extensiveness of spatial segregation; its most extreme form is represented by the institution of *kulle*. This itself varies greatly according to time, place, class, and so on, but it has been the ideal in urban Hausaland since the *jihad* of Usman dan Fodio in 1803 (see Pittin 1996:180f.). Little girls learn that the women's quarter is off-limits to boys and men, save the household head.

"The form and layout of the Muslim compound reflects the preoccupation of the Hausa with privacy" (Moughtin 1985:68). In Northern Nigeria, the Hausa compound is walled, fortress-like and inward facing and it "creates an immediate physical presence and is in certain respects an instrument of ideological and spatial control" (Pittin 1996:182). And as I have written about Accra's housing more generally, "it is particularly women for whom the . . . compound is an enculturating space" (Pellow 1991b:199; see also Pittin 1979, 1996; and Mack 1991, 1992).

It is also an entertaining space—for entertaining other women, both family and friends. And it is here that the newly-married woman displays her dowry, known as *ƙayan ɗaki* ("things for the room") that she brings into the marriage. Some of the *ƙayan ɗaki* are practical utensils essential to running the household. But of greater importance to the woman's status are the decorative objects and all conform to the same collection. In the old days in Niger, it was calabashes: "Here in town you would line them all up, and you'd parade around the town with them, to take them to the bride's new home" (Cooper 1997a:94). More recently in Hausa communities in the north as well as in Accra, *ƙayan ɗaki* have consisted of brightly-colored, enameled, Czechoslovakian-made bowls, brass bowls, porcelain soup tureens, Chinese-made enameled bowls, and irides-cent pyrex casseroles. These items are amassed for their own sake, not to be used but to be displayed, as status symbols and forms of stored female wealth (Schildkrout 1983; Cooper 1997a). They enhance the women's symbolic capital. The *ƙayan ɗaki* represent a purely female type of capital; while the fact of a woman in seclusion reflects her husband's solvency, her display items are hers, not the household's and are not necessarily reflective of the household's well-being.

Throughout Hausaland, "the repetition of similar objects is associated with *arziki*, or prosperity" (Cooper 1997a:95). And all of the women know what each of these items is worth. Because of the rules of seclusion, unrelated men like friends of the groom do not see the *ƙayan ɗaki*, but women who attend the marriage are keen on evaluating their worth. Over time, women add to their collection, buying more pots or bowls with money earned or skimmed off the household budget. Some women accumulate hundreds, stacking them in high columns on the floor, in cases, and atop the wardrobe. This collection is their capital—in theory to be sold, for example, in event of divorce, or to cull from for one's daughter when she marries.[3]

Also of interest "is the design and spatial placement of features and house furnishings controlled by women," as Lyons has detailed in her study of house-hold design in north Cameroon (Lyons 1992:iii). This may draw attention to women's activities not necessarily valued by men. Indeed, in the Hausa quarter Sabo in Ibadan, Nigeria, Abner Cohen found that husbands were annoyed by the mountains of bowls. "A current, sardonic, complaint among the married men of the Quarter is that, because of the bowls, a man cannot nowadays find space in his wife's room for even his morning prayers" (Cohen 1969:68). Clearly gender ideology plays a part in the configuration of domestic space.

According to Mack, the prototype for Hausa domestic space in Kano is the Emir's palace "because it is the most traditional and conservative" (1992:79).[4] I follow Mack by proposing Malam Bako's compound as the ideal house design in Sabon Zongo. While it is larger and more elaborate than those of his followers, it serves to illustrate the layout of and the principles of social organization encoded in Sabon Zongo housing (Figure 19).

As among the northern Nigerian Hausa, the perimeter is rectangular and the *cikin gida*, the interior courtyard where the women lived, could only be entered through a series of entrance halls. To maintain the wives segregation, there is a *zaure* (entrance hall) at the front of the compound, where Mallam Bako met with elders and judged disputes and where visitors could camp.

True to form, none of his wives' rooms, nor the rooms of his sons' wives, are directly accessible from the forecourt, thereby keeping the women out of view. There are two inner courts. That to the right off the *zaure* leads into the rooms of some of Malam Bako's adult sons and their wives. There was also a stable here, where the Malam kept horses. The court to the left could be entered only through a second entrance hall (*shigifa*), which also has a *zaure* and where only close associates or especially important persons would be entertained. The second entrance room opens into the *cikin gida*, where the household head had his own room.

Once Malam Bako relocated to Sabon Zongo, all of his wives and children, except his son Hamisu, moved from Zongo Lane. Hamisu was acculturated to the Ga and saw no reason to move. So Malam Bako had his other sons remove all of the roofing at the Zongo Lane house to force Hamisu to move. Over the years, seven of Malam Bako's nine wives lived in the Sabon Zongo palace.

By the early 1980s, four of Malam Bako's sons—Hamisu, Abdullahi ("Baban Inda"), Abubaka Garuba ("Baban Ayi"), and Issaka ("Dan Baba")—were still living in the family house in the area where Idrissu's room had been, all having lived there as adults with wives (Alhaji Hamisu 6/2/1982). Gambo, a fifth son who taught at the family Koranic school located in the rear *zaure*, lived in the compound next door until his death in 1998.

The current residents and their relationships are detailed on the accompanying genealogy (Figure 20). The family head is Issaka Dan Baba. As in the early days of the community, the residents are family only. Malam Bako's children all inherited land and on their land they built and rented to tenants. But, observed Hamisu (6/4/1982), "nobody can come and throw me out of my rooms." When Hamisu died, his wife could continue to live there till she married or died (the latter). Any of his children could come and live in the house. But they are not supposed to sell or rent rooms in the family's house. The grandchildren living in Malam Bako's rooms in the old *cikin gida* have begun renovating rooms.

While most of the residents are elderly and not working, they all formerly followed typical work trajectories: the men working primarily as tailors/embroiderers or drivers, the women as traders of prepared food (one still sells Hausa pasta and another *tuwo*, in the house) or petty goods. In this family of teachers, only one of the men teaches at Malam Gambo's Koranic school. And one man, Musa Bako's son Sai'du, is literate in English and works as a freelance journalist.

In Malam Bako's day, his wives' social and spatial relationships were highly

Figure 19
Malam Bako's House, Plan #1.

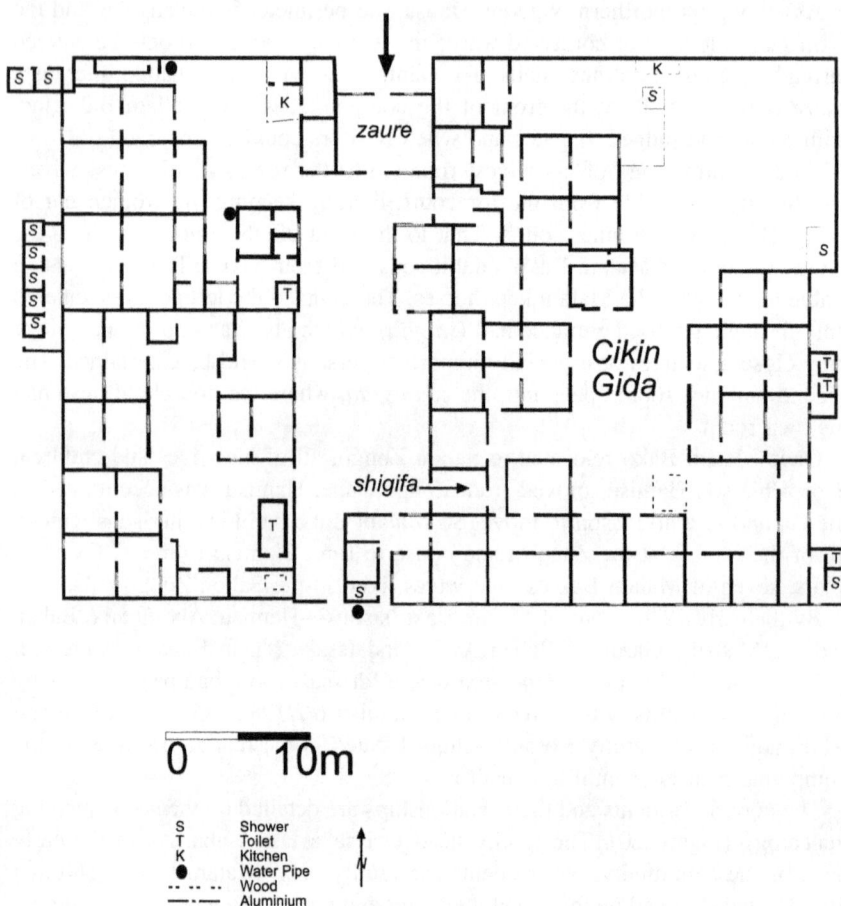

formalized. The potential for disharmony among co-wives, always high, necessitated careful regulation of their social and spatial behavior in the house: each
was allocated her own room(s) within the women's quarter for her and her young
children, and equal time to cook for and spend the night with her husband.

As their movement was carefully monitored, at least during daylight hours,
the women's most important or regular spatial relationships were with their co-
wives and children (cf. Pittin 1979). Women ate with one another and/or their
children; men ate alone or with their male friends in the *zaure*. Just as the
women's occupation of the space provided social definition to it, so the space
reminded them of their social roles (cf. Pittin 1979; Callaway 1981; Weisman
1981; Wright 1981). The only space accorded them by the culture was in the
compound; accordingly, their social roles centered on family or female-oriented

Figure 20
Malam Bako's House: Adult Resident Kin (Shaded).

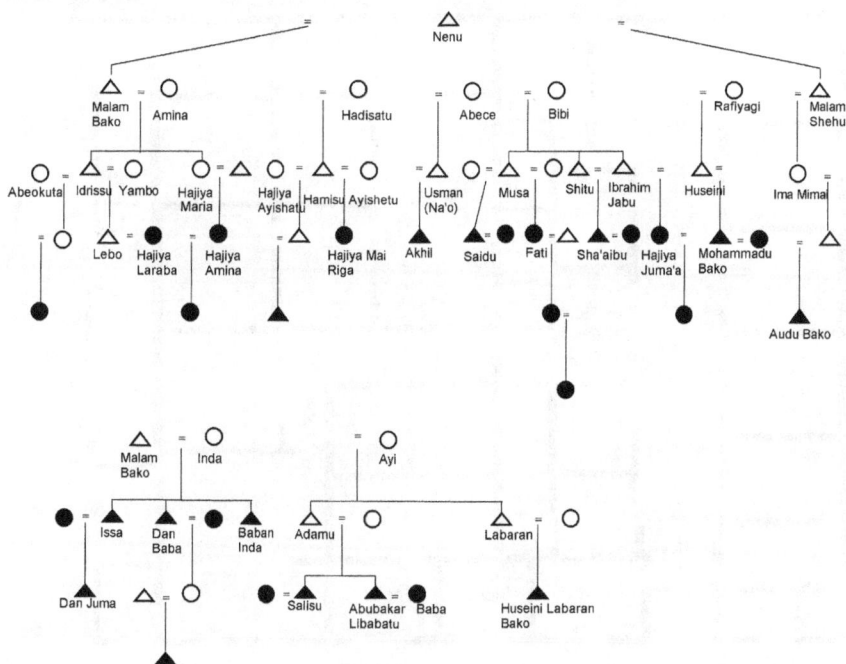

activities within compound walls. Like Hausa women in Northern Nigeria and elsewhere in the Hausa diaspora, these women amassed *ƙayan ɗaki*.

Down the road from *Gidan* Malam Bako lived Sha'aibu Bako, the recently deceased chief, his third wife Saratu and various grown offspring. Their compound (Figure 21) is across the street from the Night Market in the area nicknamed *makwala*. Sha'aibu's brother Lebo was the most senior grandchild of Malam Bako; after his death, Sha'aibu held that status. Sha'aibu was born in the family house at Zongo Lane and at the age of thirteen moved to Malam Bako's new house in Sabon Zongo. At the time that Malam Bako was building his own house in Sabon Zongo, he also built a house for his daughter Hajiya (junior to Lawal, Sha'aibu's father) and her husband.

When Sha'aibu was a child, he moved to Hajiya's house. She cared for him as well as Idrissu's daughter Huseina (both children of her two brothers). Sha'aibu lived with her up till his adulthood. When Hajiya died, her house should have gone to the family, but at that time, land was not scarce, and by paying a token fee, Sha'aibu acquired ownership of it.

Sha'aibu relocated to Hajiya's house the day of his marriage to his first wife Rekiya in 1935 and has lived here ever since. When he moved in, there were only two rooms opening into the open space of the *cikin gida*. Sha'aibu enlarged

Figure 21
Chief Sha'aibu Bako's House, Plan #2.

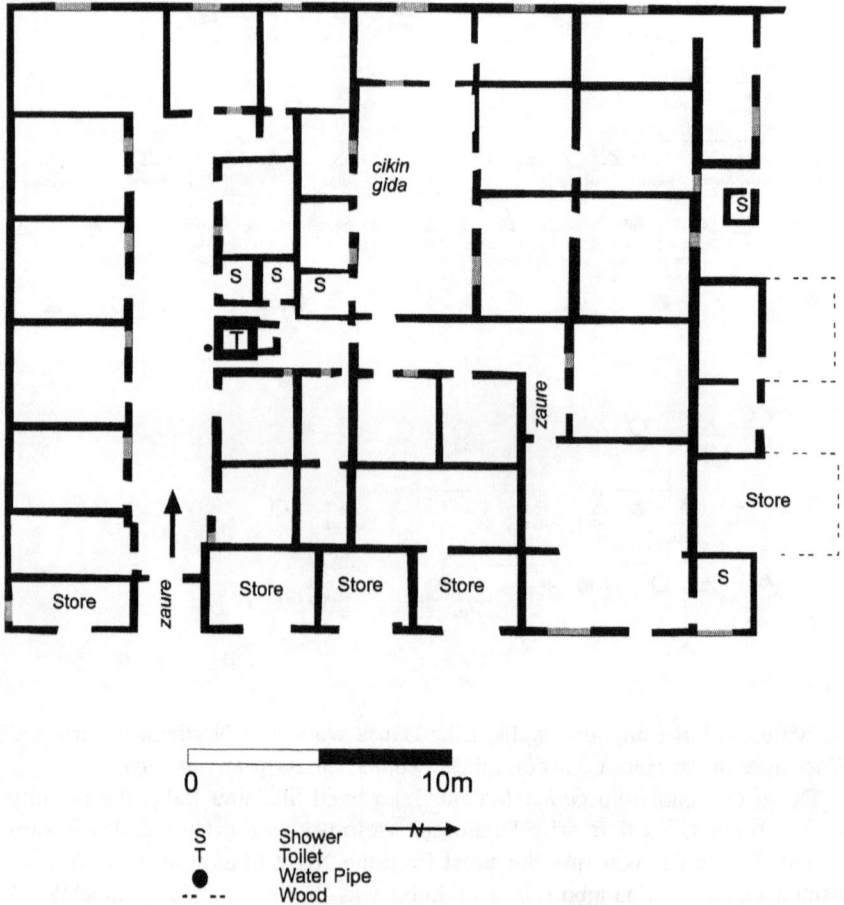

cikin gida

zaure

Store

zaure

Store   Store   Store

zaure

Store

Store

S

0   10m

S   Shower   —N—▶
T   Toilet
●   Water Pipe
-- -- Wood

the area of the *cikin gida* area and put a raffia wall around the property. Visitors had to enter through the side *zaure*. After Sha'aibu became chief August 15, 1981, he renovated and gave the *zaure* its present shape, where he would meet with members of his *fadawa* and individuals would come by to greet or consult with him. The wall of the *zaure* is the property wall. At the front are three stores.

Given its layout, Sha'aibu's house could fulfill all of the functions of traditional housing. It has a *cikin gida*, which one can get to only by crossing through at least two entryways, one of which is now his formal audience room. There is a large semi-private forecourt and a simple doorway to the *cikin gida*; the chief's room, and his wife's room within, ring a rectangular courtyard. The shower room and KVIP (which is kept locked) are for the family only.

Figure 22
Chief Sha'aibu Bako's House: Adult Resident Kin (Shaded).

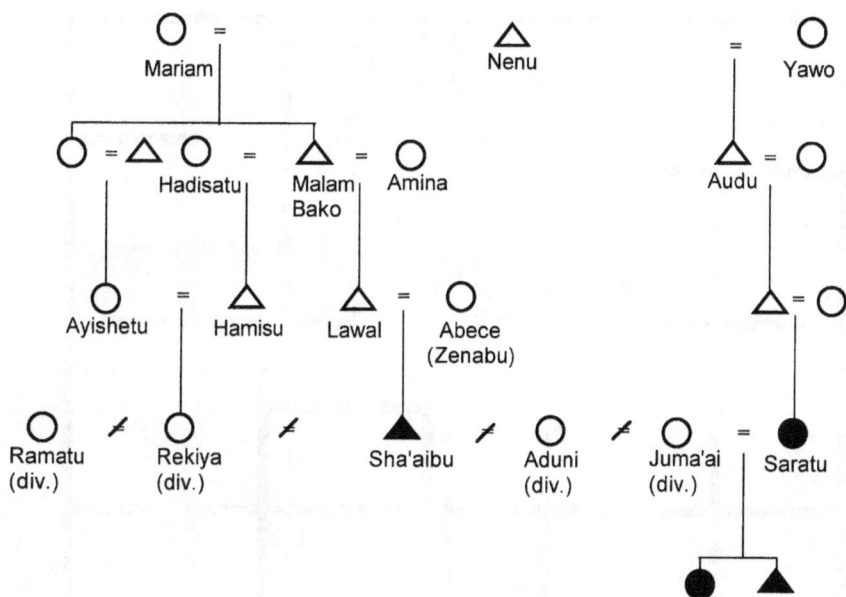

Sha'aibu's compound also represents a modification of his grandfather Malam Bako's space: in addition to housing his immediate family, he rented twelve rooms to twenty-two adult tenants (in June 2000, fourteen Akan, seven Yoruba, and one Ewe) and kept a spare for visitors (see Figure 22). Their rooms, and Sha'aibu's as well, are accessed through the original *zaure*. Thus, because of the strangers entering, principles of Hausa spatial organization take on an altered form.

The chief's wife is responsible for domestic tasks, but she has considerable mobility—certainly more than Malam Bako's wives did. She attends celebrations of life-cycles events but in the company of other women. When out, she wears her head veil over her shoulders. While she no longer has primary relationships in the house with co-wives (she was Sha'aibu's only wife for years), she spends much of each day with her married daughter, who virtually lives there, often with a child in tow. The women engage in all sorts of grooming activities, and also cook, eat, and gossip. If the chief was not out, he divided his time between the *cikin gida* and a room between the *cikin gida* and his audience room, where he prayed, read, and napped out of sight of family and subjects. The tenant women at the other end of the house have re-defined the *zaure*, through their daily practices of cooking and washing dishware there.

The Badamese house is located down the main north-south road from Malam Bako's palace, between the palace and Sha'aibu's compound, in the heart of

Figure 23
Mohammed Badamese House, Plan #3.

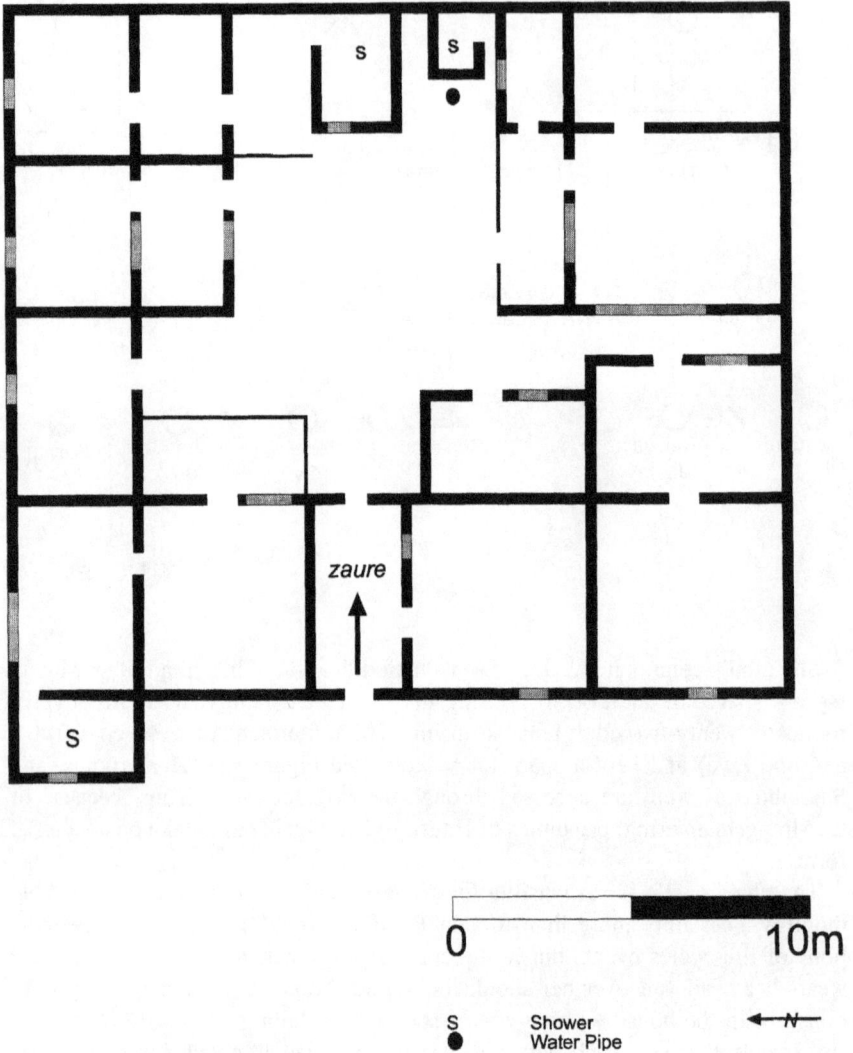

Kan Tadu (Figure 23). All of the residents are Hausa and all are members of the Bako family: the original owner, Mohammad Badamase, married Malam Bako's daughter Mariam (see Figure 24). Thus, the senior generation in the house are first cousins to Sha'aibu (his father Lawal and their mother Mariam were full brother and sister). While inherited rights to the house have been transmitted patrilineally through a non-Bako family member, as with Sha'aibu they originated with a Bako woman. One of the oldest houses (Tahiro, a resident

Figure 24
Mohammed Badamese House: Adult Resident Kin (Shaded).

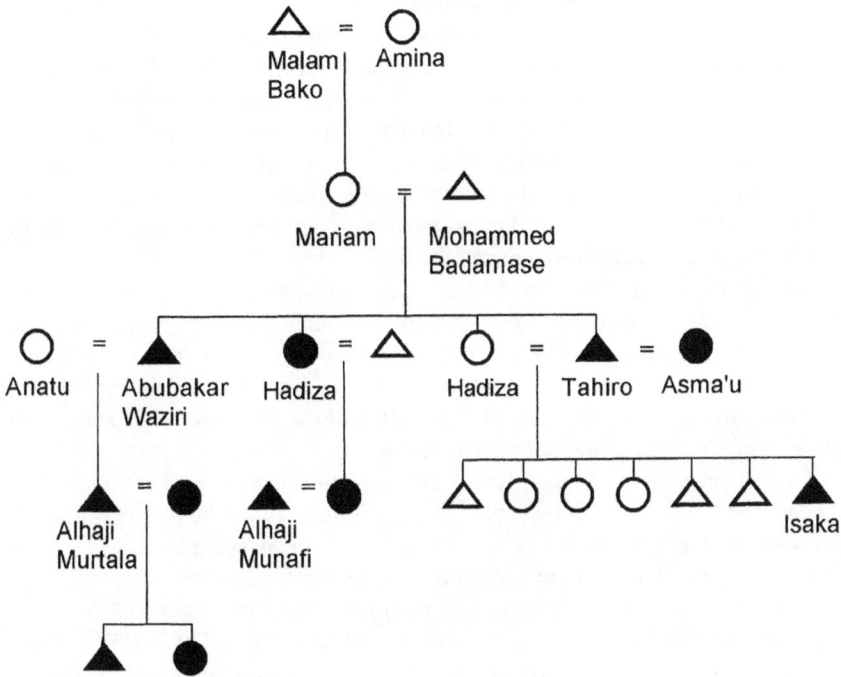

in his sixties was born here), originally it consisted of just three front rooms and the *zaure*, with an outside wall. It has clearly been renovated: it no longer has a proper wall, except in the front; the entire structure is concrete block; there are seventeen rooms. It is painted bright pink, with a paved compound yard, and the verandahs are framed by block walls, the blockwork Asante decorative design. The compound has one central yard, in effect the *cikin gida*, and there is a proper *zaure*, about 2 by 4.5 meters; one room (one of the original) opens directly into the *zaure*. There is one water spigot at the far end of the yard, next to two shower rooms; a third one is attached to the elderly Alhaji Murtala's room. There is burglar proofing on the out-facing windows, and the door to the *zaure* is locked nightly around 11:30 P.M.

As in most compounds with active people, the day begins early: by 6:30 A.M., the women have washed laundry and children are being bathed and their teeth brushed by the water spigot at the rear. While Tahiro is the only resident tailor (his son and stepson sew as well), he has tailors and embroiderers who work for him and until 1998, when he rented a shop down the street, they sewed in the double room adjacent to his sitting room. At 8:15 A.M. the first of the tailors begins work, with rock music on the radio. Tahiro sews on the verandah in front of his sitting room. He is periodically interrupted by people coming in seeking his services as a "bone setter" (chiropracter), a talent shared by others in the Bako family. Tahiro does his chiropracty inside, on the floor. The other men are "general merchants." The women in the house engage in *jojoma* trading and Tahiro's wife sells fried groundnuts at the house.

Hausa grandmothers continue to maintain a special relationship with their grandchildren. Throughout Sabon Zongo, it is normative for women to park their young children with an elder female in the family (often the maternal grandmother) during the day and even for sleeping at night. Until her death, Hajiya often had family children with her. On Saturday mornings, when the children did not have school, they would lie around the old woman's room to watch cartoons on her television set.

What is intriguing about this house is that the women spend a lot of time in the *zaure*—the old lady, senior sister, and the younger women. Meanwhile, the two senior men are always in the *cikin gida*, Tahiro in the vicinity of his room, his elder brother in a shaded corner of the compound on a mat on the ground. In other words, the women and the men in the house have reversed the customary spatial placement, the men inside, the women in the men's *zaure*.

Another grandson of Malam Bako, although considerably younger than Chief Sha'aibu Bako, Alhaji Mohammed "Numbo" Bako is the landlord of a small house (Figure 25), through a lane north of the Night Market plot, near the core of the old community. His father Sai'du's sister Hajiya Kakimatu was the original owner of this house. Numbo was born and raised in *Gidan* Malam Bako. He liked living in the palace "because of the old fathers there" (6/4/1995). When he married in 1969, he moved to his aunt's house, "because people in this house [were] not many." He ultimately inherited it from her. Mohammed Bako went to secondary school, applied his knowledge of Hausa language and now has a Hausa-language program on the Ghana Broadcasting Corporation radio and television stations.

Mohammed's house is mud and wattle, repaired with concrete. One of the outside add-on rooms is wooden and an outside structure is built out of aluminum sheet. There is no bounding wall on three sides, though at one time, the compound was a simple rectangle, with north-, east- and west-facing walls of rooms windowless on the outside. Now two of the four walls is windowed facing out. On the eastern side, where only one room has a window (so that four rooms are, in effect windowless), there is a small space and then an outer wall that continues around to the front for 3.5 meters (one room-worth). The western, southern, and northern sides are bounded by a lane, and the compound's kitchen, an aluminum shed, is across the open space opposite the front entrance.

There is a central yard, although it has been eaten into by a verandah on the east and an add-on room for the landlord on the west. The shower room, which may be used by everyone, is located outside of the compound and ratchets up the concept of public privacy. As the landlord himself laughingly observed, there's no such thing as secrets here. The women all cook in the compound not in the kitchen, each appropriating her own corner of compound space. They bath

Figure 25
Alhaji Mohammed "Numbo" Bako House, Plan #4.

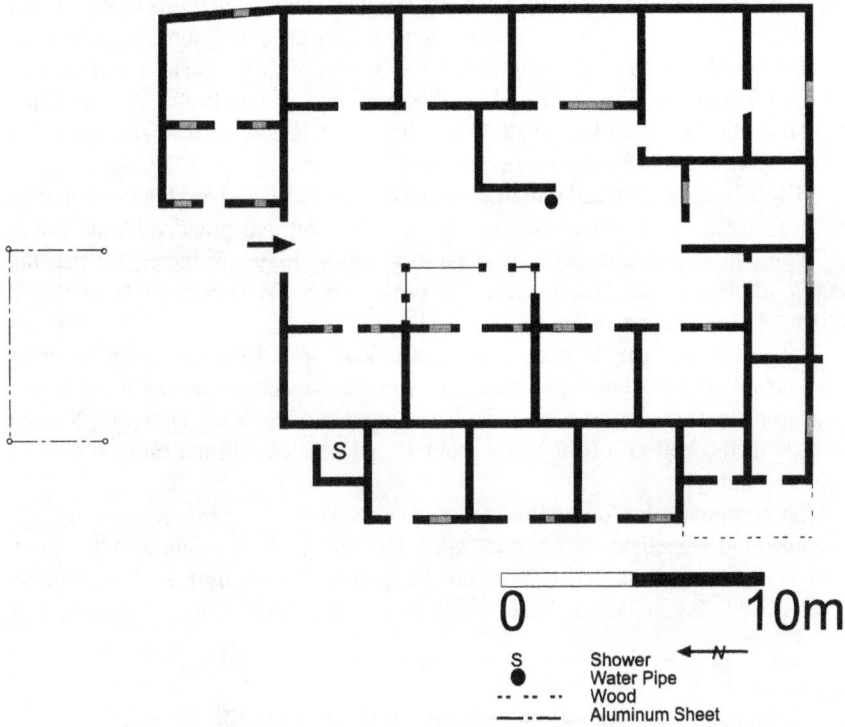

0   10m

S   Shower   ←—N—
●   Water Pipe
-- -- ·· Wood
——·—— Aluminum Sheet

the young children in a basin in the compound or by the spigot outside on the lane.

In this compound of twenty adults, only the landlord, his sister and her son, are Bako family members. The others, all tenants, include southern Ghanaians (Akan and Ewe), northern Ghanaians (Frafra), and Zabrama. Five are non-Muslims (see Figure 26). It is like the customary Hausa compound, where people see what you are doing, but unlike the Hausa compound those who do are not necessarily family.

Some blocks away, not in the core area but several blocks to the west in Unguwan Zabrama, is the Al'wali property (Figure 27). Mohamadu Al'wali migrated to Zongo Nenu in Central Accra from Kano. He married Malam Bako's daughter Hajiya Maria (her mother was Amina). He was allotted property in Sabon Zongo by Malam Bako, whom he followed to the new community, and his name is listed on Malam Bako's map of Sabon Zongo. He became Chief Idrissu Bako's *maaji*. The compound is not a Bako family house, despite the early owner's connection or that of the current household head Tanko Al'wali, who married Saratu, the daughter of Malam Bako's daughter Ayi. Sakinatu, the

daughter of the original landlord (and sister to the current household head), was
at one time married to Yahaya, the husband of Hawa Mai Danbu (daughter of
Nenu's daughter Rabi). Tanko Al'wali's mother, Hadiza, had also been married
to Malam Alhassan, son of Malam Garuba, further underlining the interconnectedness (Figure 28). One of their sons, Inanu, who was also a half-brother
to Tanko Al'wali, lived in the Al'wali compound in the 1950s. At that time,
Sabon Zongo was a CPP stronghold and Inanu was a core activist with the CPP;
thus, the compound became a center for CPP activity.

Al'wali's aged sons and daughter—Tanko, Dan Ladi and Sakinatu—continue
to live there, along with a number of their children and grandchildren. Tanko
Al'wali, the compound head, is the most senior. Like his father, he became
maaji, though to Idrissus's successor Lebo Bako. He subsequently switched
alliances and became Adamu Damaley's *galadima*.

The location of the Al'wali compound is known as *Unguwan* Damaley after
the self-proclaimed chief (his house is around the corner on Korle Bu Street
next door to Damaley Mosque). The area can even be called *Gangare*, located
as it is at the bottom of the slope from *Kan Tudu*. During the rainy season, it
is very muddy.

The compound has an enormous unpaved central courtyard, entered through
a *zaure* and ringed by rooms that open into the yard. It is about 420 square
meters, a lot of room, because the involution found in many (see, for example,
Gidan Baki, Figure 35, and the Kariki house, Figure 37) has not occurred. It

Figure 26
Alhaji Mohammed "Numbo" Bako House: Adult Resident Kin (Shaded).

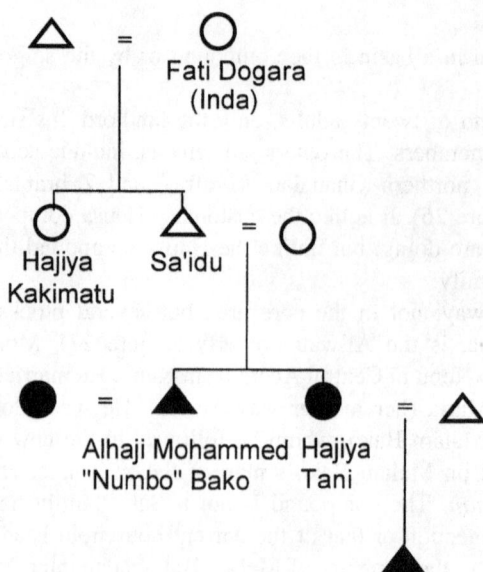

was a large enough piece of property to begin with and the descendants who would be heir to it did not proliferate—only five adult members of the family live there, so there are plenty of rooms. Moreover, with few exceptions, living quarters consist of only one room and not two. The openness of the yard is broken up by an animal pen and a huge pile of firewood, for sale by Sakinatu Al'wali.

I initially thought of the compound as uncomplicated, because of the yard's clear definition. I also had not taken into account the "add-ons"—rooms built on the outside by tenants—as well as the nooks and crannies at the corners.[5] In fact, it is very complicated, because nothing is uniform. It helped me understand why the housing on the survey map is so oddly shaped. Inside there are few straight lines. The compound quite simply is not rectangular.

The building materials vary from original structure to add-on to add-on—the old-fashioned mud wall, cement block, wood of varying kinds, iron. Wood and aluminum sheets are particularly evident on the outside rooms. The kitchen, shared by all, is a wooden lean-to, with attached pens for sheep and chickens. The joint structure is composed of wooden boards, panels, 2×4's, air conditioning vents, metal peg board sheets, chicken wire, and metal burglar proofing. The roofing of the housing is primarily rusting galvanized zinc, supplemented by aluminum and asbestos. As in most of the older properties, the roof is held in place by stones, broken furniture and wooden stools. There is only one outside wall (cement block) on the north side, which connects with an aluminum sheet wall, about five meters long, where there is no chamber and thus closes off the compound where it would otherwise be open. All of the structures facing the wall are unroofed. There are lanes bordering two of the sides, the road, so badly rutted it is not navigable by car, on the fourth.

Forty-three adults live here. The majority are tenants, including Zabrama, Dagomba, Frafra, Asante, Kwahu, and one Kotokoli. But more than one-third of the households are Hausa. There is a "condo," one room purchased from the Alwali's by a Hausa man, who sells shoes in Makola Market. He does not own the land but he does pay taxes. Tanko Al'wali knows all of the people in his compound well enough that he can go through the compound room by room and tell ethnicity for all and work for almost all. Life here is not anonymous. Typically, Al'wali hangs out with a group of male friends across the lane from the house, where there is a lean-to with a bench. In years past, he and his friends would have sat in the *zaure*, which at his house is a partial structure—there is no door at the inner edge. Now his brother, who is blind, is often found sitting or sleeping on a bench in the entryway.

COMPOUND SPACE—VARIATIONS ON A THEME

Alhaji Yaro's house in Unguwan Zabrama (Figure 29) is a variation on the synthetic Hausa theme. His compound is a genealogical and spatial extension of the Abokin Ango house, which is down the block and across the street from

Figure 27
Al'wali House, Plan #8.

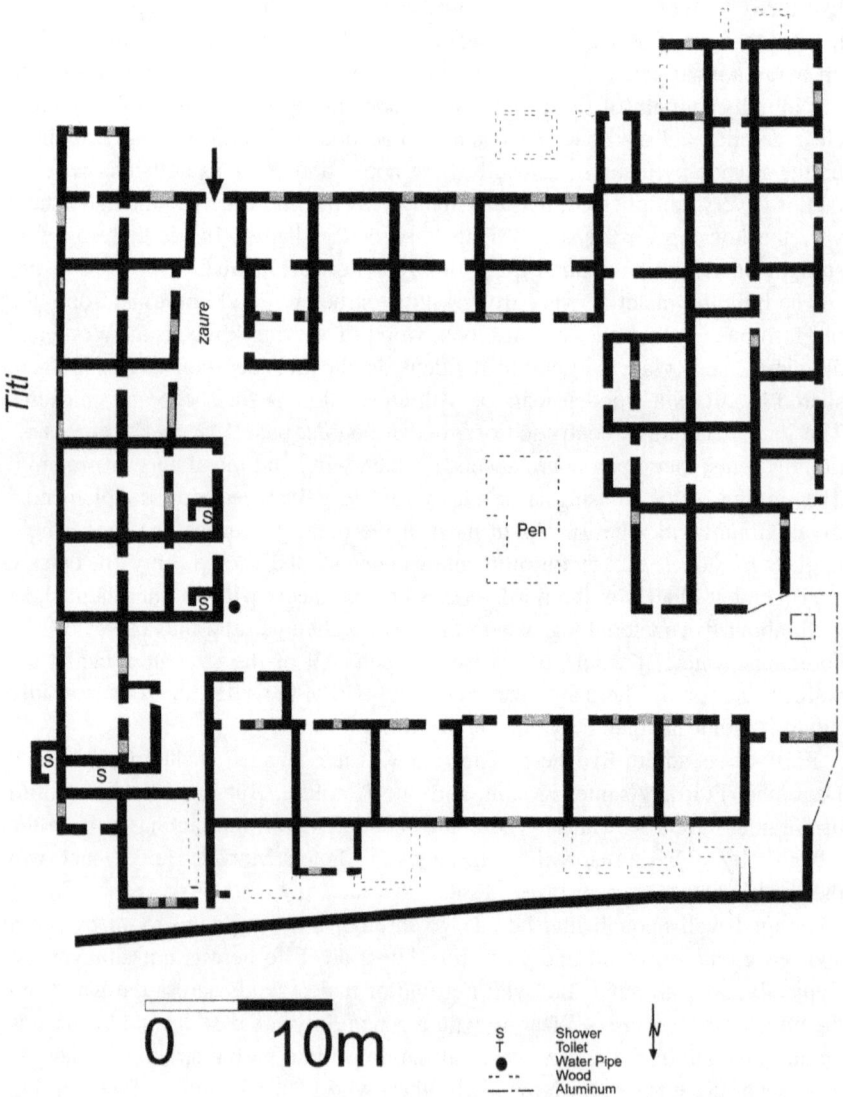

Abokin Ango Mosque. The first landlord was Abdula Dodu, a brother to Musa
Abokin Ango, who married into the Garuba family: Dodu's brother's wife
"Azumi" was Malam Garuba's son's Badamase's daughter (see Figure 11).

The property is enormous, both in space and number of inhabitants. Like the
classic form, it was built around a courtyard and retains the courtyard. Unlike
the classic form, however, it is now in four sections with four courtyards,

Figure 28
Al'wali House: Adult Resident Kin (Shaded).

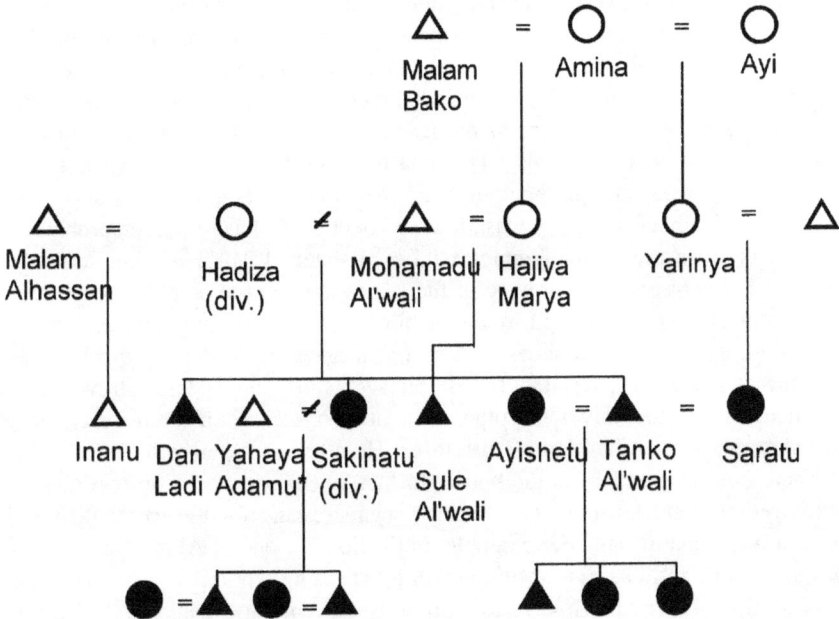

Malam
Bako   = Amina   = Ayi

Malam
Alhassan   =   Hadiza
(div.)   Mohamadu
Al'wali   = Hajiya
Marya   Yarinya   =

Inanu   Dan   Yahaya   Sakinatu   Ayishetu   Tanko   Saratu
Ladi   Adamu†   (div.)   Sule   Al'wali
Al'wali

*Alhaji Adamu Yahaya's father

the two rear sections clearly the oldest in physical terms, the front left the most modern. Alhaji Yaro, Dodu's son, built all four sections. The intial quadrant in the south east corner is where he and his father lived till their deaths (Yaro died in 1997). The *zaure* of the compound leads into his section. Over time, and with need, he built the second, third and fourth quadrants for his children, each with its own central yard. The lane into the property in effect has four termini, one at each of three compounds and one at the *zaure* that leads into the first-built quadrant.

All of the compound sections are paved. The main part of the property is mud and wattle; the additions and repairs make use of every possible material: wood, concrete, zinc, aluminum, asbestos. Seventeen rooms were built onto the outside of the house on three sides, jutting into lanes and alleys, by Alhaji Yaro; the walls and verandahs were constructed by tenants from wood, iron and cement block. The roofs are zinc, wood covered by felt, and aluminum.

Alhaji Yaro's room had an old-fashioned clock on the wall, a ceiling fan, piles of belongings, and floor mats for sitting. The room and chamber behind, however, were spacious. His wives have their *ƙayan ɗaki* in their own rooms. In the latter years of his life, Alhaji Yaro was blind and his feet were terribly swollen. Every day, he sat and dozed on the chair outside in front of his room, under an overhanging roof.

The property has a very extensive gutter system because of the way the house is sectioned. Each of the four has its own system of collection, which empties outside, including all manner of waste. Alhaji Yaro had a pan toilet (in Section #1). When we were measuring Section #2, there was a strong odor of urine and a child was peeing in the depression next to the gutter. This was not unusual: I noticed one of Alhaji Yaro's wives poured urine from the chamber pot into the gutter that runs through the compound. And then, as is the norm, she poured water from a rubber teapot, to wash it away. Section #2 has sanitation problems, I think, because the senior female member, a sister of Musa Abokin Ango, is blind and cannot oversee the state of the semi-public space. Alhaji Yaro's Section is not dirty, just cluttered by tables piled with household goods, clumps of old wood, egg crates, old shoes, and so forth. Section #4, the last quadrant, is certainly the cleanest, has the fewest piles of stuff and is least strewn with oddments. It has the only water pipe in the property. Three quadrants each have one shower room, Alhaji Yaro's has three. He also has a pan toilet.

There are many tailors in the house. In fact, every one of the professionally-employed resident kin does tailoring (or seamstressing for the women), much of it in individual rooms. For example, in Section #3, one of Alhaji Yaro's sons has a machine in his sitting room, which is where he works.

A total of 140 adults live in this property, seventy-six inside, sixty-four in the outside rooms. The degree of genealogical relationship, as in most houses, dictates who lives where (Figure 30). The most interior, Section #1, is where the elder, his wives and children have always lived. The furthest from the family core are the outside rooms, all occupied by tenants, with one exception: Alhaji Yaro's brother's grandson lives in the last room on the alley just behind Section #1. There is also, as one would imagine, far less ethnic variability within the compounds, than in the outside rooms. Section #1 is all Hausa, with one Zabrama and one Yoruba who have married into the family. Section #2's three Hausa are family, joined by seventeen northerners (Kusasi, Dagbani and Sisala) and some Kwahu. Section #3 is primarily Hausa, only one of whom is a tenant; the other tenants are Zabrama, Kotokoli, Asante and Kwahu. Section #4's only Hausa are family, the balance of seven tenants Zabrama and Akan (Asante, Akwapim and Akim).

Alhaji Yaro's cousin, his father's brother's son, was Ali Ango. For a number of years, Ali Ango had two wives. He kept both of them in seclusion in the main family house, down the block and across the street from the landmark Abokin Ango Mosque. In 1967, he took a third wife, Hajiya Kubra, a woman from the Bako family, and installed her in a room in Section 2 at Alhaji Yaro's. Unlike the first two wives, however, she refused to be put into *kulle*. As a consequence, the first two wives rebelled and refused to remain in seclusion.

One block west on Korle Bu Street is *Gidan Makaranta*, the school house (Figure 31). One of the involuted compounds, it is named for the Koranic school

(Fijr Islamic Primary School/Islamic Education School) that is located within and that the family has owned and run for years. The schoolroom periodically also houses refugees with no place to sleep.

The original owner was Fati Mohammed, a neighbor of Malam Bako's at Zongo Lane, where she had lived after migrating to the Gold Coast from Northern Nigeria. Fati followed Malam Bako to Sabon Zongo and he gave her a piece of land. (Her brother Abdullahi married one of Malam Bako's ex-wives.) In 1944, Fati's son Baba Goldsmith brought his two wives Kande (the senior wife) and Amarya from the outlying area of Fadama to live with him in his mother's house (his sister lives in Fadama to this day). Baba Goldsmith built a new room for Kande, but Kande's son Muhammad was getting married, so Kande gave him and his bride that room. (Mohammed married Basira, a great-granddaughter of Shekara, the ex-wife of Malam Nenu). Kande took Amarya's room, and Amarya took a tenant's room. It has stayed that way up to now (Figure 32).

Here as in many of Sabon Zongo's compounds, over time the space has been adapted and elaborated upon to meet the needs of an expanding family leading to involution (the shaded area in Figure 31). At least fifty years ago, Baba Goldsmith built a free-standing wooden chamber/hall in the central courtyard for his senior wife Kande; when she moved into another room, Goldsmith rented the middle room to a tenant. The room deteriorated. In 1969, Bako Goldsmith died. Everyone was given a share of the house. Kande's eldest child Hajiya Efisa ("Dodowa") re-built the middle wooden room, adding a little verandah. She gave it to her sister Hasana, who was living in Nigeria. A brother Huzefa was advised by a half-brother to trade his inherited piece of property with Hasana, and he did so. In the mid-1990s, when he had some money, he rebuilt the middle structure in concrete, finishing the foundation and the walls and framing the doorways and windows. Then he ran out of money, and for several years the two rooms were roofless and filled with debris. A few years later, he put up a roof, providing another spot for compound residents to sit out of the sun. It is now occupied by tenants. What once ate into the central space has now consumed it.

When Muhsin, the youngest of Amarya's seven children, was marrying in 1994, he converted the store on the western outside wall of the compound into a chamber and hall for him and his bride. As part of the marriage process, he had to acquire a large wardrobe for their bedroom; it is there that she, like every Hausa woman, has stacked her *kayan daki*. They also have a shower with a shower head.

Two of the compound's four sides are bordered by an outside wall—the rear (south) and interior (east). From the floor plan, one can see how the stores at the front and to the right (west) were probably created out of the original wall. The entrance at the front no longer has a *zaure* (and the gate no longer locks) but in times past did. There are two bucket bathrooms used by everyone who lives in the compound, and one spigot shower built by Muhsin on the verandah

Figure 29
Alhaji Yaro's House, Plan #6.

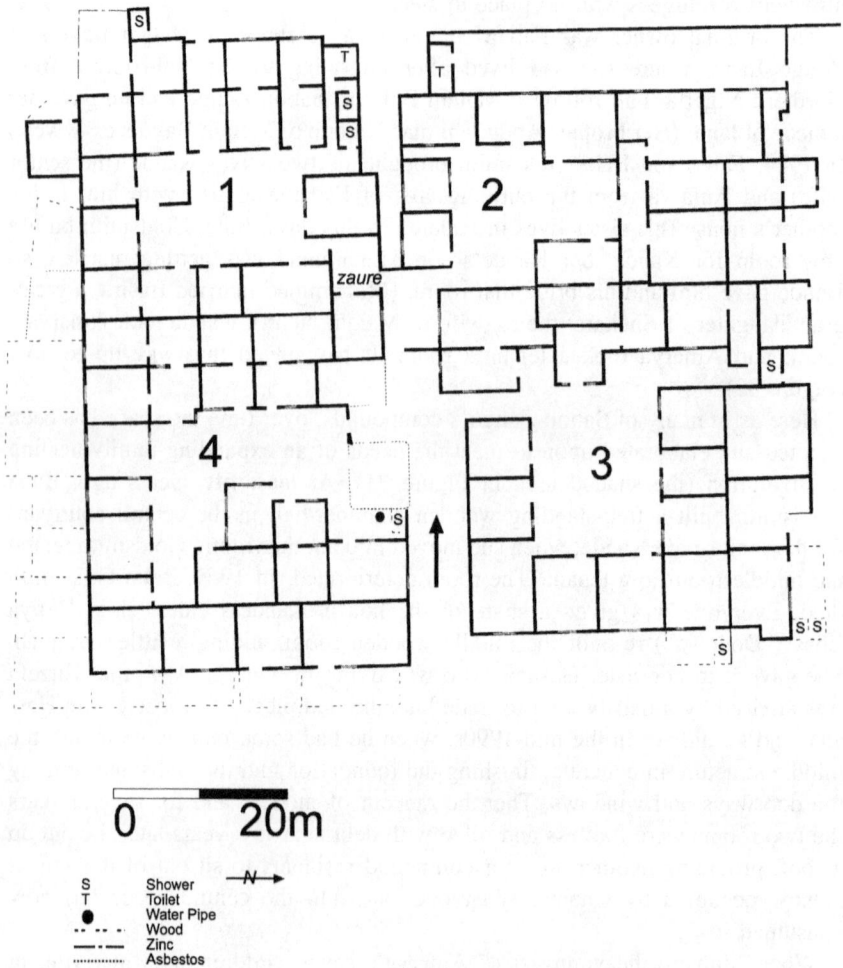

```
0        20m
```

S   Shower   —N→
T   Toilet
●   Water Pipe
–··–··– Wood
—··—·· Zinc
············· Asbestos

outside his set of rooms. The water spigot located outside the front entrance is kept locked. There is a second pipe inside Muhsin's quarters, near his shower.

There are forty-one adult residents, almost half of them Hausa; the balance (Wangara, Kotokoli, Busanga and Fante) are all tenants. The tenants, while in the majority, are not especially evident, because multiple numbers share rooms. Moreover, they are away at work during the day. This is when the adult kins-women of the compound and their daughters and grandchildren are particularly evident. Everyday, they congregate on the raised verandah outside one of the rooms. They eat there; they pray there; they doze and they chat. Until her death in 1999, Kande sold tobacco from inside. Amarya's daughter Fati who lives at

i Yaro's House: Adult Resident Kin (Shaded).

ion 1.

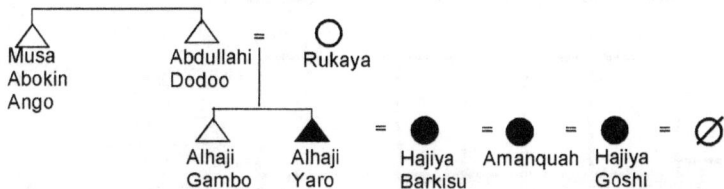

ion 2.

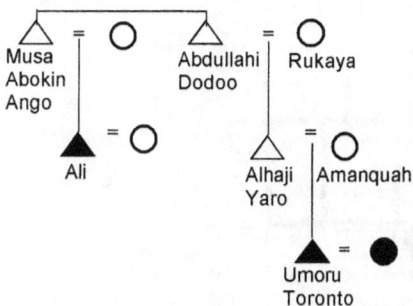

ion 3.

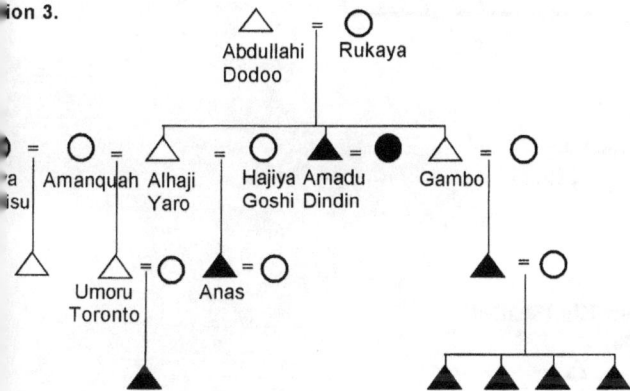

ion 4.

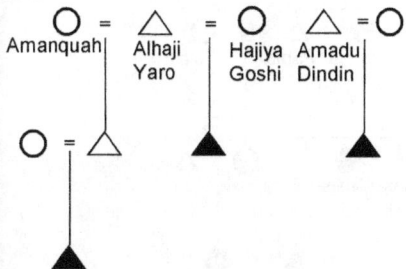

Figure 31
Bako Goldsmith (*Gidan Makaranta*) House, Plan #7 (Involution Shaded).

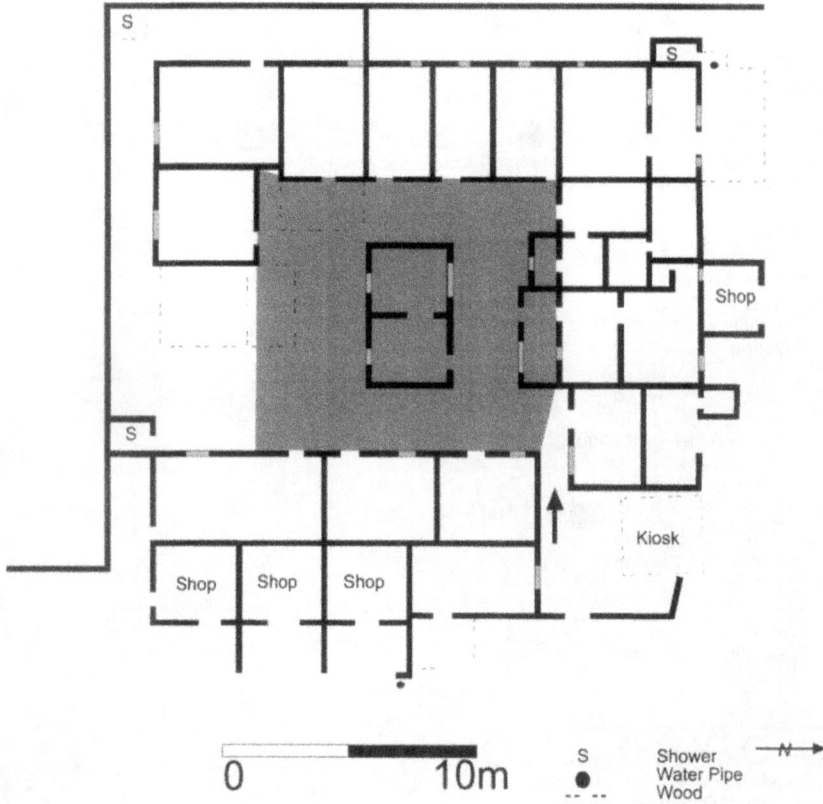

Figure 32
Bako Goldsmith's House: Adult Resident Kin (Shaded).

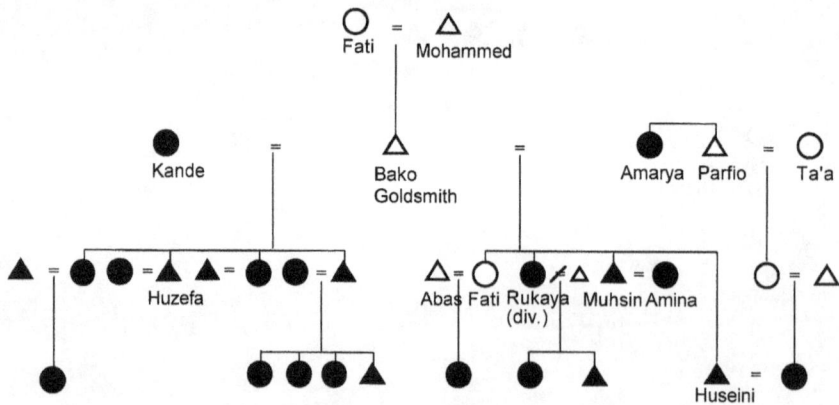

Gidan Baƙi (see Figure 35), makes pasta (*taliya*) and brings the finished noodles to her mother's house to sell. She hangs out with the other compound women kin. For several months, she set up shop late in the afternoon just outside the compound under a roof, frying and selling yam, cassava and sweet potato. While the foot traffic for prepared food selling is good outside of her own compound, she came to sell at her mother's for reasons of tradition.

As is true in many local Hausa families, once Amarya's grandchildren reach the age of five, most of those living in Sabon Zongo stay with her at night; they generally sleep on mats on the cement floor in her room. When her daughter Rukaya left her husband after 20-plus years of marriage, also following tradition she returned to her parent's house, bringing her daughters (one of them only a baby) with her. Certainly in this house, the compound space is monopolized throughout the day by the family women, resident and non-resident. It is rare to see non-resident men within, in part perhaps because the elders are women. But several of the adult family men are around, because they teach at the family's Koranic school.

Up the side road from *Gidan Makaranta* is the compound of Haruna Bawa Allah (Figure 33), another unrelated follower of Malam Bako, whose name appears on the early map as one of those allocated property in Sabon Zongo. Haruna Bawa Allah came to the Gold Coast from Sokoto State; he was a herbalist, who travelled around Accra curing people. "He lived here in the bush before anyone, because he had very strong medicine" (Papa Carlos, grandson, 6/9/2000). A mural on the front outside wall states that Abu [bakar] Bawa Allah is "a licensed herbalist, who deals in sexual weakness in men, women's problems, and. . . . Seeing is believing." Bawa Allah's wife Hanatu ("Amarya") had lived at Opera, near the old *zongo* area. He met her through his trade.

The house, on the edge of *Kan Tudu*, sits on a rise: along both roadside walls, it is several steps up. Shops open onto the outside verandah. To the left of the entrance is a locked water pipe. The old *zaure* is framed by a large-leafed tree known as *gujiya*, and throughout the day residents and friends sit there in the shade.

The compound house is in effect divided in half, the tenants primarily on the western side of the property, where they share one bath. The yard is paved and is about 356 square meters—except that a structure containing six rooms was built in the middle, another example of involution (see shaded area of Figure 33). The first middle structure ("extension") was built by Musa Bawa Allah, Haruna Bawa Allah's son, for his wife Hajiya Mari. The second middle structure, built in the mid-1990s, was built by Isaka, son of Musa Bawa Allah. There are currently tenants living there.

There is a locked standing pipe inside the compound and seven bathrooms, two of which are opposite the senior kinsman's room and one, with a shower head, kept locked. There are also two kitchens, where women may keep their utensils; unless it is raining, all cook outside. The property is completely unwalled and the four rooms at the rear—combination bed/sitting rooms—are windowless.

Figure 33
Haruna Bawa Allah House, Plan #10 (Involution Shaded).

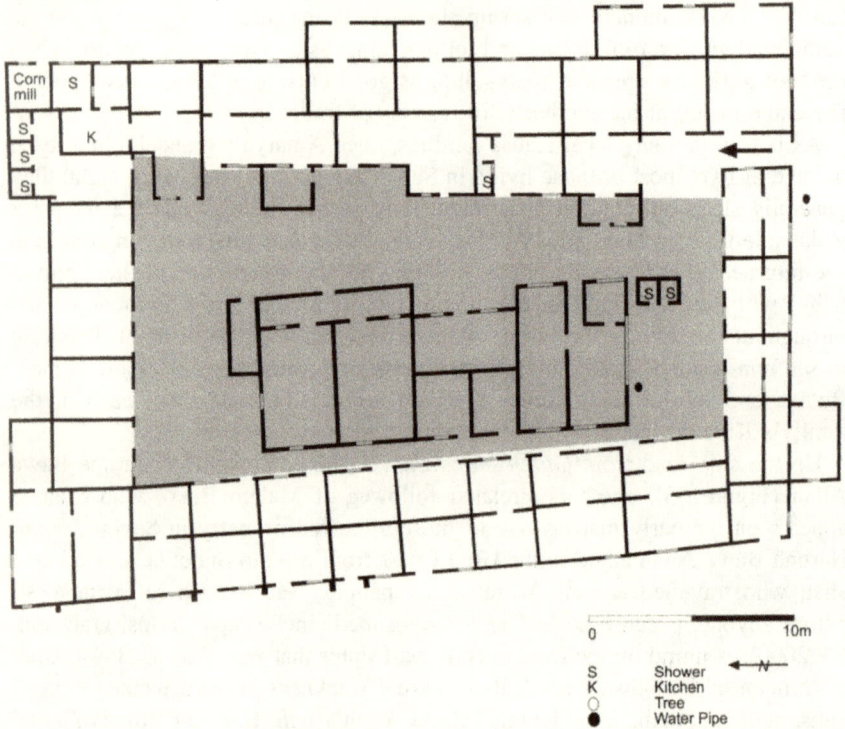

S	Shower
K	Kitchen
○	Tree
●	Water Pipe

Figure 34
Haruna Bawa Allah House: Adult Resident Kin (Shaded).

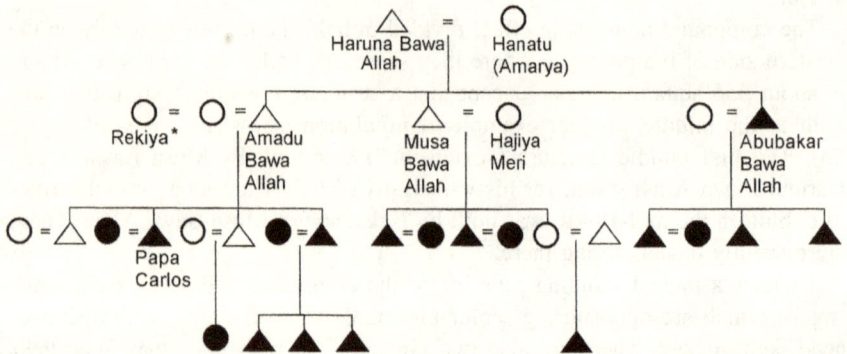

*Divorced fro Sha'aibu Bako

Haruna Bawa Allah was succeeded by his three sons, of whom only Abubakar Bawa Allah was still alive when I was interviewing in the compound.
This house has forty-five rooms, and many of the residents have a chamber/hall
arrangement. The last son of the original owner has two single rooms with a
verandah, and his own shower at the front of the compound. The widow of one
of the sons of the original owner has two rooms and her own shower. Here genealogy does not necessarily dictate location or size of living quarters. For example, a husband and wife who are tenants have two rooms, whereas a
grandson and his wife have only one. Two rooms were built on the outside using cement block. One is quite finished looking and painted pink; the second is
in effect an entryway built on with a door to a room from that side. One resident, a grandson of the original owner, has a two-room "almost self-contained"
house, with fancy masonry and window screening. In fact, he lives primarily at
another house, Bawa Villa, in the newish community Awushie, about 20
minutes away.

Forty adults live in this compound (see Figure 34). Seventeen are Hausa, all
of whom are members of the Bawa Allah family; the other twenty-three are
tenants, except four who are married to family members. The non-Hausa include
four Zabrama, six Kwahu, two other Akan, two Ga, five Ewe, one Kotokoli,
two Dagarti, and one Yoruba. In this Muslim Hausa family compound, one-half
of the residents are not Muslims; the two Ga women and one of the Kwahu
women are.

There are always people in the compound: one of the male kinsman is an
architectural draftsman and works in his room; a couple of the elders are retired;
and a couple of the younger kinsmen are unemployed. One of the Akan owns
a chop bar in front of the house. Stopping by at 5:30 P.M. residents are beginning
to return from their work day. Some sit outside under the tree or on the verandah.
The groundnut seller was preparing wet groundnuts to sell (it was the season).
A bit before 6:15 prayers, the senior kinsman brought a stool out of his room
and, like always, sat near the shower room at gutter, doing ablutions for prayer
at home before going to the mosque. Some of the children and some of the
adults were bathing. Fufu was being pounded for the evening meal. The air-
dried clean laundry was taken off the lines that criss-cross the yard.

Leaving the Bawa Allah house and walking east through *Kan Tudu* to the
Night Market field, crossing the field, passing by two of Sabon Zongo's most
beautiful full trees while continuing on for another two blocks, one enters the
edge of Ayigbetown, also known as *Unguwan* Tripoli (because of the house
where they used to show films) or *Sabon Gida* ("new house"). The compound
on the corner of Ancobra Street, kitty-cornered from Idrissu's Mosque, is called
Gidan Baki (Figure 35). *Gidan Baki* exemplifies the problem of property inheritance when the family is large and the options for building are limited.

It was founded by Salisu Abubakar, a son of Malam Garuba, first Chief Imam
of Ghana. He was one of the signatories to the letter announcing Idrissu Bako's
elevation to chief. He married Hajiya Meri, a daughter of Shekara, ex-wife of

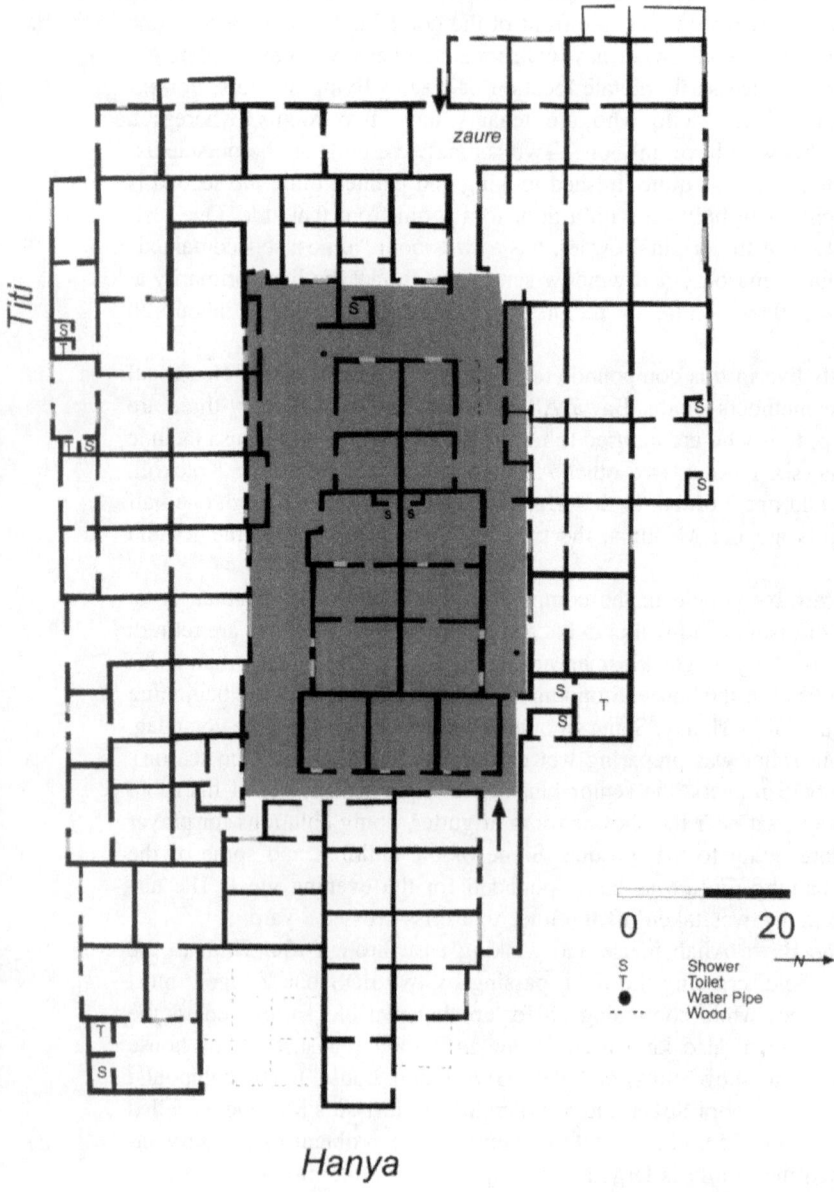

Figure 35
Salisu Abubakar (*Gidan Baƙi*) Housem, Plan #13 (Involution Shaded).

Figure 36
Salisu Abubakar House (*Gidan Baki*): Adult Resident Kin (Shaded).

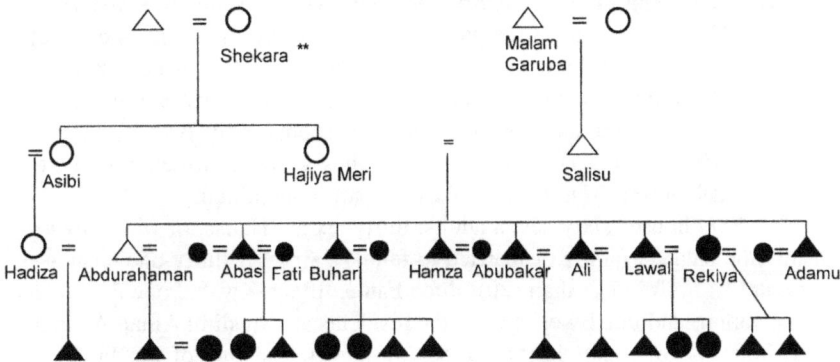

**Ex-wife of Malam Nenu

Nenu; his brother Badamase married Abu, the daughter of Nenu's brother (see Figures 11 and 36).

While there are tenants in this compound, it is thought of as a family house—twenty lineal kinsmen live there. All of Salisu's children (including the eight sons and their sons living here now) were born in this house. His son Ilyashu lives elsewhere in Sabon Zongo, and that is because he succeeded in building his own house (see Figure 41). The living quarters of the sons tend to be more elaborate than those of the other residents—including chamber/hall and verandah and shower—and for the elder, there are three rooms and also a pan toilet.

In local parlance, *Gidan Baki* is bordered on two sides by a *lungu* (an alley, only walkable), on one side a *titi* (street, where there is actually public transportation), and on one side a *hanya* (road, walkable only because of its condition). The house is a superb example of the involuted compound. As at Bawa Allah's house, there is no yard. But it is a larger plot (approximately 1,114 square meters as compared to Bawa's 950 square meters), the rooms are smaller and there are more of them. *Gidan Baki* has eighty-seven rooms, while Bawa Allah's has fifty-eight (as everywhere in the community, sometimes a "residence" consists of one room, sometimes two or more), and more people live here. Moreover, involution has made it a far more complex structure, more like a maze. It is impossible to walk straight through. It has two entrances: there is a *zaure* on the southern *lungu*; on the *hanya* at the opposite end, the entrance is like a hallway, framed by the outside wall of the house next door. Abubakar, the senior brother-owner, controls his wing of the compound, locking the *zaure* gate around 1 A.M. when the tea-seller comes in; the other end is not locked because night owls will pound to be let in.

The compound is built from cement block, though add-on rooms are wood. Many of the rooms lack windows, and since everyone shuts and locks the door to their room at night, it means that people sleep in airless rooms. With no courtyard, air cannot circulate and residents have little area in which to gather. There is barely room to hang laundry. On Alhaji Hamza's side (the *titi*), Asante decorative blocks frame the veranda. This side is where the senior men live; it is also on this side that there are three of the four pan toilets, which along with three of the showers are located inside the seniors' "apartments" and for seniors' use. The compound boasts another six shower rooms, only two of which are located within the semi-public domain (and thus available to tenants). Part of the roof is galvanized iron, part is asbestos, part is aluminum.

Gidan Baƙi houses sixty-seven adults; thirty-six are Hausa, of whom four are tenants (the balance family or married to family). Another thirty-one tenants are Zabrama (3), Frafra (7), Akan (20): three Fante, fifteen Kwahu, one Asante and one Akwapim) and one Ewe. Most of the residents are Muslim: Alhaji Abubakar is the imam at *Masalaci* Idrissu across the street, and one of the Frafra's is Muslim. But one of the Christian tenants is the pastor of Jesus Generation, an evangelical church. Some residents complain about the loud Christian singing at all hours by him and his two sisters who share a room on the north side. Painted on the wall next to their door is the aphorism "I Try to Make Them Understand."

A number of the Hausa residents use the home or its vicinity in pursuing an occupation: a shoemaker works next to his room; two pasta sellers and a *pinkaso* trader prepare the foods to sell; the kerosene and fruit sellers sit in the doorway; and the tailors sew in the kiosk outside. Fati, whose family owns *Gidan Makaranta*, hangs her pasta to dry on clothesline in her veranda. She then carries it to her mother's in a basket, selling some of it there, sending the rest with one of her daughters to hawk around the community.

The complexity of *Gidan Baƙi* is matched, even exceeded, by the Kariki compound (Figure 37). The latter is located in *Gangare*, about three blocks north of the *Baƙi* house and just west of Gaskiya Cinema near Oblogo Road. Indeed, the modern storied buildings on Oblogo provide a jarring contrast to the dirty white-washed walls and rusted roofing of Kariki's compound. The property has 128 rooms and is locally referred to as *gari guda* (an entire city). Like *Gidan Baƙi*, one cannot really tell how large it is, because it has no setback from the road or alley. Like Alhaji Yaro's, it has generated more than one section. But unlike Yaro's, the three house sections are of different shapes and sizes and like *Gidan Baƙi*, the involution occurs in two of them, albeit in varying ways. For many years, the Kariki family had the land to keep expanding, by building the two additional compounds on either side of the original one. House #3 was built in the 1970s.

The senior member is Alhaji Abdullahi Kariki, son of Musa Kariki, grandson of Ali Musa. Ali Musa migrated from Kano to Salaga in the north of Ghana. His son, Musa Kariki, was born in Accra. He followed Malam Bako to Sabon Zongo and was given the plot of land. He was one of the signatories to the letter announcing Idrissu Bako's elevation to chief. And while the Kariki family is not related to the Bako's, when Idrissu Bako became chief, he chose Musa as his Sarkin Fada. Musa's son Abdullahi was Sha'aibu Bako's Sarkin Fada. Moreover, Abdullahi is married to Ramatu, daughter of Idrissu Bako.

There are 105 adults living in the three sections that were built sequentially (see Figure 38).[6] The "family house" was the first built by Musa Kariki; Abdullahi was born in this house and has always lived here. This segment has the most obvious compound yard, with a tree in the middle. The rooms clearly ring the yard, which is entered through a proper *zaure* from the road. This house is home to thirty adults, and today one-third of them are tenants. All of the Hausa (eighteen adults) are family (two work overseas but keep rooms here). The tenants include Dagomba, Mamprussi, Zabrama, Wangara, Ewe, and six Akwapim. One of the tenants (a Mamprussi) is Muslim.

House #2, like House #1, is entered from the road, but the entryway is an unroofed hallway. It was built adjacent to House #1 by Abdullahi's father, for family and also for tenants. This segment is long and narrow, its depth the same as the other two combined. It encompasses two vestigial courtyards—a long one just inside the entryway, which has been consumed by a block of three rooms, a minor one in the rear. The house has fifty-three adults: thirty-four Hausa, of whom nineteen are family and fifteen tenants; the balance of the tenants are Busanga, Kotokoli (5), Akan (9, primarily Kwahu), and four Ewe.

In 1999, Abdullahi built a mosque in the unoccupied front rooms of House #2.

House #3, to the rear of House #1, is entered off the *lungu*. It was also built by Abdullahi and like #2, for both family and tenants. Abdullahi also constructed a set of rooms around 1992 that consumes what had been the courtyard. They belong to a son who has been living in the United States but retains his property rights here. There are twenty-two adults resident here: nine are Hausa, of whom four are tenants; the rest are all tenants: four Zabrama, and then Buzanga, Kotokoli, Yoruba, Ewe, and Fante. Until Abdullahi's second wife Meri died in 1996, she lived in this compound.

In terms of amenities, House #1 has the sole water pipe, which means a lot of traffic from residents in the other two houses coming to fetch water. All three houses have shower rooms: House #1 has three showers, one of which is within a verandah; House #2 has six showers, two of which are attached to individual rooms; and House #3 has two showers, one of which is in Hajiya Meri's room. The compound yards are paved. The structures are mud or cement block. The only wooden structures are outside attachments.

Most of the residents who work or trade do so elsewhere in Sabon Zongo or Accra. A number of the Hausa, however, are able to pursue their occupations in or near the house: the women who make *taliya* do so in their respective rooms; the malam teaches in the house; a number of the tailors work in a shop just outside or in their rooms; a male family member sells TV licenses in a kiosk outside; and women cook and sell porridge, *kosai* or *masa* out front or in the alley. There is also an Ewe "washman" who launders and irons at his home on

Figure 37
Musa Kariki House, Plan #19 (Involution Shaded).

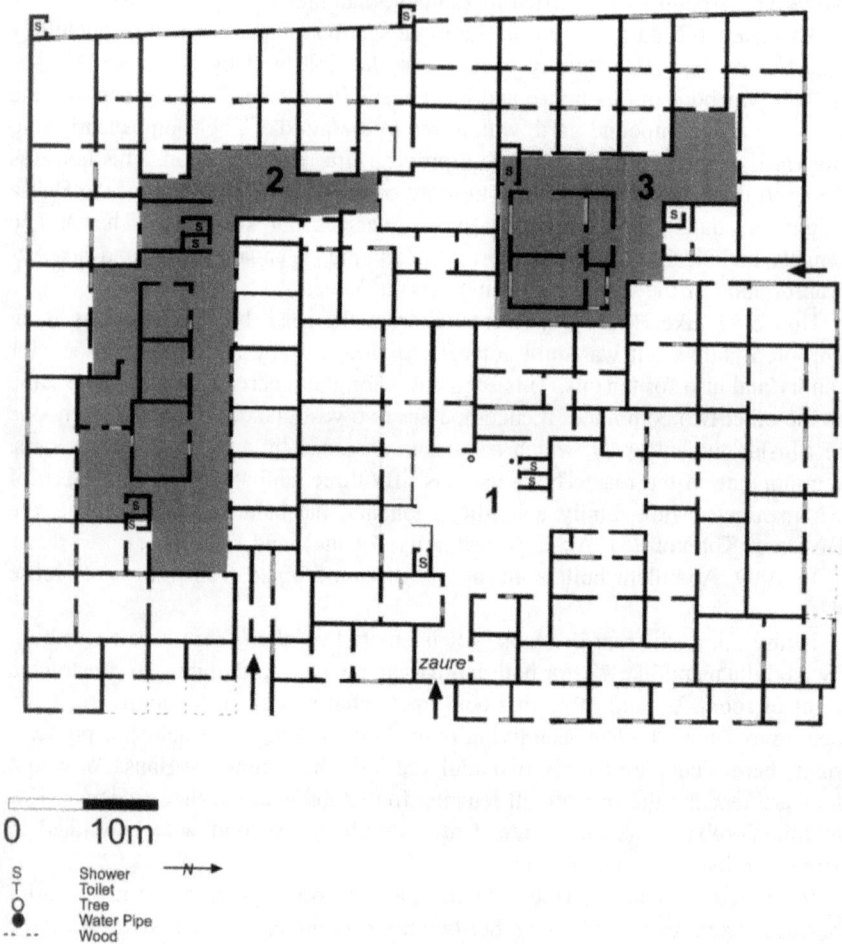

```
0        10m

S      Shower         —N—▶
T      Toilet
O      Tree
●      Water Pipe
-- --  Wood
```

the alley and whose wife is a petty trader in the doorway. The tailors who work at home include an Asante man and wife.

It is House #1 particularly that has the feel of a traditional compound, given the formal *zaure*, the tree and water spigot, the particular kin who live there, the women gathering in the compound yard. But it also expresses the social changes that have occurred over time: non-family, indeed non-Hausa and non-Muslims, hiring rooms there, the blurring of male-female separateness as women engage in trade outside of the house and as at Badamase's, claim the *zaure*. The Hausa men of the combined house never hang out in the *zaure* but are often found in front by the road, sitting on benches along the outer wall or across the road under a shelter.

Figure 38
Musa Kariki House: Adult Resident Kin (Shaded).

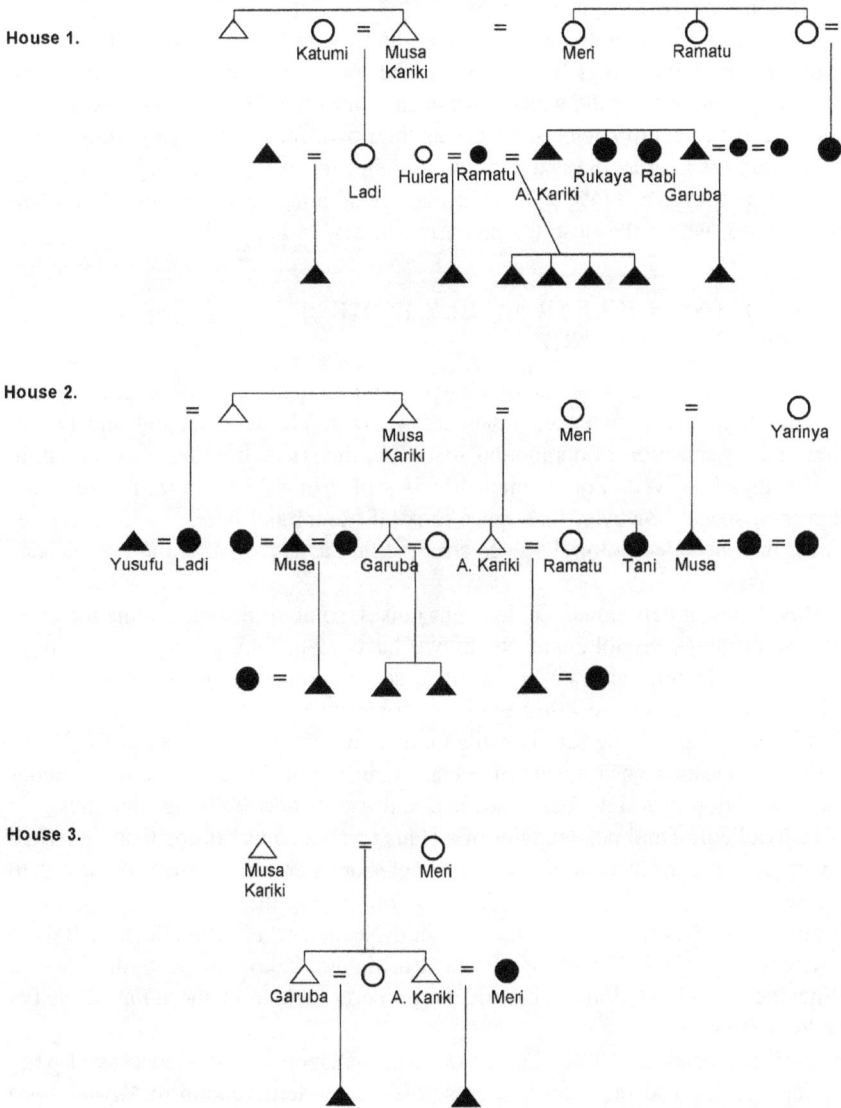

At four every afternoon, male friends from around the community convene in the road down from the *zaure* to play cards.

In all of the involuted houses I have just detailed, one no longer traverses the yard in full sight of everyone. The yard is gone and one walks along lanes that snake through the compound around the newer structures. The rationale of the courtyard, whether climatic or social, is lost. The interior of the compounds that have undergone involution are reminiscent of the narrow meandering lanes of the original *zongo* in Central Accra.

And yet, a compound space is created and used. The conceptual division of cooking and eating areas carved out of the whole has been actualized by the physical boundaries of the walls to these structures that fill in the yard. Residents still manage to claim enclosed spaces as their own for sleeping or getting in out of the rain (as long as they have rights to them; for example, if they are tenants, as long as they pay rent); and residents "own" areas in the semi-public compound yard, which they use for preparing meals, eating, and so on.

TENANT AND NUCLEAR FAMILY HOMES:
EXTREMES OF CHANGE

Since the early days of Sabon Zongo, with changes in society at large that have included independence, urbanization, economic development and migration, the organization of compound space and the social life that goes on within has changed as well. For women, life is still primarily organized around the domestic space; however, that space looks different and is less exclusively defined. Its embedded cultural values are modified as is the particular significance of the space.

Development here comes in different guises, some of it social, some material. Family holdings predominate but as we have seen, family houses have been modified to incorporate non-kin. In fact, some compounds have been built for tenants only, and at the other extreme, some have been built for the nuclear family only. Redefining family obligations and units of cohabitation for Hausa calls into question basic tenets of social organization. Material change includes the installation of toilets, better setback and use of new building materials.

Hajiya Pedro Onukpe, daughter of a Hausa woman and Yoruba man, inherited her house (Figure 39) on Korle Bu Street from her father. He had moved to Accra from Nigeria, living first at Tudu before buying the Sabon Zongo property from Malam Neze, a Fulani man. Malam Neze, one of Chief Idrissu Bako's advisors, was given the piece of land by Malam Bako and he built a house. When he moved to Odonkor, he sold the property to Alhaji Umoru Faruk, Hajiya Pedro's father.

Until her death in 1996, Hajiya was one of Sabon Zongo's successful petty capitalists. She had the stacks of casseroles (a modern version of *ƙayan ɗaki*) in one of her rooms. She owned other houses/rooms in Sabon Zongo, a small "fleet" of taxis (three), two private cars, was a wholesaler of toothbrushes and tooth paste and had a store in Accra. When she died, her daughter found a staggering amount of Dutch wax cloth among her possessions: more than 400 sewn outfits, more than 160 half pieces (six yards each) as yet unsewn. Moreover, she had built a duplex with all the amenities in Awnshie, a peri-urban area about 20 minutes away.

Hajiya Pedro's compound is compact and though on paper it looks neat, when I was there in 1995 and 1996, it was actually shabby. The compound was compact, the yard dirt, the platform-like edging in front of the rooms cement. A hen coop and a pen were used to keep the animals inside at night. The kitchen was for storing utensils, as all cooking was done outside. The front wall was a combination of cement block on one side of the doorway and aluminum on the other. Atop the wall was broken glass, to discourage thieves. On the cement was written:

Mallam Umaru
General Merchant
Herbalist for Treatment
of all Diseases of Men, Women
& Children

and beneath the sign was a cement prayer platform. There was no longer a resident herbalist, though there was a church prophetess (Christian) and a soothsayer (Muslim).

A ramshackle but effective wooden pen was built outside in front for the sheep her son Zakari washed every week. Hajiya had planned to tear down the wooden rooms in front and behind and replace the wood with cement blocks. Indeed, in spring 2001, the front was being rebuilt and a second floor "raised," paid for by a son living in Germany. The house has fourteen rooms. Hajiya kept three for herself—a chamber/hall combination for sitting and sleeping and a single room as a storeroom. Her bedroom in the southwest corner contained piles of clothing. At times, Hajiya slept on a mat on the floor.

There were eighteen adults (see Figure 40): the five and one-half Hausa/one-half Yoruba all family, the two Wangara tenants Muslims, the Frafra, and Kwahu tenants Christian. Two of Hajiya's grown children live and work overseas, in addition to the son in Germany, a daughter in Liberia. Significantly, like members of family houses all over *zongo*, they maintain their ties by holding onto their rooms; in this case, this is at the mother's house, where her last husband lived till his own death twenty-nine days before hers. Hajiya's son was a fitting mechanic in front of the house; the soothsayer worked in his room, and three of the Kwahu women owned the provisions store across the street.

Like Hajiya Pedro, Ilyashu Salisu owns his compound, known as "Small London" (Figure 41). Unlike Hajiya Pedro, he built it himself. Ilyashu is a member of the *Gidan Baki* family, a grandson of Imam Garuba. He was a worker at the Pepsi factory when he bought the land in Municipal (Ayigbetown) from Lebo Bako before Lebo became chief. Ilyashu spent nine years (1957–1966) building the house. From 1966 until 1985, he had tenants living here while he remained at his father's. He moved in with his wife and sons in 1985. Ilyashu has a chamber/hall, with a verandah. But his spatial allocation is no

Figure 39
Hajiya Maimouna Pedro Onukpe House, Plan #19.

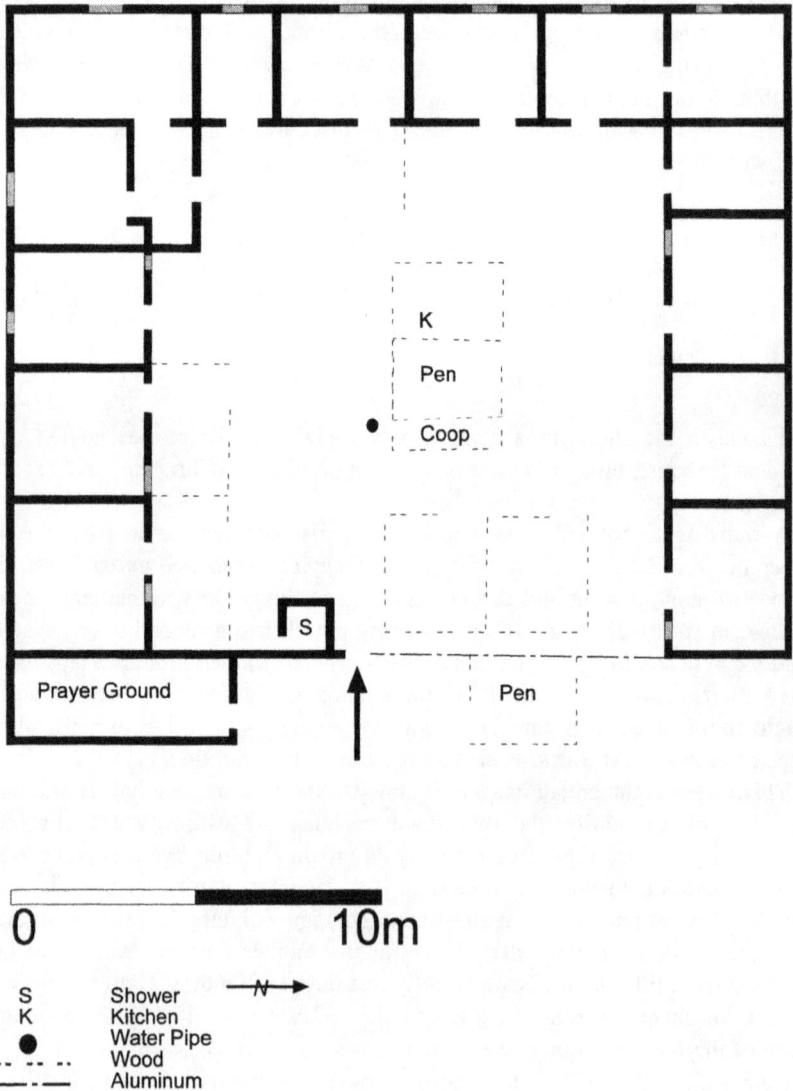

0 ——————————— 10m

S   Shower   ⟶N⟶
K   Kitchen
●   Water Pipe
-- -- .. Wood
——-—   Aluminum

greater than some of the tenants. His quarters are opposite the compound entrance.

Twenty-four adults live in this compound, only six of whom are family (see
Figure 42). Several of the tenants, including Akan and Ga, have lived in this
house since 1980; another Ga, who is a friend of the son and became Muslim,
has lived here since childhood. The six Hausa are all family. In addition to Ga

Figure 40
Hajiya Maimouna Pedro Onukpe House: Adult Resident Kin (Shaded).

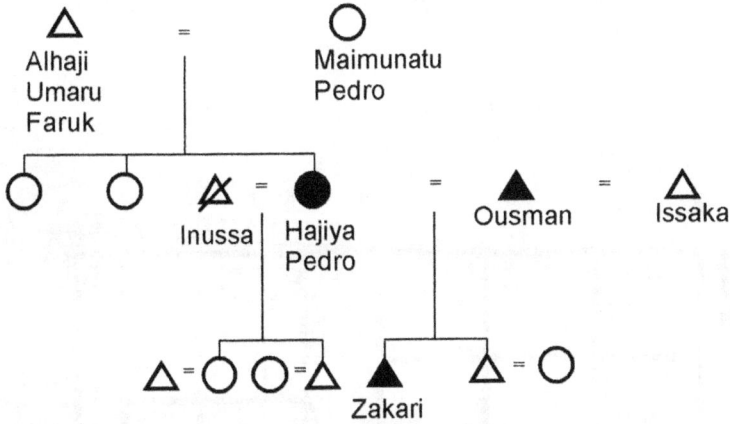

(3) and Akan (10), the tenants are Kotokoli, Busanga and Gao (Timbuktoo Mosque, and some Malians, are nearby).

This house represents an interesting cross between a traditional compound and a single family house. It is rectangular, it has a central yard, everyone shares the semi-public space—for cooking, hanging laundry and so on. There is a wall at the back of the compound, and four rear rooms are entered from the space created. Yet the compound sits alone like a single bungalow. It is built entirely from concrete blocks—only the doors and animal pens are wooden. The roof is not rusted and it is properly attached. The compound shows little signs of wear and tear. The yard is paved and it is clean and tidy. There is a front gate, which is locked at night, but nothing akin to a *zaure*. To the right of the front doorway is a separate room for a corn mill. The family raises rabbits for the children to sell. An unroofed patio with decorative cement blocks leads from the yard into Ilyahsu's rooms. There are two shower rooms and a KVIP, the latter for family only. Near the toilet there is an animal pen and a hen coop. In front of the compound, there is another animal pen and a kiosk which houses the electronic business of one of Ilyashu's sons.

Residents pursue a variety of occupations in or near the house. In addition to the electrician, there is corn grinding and kenkey preparation and sale; a seamstress works in the house; and a Muslim woman who sells gari, sugar, groundnuts near the front door. (One of the Ga women residents sells kenkey at her mother's in Accra.)

Ilyashu noted he has never had to contact an agent to fill a vacant room in the compound. When tenants are packing up, people seeking lodging come in and ask. So renting has been entirely by word of mouth. But just as this house began as a rental property only, so it can evolve into a new family house, for

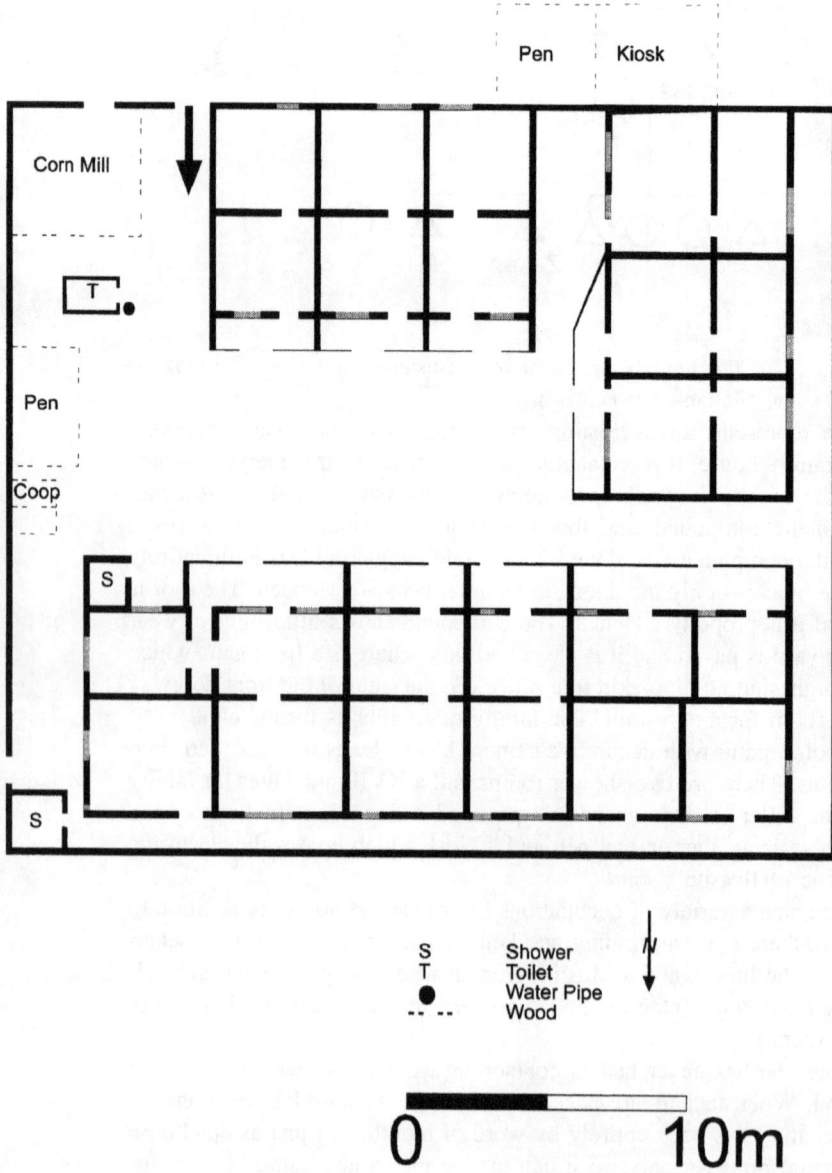

Figure 41
Ilyashu Salisu ("Small London") House, Plan #18.

Pen   Kiosk

Corn Mill

T

Pen

Coop

S

S

S   Shower
T   Toilet
●   Water Pipe
-- --   Wood

0   10m

Figure 42
Ilyashu Salisu House: Adult Resident Kin (Shaded).

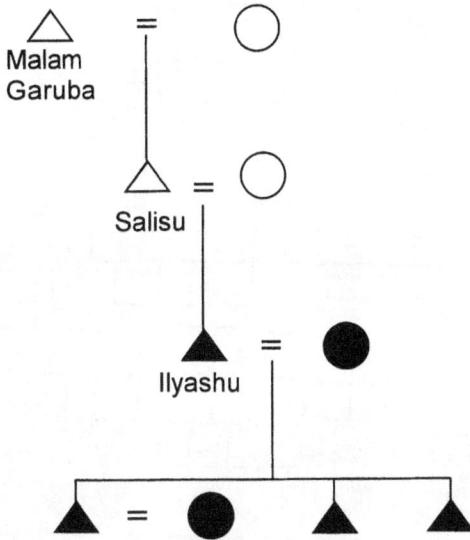

Ilyashu's line. As his sons marry and have children, he will have a place for them.

Some blocks south in Ayigbetown lives Alhaji Baba Mai Doki (a.k.a. Suleiman Bako), a son of Idrissu Bako and one of Sabon Zongo's highly respected elders. His residence is opposite *Gidan Baƙi* in a compound that he co-owns with his sister. He also owns a fair amount of rental property in Sabon Zongo, including the housing one-half block east that wraps around the mosque named after his father. The property (Figure 43) includes the mosque (*Masalaci* Idrissu), a small compound on the north side, and rooms all the way round the back that open out onto the empty space. On the south side of the mosque is a pen with lots of sheep but there is also usually a horse there. The house (really individual rooms) was originally a stable, which may explain why little of it is mud or cement—almost all is built out of wood.

Idrissu built the housing currently behind the mosque for family. There were four rooms and a wall was made out of zinc. When the residents died, he began to rent out rooms to tenants. All around were fields. A fine horseman, Baba Mai Doki (Baba the horseman) went to Nigeria in the 1950s and brought back two horses: Fear God and Fear Judgement. Baba constructed three rooms, two for horses, one for a horse boy. He built stables on his property the year that Queen Elizabeth came to Accra (1960). Inside the stable house, there are seven stable rooms, which have housed as many as twenty horses. There is the semblance of a courtyard, with a dirt floor, and rooms open into the yard on two sides. They house the boys and men (and their families) who work with the horses.

Figure 43
Alhaji Baba Mai Doki's Rental Property (Suleiman Idrissu Bako), Plan #14.

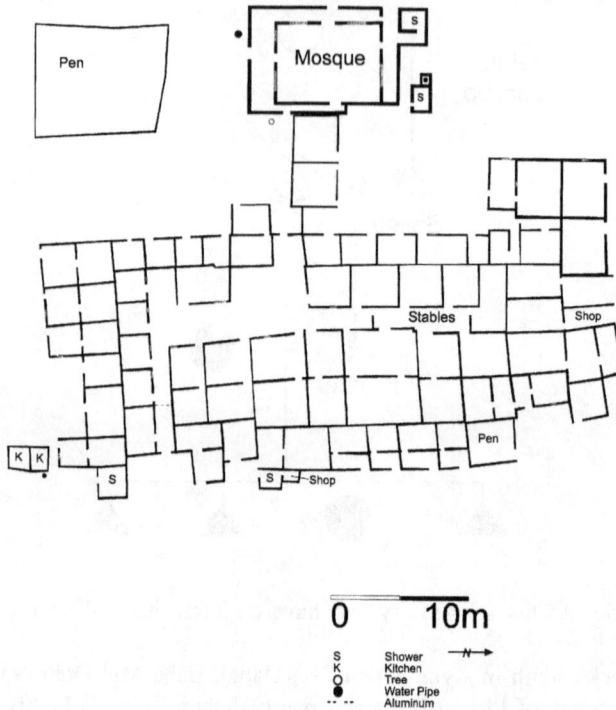

As the number of horses waxes and wanes, the stables outside near the mosque are enlarged or reduced. In 1996, a turkey coop that was not being used was disassembled. With the addition of wood from the outside stable that was also taken apart, a room was built near the stable boys for a trader in men's clothing from Baba Mai Doki's family in Zaria, Nigeria, who planned to come periodically to sell embroidered *baban riga*.

The story of Idrissu's Mosque, according to Baba Mai Doki, is that one day in the 1970s, a Syrian man asked who owned the land in front of the stables. He said he wanted to build a mosque and give it to Baba. He asked if Baba could come up with a plan. Baba said yes, brought him a plan, and the man agreed. He asked if there were workers; Baba said yes. The man brought earth, cement, stone. Baba found workers, and he and Alhaji Huudu, a son of Lawal and first cousin to Baba, oversaw the task. It took three months to build the mosque (Baba Mai Doki 6/1/1996). When Alhaji Huudu was still working as a tailor, his workroom was across the road. Now that he is retired, he hangs out at the mosque all day, taking the role of *madubin masalaci* ("the eye glasses of the mosque"). Baba now boards and trains race horses for owners who live elsewhere in Accra. Throughout the day, he too sits alongside the mosque, overseeing horse care and watching his goats. Everyday, men and women come to ask his counsel on a variety of concerns.

All 58 adult residents are tenants. They represent a breathtaking melange of ethnicities: almost half are Ewe and one-quarter Hausa; the rest are Yoruba, Wanagara, Adar, Fulani, Barga (Benin), Chamba, Ga, Kwahu, Fanti, and Asante. Along with countless children, they live in seventy-one rooms in this sprawling property of varying shapes and sizes. Only three rooms are landcrete; the rest are wooden. Each room or set of rooms is entered from outside.

This property lacks any of the boundaries normative in Ghanaian or Nigerian housing. At the large back end, there is nothing akin to the work and socializing space of a courtyard. The residents cook outside their respective doors, which in many cases means out in the public. Some on the field-facing east side have built-on an outer roofless room, for activities such as cooking and washing that would customarily be carried out in the yard. On the other side, framed by the southern end of the mosque and the wall for the stables and their yard, tenants have built verandahs at the front of their rooms. While clearly visible to the public, they are symbolically separate.

On the north side of the mosque, here a small compound has emerged, formed by rooms and the back of the mosque. At the road side, there is no outside wall. In years past, there was a tall pile of blocks; now there is a kiosk. The "compound" has a water pipe and shower. There is considerable activity here, social and work related, as three members of the local *bori* troupe have lived here for years. *'Yan bori* who live in Sabon Zongo as well as adepts from elsewhere in Accra come through daily to greet or to consult Tabaraka, the *magajiyan bori* (head of the bori troupe). Tabaraka had cooked and sold *tuwo* for at least fifteen years; when she returned from *haji*[7] she calculated that the market no longer made it worthwhile. One of the other women took up her spot in the yard to prepare another type of food to sell. One of the *'yan bori* makes medicine, which people may come to buy.

Around the back of Tabaraka's enclosure, there are others who ply their trade at or near home: one woman has a store near her room; a petty trader sells in front of house; a soothsayer has his office; an Asante woman prepares women's medicine, which she hawks on the streets; and a seamstress sews with her apprentice. Those working with the horses in Baba Mai Doki's stables are out at dawn with the animals, walking them to the beach to train; later in the day, they have them tied up opposite the mosque, where they feed, water, and brush them.

Across "town" from Baba Mai Doki's in Ojo, on the edge of *Kan Tudu* near the Freedom Market, there is another tenanted compound (Figure 44), this one owned by Alhaji Mumuni.[8] His father was a Kanuri who came to the Gold Coast as a trader but also bought farms in the interior. They came here from Mangoase (near Kumase) when Mumuni was nine and one half. According to Baba Mai Doki (6/10/2000), Mumuni and Dan Baba (the last surviving "child" of Malam Bako) are close friends, and after Mumuni's father died, Dan Baba

Figure 44
Alhaji Mumuni House, Plan #12.

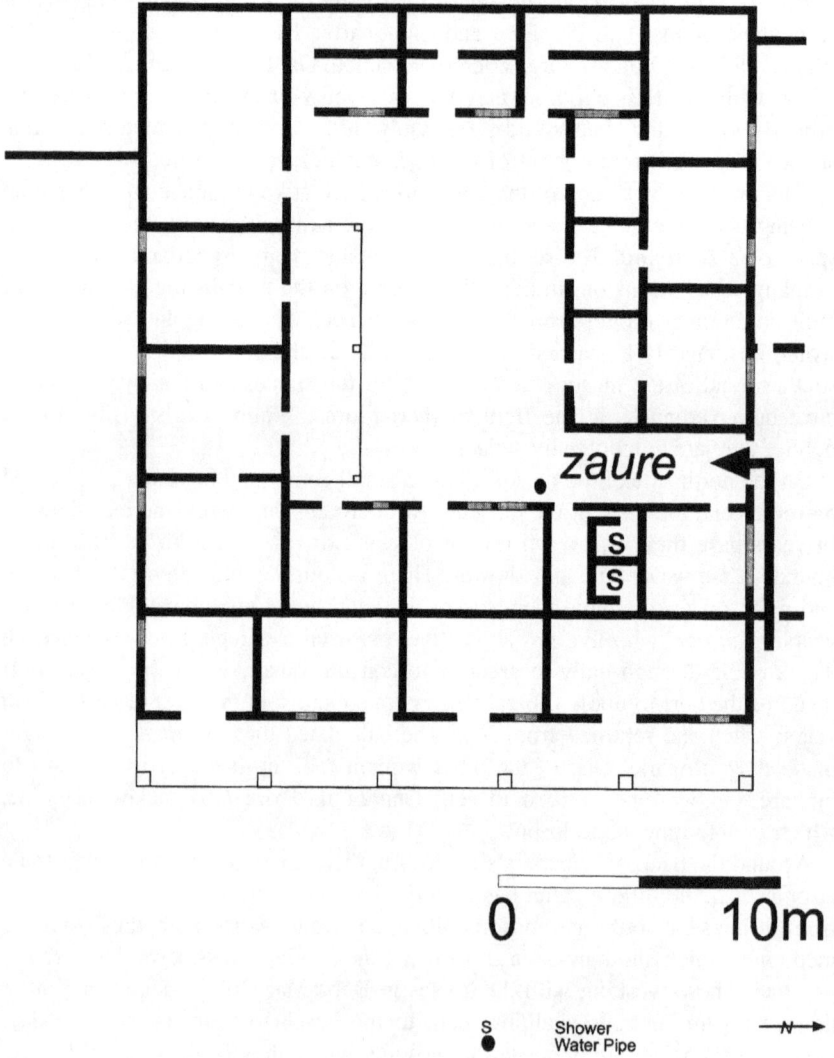

zaure

0   10m

S   Shower
●   Water Pipe   —N→

Figure 45
Alhaji Mumuni House: Adult Resident Kin (Shaded).

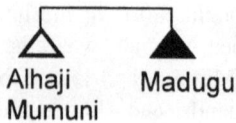

Alhaji   Madugu
Mumuni

made it possible for him to buy a piece of Bako family land on Market Street. He subsequently acquired this second property, and his brother is the resident overseer.

The property sits near the top of the incline, one house down from Market Street, on a road that cannot be navigated by car and barely by foot because of the ruts and rocks. Looking south from the front gate, one can see Freedom Market. The compound does not have a surrounding wall as such, but it is bounded: at the roadside by four stores entered from a roofed verandah, on either side by a lane separating the house structure from the house next door. At the rear, the rooms are windowless (as if walled in). The house is built from cement block.

The front gate, next to the tailor shop off the verandah, is locked around midnight. Walking along the lane toward the interior of the house, one comes to the *zaure*, through which one enters the non-obstructed central yard. As in all compound yards, at any given time during the dry season, there is clean laundry hanging. The rooms facing one another across the width of the yard have verandahs as well as cross-ventilation through out-facing windows. The rooms at the two ends have neither verandahs nor windows to the outside. There are two shower rooms next to the standing water pipe.

The house was previously Ewe-dominated. Then in 1992, a Sisala man moved in and in addition to his wife, seven other Sisala moved in as well (Figure 45). Of the eight, six deal in charcoal ("confirming" the ethnic stereotype). One is an educated man and works as an accountant, but both his parents were charcoal sellers. His wife, a trained seamstress, sells charcoal with her mother because she can earn more than by sewing. There are still five Ewe residents, three Kwahu and two Fante (he is the oldest tenant and chairman of the tenant's association), one Zabrama and one Malian. The Hausa man (and his wife) are tenants without paying: he is the caretaker for his brother the owner; he lives in the large chamber/hall that was originally the landlord's apartment and the tailor shop out front is his.

The configuration and use of the compound is reminiscent of a family house. It is women who use the compound space during the day. In that time period, there is no man in evidence, unless he is going to bathe. As in all compounds with Muslim residents, the day begins early. The observant men are up by 4:45 A.M. to do ablutions and pray—either in their rooms or at one of the local mosques. And as in all compounds in the community, by 6 A.M. the women are actively engaged: washing laundry and the last night's dirty dishes in their space in the compound; putting away cooking utensils in their cupboard outside of the room or on the porch if one has one; washing one's face, washing children, brushing teeth near the spigot; bathing babies in large basins. Once the children of the house are off to school, there is not a lot of activity in the compound, until late afternoon/early evening, when the men and women working out of the house return.

Figure 46
Abdullahi Mohamadu "Gongadi" House, Plan #17 (Involution Shaded).

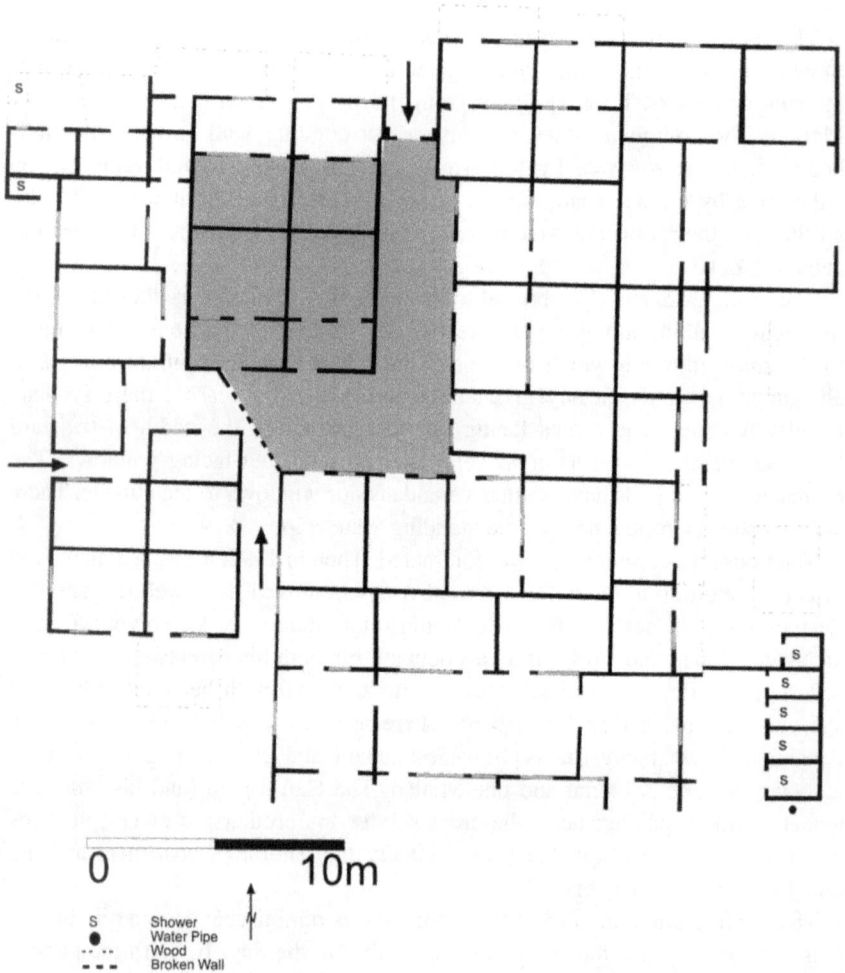

An intriguing variation on the theme of tenancy is evident at a compound in the Sunshine area of Ayigbetown. Up the road from Timbuktoo Mosque, across the street from Tumba Mosque and an open field and next door to Kataki Mosque, the compound (Figure 46) sits on Bartholomew Street, the eastern cut-off of Malam Bako's Zongo. This is a very mixed neighborhood. According to one of the residents, it is primarily Ga who live behind Tumba and up the street, Ewes—this is after all Ayigbetown. It is also sparsely built up and populated, with wide roads and wide open spaces.

The "landlord" is Abdullahi Mohamadu, whose nickname is Gongadi ("gun

Figure 47
"Gongadi" House: Adult Resident Kin (Shaded).

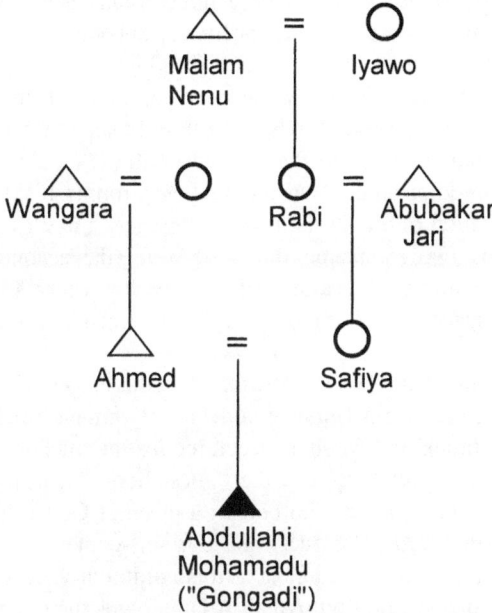

guarding"), a Hausa-identified man whose mother is from the Bako family (see Figure 47). Her mother was Nenu's daughter Rabi. His father was a Wangara man and the land was his. His house was small—Gongadi says they lived in a grass-roofed shack. His father built the little unroofed Kataki Mosque next door in 1943 and it is still in use. Situated as it is on a lane, not on a proper plot, should the street grid ever be reclaimed, Kataki would have to be demolished or relocated.[9]

Gongadi developed the area after inheriting it. According to his kinsman Sule Bako, around 1962 Gongadi was demolishing zinc structures to renovate. He started with cement from the base (building a dwarf wall) then halfway to the top he built with zinc. He was well-to-do and had enough money to build only with cement but thought the combination would be better. Sule convinced Gongadi to do it all with cement blocks.

Gongadi developed money problems and began selling off the property. There are now seven different resident owners, each of whom owns a piece of the compound. Alhaji Abu owns a room in the house. As mentioned earlier in this chapter, he also bought two adjacent rooms which he had demolished, intending to create a self-contained flat (the architect labels it a "single storey house"). This will include a living room, bedroom, kitchen, and bath/WC. Another man, Muniru Dan Juma, related by marriage to the Bako family (his mother's mother was the sister of Lawal Bako's wife), lives in *Kan Tudu* but owns two rooms here. Alhaji Adamu's brother owns one room. Two women, one of whom lives in The Netherlands, also own rooms in the compound. Gongadi's penury is indicated by his quarters—he owns only three rooms and sleeps in a barely furnished room that is located on the north side, outside of the compound.

The compound has three different sections: 1) an L-shaped building. The entrance to the compound (formerly the only entrance) on the north side, the mosque side. It has a door that closes; 2) a middle section was added on, and a wall was built diagonally from the far end of the L (south end) to the new west end of the middle; and, 3) an addition: six rooms inside, including the unfinished construction of one of the resident "owners"; two rooms on the south side (outside) plus two rooms on the north side (the second with an outer wooden wall). The interior diagonal wall was broken down to create the new larger compound space. There is a doorway to the outside at the south end, but no door.

The three sections of the house correspond to the stages of construction and the materials used: the original house, built out of cement block, was added to with used cement block and wooden structures for the outside rooms, and then cement was used. A fourth stage is the "guest house" constructed by Alhaji Adamu, a cousin of Gongadi's, who bought a piece of Gongadi's plot but lives in his own house in Katifa. The guest house is self-contained with rather monumental facing, unusual in the context of this community. It has been planned with indoor plumbing. In addition, Alhaji Adamu owns the five showers in front of the compound and he has also constructed a proper cement gutter that runs along the street in front of the showers.

Within the house there are two shower rooms and residents have access to water at the tap outside near the public showers. There are four rooms north of the showers (at the side of the compound, on the outside), each of which has a small verandah. The latter have no courtyard—each set of rooms is entered from the front yard. Gongadi built and then sold off these rooms when he needed money. A Kwahu tenant in one of the side rooms, a rather elegant and educated woman who has fallen on hard times, put up a partial wooden wall in front of her front yard where she sometimes sits "so people can't see." When her new landlord wanted to renovate that side of the compound, she had to move to a smaller room.

There are forty-one adult residents here. Only three of them, including Gongadi, are Hausa. The three of them, the six Zabrama, two Mossi and one of the four Frafra are Muslims. The Christian balance are Akan (19, of whom 11 are Kwahu), Ga (three), and Ewe (four). Three of the men work in Forex Bureaux (buying and selling foreign exchange), typically plied by Hausa and Zabrama (as is here the case). Only one woman, a seamstress, works at home.

Up the street from Gongadi in the area of Ayigbetown known as Stable is the compound of Hajiya Hasana Adamu (Figure 48). She is a member of the Limam family, community pioneers who built the mosque around the corner from Chief Sha'aibu's house. Hajiya, an elderly woman who had a stroke in

1999, has never lived in the Ayigbetown house; she lives in her father Imam Limam's house in *Kan Tudu*. She bought the Ayigbetown house in the 1970s. According to Chief Sha'aibu (6/9/2000), the land was owned by a half-brother to his father Lawal and it was he who built the house. He sold it to a Hausa man who moved to Zaria, Nigeria, and Hajiya Hasana bought the house from him. It has served Hajiya as a rental property. Until one of her daughters married in the mid-1990s and moved there with her new husband, the house was occupied by tenants only.

This is a new version compound. There is a wall only on the east side; the other three sides are the outside walls of rooms, all windowed. There are two entrances, common in many compounds, but no *zaure*. The entrances are directly across from one another, as if they are at either ends of a lane. The shared yard looks more like a corridor than a central space.

The apartment of Hajiya Hasana's daughter and son-in-law is in the southeast corner and consists of a foyer, two rooms, and a shower. They also made an interesting physical alteration to enclose their corner of the compound: they put up a high wall with a solid (wooden) door. This created an unroofed patio area, with flowers (unusual, since in most houses, goats are free to wander in and will eat any vegetable matter), giving them a bit over twelve square meters of extra space. Closing off the area also affords them sole access to the water pipe. As an interesting side note, in this patriarchal culture (Hausa), it is the norm for the bride to move to her husband's or his father's house; it is also Hausa tradition for a man not to stay in the same house as his in-law, except in extreme cases. In this case, since the younger woman was already well-situated, and her mother lived elsewhere, it made practical sense for her husband to move in with her.[10]

As in all compounds, each household does carve out a space near its door for a coal pot and other cooking utensils. Because the water spigot is not accessible, each household also has a large drum of water. The kenkey lady cooks in front of her door and sells her product from a table in "her" compound space.

In addition to the Hausa couple, there is one other Hausa resident. The rest of the tenants are two Akwapim, one Kotokoli and thirteen Ewe—the house, after all, is in Ayigbetown.

The next three landlords—Alhaji Bebe, Alhaji Sule Bako, and Alhaji Adamu Yahaya—dwell in far less extensive compounds, with family members and primarily immediate family, thus opening the door to nuclear family living.

Alhaji Bebe was born in Makafai, near Bako B.K.'s Mosque. When he came of age, he himself moved to a rental room in Ayigbetown. He married. In the late 1960s he had money—*doki ya gudu* ("the horse was running"). He bought several properties—in Alajo, Dansoman, Shukura, and a piece in Sabon Zongo he named Akwei Allah Villa. His land in Sabon Zongo, across from *Gidan Makaranta* and next door to Bawa Allah, was originally owned by Alhaji Tsoho from the Dan Kambari family.[11] Alhaji Tsoho put up two swish buildings. When Alhaji Bebe bought it in 1969, there were only the two rooms on the property. He demolished them and built new ones from cement block.

Figure 48
Hajiya Hasana Adamu House, Plan #16.

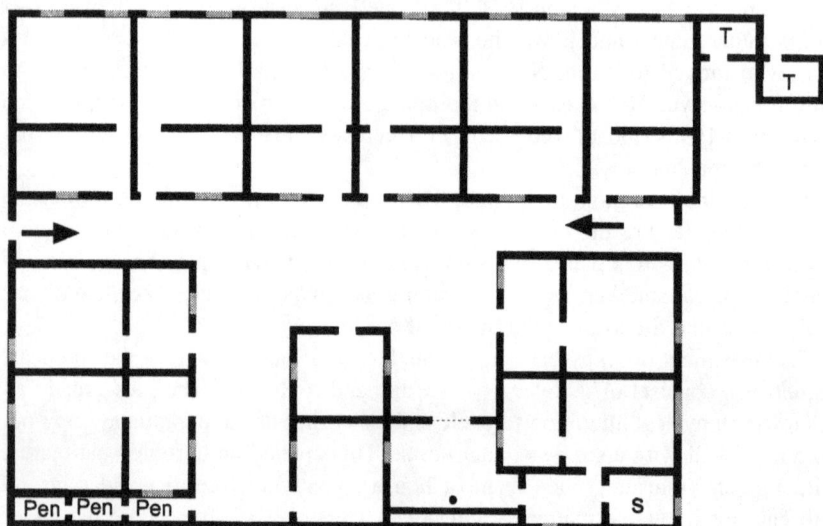

He transformed the property into a modern compound (Figure 50) for his immediate family. Actually, his compound is a cross between old and new—enclosed and completely walled with a proper iron gate, it fits the Hausa prototype. Alhaji lives here with his two wives and their children. But in addition to his conjugal family, he also has tenants. In 1972, after building two additions for family, he fell on hard financial times and quickly rented them out. (He had also built homes in Alajo and Shukura but when his trading business suffered, he was forced to sell them.) He has seven tenants, five are Kwahu, two are Fante, all are Christians. "Muslims and Christians live together with no worries. They practice their own religion and customs. If one disturbs the other, he asks forgiveness" (6/3/1996).

When Alhaji's two daughters married in August 1997, he was able to accommodate about two hundred men in the compound yard who came to hear the

Figure 49
Hajiya Hasana Adamu House: Adult Resident Kin (Shaded).

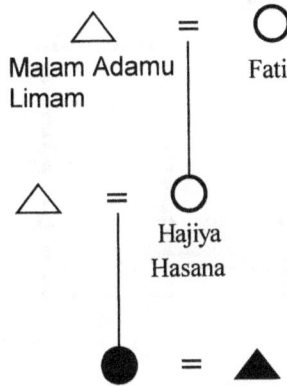

young women read the Koran. Meanwhile, the street outside was filled with women cooking or sitting under a canopy and waiting for the women's celebration. It is intriguing that *zongo* tradition has solidified sufficiently that even though there was room at Alhaji Bebe's, the women's *biki* was held in the street.

Each of Alhaji's wives has her own set of three rooms. His senior wife's quarters are to the left, the junior wife's to the right, and his are in the middle. Thus, the three adults and their children live in the row of rooms, just opposite the gate. The buildings are cement block. The walls and buildings are a soft yellow, the gate and trim are teal blue. The capacious compound yard (58 square meters) is paved. There is a beautiful shade tree in the middle. Two of the rooms are "self-contained"—with kitchen, toilet and shower. A verandah wraps around the inside of the yard, from which one enters each room or set of rooms. The compound is very neat and always fairly quiet.

One block east and two south on Hide Street, Sule Bako, Chief Sha'aibu's son, built his own house (Figure 52). Sha'aibu divorced Sule's mother when the son was very very young, and Sule went to live with his great grandfather Malam Bako's most senior wife Amina. When Amina died in 1959, Sule moved to the home of Lawal, his father's father, in the house next to Malam Gambo. Sule is the most educated of his father's children, not to mention all of Sabon Zongo. There is only one other person in the community who has gone to university. When life got hard in Ghana in the 1970s, Sule moved to Nigeria where he taught secondary school. He returned in 1981 and built this house. But he did not move in until 1988, again living at his grandfather Lawal's house. When Sule and his wife moved into this house, one of his sons took the room vacated at Lawal's (see Figure 53).

Sule Bako's property like Bebe's has a real, complete concrete wall that bounds the entirety. The entry is through a metal gate. The main house sits in the middle of the compound, eliminating the central yard. Because the house

Figure 50
Alhaji Abubakar Alhassan "Bebe" House, Plan #11.

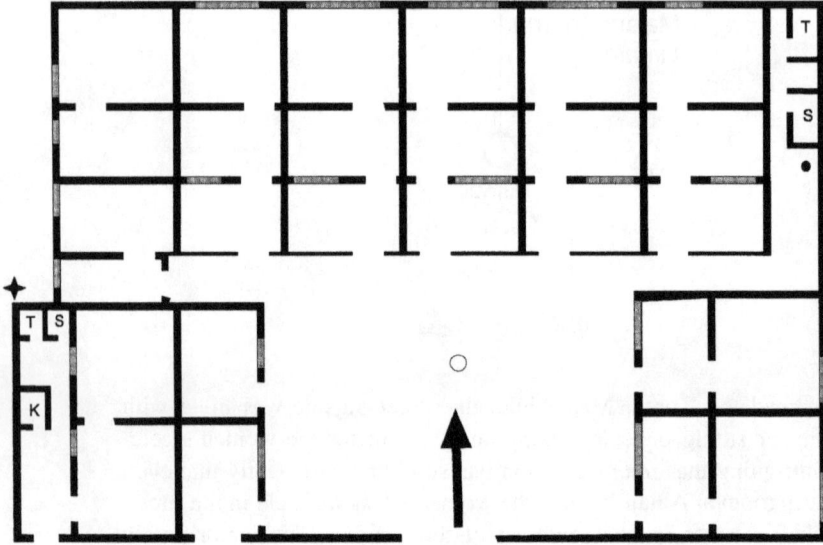

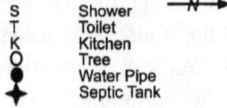

0   10m

S   Shower   —N→
T   Toilet
K   Kitchen
O   Tree
●   Water Pipe
✦   Septic Tank

Figure 51
Alhaji "Bebe" House: Adult Resident Kin (Shaded).

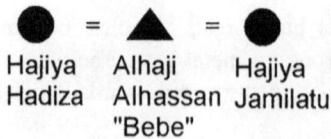

●   =   ▲   =   ●
Hajiya   Alhaji   Hajiya
Hadiza   Alhassan   Jamilatu
             "Bebe"

has rooms with specific functions, like a sitting room, dining room, kitchen, store room—all of which are normally accommodated by the courtyard—and only one family, the loss of the large outside space is not problematic. In any case there is yard space to the side and in the back. The compound is light and airy, the yard cemented. While the kitchen has a stove, Sule's wife often cooks outside on the front door stoop on a gas burner (with a gas balloon). She has fufu pounded outside in the compound as well.

There are also three single rooms at the rear of the compound—what would be considered "boys' quarters" in the suburbs—with a shower. According to the original plan for the main house, there is a WC next to the indoor shower. But Alhaji Sule ran out of money and did not install a septic tank. He did, however, install two KVIPs in the compound yard. And nearby, he also built four showers. In 1999, Sule demolished the KVIPs; he built three WCs outside in their place and installed one in the house.

Alhaji Sule owns five taxis and manages the transport business from the house. In addition, he deals in services: he sells showers; he sells toilet access, and in the mid-1990s, he broke through the wall in front of his compound and built a tailoring shop (his wife is a trained seamstress and one of their sons is a tailor) and a hairdressing shop to rent out. Five adults live in this house— Alhaji Sule, his wife, two of his grown children and a cousin of his wife. All of course are Hausa. As the landlord, Sule "owns" the sitting room; this is like the old-time *zaure*, where he sometimes entertains friends. His wife has her own room for her *ƙayan ɗaki*, and the kitchen "belongs" to her. The boys' turf is outside.

The final sampled house is that of Alhaji Adamu Yahaya in Katifa/Ayigbe-town (Figure 54). As the story goes, the land that it sits on was sold by Lawal Bako to a Hausa man who decided to return to Nigeria to die. He in turn sold it to Alhaji Adamu who built a house on it in 1979. Should the municipality decide to lay the roads that have been mapped, the house will be bulldozed.

Adamu's father's father Abubakar came from Nigeria; he was the first imam of Kwashima. After he died in Kwashima, Yahaya (Alhaji Adamu's father) came to Sabon Zongo. He lived in *Kan Tudu* and married Hajiya Hawa Mai Danbu, daughter of Malam Nenu's daughter Rabi. Alhaji Adamu was born in *Kan Tudu*. His whole family is here.

Adamu is an agent for pilgrims to Mecca. He is also an art trader. And he is one of the "shower entrepreneurs" in Sabon Zongo. While the showers built out in front of his house are "not for me," he owns public showers in Ayigbetown at Gongadi's, as well as four public showers behind *Gidan Baƙi*.

His house is self-contained and only Adamu's nuclear family (wife, daughters and young son) live there (see Figure 55). It is nicely designed, with a paved compound and a roof over the capacious verandah. Unlike the typical compound house, the rooms here are not designed to be multifunctional; rather, they are designed and furnished for specific purposes. There is a proper kitchen off the compound, outfitted with sink, counters, cupboards, an electric stove and a table-

Figure 52
Alhaji Sule Bako House, Plan #5.

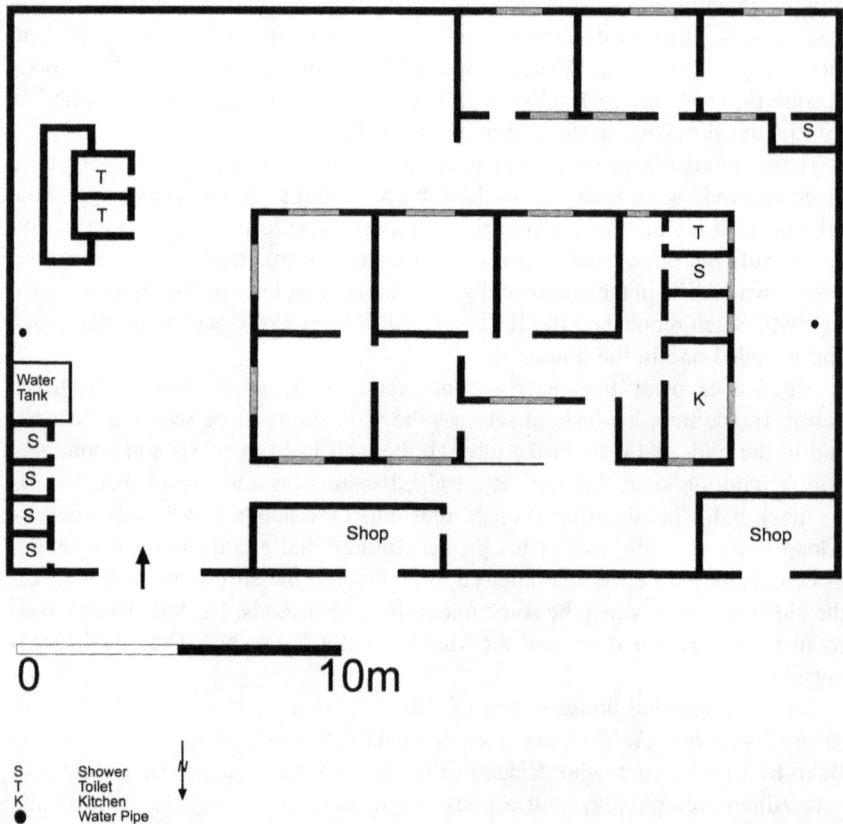

top fridge. The hall (living room) has rugs, drapes, sofa, chairs, an étagerè (with stereo and tureens) to divide off the dining room. There are an overhead fan and lights. A second étagerè holds the television and VCR. The dining room has a table and chairs. Alhaji Adamu, his wife and their young son sleep in one of the chambers, where Hajiya keeps her *ƙayan ɗaki* in a large wardrobe. The second chamber sleeps the three daughters; since marrying, they come and go with their babies. On return from *haji* several years ago, Alahaji Adamu brought back a satellite dish. So while he has no WC in his house, he can watch television programs from the Middle East.

Adamu also owns a plot in Dansoman—150' × 150'—which would build a much bigger house than here. Friends and business are elsewhere and "Here it is a ghetto—there are so many people around you." Sometimes, he says, people don't want to come to see him because they want to come in secret, and in Sabon Zongo, there are no secrets. Yet he likes living in Sabon Zongo, "because

Figure 53
Alhaji Sule Bako House: Adult Resident Kin.

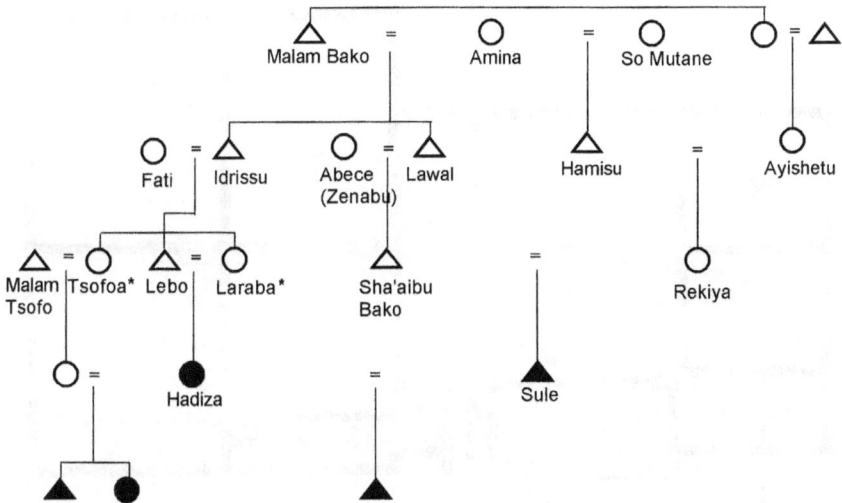

*Laraba and Tsofoa are great granddaughters of Malan Garuba.

I have many friends and family." It is important to remember that this man does not have agnatic ties in the community and his father did not own property in the community. He so wanted roots here that even though his property lies in the path of a potential road, he built his house. "But sometimes," he adds, "I want to run away, because people come to beg for money. And even if I don't have any money, they don't believe me."

MARKING SOCIAL CHANGE

Residents are attached to the *zongo* because of its cultural values and social relationships. These are embedded in its physical order and social institutions as expressed in the built form of the compound house and its evolution over the last eighty-plus years.

Sixteen of the landlords surveyed are Hausa, two are half-Hausa, one is Kanuri. Twelve of the houses hail from the early days of the community; they continue to house at least some family descendants. Only one of the properties was built specifically for tenants, starting as horse stables. Four were built on land purchased or inherited from Bako descendants in the last twenty or thirty years. All of this latter group house nuclear family members, two of them also renting rooms to tenants. All but one of the four men who built these last houses could have remained in family housing within Sabon Zongo but chose to move out into his own compound.

When the owner is a resident, he/she normally lives on the inside, as opposed to living on the outside, in a room added on. The son of the original owner of

Figure 54
Alhaji Adamu Yahaya House, Plan #15.

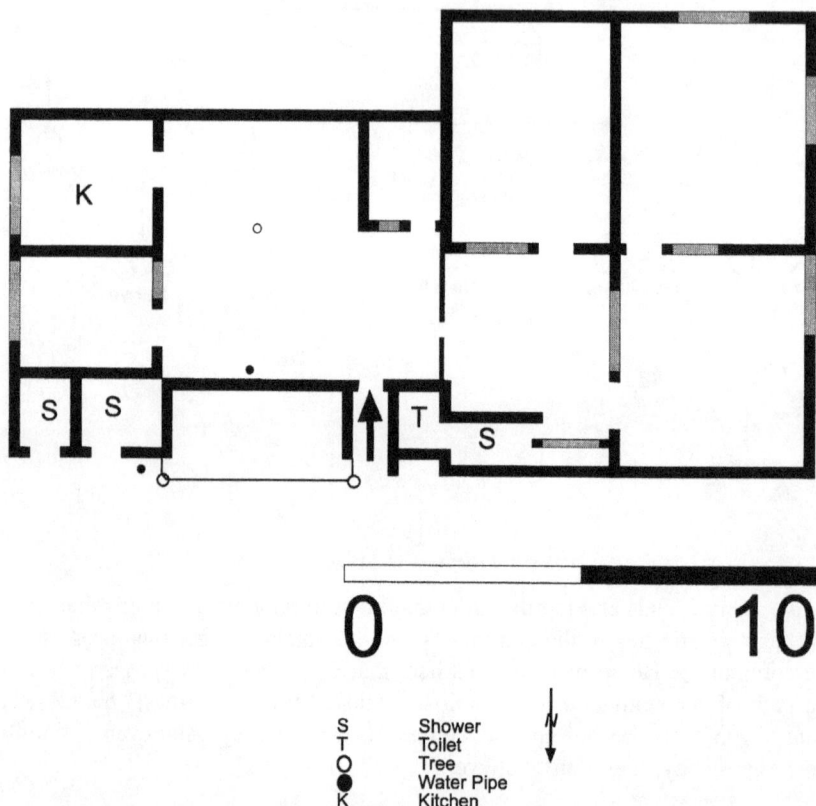

```
S   Shower
T   Toilet
O   Tree
●   Water Pipe
K   Kitchen
```

#17 (Figure 46), who should be the landlord, is the exception. Because he spent all of his money, he sold off pieces of his patrimony, so that the compound is owned by several residents. He has ended up in one of the outside rooms. Where others live, who gets only one room as opposed to a chamber/hall, is often the luck of the draw—who happens to come along just as a room is being vacated and moves in.

At Badamase's (Figure 23), in her later years Hadiza Bako would watch the world go by from the protection of the *zaure*, while her brother's wife sat nearby and sold groundnuts. At Sha'aibu Bako's house (#2, Figure 21), his tenants use the *zaure* as a workspace to cook. At Sarkin Fada's (#19, Figure 37), when his daughter died, the women mourners took over the inside of the compound, including the *zaure*, while the men sat on benches outside across the street from the *zaure*.

But people are also talking about larger changes. "You see [proper] buildings in Ayigbetown or near Zongo Junction; why not in *zongo* [the old core]?" (Ba-

Figure 55
Alhaji Adamu House: Adult Resident Kin (Shaded).

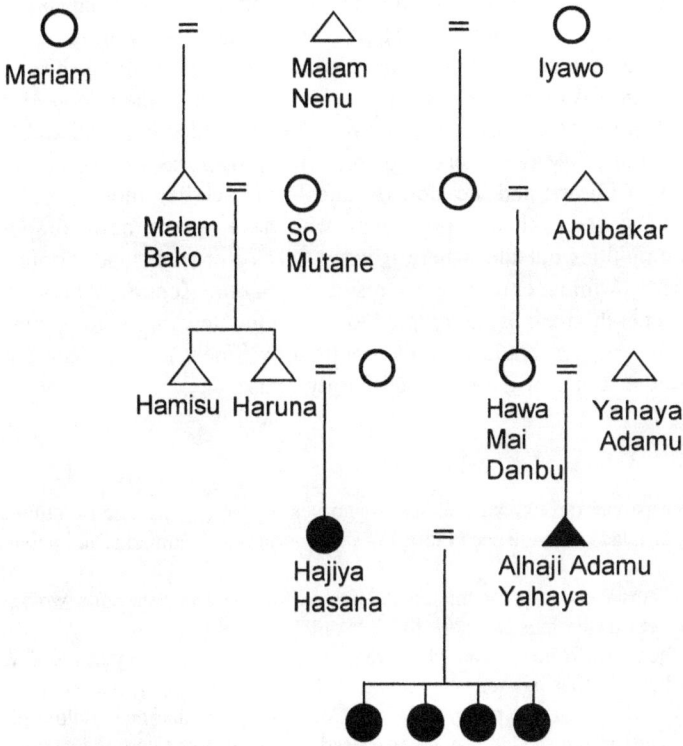

bah Alargi). When I asked Tahiro if he had the money to renovate the house what he would do, he replied that he would build stores on the ground floor at the front and on the north side, and then he would build a second floor with his room. People have been able to buy land and put up buildings outside of the nucleus. There are very few houses with indoor plumbing (septic tanks), though as noted, this is changing.

In *zongo*, you don't have it [in the old part of town] unless you raze the house and put down a new building. [In Ayigbetown, however,] that one is undeveloped land. That's where the development in zongo is going on, because there are no houses there. Or somebody too will buy a house and develop it—like Timbuktoo [next to Timbuktoo Mosque on Korle Bu Street]. He has a toilet and everything. Just like Ila's house [the former Member of Parliament] and Butcher House [a storied building on Oblogo, whose owner bought the land from Malam Bako]. So that is what we are doing—we are trying to develop our area. (Mohammed Bako 6/6/1996)

Indeed, there are now pockets of new kinds of building going on throughout Sabon Zongo. On Harmattan Street, a block up from Idrissu's Mosque and the rental housing on Garuba family property, there is a new two-story building. It is one room deep and one room wide. It houses a communication center and a row of flush toilets. Nearby, within the compound that is an extension of *Gidan Baki*, new rooms are being built. Hajiya Pedro's house is getting an overhaul: at the front, a second floor has been added and the front wall has been disman- tled and rebuilt. As was true for the new structure inside the *Gidan Makaranta* compound, some of the new construction is being funded transnationally, by the descendants of property owners who are working overseas—some in Saudi Ara- bia, others in Europe and the United States—and sending money home.

There have been others with money who have put up new compounds in other communities outside, where it was easier to procure land. Some rent out the property while continuing to reside in Sabon Zongo. Others from the younger generation are being tempted to move out. New multi-story construction within Sabon Zongo could give the community a new lease on life and better guarantee the future of the extended family house.

NOTES

1. Like people throughout the city, zongo-ites do not use their house numbers; they identify their place of residence in terms of neighborhoods, landmarks, and popular house names.

2. The AMA tax map for this block of *Unguwan Makafi* lists only two very small structures next to the mosque, both for "Makafi," i.e., "blind."

3. In fact, I know no woman who, even *in extremis*, has sold any of her *ƙayan ɗaki*.

4. Barbara Cooper has seen few compounds in Maradi, Niger, that emulate the ele- ment of the *cikin gida* and disagreeing with Mack suggests that one could argue that if the chief keeps to the model, no one else need do so (personal communication).

5. We also had to work around people, laundry, cooking pots (I burned my leg on one), people using facilities like shower rooms, and the children.

6. I have referred to each section as a "house." They are not households; rather, each of the houses encompasses numerous households. In most cases, household equates to a room or set of rooms occupied by a group of people who eat from the same pot.

7. Tabaraka, and the other *bori* members, see no conflict between her commitment to Islam and her participation in *bori*.

8. Curiously, when I interviewed at the compound in 1995, I was told that Alhaji Mumuni was the original owner and the current owner is Marya Mai Yake who lives elsewhere in Sabon Zongo.

9. Tumbaa, another unroofed mosque, was built across the street in 1996.

10. Though a Hausa male friend of mine says that no self-respecting (Hausa) man would do so, as it weakens his position in the marriage.

11. Malam Garuba's daughter Nana married Dan Kambari and had five children; one son, Abdullahi, married and Tsoho was his son.

8

COMPOUND SOCIAL SPACE: TRANSFORMATIONS THROUGH LIVING

When asked to imagine changing the house, the women of *Gidan Makaranta* said they would like to rebuild the mud with cement blocks and make it more self-contained. Minimally, for everyone to have a chamber/hall combination with a longer hall and a shower inside; maximally a sitting room, bedroom, kitchen, bathroom (tub and toilet). Should they recreate the *zaure*? No, because it is old fashioned.

And what about changes in the community? "The settlers [tenants] are very few. At first there were Ewes and Zabramas. The Zabramas have almost vanished from the area. Gradually as they left the Kwahus who came to Accra for trade look for accommodation in zongo, and their population is increasing. Their children go to school. How they can influence us is going to be very difficult, or take a long time, because we don't have contact with them. We regard them as settlers—looking for accommodation temporarily. When they get what they want they go away. If they are rich enough to put up their houses, they do it; and in the end go away. So some of us don't see why they should influence us. Rather, we would like to influence them. So their children speak fluent Hausa, but we don't speak fluent Twi. . . . The point is we will not allow them to influence us, we will influence them. And that is being achieved by way of language." (Sule Bako 6/14/96)

This chapter is about the compound as an instrument of enculturation.[1] In Chapter 7, I examined the spatial transformations that have transpired in Sabon Zongo's compounds. In this chapter some of the social transformations enabled by that socio-spatial context, the reproduction and change in the practices and the spacetime that the compound embraces and enables are considered. Each compound encompasses a social geography of identity. It is my opinion that the compound's changing socio-spatial order occurs through several features: 1) person-place linkages, the landlord who comes by his/her property as an heir, the new buyer, and the tenant; 2) the conceptual division of space; and, 3) public privacy, a term I have coined that sounds like a contradiction but is actually a social dialectic. These features enable enculturation into new roles and relationships.

The compounds are born of Sabon Zongo's social and spatial system, they represent a microcosm of that socio-spatial system, and it is within (and through) the compound that the basics of community membership are conveyed. The spatial outline and social arrangements within the compound walls correspond at least in part to the salience of kinship in the community and in the given compound.

The compound house is generally significant because of the activities and relationships it anchors, because of its flexibility in accommodating activities.[2] Its spaces are encoded to privilege family connections. Yet, the house embodies tensions between lineage culture and urban/community culture. Within and through these spaces, transformations do occur, markers of what I call *zong-wanci*.

THE DRAW OF SABON ZONGO

Sabon Zongo residents are strangers to Accra. They have been primarily Hausa and other Muslims, but even non-Muslim southern Ghanaians have moved there. Owners, buyers and renters all have reasons for moving in or staying. There are those who live there because it is their birthright. Genealogical rights to housing, unlike simple tenancy, carry two different types of privilege: the first is the guarantee of having a place to live, and without cost—clearly crucial to an underemployed or underpaid population; the second is the chance to have an impact on the community. According to one tenant, some people claim their fathers founded Sabon Zongo and if you're not related to the Bako family, you're nobody. This is because you are not "indigenous" (Bawa Sisala 5/31/96), though of course none of the original Hausa landlords were indigenous; all came into the community as strangers. But like the children of those adopted by a family, the contemporary progeny of the original propertied strangers carry a kind of legitimacy or pedigree that tenants (or even new owners without primal ties) do not. Thus, they stay. Others have a history with the community and want permanence there. Alhaji Adamu, for example, both grew up there in his father's rented space but also married into the Bako family.

Some who live in the run-down houses could live elsewhere but stay because of the connections. Mohammed Bako says he lives here because it is peaceful, which he translates in part as no problems with water or electricity. Moreover, "we [Bako family] are all here." Hajiya Maimouna Pedro built a large self-contained, house in Awushie. The house has a WC and bathroom, kitchen, sitting room, and four bedrooms. It sits in a large concrete compound, separated from a second house (which she rents out) by a carport. She would not live there. She preferred her *zongo* house, with no toilet, no showerhead bathroom, a dirt compound. "*Sai* caterpillar [unless bulldozed out of this one, she would not move]" says her son. As she said, "Why [move]? I have everything here! and my sisters are here" (6/9/1995). In fact, none of her children want to live at the Awushie house. They perceive it as being in the middle of nowhere, especially as compared to *zongo*. It is "far" (if one has no private transportation) and has no community life, or anyway, not the vibrant and congested life her sons love. Awushie is developed but no one is outside. There are no activities. Pedro built the house there as an investment.

There are those Hausa/Muslims who want to live in Sabon Zongo but despite having money, are not successful in buying a piece of land. Across the street from Sha'aibu Bako's house is the Night Market property that is owned by nine people, all heirs of the original Garuba owner. It can be torturous trying to sell a piece of property when so many individual owners must be placated. By the same token, there is land in back of Baba Mai Doki's described property, which is still unclaimed because so many have rights to it that if they split it up, they'd each get a piece the size of a table. So, there are those who build houses elsewhere but they rent in Sabon Zongo (Sha'aibu Bako and Alkali 5/4/1982).

One of the more interesting questions is why a religious, ethnic, and national diversity of people move to Sabon Zongo today—to what extent is it simply economics or is there more involved? According to broker Bashiru Shadow, a housing agent (3/15/1995), *zongo ya sauki*, that is, the rent is okay. Clearly, a house search is constrained by what the searcher can afford. Suburban areas like Roman Ridge and urban areas like Adabraka are beyond the means of a person without means. Thus, the search must begin in an affordable area, after which one can zero in on what is available and at what price.

The non-Muslims tend to move in for reasons of economy and availability. But according to Shadow, people move to Sabon Zongo for other than financial reasons. It is known as a Muslim area, but non-Muslims also live here. Many of the latter are comfortable living here and they overlook the physical defi- ciencies. One Akan man had been an accountant at the Ambassador Hotel. When the hotel closed down in the 1980s, he became a Lotto agent. His kiosk is right in front of his room. He exhibits no apparent bitterness about the change in his life and asserts that he is content living in this community.

The salient question is, what constitutes comfort? To which I would reply, the ability to satisfy social and cultural needs. For example, if one wants to keep goats (common for the *zongo* dwellers), Accra's suburbs are not the an- swer. While such areas are gracious and well-appointed, ordinances prohibit residents from raising animals. "If you stay here, it's like living in Northern Nigeria—you can buy *fura*, everything. Hausa who come from Nigeria prefer staying in *zongo*" (Mohammed Bako 6/4/1995).

Migrants like to live here because "here there are friends, no worries" (Shadow 3/15/1995). The non-Muslims report that the rent is affordable and that they are not subject to discrimination. A Kwahu tailor, whose shop is located in *Unguwan* Zabrama across from Hajiya Maimuna, came in 1973 to work here, because his senior brother had a place here in Ayigbetown. He moved to Ayigbetown and in his house there are Kwahu, Ewe, Fante, and Asante. He decided to stay in Sabon Zongo because "there is peace" (Alfred Mercy 5/30/1996). Others who come from the interior, from the bush who are not Muslim, "cannot live among the Ga, because the Ga look down on them. Here nobody does" (Bashiru Shadow 3/15/1995). People come here because they feel at home. "*Muna da free*" [we feel free, at peace]. Those from non-urban areas live the same way here as in the hometown. "It's like a *kauye* [village]." One Ewe man moved here from the Volta Region in 1947 and lived here till 1993; he left only after building a house in Togo. A Kwahu woman who has fallen on hard times, rents a room in Ayigbetown: "No problem here. No problem from my landlord. The neighbors don't hamper me. If there's no problem, you can stay."

People also have practical reasons for living in Sabon Zongo—people of a variety of ethnicities. For example, just as an Akan who deals in kola must speak Hausa, he must have easy dealings with the people, and living in Sabon Zongo accommodates such needs.

HAVING CAPACITY

In her study of a Hausa community in Niger, Barbara Cooper observed that property is crucial—not just as a material asset, "but also because it creates, defines, and facilitates social relations"(Cooper 1997b:210). This is also true in Ghana, where rights to land accord rights to roles and statuses and land ownership is traditionally kin-based (Ollennu 1962; Pellow 1991a), and it is also true in Sabon Zongo.

Alhaji Hamisu, one of Malam Bako's sons, observed that property is a sign of respect: "when you have cows, land, houses, some people respect you, others hate you—it is good to have these three, because then you know that you are somebody" (6/4/1982). Baba Mai Doki, a respected elder, and his sister own many properties together—"*muna share*" (we share)—which he believes gives them considerable status (Baba Mai Doki 6/1/1996). In line with Hausa Muslim law, in the Hausa families in Sabon Zongo land and family houses are inherited two to one, male to female.

We see the relation of property ownership to status in Sabon Zongo today. For example, on August 1, 1933, when Idrissu was chosen to succeed his father Malam Bako as chief, community elders of Sabon Zongo sent a letter to the Jamestown Ga chief, asking him to inform the District Commissioner, that they had "elected and installed according to our customs, the son of Malam Bako by the name of Malam Idrisu Bako (alias Malam Tumbi) to be our Head." Of the forty-three signatories, thirty-four identified by the current elders had all been property-owners (indicative of patron status); those properties are still in their families today, and many of their current resident heirs are still important community members.

"If you don't own a house," observed Chief Sha'aibu Bako and Alkali (his judge), "how do you show 'capacity'?" They go on: Some people have no sense; they hire a place. During the Colonial period, on Kingsway (department store) side, there was the DC (District Commissioner) Court. The Government called together all Muslims in Accra—they wanted to know who had a house. They called all of their names. Only one man, Mamman Atta, did not have a house. Everyone shouted, "Oh, you don't have a house!" and shamed him (Sha'aibu and Alkali 5/4/1982). On the other hand, by owning houses inside and outside of *zongo*, Hajiya Pedro shows she has "capacity."

While it is true that Malam Bako and his followers were strangers and thus lacked legitimate rights to land, as we have seen in Chapter 3 Bako was awarded custodial rights.[3] As the patron, Malam Bako could then allocate the land as he saw fit. And as detailed in Chapters 6 and 7, the majority of the current landlords of Sabon Zongo are descendants of the men and women who were allotted plots on which to build in 1912. Those owned by others are located primarily in Ayigbetown and the southern periphery, the latest and least densely populated.

There is a certain amount of mobility between houses, both for kin (at the least, non-paying residents, at the most owners) and tenants: through kin connections, through marriage, through money. For example, Mohammed Bako, grandson of Malam Bako (his father was Saidu), was born in *Gidan Malam Bako* (Malam Bako's house). When he married in 1969, he moved to the house of his father's sister, Hajiya Kakimatu, "because people in this house are not many," and through kinship and inheritance rights, he is now the landlord (Mohammed "Numbo" Bako 6/4/1995). When Amina Musa Ango, granddaughter of Musa Abokin Ango, married Muhsin Barko, grandson of Fati Mai Gujiya (one of the early supporters of Malam Bako and thus an original landlord), she moved around the corner from the Abokin Ango family house to the Abdurahaman Bako Goldsmith family house (a.k.a. *Gidan Makaranta*).

Residence patterns for the Hausa are traditionally patrilocal, minimally virilocal. Today, as observed above, there are young men who bring their bride to their father's house. According to the elder (and Bako son) Alhaji Hamisu, "when you have room in the house, then you have to" (6/4/1982)—unless you have room elsewhere and want to live separately, or if your father has land and money and doesn't want you to stay in the house with him, then he can build for you. In this Hausa-created community, it is unusual for a man to move with his wife to her father's house, although it has happened. Alhaji Hamisu also recounted the story from the days before Sabon Zongo of a friend of Malam Nenu who came to Ghana with his son Audu Bawa. They lived at Zongo Lane. The father died, Nenu took Audu Bawa as his son and then gave his daughter Adama to him as a wife. The young couple then lived at Nenu's at Zongo Lane (Hamisu 6/4/1982). Their son became one of the early landlords at Sabon Zongo

(Malam Bako was his mother's brother by the same father), and his son Ila was elected assemblyman and then member of Parliament in 1992.

A more recent example is that of Alhaji Huudu, a son of Malam Bako's son Lawal. Huudu married Halimatu, great-granddaughter of Shekara (former wife of Malam Nenu), in 1957. Shekara had been a co-wife to Malam Bako's mother, so even though she was divorced by Malam Nenu, Malam Bako gave her two pieces of land in Sabon Zongo. She gave the land to her daughter's daughter— Halimatu's mother, Hajiya Telefi. Telefi built a house on her plot in Unguwan Zabrama. When Halimatu and Huudu married, they lived at Lawal's. But the other women didn't get along with Halimatu. So Huudu and Halimatu moved to the house owned by her mother, while her mother lives in her own house at Zongo Lane (Alhaji Huudu 6/14/1996).

Two questions emerge: 1) How have Hausa landlords or landlord families held onto their property? 2) How have the non-Hausa acquired property? Over the years, throughout Ghana individuals have been granted freehold titles by stools and families. In Accra, private lands constitute a very small percentage (Konadu-Agyemang 2001:134) and there is no evidence that the originally al-located Sabon Zongo land itself can be sold. First of all, "the Hausas acquired a usufructuary title to the Sabon Zongo land . . . It is clear also from the evidence of Manche Ababio [James Town Ga chief] that he did not alienate the allodial titlebto Sabon Zongo land to Malam Baako [*sic*]" (Chief Lebbo Baako v. Alhaji Adamu Damanley and J.P. Allotey (alias) Nii Amane Akwai II, Acting Sempe Mankralo, The High Court of Justice, Accra, Ghana, 12/23/1981:5). Anyone granted a piece of land owns the right to use that land. Upon his or her death, if the family abandons it, it then becomes vacant Ga stool land. Thus, the acreage was given to Malam Bako; he or his family in turn allocated parcels to others. As long as they continue to use them, they may keep them. But, they only own the right to use and benefit from the land, whether that means building a house or growing a garden. When Sabon Zongo people talk about "buying" land, in fact they are still only buying the rights to use it.

As is the case throughout Accra, families are loathe to alienate corporately-owned compounds. For descendants of early settlers in Sabon Zongo, the family compounds carry symbolic capital. They are material connectors to the founding of the community, and they are proof of pedigree. As Peter Marris wrote about the over-populated and poor inner-city area of Lagos, "through its courtyards ramified a network of family relationships sustaining an intricate exchange of mutual support" (Marris 1979:421). Such housing enables survival through so-cial support, but it also enables survival in a real physical sense, proving able "to invoke free accommodation for the poor" (Korboe 1992:1159).

Some people with no genealogical ties to the Bakos have succeeded in ac-quiring pieces of land. They include men and women with long-standing Sabon Zongo connections who were never tenants, who grew up in patriline-owned property, or who have connections with the patrons of the community, elders of the Bako family. For example, the owner of one of the sampled compounds,

Alhaji Mumuni, is a close friend of Dan Baba (Malam Bako's last surviving child). After Alhaji Mumuni's father died, Dan Baba made it possible for Mumuni to buy a piece of land. The Gaskiya Cinema sits on what was empty space. Baba Mai Doki, Idrissu's son, loves going to the movies and when an Akan man asked about opening a theatre, Baba Mai Doki arranged for the rights to build the movie house (though the land is still in the Bako family).

Property in *Kan Tudu*, the core of Sabon Zongo, is not available. Outside of the core, where it is less densely populated and there is far less street life, some buying and selling of land is still possible, especially in the southern less-built-up section of Ayigbetown. But it is uncertain. You specify the amount of land you want, you build your own structure, you tell the landlord what it cost to build; then the landlord accepts the cost, by dividing the cost by the amount of rent you would otherwise pay per month. When the number of months is over, the agreement is over and a new one is necessary. If the landlord wants you out, even though you built it, when the agreement ends, you are out.

The owner of Timbuktu Mosque, in the Sunshine area, is a Zabrama man. He had lived nearby, got into business gradually and made some money. With the help of Sule Bako, the chief's son, he bought the land from the Bako family. The southeastern part of Sabon Zongo, Ayigbetown, sports several new houses, some built by non-Bako people who bought the land. Alhaji Adamu Yahaya has a history with the community and succeeded in buying a piece of land from a man who had bought it from Lawal, a son of Malam Bako. Yahaya says his whole family is here—*muna da yawa*, we are many—which is why he chose to stay (Alhaji Adamu Yahaya 6/11/1996). But he was also fortunate enough to be able to build, rather than be reduced to renting space. Alhaji Babah Alargi, the Hausa engineering consultant, mused aloud that there are "proper" buildings in Ayigbetown and at Zongo Junction, but not in *zongo*. People have been able to buy land and put up buildings outside of the old nucleus. "With the zongo [the old core], it's a pity—no improvement. . . . Even in Nigeria, the family houses have improved" (Alhaji Babah Alargi 5/12/1995).

One can also buy/sell single rooms in compounds. This is similar to condominium ownership. To do so, one must go to the Lands Department, and they will assign the room a new number. There are advantages and disadvantages. Agent Shadow thinks it is a disadvantage to the seller, because he loses a piece of property. But if it is family property and the resident wants to move out, selling off his piece will give him cash in hand. For the buyer, if the house is more than eighty years old, the cost is low and he can live there forever. For example, for a new chamber/hall for sale in a compound, someone offered ₵800,000.

There are a couple of examples of such "condo" ownership in Sabon Zongo. At Tanko Alwali's, house number B67/2, a huge open compound in Unguwan Zabrama, a tenant bought one of the rooms (number B67D/2). As I noted in the last chapter, a landlord in the Sunshine section of Ayigbetown had so many financial problems that he sold off most of the compound that he inherited from his father. One of his tenants bought three rooms and has had an architect draw up plans to create a self-contained apartment—including sitting room, bedroom, kitchen, shower and WC.

One view from within the Bako family is that, first of all "the settlers are very few" (Sule Bako 6/14/1996); that initially there were Ewes and Zabramas (hence the creation of the neighborhoods Ayigbetown and Unguwan Zabrama), that the Zabramas have almost vanished from the area, and gradually the Kwahus who came to Accra for trade looked for accommodation in *zongo* (ibid.). But more importantly, it is not believed that these tenants influence the Hausa residents. "Because we don't have contact with them. We regard them as settlers—looking for accommodation temporarily—when they get what they want they go away. If they are rich enough to put up their houses, they do it; and in the end go away. So some of us don't see why they should influence us. . . . The point is we will not allow them to influence us, we will influence them. And that is being achieved by way of language [Hausa]" (ibid.).

BECOMING A TENANT

Rapoport has observed that a significant element of the courtyard house is that it fulfills the individual's need to get away "while still in the familiar territory of the family or clan group" (Rapoport 1969:82). This is no longer the living situation for the majority in Sabon Zongo given the large number of tenants or settlers living apart from family in the midst of strangers, but the house form still works as daily exchanges persist.

In Sabon Zongo, tenants are referred to as *bako*, by which is meant "settlers," though the word really means "guest." "No matter what your position, they won't accord you your respect due," complains one tenant. An important element in one's social position is where one lives. And yet, from my own sample we can see that there are far more than a few settlers who are not related to *zongo* founders: of the 714 adult residents, more than half are tenants. And some who are educated even believe they have influence. The association Ghana Muslim Youth Research, formed by a cross-section of educated Muslim youth about seventeen years ago, became known to diplomatic missions from Islamic countries. Some believe this worries the Bako family and those landlords of Sabon Zongo, who think that anything that comes to Sabon Zongo should come in under their control.

Konadu-Agyemang (2000:82) characterizes the process of a migrant to Accra finding a place to rent "a nightmare." He has found that it takes such a person on average two-plus years. In the interim, many camp out with friends or family. Those without such ties may sleep in classrooms (like in *Gidan Makaranta*) or the workplace. In Sabon Zongo, tenants generally find a room through one of the following ways (M. Barko 6/30/1996). First, agent or broker (Hausa, *dillali/iya*): for some time, local room agents have been the main source of finding a room. In 1996 there were three known people involved: Basiru Shadow, Issah Bola, and Awudu Keeper. The agents charged a registration fee of ₵5,000 and 15 percent of the total rent advance paid if the deal went through. For example, two Akan (Fante) brothers who share rooms in what is predominantly a Hausa family compound gained access through the agent, Issah Bola. Basiru Shadow is a driver by profession and his station is at Arena in Accra. He says that the landlords in all of Accra know him, so when they have a vacancy, they tell him. By the same token, local residents know that Shadow is a broker, so when prospective renters are looking for a place to live and know someone living in Sabon Zongo, the friend leads them to Shadow. Second, friends or relatives: another Akan, who has a Lotto kiosk said he first lived nearby at Abossey-Okai. When he needed to move, he told his friend who contacted his landlord, who also happened to have a vacant room at a family house. Third, by asking around: this was particularly common years ago, when there were no agents working the community. For example, about twenty years ago, a Kotokoli migrant was looking for a room. He happened to be asking at a Hausa family house just when some Zabrama tenants were moving out. They vacated the room, and he got it. More recently, a Kwahu woman died in one of the rooms at the "stables." The word got out and as soon as the woman was sent to the morgue, some people came looking for her room. All three modes ultimately work through the network.

In 1995 the average cost of a chamber and hall was ₵5000–6000/month (when the equivalence was $1 = ₵1360); there are other inexpensive housing areas in Accra. At Zongo Lane, the houses that are zongo-like are comparable in price to Sabon Zongo. The rent is higher elsewhere, like in Nima and Abossey Okai, or the newer Muslim areas of Russia and Mataheko at ₵12,000.

The cost depends on the house itself and negotiation with the landlord. The more modern houses are more expensive. For example, the owner of Butcher House (a modern, multi-story building with apartments on Oblogo Road) wanted to rent out the top floor, which is two sets of two rooms with a kitchen and a flush toilet for ₵30,000/month.

The landlords want an advance, usually three to four years of rent. This is not peculiar to Sabon Zongo—it began around 1980 in Accra, although the amounts requested were low. Since 1985, landlords have demanded large amounts. Some analysts see rent advance as a means of offsetting Structural Adjustment-produced costs and/or a reaction to a government Rent Decree to (unrealistically) lower costs (Konadu-Agyemang 2000:82); others understand it as a way to increase net present value of low rents during times of inflation (Tipple 1999:277). What is particularly hard in Sabon Zongo, however, as in other poor areas is that prospective residents have a hard time coming up with that kind of money.

At the same time, everything is negotiable. For example, one landlady wants ₵8000/month (times 48 months) and Shadow got her to reduce the monthly rent to ₵7000. When the time of the advance is finished, the landlord and tenant make a new deal. The agreements are always in writing, with witnesses—maybe month to month, maybe year to year.

In 1995, Umoru, a former resident of Sabon Zongo who had re-located to Kumase wanted to return. He heard through one of the Bako family members that there was a room in a compound around the corner from the chief. It was a single room, about 8 × 10, with one window. There was no electricity, although the last tenant pulled electricity in from an outside wire. The zinc roof showed through in at least two places, which meant it probably leaked during rains. Only part of the roof had a proper ceiling, and that was stained, probably because of the roof leaks.

The price was negotiable. First the landlord asked ₵5000/month plus three-and-a-half years in advance; when the renter protested, the landlord countered with ₵4000/month, but still three-and-a-half years in advance. The price per month seemed far too high for just one room; in Kumase *zongo* at that time, they were charging ₵2000 for two rooms (a chamber/hall combination). What particularly concerned the man seeking lodging was not so much the size or monthly rent for the room; rather, it was that the landlord only wanted three-and-a-half years rather than five years in advance, which he read as meaning that at the end of that time, he could throw him out.

Whether a resident does or does not own his/her space, renovation of any kind (often even fundamental) comes out of his/her pocket. When Umoru the prospective tenant observed to the landlord that the room he was considering renting needed fixing, the landlord was not interested in doing it. Often, there is no negotiation on this point. Property improvement and repairs on rental properties are not necessarily regarded as capital improvements, that is, for the owner's benefit. Moreover, there is no house insurance in Sabon Zongo, so, for example, when Baba Mai Doki's tenanted house burned down, he had to pay to rebuild it himself. He allowed that if the roof goes bad over a tenant's room, the tenant is responsible for replacing it *but* he/she can then deduct the cost of repair from the monthly rent. However, the landlord does not pay for improvement inside—"*Suna kwana cikin*" (they are sleeping inside, thus it is their responsibility)—and when one of his tenants laid a cement floor inside, and on the porch/verandah outside, that was his choice.

People do not always look kindly upon the use of shared (public) space for private aims and aspirations. As a result, those who are owners may have problems making improvements on their property, because they are not the sole owners. One man wanted to put a flush toilet into his mother's house. To do so meant installing a septic tank outside and then passing a pipe under the room to connect with the toilet. He finally succeeded in 1986, but he had terrible problems because the room over which the pipe would be laid had not belonged to his father, and his father's father's wife's "rival" (co-wife) objected (Alhaji Alhassan Sulley 7/1/1996).

By the same token, the agent Shadow and a variety of tenants aver that a room that Shadow would not even use as a pen for animals houses three Kwahu men who do not have much money. They live here till they can afford something better. On Korle Bu Street there is a room built-on to the outside of a compound which in the past has been a storefront. It has neither door nor windows—the street front is not enclosed. The floor is dirt and there is no electricity connected. For about one year in the mid-1990s, a group of Chadian refugees lived there.

But here it is also tight—maybe one can find only a single room and one wants something bigger. For some, Sabon Zongo is like a stepping stone, and they will move on. Others may even want to buy in Sabon Zongo. One of the educated tenants mused about the divisions in Sabon Zongo. "They [the Bako family] believe that . . . if they don't do the roads, no one should. How do you control people if you are not educated? So it came to pass that all who are educated are not part of their family and control everything." While some of what he was saying was hyperbole, it holds more than a germ of truth. We know that the old landlords, mainly Hausa, were afraid to send their children to Western schools. The less educated they and their children are, the less they control in terms of knowledge, the less they can help develop the community.

Sabon Zongo has a history of development associations, each of which see its charge to help improve the physical environment. Asking whether a recently-established organization includes *zongo* tenants, a member replied, "Well, we didn't include the tenants actually, but we invited just few of them to take part, because as tenants, they are also part of the area (Mohammed "Numbo" Bako 6/6/1996).

COMPOUND-BASED ACTIVITIES

Life is often organized around domestic space, with the same space serving different purposes, perhaps for different people, through coincidental and sequential use. The compound, as a spatial locale, provides the settings and the contexts of interaction among the residents and with visitors from outside. As a social locale, it is performative (cf. Sahlins 1985). It is a lived world, an arena of action while also constructed by action (Munn 1986:8). The house is also a staging area to express distinctions of age, sex, rank (Douglas 1973), identifying certain actors with or assigning them to certain spaces.

It is largely through living their lives in the compound that people have played out their social identities, since residents' social identities correlate with their niche in *zongo* history through the compound space(s) they occupy (cf. Lobo 1982). Cultural rules and norms that guide the activities and behaviors, are reinforced and reproduced through the repetition of those daily activities in which people participate.

The social attributes of ethnicity, religion, hometown provenance, and customs are differentially incorporated into the Sabon Zongo houses, even the Hausa family houses. Its residents are far more varied, coming not only from different families but even different ethnic groups and religions as well. Their complex of customs and practices is anchored spatially and is transacted temporally, while the compound itself has been re-defined to extend beyond the compound walls. Over time, these practices, which Munn characterizes as "*intersubjective spacetime*—a spacetime of self-other relationships formed in and through acts and practices" (Munn 1986:9), undergo spatial, temporal and socio-cultural transformation through performance or action.

Sabon Zongo's compounds, like those elsewhere in Accra, introduce immigrants to city life in general and to *zongo* ways in particular. As elsewhere in Africa, it is the compound yard that carries primacy as a space for work and play, in large part due to climate: rooms are generally small and often not well-ventilated. The living unit (whether family or roommates) has exclusive control over their own indoor space to use as they see fit. But it is rarely spacious. Thus, private physical and social space for the individual resident is minimal.

The compound yard is a semi-public/semi-private space, where most activity takes place. It is open to all occupants. When non-residents (friends and customers of residents, ambulatory traders and bankers) enter, according to local courtesy they announce their arrival. Each household "owns" a conceptually delineated section, where the respective woman cooks, family members eat, children are bathed, clothing and dishes are washed, residents and visitors socialize. In Sabon Zongo, the coal pot symbolizes the family unit.[4] According to the Urban Preparatory Study's analysis of Sabon Zongo, each house (compound structure) encloses a multiplicity of such units: in 45.6 percent of the compounds, there are six to ten households, in 33.3 percent, one to five, in 17.5 percent, eleven to fifteen (Government of Ghana 1992:22). The overwhelming number of households are composed of only two to 4.9 people (86 percent), the balance evenly divided between those of less than two or five to 9.9 (Government of Ghana 1992:23). The Urban Preparatory Study's analysis is based upon a study population of 246, from infancy to age sixty-five-plus. The Study calculated the average number of households per compound at 7.7, the average household size at 3.2 persons, and the average room occupancy 2.7. In my Sabon Zongo sample, each home has an average of forty adult residents.

The physical structure of the house and yard encapsulates or encodes social understandings and values—what Mitchell (1991) refers to as "enframing." This has helped create the order manifest in the social system of the occupants. Boundaries define the interactions. "The boundaries may be physical, they may be conceptual, rigid, or permeable, of long or short duration. People live in physical proximity to one another; their copresence is interconnected and regulated by the *durée* of daily existence" (Pellow 1991b:190).

The boundaries are thus delineated through daily incidents of exchange—the sharing of space through engagement in or observation of talk, domestic needs and duties, joint rituals, commercial enterprises, intangibles of genealogical entanglement and remembered histories. Even as spatial differentiation is not great, the sequencing of activities is. Early in the morning, from 6 A.M. till 8 A.M., the same corner of the compound may be used to prepare breakfast, to bathe young children, to feed the children, to wash the dishes, to wash laundry, to hang the wet wash. Routine activities reveal some seasonal variation, for example, cooking inside during the rains. Thus, social composition and physical form are both constitutive of social and cultural values and implicated in the routines people engage in and the manner of exchange.

The heterogeneity of Sabon Zongo's compound in the context of *zongo* life encourages new forms of interaction, new roles, new identities. Islam impacts on everyone's life, whether a believer or not. For the Muslims, it is convenient. By living here, they can satisfy religio-cultural standards. In this community of thirty mosques, no compound is far from one. By praying together daily, the men create or solidify their networks. For the Muslim women, prayer in the compound is convenient, in the sense that it is not alien. During Ramadan, everyday from 3:30 to 5:30 at Bako B.K.'s mosque on Korle Bu Street, there is preaching. Also during the fast month, pre-dawn prepared foods are available. For the non-Muslims, there is a familiarization of the dailiness of Islam, as co-residents create a sacred space by laying a prayer rug by their room to pray or ready themselves for celebration of the Prophet's birthday. So in addition to enabling basic family routines, this shared space exposes individuals to one another's customs and culinary traditions, even encouraging interaction among these members of different ethnicities and religions.

People know each other, certainly by sight, but often by name, occupation, ethnicity. Even in populous compounds, landlords can identify their tenants. Sarkin Fada's house (actually three houses) has 128 rooms and an adult population of 103, which includes ten ethnicities. He knows all of the people in his compound well enough that he can go through room by room, noting ethnicity for all and work for almost all. His personal familiarity with his neighbors, most of whom are not family, is hardly unusual and argues against characterizing all urban living as anomic or anonymous.

If there are facilities like a shower room, they are shared. But, which facilities one might use is a function of one's place in the compound's social order—family or tenant, and if family, how close to the landlord. For example, in Bawa Allah's compound, there is one shower room (with a shower head) and one standing pipe at the front of the compound; both of these, for the use of the compound elder, are kept locked.

Children tend to have the run of the place. The compound yard is their playground, although Sabon Zongo is so village-like and many of the roads are lanes without vehicular traffic, that the street is perfectly safe. They are also comfortable wandering in and out of people's rooms—"unlike adults, [children] seem to feel no restrictions—social, psychological, or territorial. They often disregard boundaries and trespass where adults would not dare" (Pellow 1991b: 199). But they also do have their "assigned" spots. Since families tend to have at the most two indoor rooms where they sleep (chamber and hall), and normally one bed, the children either share the adults' bed or are consigned to mats on the floor. Young children are generally bathed not in the shower room, which is reserved for adults, but in the family's corner of the compound, near the spigot, or even outside of the compound alongside the gutter.

It is also as a site for income-producing work that the courtyard space is fundamental. Throughout Africa, indeed much of the developing world, housing is a potential resource as a site for informal economic enterprises. Reviewing the international literature, Rogerson (1991:341) observes "that income from home-based enterprise is often vital to the financing of dwellings and their improvement in poor urban communities."

It is particularly common to see women preparing and selling from the compound yard foods that one can find all over Accra, such as *kenkey*, or Northern Nigerian specialties, such as the staple *tuwo*. Others sell oil and firewood in the compound, or corn (which is ground in a room off of the entrance). Compound residents also use its various other spaces for income-producing activities. The courtyard is used by residents simultaneously and sequentially. There are those who convert their sleeping room into a workplace during the workday: to do seamstressing/tailoring, ironing, architectural drafting, shoe repair; to make pasta (*taliya*, a Hausa favorite); to hold school classes as a *malam*; to do soothsaying, make and prescribe folk medicine. Some are lucky enough to have access to an extra room for their work.

Others are able to press their appliances into service. Women with freezers often sell "ice water" and "ice cream." Accra has a clean water system and plastic bags are cheap and readily available. Sellers generally fill a large basin with water, strain it through a funnel into individual bags, tie each, and put it in the freezer. All over the city, one can buy bags of cold water. In Sabon Zongo, some women sell from their freezer; community residents know who is in business through the gossip network. Other women sell from shops. Still others hawk from a tray carried on the head as they walk through the community. Vic, who lives in Ayigbetown, sells ice water. "As I have a fridge, I have to make it for my neighbors. . . . If I don't and I say it's finished, people won't believe you" (6/17/1996). "Ice cream" consists of frozen, colored and flavored water in cubes or varying plastic-enclosed forms. Those with a window that faces the street or lane can utilize it as a store counter.

Indeed, they may even use the out-facing room as a shop—which, at night, may serve as the sleeping room. Or, those who actually own the property (or whose family does) may have the space to create a small shop out of an already-existing room, or wall off part of a room, or even carve a section out of the compound wall to build a shop—for a tailor, a laundryman, a hairdresser, or a chop bar (restaurant) out front.

Exiting the prototypical Hausa compound, one passes through the *zaure*. In some *zongo* properties, women of the house sit there and sell their goods. Other women situate their business outside but nearby, often in the shadow of the compound wall. There are the simple traders, who sell petty goods; produce, like bananas and oranges, and peanuts; cooking ingredients, like raw rice, to-matoes and pepper; and bread. Then there are those who are prepared food sellers. Some prepare the foods at home and carry it outside to sell; others cook and sell outside. The full complement of typical Northern Nigerian prepared foods are found nowhere else in Accra. Thus, just as the Hausa housewives all have their favorite purveyer of Ga *kenkey*, so many of Sabon Zongo's southern Ghanaian women send their children out for Hausa *wake*.

Some compound properties also include a yard outside, where men engage in various businesses; others living on a lane with little foot traffic may claim a space there. They engage in such activities as fixing appliances and cars, keeping sheep and goats, washing clothing, carpentry.

According to AMA records, there are 267 mixed commercial/residential struc-tures in Sabon Zongo. These include the Oblogo Road storied buildings, which have apartments upstairs and storefronts at the street level, as well as small shops that are built onto the compounds and entered from the street or lane. Many of these are provision stores, tailors/seamstresses, hairdressers, and chop bars. Some of the businesses belong to individuals resident in the given com-pound; others are owned by outsiders (from elsewhere in Sabon Zongo or even from outside) who rent the space.

Finally, there are those who work in a kiosk. Some are free-standing but many are in front of or somehow attached to a compound. Some of the shop-keepers are men, some are women. The women's occupations include selling provisions, sewing, and hairdressing; the men work in electronics (sale and repair of), selling lotto tickets, and as tailors.

PUBLIC PRIVACY

When Malam Bako founded Sabon Zongo, his followers built their com-pounds to accommodate the (Hausa) extended family unit. On the socio-spatial continuum of public to private, the original Sabon Zongo compounds were transitional in nature, open interior space encircled by living units and providing a link between the exterior of the compound and the interior living area of the family. Passing through the front vestibule, one transits from the exterior, public space to the interior, private household space (Prussin 1986). Unlike all court-yards and compounds, they specifically incorporated principles of Hausa/Muslim social and spatial organization. The gradations of privacy, set from the entrance hut, the *zaure* "mediating between public and private space, grew more pro-nounced, presumably reflecting a psychological response to 'protect' or 'guard' an opening under conditions of increased density" (Prussin 1986:212).

While privacy is a culturally variable concept (Altman 1974:24; Rapoport 1980b:31; Moore 1984:262; Howell and Tentokali 1989), people everywhere find ways of creating boundaries between themselves and others. In Sabon Zongo, the extended family no longer necessarily lives together, although for the founding families, that would be the ideal. In most cases, there are non-family members (tenants) resident as well. Their own enclosed space—perhaps only one room, in some cases a sitting room and bedroom—not only is rarely spacious, it also lacks an indoor kitchen and bathing and toilet facilities. Cooking is done in front of one's door. Shower room and toilet, if they exist, are situated in the compound yard and shared among compound dwellers.

Because the public/private distinction is visually minimal if not absent altogether, residents engage in what I have termed public/private behavior or public privacy (Pellow 1996b:126). On the one hand, individuals engaged in an activity behave as though no one else is present, while on the other hand, those present follow various rules, such as visual avoidance, to allow the other to use the shared space or walk through it without visual transaction or intrusion.

Those using the compound yard are often in full view of one another. Little is invisible to co-residents. There is no such thing as secrets here: "When you are going to bath, you have to hold your bucket—people see that you are going to bath" (Mohammed Bako 6/6/1996). Visitors may be entertained inside, but to get there they often must walk through the shared space (unless the resident's rooms are add-ons from the outside). Residents are socialized in compound ways through a mini-social system, cued in part by physical elements, in part by social ones. There is an order to the compound, and the behavior of residents such as respecting others' privacy or seniority suggests that on some level they are aware of socio-spatial rules of engagement. This shared morality of user behavior makes possible an easygoing sharing of the common space. They may choose to interact, but they might also choose not to interact.

The choice is a function of the particular activity. In this largely Muslim community, women in particular tend to observe the five daily prayers at home (unlike the men, who generally go to the mosque). They may do so inside or in the yard, and by laying out a prayer rug delineating a conceptually enclosed space which others will not violate.

Compound residents also have differential rights to facilities (toilet, shower) depending upon their status (member of the landlord family or tenant and degree of seniority). This in effect represents another side of public privacy—it is as though these conveniences are located within someone's private domain and thus accessible to him/her (or guests) only. In the Small London compound and Sule Bako's house, there are toilets (a KVIP and WCs, respectively). Visible to all, they are padlocked and the owner holds the key. In a more Western version, Alhaji Hamza's shower room and toilet (pan toilet) are in rooms built into his quarters at *Gidan Baki* and thus literally do lie within his private domain.

GENDER ROLES

Over the last eighty-plus years, compounds have expanded in size through kinship lineally and collaterally, but also by adding tenants. The householders have come to tolerate a mix of ethnicity, of religion, of varying customs. The tradition of seclusion, still the norm in urban northern Nigeria, is long gone in Sabon Zongo.

Seclusion bespeaks a delineation of the practitioner's range of social contacts and activities, which is expressed in physical space—the sequestering of women in an exclusive and private domain, the division of the household into male and female sectors, indeed, the division of the world into male and female domains, and the contrivances employed to advertise this fact to those outside the household and to socialize those within the household. It is the manner and mode of physical confinement. Men seek to exert social control by trying to impose spatial control over the adult women of their compounds, defining the house as the container of women and restricting women to it (Callaway 1987). Women may concur, but talk and action are different. Indeed, as Pittin observes, spatial boundaries may reflect social boundaries that "undergo revision, resistance, and renegotiation" (Pittin 1996:184). Men in fact have little control over the women's interaction within the compound, as they are so rarely there; by the same token, if the husbands travel, women may take advantage of their absence to leave the house (Schildkrout 1983; Pittin 1996).

The Koran in fact is ambiguous on how wifely modesty is to be enforced, and this has generated a range of modes of "symbolic shelter" to protect the honor of men and the family. Variability in modes of such shelter conveys the differences implicit in the female experience, say the spatial confinement of seclusion as opposed to veiling, and the attendant freedoms and constraints (see for example Vatuk 1982 for India; Odeh 1993 for Iran; Bourdieu 1979 for Algeria). The twin customs of veiling and secluding women, overseen by men and imposed upon women, are two types of "symbolic shelter" that protect the honor of the family.

But even in Malam Bako's house, the heirs have brought in tenants, albeit all Hausa. "How can you 'make *kulle*' with tenants?" asks Malam Gambo, who died in 1998. The fact that seclusion has not operated in the community, that compounds include unrelated persons (tenants) does not mean that, as one proud Hausa husband declared, "women can just go roaming about." The Hausa value of *kunya* for women is maintained, albeit in an altered form.

As we have seen, many women who work now situate themselves in front of the outside wall of the compound, or just under the eaves or in the doorway, plying their trade or spending time with friends and family. In a sense, they are making their trading space liminal. Turner's use of liminality (1969) connotes a condition of ambiguity. As he writes, "liminal entities are neither here or there; they are betwixt and between the position assigned and arrayed by law, custom, convention, and ceremonial" (1969:95). To be in a liminal space might include engaging in behavior that is ambiguous or socially defined out of bounds. In the old days of Malam Bako, a woman selling outside would be socially out of bounds. One's doorway or the street near one's own or mother's house might be construed as ambiguous or even an extension of the house. As a corollary to public privacy, the ambiguity expands the women's permissible spatial domain.

As observed in Chapter 7, women's domain has also extended into the *zaure* (Figure 56), made possible because the social construction of that space has been

Figure 56
Women Using the *Zaure*. Courtesy of the Author.

re-defined. Women are not secluded, men are not confined to this peripheral area. But it is also the case that Hausa men and men of other ethnicities as well who live in Sabon Zongo tend not to hang around the inside of the house, although some, such as tailors, may work in a shady spot in the compound or an inside room. Men have a variety of gathering spots, as discussed in Chapter 6.

CHANGING ROLES

Since the establishment of Sabon Zongo, there has been a decrease in polygyny and the absence of seclusion. The community and its members have become far more metropolitan. Tenanting is typical. In analyzing the mutually constituted social and spatial changes, how do we disentangle longer-term patterns (historical shifts) from cyclical patterns (due to settlement growth, depth of residence, phase in the family cycle)? Is it conceivable that seclusion or some equivalent might return to the stranger community? Have the shapes and sizes of compounds and the attendant or determinant social behaviors really altered, or do they just belong to a particular moment in time? The desire for "self-contained" units is not related to seclusion, to the desire to "do *kulle*" in an easy manner. In contemporary Accra, there are nightly showings of soap operas like *Sunset Beach* and *The Bold and the Beautiful.* The Sabon Zongo women, even those who do not understand English, watch and connect with the people and their stories—everyone is beautiful, lives graciously or aspires to do so. It is the stuff of fantasy.

But there are those, even in Sabon Zongo, who can actually imagine themselves living in a self-contained home. And some of them have actually built such homes in the outlying areas of Awushie and Shukura. There is a dimension of education here or at least cosmopolitanism, to the extent that they have traveled and/or lived abroad. They would not express this as a need for privacy; one man, for example, is building a modern version of an extended family house. So there will still be shared semi-public space, but everyone will have his/her own bedrooms and full bathroom. What it gives them is "capacity" and re-defined social status, marked by re-defined housing, within their community.[5]

NOTES

1. I have written elsewhere (Pellow 1991b) about Accra's compounds as enculturating space.

2. Vestbro (1975:34f.) has made a similar demonstration of the versatility of the urban Swahili house in Dar es Salaam: the spatial organization is not designed for strict differentiation of household activities, the ground plan can be changed within limits of the basic structure, and it may be extended by adding new rooms. It is also technically adaptable, with the capacity to absorb innovations in building techniques, materials, and facilities.

3. Indeed, his grandson Sha'aibu's power as chief is characterized by Sha'aibu's *maji dadi* as *a kan kasa* (over land) and its subjects (Musa Alhassan 28 May 1996).

4. Not only is this true throughout Africa, as observed by Levine and Levine on the Gusii of Kenya (1991); in medieval Europe, households were determined for the census by enumerating hearths (Contamine 1980). I have written elsewhere (Pellow 1991b) about Accra's compounds as enculturating space.

5. See for example, Kent (1984) for similar observations about Navajo traditional housing.

9

CONCLUSION: *ZONGWANCI*

Place has a unique reality for each inhabitant; even though meaning may be shared, there are likely also to be contested views (Rodman 1992). By extension, individuals produce and reproduce a unique place. Collectively, in a larger geographic field of experience, a place is a listening post to other places.

Sabon Zongo was consciously established as a place. It was created as a refuge for people who felt their practices were in jeopardy. Sabon Zongo has a distinct local public culture and distinctive domestic and public spaces, the two dimensions intertwined temporarily, then reproducing and altering one another and creating what I call *zongwanci* or zongo-ness. The public events and festivals, the daily street activities and foods sold, through which residents construct community are distinctive to the people and the place.

Layers of past meanings are embodied in the place. They are used to authenticate rights and responsibilities. Sabon Zongo represents the vision of a single family, the Bakos. But the community is far more complex than that of the Bako landlord group. The community is also far more complex ethnically than it was in its origins. The social change and its various kinds of diversification carry new meanings and they are manifest spatially—the proliferation of new neighborhoods (some with occupational specializations, others socially unique), new community services, the adaptation of the public spaces and of the compound house and yard.

Non-*zongo* Accra dwellers negatively perceive the community as separate and different from southern Ghana. Many consider it an enclave of aliens, others an enclave of northern Ghanaians. Ghanaians who have never been to Sabon Zongo talk about how run down and unattractive it is. They imply that the place is somehow unsafe or make disparaging remarks about the behavior and practices of people who live there. Invariably, such people also express disbelief when told that southern Ghanaians live there.

Sabon Zongo's physical landscape is different from most other communities in Accra's mosaic. There are certainly similarities with some of Accra's other *zongos*. Cultural symbols or landmarks (icons of landscape), such as the Zana and Abokin Ango Mosques, are also found in Nima and Lagostown, distinguishing them like Sabon Zongo as places apart from metropolitan Christian Accra. Driving along Oblogo Road in the evening, the men hanging out on the steps of the Gaskiya Cinema, like men hanging out near the overhead pass in Nima, *look* foreign, many garbed in their flowing gowns and hats.

Zukin (1995) reminds us that social differentiation can be subtly implied through visual and spatial cues and strategies, and that culture is intertwined with capital and identity. Smart and Smart (1999) and Bestor (1999) provide anthropological examples of the latter phenomenon for Hong Kong entrepreneurial activity and Tokyo's fish market, respectively. Sabon Zongo's cultural marginalization has been reinforced through negative perceptions of poverty and foreignness, and through the language of exclusion and entitlement—by the city at large and by the local elite and landlords.

But the same cultural markers that carry pejorative implications for outsiders carry a positive charge for many insiders. Residents see advantages to living in Sabon Zongo: the small-town contacts, a public culture that draws in everyone through social encounters and cultural practices, symbols such as the mosques, compound forms, foods, night market, the gendering of visibility and space usage, and even the alternative of a native court. Their social practices create a socially meaningful world. Community routines and interpersonal ties cross-cut and anchor relations in time and place. The houses they live in and the public spaces they traverse are filled with meaning that infuses their daily interactions. Sabon Zongo is a "place to belong to" in the midst of so many other (possibly anonymous) places in Accra. It recalls the phenomenon of "place attachment" (Altman and Low 1991).

When Sarkin Fada's daughter died, men heard about it at 6:30 A.M. after praying at the mosque. When Alhaji Ila's mother-in-law died, the muezzin announced it as part of his dawn call to prayer. Public privacy kicks in as such details of individual family life are shared with the collectivity. Phenomena of global magnitude also impact on the social and spatial configuration of Sabon Zongo. Many people have televisions, and those who do not share with those who do. It is unclear exactly how or to what extent television influences people's beliefs and desires.

One Saturday morning, I was sitting with a woman on the dirt floor of her room just talking. The room was just large enough to hold a double bed, cabinet with dishware, chair and television. The old black and white television was on and CNN's Style show from Paris was broadcasting. My friend did not understand English and the television basically provided background noise. Who knows how much she gleaned from the program, if she was even interested in it. But there is no doubt that television and news magazines and the like provide exposure to new and different lifestyles. Certainly those women who told me that they wanted to live in houses that are not old-fashioned have some image of what that might be.

Hausa who come from Nigeria prefer staying in *zongo*, because they can find everything they are accustomed to in their homeland. People claim they stay here because there are no problems with electricity or water (especially water, needed by Muslims for ablutions before the five daily prayers). Life here enables continuity in tradition and traditional alliances. "I was bred here, grew here, therefore want to stay here." "We are all here" [that is, the Bako family members]. Chief Sha'aibu Bako's highly educated son Sule Bako mused: "I don't want to shun my people, because of my background. I don't want to leave my parents. I was born here and bred here, so now that I have developed out of them, do I run away from them? No matter where I go to live, I will . . . come to them" (6/14/1996).

But Sabon Zongo's population, and thus the cultures it incorporates, has diversified considerably. Initially, its population was Hausa; they came in order to live in peace and practice their religion, separate from the other Muslim groups. Today, many different ethnicities live in Sabon Zongo; many of them are southern Ghanaians, strangers to Accra. Moreover, many of those now resident in Sabon Zongo are tenants, not house owners or relatives of house owners. While Islam continues to define Sabon Zongo, many of the northern and southern Ghanaian residents in fact are Christians. These different groups of people have brought along different kinds of cultural baggage. The simple fact that they lack historical or genealogical connections with the community and its founders, that they are of different backgrounds, opens the door to new ideas and behaviors. It helps alter the habitats of meaning.

Many non-Muslims have moved to Sabon Zongo and express satisfaction with living there. They say it is peaceful, there is no discrimination against them, and the rent is affordable. As residents, they have ties to the locale via exchange of all sorts (social, material, political, occupational), forms of consumption (of foods, clothing, celebrations), through patron-client relationships.

Residents, tenants and owners, Christians and Muslims—all these people speak of a kind of overarching morality as another reason for people staying on in Sabon Zongo beyond the cost of accommodation and the social ties. They celebrate the village morality of their community-in-the-city. Musa Alhassan, one of the chief's cabinet members, refers to this as one overriding culture. He observes that if you are a stranger in a country and the people have tails, you must wear a rope. By extension, southerners living in Sabon Zongo come to know of the life-cycle activities celebrated by the northerners and many participate.

Neighbors are "the eyes of the street" (Jacobs 1961). Residents do not worry about crime, but speak of "respectable thieves": "we know everybody" (who the thieves are) and if something goes missing, people often know who might have "borrowed" it and go collect it from them.[1]

This is not to say conflict is absent. Genealogical pedigree and relationship to the community's mythic past and the heroes celebrated can be and are divisive. Pockets of dissatisfaction derive from social divisions that are spatially manifest. In some cases, the issue is whether or not one is a member of the Bako family (connected through genealogy). In other cases, it is the issue of whether or not one is a house owner (not necessarily genealogical, but more often than not of historical origin). Often, it is the spatial core-periphery split, which is also tied to both genealogy and history. The primary spatial oppositions are up/down, and they are most visible in old *zongo*/Ayigbetown: as "up" is equated with *Kan Tudu* and the original *zongo* nucleus, whereas Ayigbetown is "down," being the most recently settled and most clearly for non-Bako, non-Muslim, even non-Hausa residents. Just as some *Kan Tudu* residents consider Ayigbetown peripheral to the core of Sabon Zongo (socially, politically, economically), there are those in Ayigbetown who do not identify themselves as residents of Sabon Zongo—they happen to live there, do not follow the chief, do not relate to the community's kin-based history.

In fact, a number of members of the younger generation observe that the family basis of the community is a real obstacle to development. The elders don't like those younger to tell them what to do, and they are afraid of progress.

But despite its physical shabbiness, the Hausa, other Muslims, and even southern Ghanaian Christians like to live in Sabon Zongo. Beyond economics, for the Hausa and Muslims it is the pull of network coherence; for the Christians, it is the peacefulness and non-danger that is appealing. Well-to-do men reside there but do not own homes, simply because they are not heirs to early house-owners and there is no place to build. Some build houses in Shukura, Lagostown, and Abossey Okai, but rent rooms in Sabon Zongo. They do not move into their owned properties outside Sabon Zongo, because

if you go live there, people take it like you want to go out from Muslim society. There are no mosques around there. And then if anything happens, you don't hear it quick. Things will happen, and then they will just pass before you hear it. [Within the *zongo* it is] easy for you to hear, because you are with the people and then people still regard you as being with them. As soon as you go [to the suburbs] then they think that you are making yourself too big for your people. (Hamidu 1982)

People stay in Sabon Zongo because of ties, roots, traditions, and even a comfortable inertia. Hausa cultural patterns and genealogy are key to understanding how Sabon Zongo works: regulating relations among people and impacting on the community's social, institutional, and spatial structure. While over time Sabon Zongo has reproduced its socio-spatial order, it has also produced, changed, and evolved into a different kind of community, one based upon a collective identity that transcends ethnicity. There have been shifts in spatial and social practices due to ethnic diversity, economics, dilution of ritual orthodoxy, acculturation through connections with urban living. Changes have resulted from conflicts, political pragmatism, and detachment from Hausa or Bako authority and ownership. Sabon Zongo has expanded considerably from its early days. It is also no longer a place apart from the rest of Accra. It lies within the Municipality and is serviced by the city; its citizens vote for an Assemblyman, who sits on the Accra Metropolitan Assembly, as well as a Member of Parliament who represents Sabon Zongo as a part of a larger parliamentary district.

Many residents identify with Sabon Zongo through their particular neighborhood (*Kan Tudu, Unguwan* Zabrama, or Ayigbetown) and its public culture. They also identify with Sabon Zongo through their relationship to the Bako genealogy. Their compound houses, with the involution that has occurred over time, are staging areas for their domestic, ritual, entrepreneurial lives. Sabon Zongo's social and spatial structures are basic to the social order. And the representative cultural symbols "have material consequences" (Zukin 1995:268), as for example, in the housing, which in turn play out socially. The spatial changes in the compounds are intertwined with changes in social roles and behaviors. Is involution of the courtyard bound to happen no matter what? As more second and third generation zongo-ites increase their financial wherewithal, for example, by working overseas, will they make involution into a tradition by continuing to build in? Will they build up, as Hajiya Pedro's son is doing? Or will they buy property outside, build there, and move there? Are these various solutions predictable outgrowths of particular historical circumstances, different, for example, from the domestic cycle?

Relations of power within the community, expressed materially through the use of public and compound space, have changed. Besides involution, I see the beginnings of the privatization of space, through the creation of nuclear family compounds and the purchase of "condos." Both Hausa and non-Hausa-affiliated residents have altered/modified the "performative" structures that enable spatial usage resulting in new forms of interaction, roles, identities.

Ultimately, Sabon Zongo is characterized by *zongwanci*, an over-arching social identity which is itself a social creation, resulting from a combination of history, social and political structures and human agency. *Zongwanci* is a kind of northern ethos that emerges from Islam and cross-cuts ethnicity; *zongwanci* is not kin-based, but it is basic to the ties that bind, to the overarching shared morality, to the attachment that residents feel for the community. It has been perpetuated through the daily activities and exchanges in which residents engage. It has also changed, as people with different backgrounds have moved in and become interactants in the daily exchange. This social practice defines the operational boundaries of Sabon Zongo.

NOTE

1. Someone who had visited me in my room took my Walkman. I had no idea who that might be and told everyone to keep an eye open for it. In a matter of days, my research assistant saw a local teenager with it and said something to him. The young man came to see me. I was then called in to his family's house to meet with him and two elders. The two men apologized to me, one of them smacked the boy, and he was sent off to live with extended family in another city.

APPENDIX

To document that "the processes of history are as much spatial as they are economic, racial and social, and that spatial histories in turn are rooted in phenomenological experience" (Foster 1996:93), I had drawn a sample of 19 compounds from Sabon Zongo's main neighborhoods: *Kan Tudu*, *Zabrama/Gangare*, and Ayigbetown. I selected compounds that are representative of different phases of social change, where occupants include extended family members only, extended family members supplemented by tenants, tenants only, and nuclear family only. Each was drawn to scale by Bossman Murey, a staff member in the Department of Archaeology at the University of Ghana. I carried out a census of all adults resident in each, which included ethnicity, religion, hometown provenance, relation to the landlord, and occupation. I also collected family genealogies, did systematic observation in the semi-public compound yards, and asked (probably an irritating number of) questions of the residents. With the exception of Chief Sha'aibu Bako's house, the census information dates to 1995 and 1996; I canvassed the Chief's compound in 2000.

Each house has an accompanying genealogy, indicating the adult residents and how they are related to the houseowner. Alhaji Baba Mai Doki's house is entirely tenanted, hence there is no genealogy.

Figure 57 shows the location of the compounds, using the numbering system of the house plans. Those of Alhajai Sule Bako, Bebe, Mumuni and Adamu were not yet built when the aerial survey map was completed in 1969. I have indicated their position and approximate shape. Some of the others have been added to since then—for example, the Kariki house did not yet have a third

Figure 57
Aerial Map of Sabon Zongo, Showing Location of Sampled Compounds.

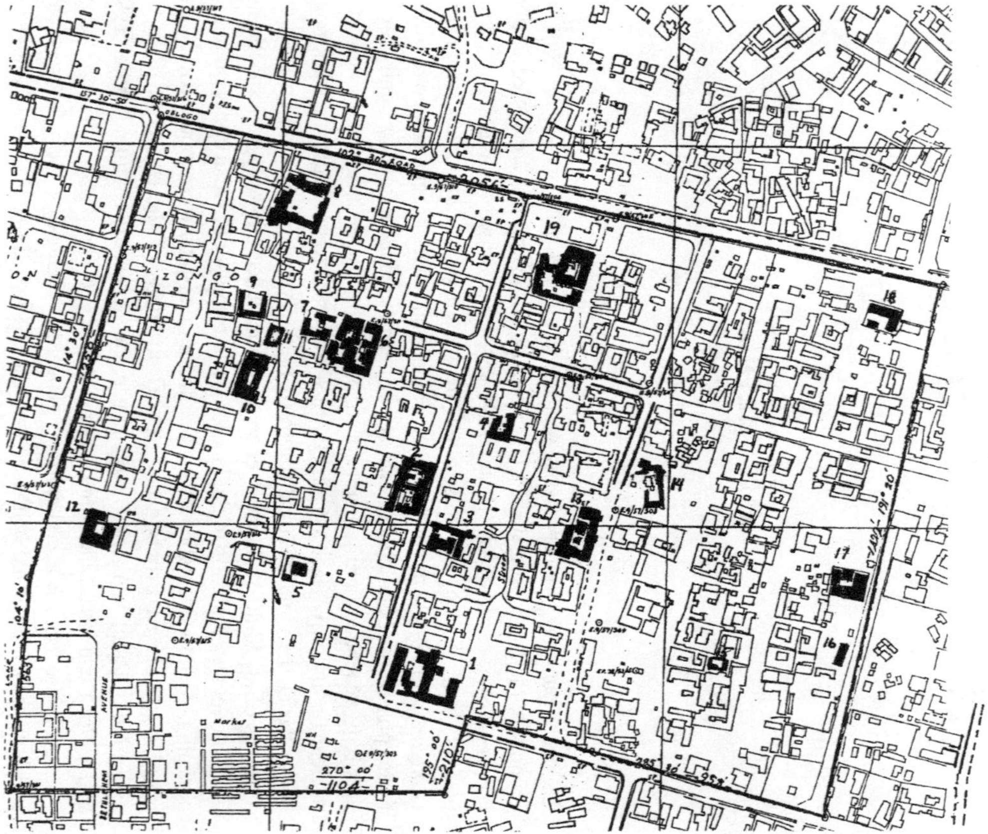

section, and its second section, like the Bawa Allah compound, did not yet exhibit the property of involution.

SAMPLE OF COMPOUNDS

Kan Tudu
1. Malam Bako's House—House Number B425/2
2. Chief Sha'aibu Bako—House Number B321/2
3. Mohammad Badamase—House number B317/2
4. Alhaji Mohammed (Numbo) Bako—House Number B328/2
5. Alhaji Sule Bako—House Number B313/2

Zabrama/Damaley
6. Alhaji Yaro—House Number B498/2
7. Bako Goldsmith (*Gidan Makaranta*)—House Number B220/2
8. Tanko Ali'wali—House Number B55/2
9. Hajiya Maimuna Pedro Onukpe—House Number B227/2
10. Abubakar Bawa Allah—House Number B282/2
11. Alhaji Abubakar Alhasan ("Bebe")—House Number B288/2

Ojo
12. Alhaji Mumuni—House Number B400/2

Tripoli/Sabon Gida
13. Salisu Abubakar (*Gidan Baki*)—House Number 350/2
14. Alhaji Baba Mai Doki (Suleiman Idrissu Bako)—House B363/2

Ayigbetown
Katifa
15. Alhaji Adamu Yahaya—House Number B251/2
Stable
16. Hajiya Hasana Adamu—House Number B424/2
Sunshine
17. Abdullahi Mohamadu "Gongadi"—House Number B255/2

Municipal
18. Ilyashu Salisu ("Small London")—House Number B123/2

Gangare
19. Alhaji A. Kariki (*Sarkin Fada*)—House Number B406/2=B21/2; B85/2; B22/2

BIBLIOGRAPHY

Accra Metropolitan Assembly. 1996–2000. *Five-Year Medium Term Development Plan*. Accra.

Acquah, Ione. 1958. *Accra Survey*. London: University of London Press.

Adamu, Mahdi. 1978. *The Hausa Factor in West African History*. London: Oxford University Press.

Addae, Stephen. 1997. *History of Western Medicine in Ghana, 1880–1960*. Edinburgh: Durham Academic Press Ltd.

Allen, Catherine. 1988. *The Hold Life Has: Coca and Cultural Identity in an Andean Community*. Washington, DC: Smithsonian Institution Press.

Altman, Irwin. 1974. "Privacy: A Conceptual Analysis." In *Man-Environment Interactions: Evaluations and Applications*. D.H. Carson, ed. Washington, DC: Environmental Design Research Association.

Altman, Irwin and Low, Setha M., eds. 1991. *Place Attachment. Volume 12: Human Behavior and Environment, Advances in Theory and Research*. New York: Plenum Press.

Amoah, Frank E.K. 1964. *Accra: A Study of the Development of a West African City*. Master's Thesis, University of Ghana.

Appadurai, Arjun. 1988. "Putting Hierarchy in its Place." *Cultural Anthropology* 3(1): 37–50.

———. 1996. *Modernity at Large*. Minneapolis: University of Minnesota Press.

Architecture, Faculty of. 1978. "Traditional Forms of Architecture in Ghana." *International Social Science Journal* XXX:449–476.

Archival Sources. NAG (National Archives of Ghana, Accra); ADM (Administration) II; SNA (Secretary for Native Affairs) 1086. Accra Native Affairs: 1878–1903 (Case No. 271/1900).

———. ADM II/I.

————. ADM II/1502 Hausa Community—Accra (Case No. 86/1912—SNA Board 133); SNA 1331/07; SNA 2288.

Ardener, Shirley, ed. 1981. *Women and Space: Ground Rules and Social Maps.* New York: St. Martin's Press.

Arn, Jack. 1996. "Creation of a Relative Surplus Population: A History of Accra, Ghana to 1980." *Review* XIX:413–444.

Asabere, Paul Kwadwo. 1981. "The Determinants of Land Values in an African City: The Case of Accra, Ghana." *Land Economics* 57(3):385–397.

Barnes, Sandra T. 1986. *Patrons and Power: Creating a Political Community in Metropolitan Lagos.* Bloomington: Indiana University Press.

Barth, Fredrik, ed. 1969. *Ethnic Groups and Boundaries.* Boston: Little, Brown.

Basso, Keith H. 1996. "Wisdom Sits in Places: Notes on a Western Apache Landscape." In *Senses of Place.* S. Feld and K.H. Basso, eds., 53–90. Santa Fe: School of American Research Press.

Berry, LaVerle. 1995. *Ghana: A Country Study.* Washington, DC: The Division: Headquarters, Dept. of the Army.

Besmer, Fremont E. 1983. *Horses, Musicians and Gods: The Hausa Cult of Possession-Trace.* South Hadley, Massachusetts: Bergin & Garvey.

Bestor, Theodore. 1989. *Neighborhood Tokyo.* Stanford: Stanford University Press.

————. 1999. "Wholesale Sushi: Culture and Commodity in Tokyo's Tsukiji Market." In *Theorizing the City: The New Urban Anthropology Reader.* S. Low, ed., 201–242. New Brunswick: Rutgers University Press.

Birdwell-Pheasant, Donna and Denise Lawrence-Zuniga. 1999. "Introduction: Houses and Families in Europe." In *House Life: Space, Place and Family in Europe.* D. Birdwell-Pheasant and D. Lawrence-Zuniga, eds., 1–38. Oxford: Berg.

Blair, Thomas L. 1971. "Shelter in Urbanising and Industrialising Africa." In *Shelter in Africa.* P. Oliver, ed., 229–239. London: Barrie and Jenkins.

Blankson, Charles C.T. 1988. "Housing Estates in Ghana: A Case Study of Middle- and Low-Income Residential Areas in Accra and Kumasi." In *Slum and Squatter Settlements in Sub-Saharan Africa.* R.A. Obudhun and C. Mhlanga, eds., 53–70. Westport, CT: Praeger.

Blier, Suzanne Preston. 1987. *The Anatomy of Architecture: Ontology and Metaphor in Batammaliba Architectural Expression.* Cambridge: Cambridge University Press.

Boeh-Ocansey, O. 1997. *Ghana's Microenterprise & Informal Sector.* Accra: Anansesem Publications Limited.

Bordo, Susan. 1993. *Unbearable Weight.* Berkeley: University of California Press.

Bosman, William. 1705. (New edition, 1967). *A New and Accurate Description of the Coast of Guinea.* Translated from the Dutch. London: Frank Cass & Co.

Bourdieu, Pierre. 1977. *Outline of a Theory of Practice.* Cambridge: Cambridge University Press.

————. 1979. The Kabyle House or the World Reversed. Algeria 1960: The Disenchantment of The World: The Sense of Honour: The Kabyle House or the World Reversed: Essays. Pp. 133–153. Cambridge: Cambridge University Press.

Boyd, A. 1962. *Chinese Architecture and Town Planning: 1500 B.C.–A.D. 1911.* Chicago: University of Chicago Press.

Brand, Richard R. 1972. "The Spatial Organization of Residential Areas in Accra, Ghana, with Particular Reference to Aspects of Modernization." *Economic Geography* 48(3):284–298.

———. 1973. "A Geographical Interpretation of the European Influence on Accra, Ghana Since 1877." Ed.D. diss., Columbia University.

Bremer, Alf. 2000. *Conflict Moderation and Participation—Prospects and Barriers for Urban Renewal in Ga Mashie, Accra.* Accra, Ghana: Visions of the City: Accra in the 21st Century.

Caldwell, John C. 1967. "Population: General Characteristics." In *A Study of Contemporary Ghana.* W.B. Birmingham, I. Neustadt, and E.N. Omaboe, eds., Vol. II: *Some Aspects of Social Structure.* Evanston: Northwestern University Press.

Callaway, Barbara. 1987. *Muslim Hausa Women in Nigeria: Tradition and Change.* Syracuse: Syracuse University Press.

Callaway, Barbara and Lucy Creevey. 1994. *The Heritage of Islam: Women, Religion, and Politics in West Africa.* Boulder: Lynne Rienner Publishers.

Callaway, Helen. 1981. "Spatial Domains and Women's Mobility in Yorubaland, Nigeria." In *Women and Space: Ground Rules and Social Maps.* S. Ardener, ed., 168–86. New York: St. Martin's.

Campbell, John. 1994. "Urbanization, Culture and the Politics of Urban Development in Ghana, 1875–1980." *Urban Anthropology* 23(4):409–50.

Casey, Edward. 1996. "How to Get from Space to Place in a Fairly Short Stretch of Time: Phenomenological Prolegomena." In *Senses of Place.* S. Feld and K.H. Basso, eds., 13–52. Santa Fe: School of American Research Press.

Castells, Manuel. 1979. *The Urban Question: A Marxist Approach.* Cambridge, MA: MIT Press.

Chazan, N., P. Lewis, R.A. Mortimer, D. Rothchild, S.J. Stedman, eds. 1999. *Politics and Society in Contemporary Africa.* Boulder: Lynn Rienner Publishers.

Cohen, Abner. 1969. *Custom and Politics in Urban Africa: A Study of Hausa Migrants in Yoruba Towns.* London: Routledge & Kegan Paul.

———. 1965. "The Social Organization of Credit in a West African Cattle Market." *Africa* 35(1):8–20.

Cohen, Abner, ed. 1974. *Urban Ethnicity.* London: Tavistock.

Comaroff, Jean. 1985. *Body of Power, Spirit of Resistance: The Culture and History of a South African People.* Chicago: University of Chicago Press.

Contamine, Philippe. 1980. "Peasant Hearth to Papal Palace: The Fourteenth and Fifteenth Centuries." In *A History of Private Life: Revelations of the Medieval World.* G. Duby, ed., 425–505, Vol. II. Cambridge, MA: Harvard University Press.

Cooper, Barbara. 1997a. *Marriage in Maradi: Gender and Culture in a Hausa Society in Niger, 1900–1989.* Portsmouth, NH: Heinemann.

———. 1997b. "Gender, Movements, and History: Social and Spatial Transformations in 20th Century Maradi, Niger." *Society and Space* 15: 195–221.

Crooks, John J. 1923. *Records Relating to the Gold Coast Settlements from 1750–1874.* Dublin: Cass.

Dakubu, M.E. Kropp. 1997. *Korle Meets the Sea: A Sociolinguistic History of Accra.* New York: Oxford.

Davidson, Basil. 1974. *Africa in History.* New York: Collier Books.

Denyer, Susan. 1978. *African Traditional Architecture.* New York: Africana Publishing Company.

Douglas, Mary, ed. 1973. *Rules and Meanings.* Harmondsworth: Penguin.

Dretke, James P. 1968. "The Muslim Community in Accra: An Historical Survey." Master's thesis, University of Ghana.

Du Toit, Brian, ed. 1978. *Ethnicity in Modern Africa*. Boulder: Westview Press.

Fernandez, James. 1977. *Fang Architectonics*. Philadelphia: ISHI.

Field, M.J. 1940. *Social Organisation of the Ga People*. London: Crown Agents.

Foster, Jeremy. 1996. "Landscape Phenomenology and the Imagination of a New South Africa on Parktown Ridge." *African Studies* (Wit. U.) 55(2):93–125.

Friedman, Thomas. 2001. "It Takes a Satellite." *New York Times*. May 8, 27.

Furniss, Graham. 1995. "The Power of Words and the Relation Between Hausa Genres." In *Power, Marginality and African Oral Literature*. G. Furniss and Liz Gunner, eds., 130–46. Cambridge: Cambridge University Press.

Gaffin, Dennis. 1996. *In Place: Spatial and Social Order in a Faeroe Islands Community*. Prospect Heights, IL: Waveland Press.

Gell, Alfred. 1998. *Art and Agency: An Anthropological Theory*. Oxford: Clarendon Press.

Ghana, Government of. 1978. *1970 Population Census of Ghana. Special Report A: Statistics of Towns with Population 10,000 and Over*. Accra: Census Office.

———. 1992. *Urban II Preparatory Studies: Accra Residential and Market Upgrading Study*. Final Report. Accra: Ministry of Works and Housing.

———. 1995. *Urban Environmental Sanitation Project (Identification of Urban Communities Suitable for Upgrading Projects)*. Accra: Ministry of Local Government.

Giddens, Anthony. 1984. *The Constitution of Society: Outline of the Theory of Structuration*. Berkeley and Los Angeles: University of California Press.

Gow, Peter. 1995. "Land, People and Paper in Western Amazonia." In *The Anthropology of Landscape: Perspectives on Place and Space*. E. Hirsch and M. O'Hanlon, eds., 43–62. Oxford: Clarendon.

Grant, Richard. 2001. "Liberalization Policies and Foreign Companies in Accra, Ghana." *Environment and Planning* A 33:997–1014.

Grillo, R.D. 1974. "Ethnic Identity and Social Stratification on a Kampala Housing Estate." In *Urban Ethnicity*. A. Cohen, ed., 159–85. London: Tavistock Publications.

Grindal, Bruce T. 1973. "Islamic Affiliations and Urban Adaptation: The Sisala Migrant in Accra, Ghana." *Africa* 43:333–46.

Guidoni, Enrico. 1975. *Primitive Architecture*. New York: Rizzoli.

Hannerz, Ulf. 1992. *Cultural Complexity: Studies in the Social Organization of Meaning*. New York: Columbia.

———. 1996. *Transnational Connections: Culture, People, Places*. New York: Routledge.

Hart, Keith. 1973. "Informal Income Opportunities and Urban Employment in Ghana." *Journal of Modern African Studies* 11(1):61–89.

———. 1982. *The Political Economy of West African Agriculture*. Cambridge: Cambridge University Press.

Harvey, David. 1996. *Justice, Nature & the Geography of Difference*. Cambridge, MA: Blackwell.

Harvey, William B. 1966. *Law and Social Change in Ghana*. Princeton: Princeton University Press.

Hill, Polly. 1966. "Landlords and Brokers: A West African Trading System." *Cahiers d'Études Africaines* 6:349–66.

———. 1970. *The Occupations of Migrants in Ghana*. Ann Arbor: University of Michigan Press.

Hirsch, Eric. 1995. "Introduction: Landscape: Between Place and Space." In *The An-thropology of Landscape: Perspectives on Place and Space*. E. Hirsch and M. O'Hanlon, eds., 1–30. Oxford: Clarendon Press.

Howell, Sandra C. and Vana Tentokali. 1989. "Domestic Privacy: Gender, Culture and Development Issues." In *Housing, Culture and Design*. S. Low and E. Chambers, eds., 281–97. Philadelphia: University of Pennsylvania Press.

Humphrey, Caroline. 1988. "No Place Like Home in Anthropology: The Neglect of Architecture." *Anthropology Today* 4:16–18.

Illich, Ivan. 1983. *Gender*. New York: Pantheon Books.

Irving, Robert Grant. 1981. *Indian Summer: Lutyens, Baker, and Imperial Delhi*. New Haven, CT: Yale University Press.

Isichei, Elizabeth. 1995. *A History of Christianity in Africa*. Lawrenceville, NJ: Africa World Press, Inc.

Jacobs, Jane. 1961. *The Death and Life of Great American Cities*. New York: Vintage.

Kaniki, M.H.Y. 1985. "The Colonial Economy: The Former British Zones." In *General History of Africa*. A. Boahen, ed., Vol. 7, *African Under Colonial Domination, 1880–1935*, 382–419. Berkeley: University of California Press.

Keller, Suzanne. 1968. *The Urban Neighborhood*. New York: Random House.

Kent, Susan. 1984. *Analyzing Activity Areas: An Ethnoarchaeological Study of the Use of Space*. Albuquerque: University of New Mexico Press.

Kilson, Marian. 1974. *African Urban Kinsmen: The Ga of Central Accra*. New York: St. Martin's Press.

Kimble, David. 1963. *A Political History of Ghana: The Rise of Gold Coast Nationalism, 1850–1928*. Oxford: Clarendon.

King, Anthony. 1976. *Colonial Urban Development: Culture, Social Power, and Envi-ronment*. London: Routledge and Kegan Paul.

———. 1995. "Writing Colonial Space: A Review Article." *Comparative Studies in Society and History* 37:541–54.

———. 1984. *The Bungalow: The Production of a Global Culture*. London: Routledge and Kegan Paul.

Knapp, Ronald. 1989. *China's Vernacular Architecture: House Form and Culture*. Hono-lulu: University of Hawaii Press.

Konadu-Agyemang, Kwadwo. 1998. "Housing Conditions and Spatial Organization in Accra, 1950s–1990s." *Ghana Studies* 1:63–90.

———. 2001. *The Political Economy of Housing and Urban Development in Africa: Ghana's Experience from Colonial Times to 1998*. Westport, CT: Praeger.

Koran. 1975. *The Holy Quran*. Text translation and Commentary by Abdullah Yusuf Ali. London: Islamic Foundation.

Korboe, David. 1992. "Family-houses in Ghanaian Cities: To Be or Not To Be?" *Urban Studies* 29, 7:1159–72.

Kulturmann, U. 1963. *New Architecture in Africa*. New York: Universe Books.

Kuper, Hilda. 1972. "The Language of Sites in the Politics of Space." *American An-thropologist* 74:411–25.

Larbi, Wordsworth Odame. 1994. "Urban Land Policies and the Delivery of Developable Land in Ghana." Ph.D. disser. University of Reading.

———. 1996. "Spatial planning and urban fragmentation in Accra." *Third World Plan-ning Review* 18(2):193–215.

Lawrence, Denise and Setha M. Low. 1990. "The Built Environment and Spatial Form." *Annual Review of Anthropology* 19:453–505.

Lawrence, Denise and Setha Low, eds. 2002. *The Anthropology of Space and Place. A Reader.* Cambridge, MA: Blackwells.

Levine, Robert A. and Sarah E. Levine. 1991. "House Design and the Self in an African Culture." In *Body and Space: Symbolic Models of Unity and Division in African Cosmology and Experience.* A. Jacobson-Widding, ed., 155–223. Uppsala: Almqvist & Wiksell International.

Levitzion, Nehemiah. 1969. "Coastal West Africa." In *Islam in Africa.* J. Kritzeck and W.H. Lewis, eds. 301–318. New York: Van Nostrand-Reinhold Co.

Leys, Colin. 1975. *Underdevelopment in Kenya: The Political Economy of Neo-Colonialism, 1964–1971.* London: Heinemann.

Lisowska, Jolanta. 1984. "The Demographic, Social and Professional Structure of the Population of Accra between 1960 and 1970." *Africana Bulletin* 32:113–129.

Lobo, Susan. 1982. *A House of My Own: Social Organization in the Squatter Settlements of Lima, Peru.* Tucson: University of Arizona Press.

Lovejoy, Paul. 1973. "The Hausa Kola Trade (1700–1900): A Commerical System in the Continental Exchange of West Africa." Ph.D, diss., University of Wisconsin.

Lovell, Nadia. 1998. "Introduction: Belonging in Need of Emplacement." In *Locality and Belonging.* N. Lovell, ed., 1–24. New York: Routledge.

Low, Setha. 1996. "The Anthropology of Cities: Imagining and Theorizing the City." *Annual Review of Anthropology* 25:383–409.

———. 2000. *On the Plaza.* Austin: University of Texas Press.

Low, Setha M. and Irwin Altman. 1992. "Place Attachment: A Conceptual Inquiry." In *Place Attachment.* I. Altman and S.M. Low, eds. Vol. 12, 1–12, New York: Plenum Press.

Lyons, Diane. 1992. "Men's Houses: Women's Spaces: An Ethnoarchaeological Study of Gender and Household Design in Dela, North Cameroon." Ph.D, diss., Simon Fraser University.

Mabogunje, Akin L. 1970. "Urbanization and Change." In *The African Experience.* J. Paden and E. Soja, eds. Vol. I, *Essays,* 331–358. Evanston: Northwestern University Press.

Mack, Beverly. 1991. "Royal Wives in Kano." In *Hausa Women in the Twentieth Century.* C. Coles and B. Mack, eds., 109–129. Madison: University of Wisconsin Press.

———. 1992. "Harem Domesticity in Kano, Nigeria." In *African Encounters with Domesticity.* K. Tranberg-Hansen, ed., 75–97. New Brunswick: Rutgers University Press.

Malinowski, Bronislaw. 1922. *Argonauts of the Western Pacific.* London: G. Routledge & Sons, Ltd.

Marris, Peter. 1962. *Family and Social Change in an African City: A Study of Rehousing in Lagos.* Evanston, IL: Northwestern University Press.

———. 1979. "The Meaning of Slums and Patterns of Change." *International Journal of Urban and Regional Research* 3(3):419–441.

Masquelier, Adeline. 2001. *Prayer Has Spoiled Everything: Possession, Power, and Identity in an Islamic Town of Niger.* Durham: Duke University Press.

Mauss, Marcel. 1967. *The Gift: Forms and Functions of Exchange in Archaic Societies.* New York: Norton.

Mitchell, J.C. 1966. "Theoretical Orientations in African Urban Studies." In *The Social Anthropology of Complex Societies*. M. Banton, ed., Vol. ASA Monographs 4, 37–68. London: Tavistock.

Mitchell, Timothy. 1991. *Colonising Egypt*. Berkeley: University of California Press.

Moore, Barrington. 1984. *Privacy: Studies in Social and Cultural History*. Armonk, NY: M.E. Sharpe.

Moore, Henrietta. 1986. *Space, Text and Gender*. Cambridge: Cambridge University Press.

Moughtin, J.C. 1964. "The Traditional Settlements of the Hausa People." *The Town Planning Review* XXXV(1):21–34.

————. 1985. *Hausa Architecture*. London: Ethnographica.

Mousset-Jones, Nicola. 1999. "Planning, Promotion and the Production of Markets: Tension in Accra's Central Business District." Master's thesis. Syracuse University.

Muhammad-Oumar, Abdulrazzaq Ahmad. 1997. *Gidaje. The Socio-Cultural Mosphology of Hausa Living Spaces*. PhD, University College London.

Munn, Nancy. 1986. *The Fame of Gawa: A Symbolic Study of Value Transformation in a Massim (Papua New Guinea) Society*. Cambridge: Cambridge University Press.

Obirih-Opareh, Nelson. 2001. "Public or Private? A Policy Dilemma of Liquid Waste Management in Accra." In *Toilets and Sanitation in Ghana: an Urgent Matter*. S. Van der Geest and N. Obirih-Opareh, eds., 13–23. Amsterdam: Council for Scientific and Industrial Research.

Obudho, R.A. and Constance C. Mhlanga. 1988. "The Development of Slum and Squatter Settlements as a Manifestation of Rapid Urbanization in Sub-Saharan Africa." In *Slum and Squatter Settlements in Sub-Saharan Africa: Toward a Planning Strategy*. R.A. Obudho and C.C. Mhlanga, eds., 3–30. New York: Praeger.

Odeh, Lama Abu. 1993. "Post-Colonial Feminism and the Veil: Thinking the Difference." *Feminist Review* 43:26–38.

Odoom, K.O. 1971. "A Document on Pioneers of the Muslim Community in Accra." *Institute of African Studies Research Review* (Accra) 7(3):1–31.

Ojo, G.J. Afolabi. 1968. "Hausa Quarters of Yoruba Towns with Special Reference to Ile-Ife." *Journal of Tropical Geography* 27:40–49.

Oliver, Paul. 1987. *Dwellings: The House Across the World*. Austin: University of Texas Press.

Ollennu, Nii Amaa. 1962. *Principles of Customary Land Law in Ghana*. London: Staples.

Onwuejeogwu, Michael. 1969. "The Cult of the Bori Spirits among the Hausa." In *Man in Africa*. Mary Douglas and Phyllis Kaberry, eds. New York: Tavistock.

Ottino, Arlette. 1998. "Origin and Ritual Exchange as Transformative: Belonging in the Balinese Temple." In *Locality and Belonging*. N. Lovell, ed., 103–24. New York: Routledge.

Parker, John. 2000. *Making the Town: Ga State and Society in Early Colonial Accra*. Portsmouth, NH: Heinemann.

Peil, Margaret. 1971. "The Expulsion of West African Aliens." *The Journal of Modern African Studies* 9(2).

————. 1972. *The Ghanaian Factory Worker*. Cambridge: Cambridge University Press.

————. 1979. "Host Reactions: Aliens in Ghana." In *Strangers in African Societies*. W.A. Shack and E.P. Skinner, eds., 123–140. Berkeley: University of California Press.

Pellow, Deborah. 1978. "Work and Autonomy: Women in Accra." *American Ethnologist* 5(4):770–785.

———. 1985. "Muslim Segmentation: Cohesion and Divisiveness in Accra." *The Journal of Modern African Studies* 23(3):419–444.

———. 1987. "Solidarity among Muslim Women in Accra." *Anthropos* 82:489–506.

———. 1988. "What Housing Does: Changes in an Accra Community." *Architecture and Behavior* 4(3):213–228.

———. 1991a. "The Power of Space in the Evolution of an Accra Zongo." *Ethnohistory* 38, 4:414–450.

———. 1991b. "Spaces that Teach: Attachment to the African Compound." In *Place Attachment*. I. Altman and S. Low, eds., Vol. 12. 187–210. New York: Plenum Press.

———. 1996a. "Concluding Thoughts." In *Setting Boundaries: The Anthropology of Spatial and Social Organization*. D. Pellow, ed., 215–225. Westport, CT: Bergin & Garvey.

———. 1996b. "Intimate Boundaries: A Chinese Puzzle." In *Setting Boundaries: The Anthropology of Spatial and Social Organization*. D. Pellow, ed., 111–136. Westport, CT: Bergin & Garvey.

———. 1997. "Male Praise-Singers in Accra: In the Company of Women." *Africa* 67(4): 582–601.

———. 1999. "The Power of Space in the Evolution of an Accra Zongo." In *Theorizing the City*. S. Low, ed., 277–316. New Brunswick, NJ: Rutgers University Press.

Pellow, Deborah and Naomi Chazan. 1986. *Ghana: Coping with Uncertainty*. Boulder, CO: Westview.

Pittin, Renee. 1979. "Marriage and Alternative Strategies: Career Patterns of Hausa Women in Katsina City." Ph.D, diss., University of London.

———. 1984. "Documentation and Analysis of the Invisible Work of Invisible Women: A Nigerian Case Study." *International Labour Review* 123(4):473–490.

———. 1996. "Negotiating Boundaries: A Perspective from Nigeria." In *Setting Boundaries: The Anthropology of Spatial and Social Organization*. D. Pellow, ed., 179–94. Westport, CT: Bergin & Garvey.

Planning, Department of Town and Country. 1992. *Strategic Plan for the Greater Accra Metropolitan Area*. Accra: Accra Planning and Development Programme.

Pogucki, R.J.H. 1954. *Report on Land Tenure in Customary Law of the Non-Akan Areas of the Gold Coast (Now Eastern Region of Ghana)*. Volume II. Accra: Lands Department.

Proshansky, H.M., A.K. Fabian, & R. Kaminoff. 1983. "Place-identity: Physical World Socialization of the Self." *Journal of Environmental Psychology* 3:57–83.

Prussin, Labelle. 1969. *Architecture in Northern Ghana: A Study of Forms and Functions*. Berkeley: University of California Press.

———. 1986. *Hatumere: Islamic Design in West Africa*. Berkeley: University of California Press.

Quarcoopome, S.S. 1993. "A History of the Urban Development of Accra: 1877–1957." *Research Review* (NS) 9 (1):20–32.

Rakodi, Carole. 1997a. "Global Forces, Urban Change, and Urban Management in Africa." In *The Urban Challenge in Africa: Growth and Management of its Large Cities*. C. Rakodi, ed., 17–73. New York: United Nations University Press.

————. 1997b. "Residential Property Markets in African Cities." In *The Urban Challenge in Africa: Growth and Managment of its Large Cities.* C. Radkodi, ed., 371–410. New York: United Nations University Press.

Rapoport, Amos. 1969. *House Form and Culture.* Upper Saddle River, NJ: Prentice-Hall.

————. 1980a. "Neighborhood Heterogeneity or Homogeneity: The Field of Man-Environment Studies." *Architecture and Behavior* 1:65–77.

————. 1980b. "Cross-Cultural Aspects of Environmental Design." In *Human Behavior and Environment: Advances in Theory and Research.* I. Altman, A. Rapoport, and J.F. Wohlwill, eds., Vol. 4: Environment and Culture. 7–46. New York: Plenum.

Rayfield, J.R. 1974. "Theories of Urbanization and the Colonial City in West Africa." *Africa* 44:163–185.

Reynolds, Edward. 1974. *Trade and Economic Change on the Gold Coast, 1807–1874.* New York: Longman.

Robertson, Claire. 1983. "The Death of Makola and Other Tragedies." *Canadian Journal of African Studies* 17:469–495.

Robertson, Claire C. 1984. *Sharing the Same Bowl: A Socioeconomic History of Women and Class in Accra, Ghana.* Bloomington: University of Indiana Press.

Rodman, Margaret. 1992. "Empowering Place: Multilocality and Multivocality." *American Anthropologist* 94:640–656.

Rodman, Margaret and Matthew Cooper. 1989. "The Sociocultural Production of Urban Space: Building a Fully Accessible Toronto Housing Cooperative." *City & Society* 3:1–22.

Rogerson, Christian. 1991. "Home-Based Enterprises of the Urban Poor: The Case of Spazas." In *South Africa's Informal Economy.* E. Preston-Whyte and Christian Rogerson, eds., 336–344. Cape Town: Oxford University Press.

Rotenberg, Robert. 1993. "Introduction." In *The Cultural Meaning of Urban Space.* R. Rotenberg and G. McDonogh. eds. Westport, CT: Bergin & Garvey.

Rouch, Jean. 1956. *Migrations au Ghana.* Paris: Centre National de Recherche Scientifique.

Rutter, Andrew. 1971. "Ashanti Vernacular Architecture." In *Shelter in Africa.* P. Oliver, ed., 153–171. London: Barrie & Jenkins Ltd.

Sa'ad H.T. 1981. *Between Myth and Reality: The Aesthetics of Architecture in Hausaland.* PhD, University of Michigan.

Sahlins, Marshall. 1985. *Islands of History.* Chicago: University of Chicago Press.

Salamone, Frank A. 1975. "Becoming Hausa: Ethnic Identity Change and its Implications for the Study of Ethnic Pluralism and Stratification." *Africa* 45(4):410–424.

Sandbrook, Richard and Jack Arn. 1977. *The Laboring Poor and Urban Class Formation: The Case of Greater Accra.* Montreal: McGill University Center for Development Studies.

Schildkrout, Enid. 1970. "Strangers and Local Government in Kumasi." *Journal of Modern African Studies* 8(2):251–269.

————. 1970a. "Government and Chiefs in Kumasi Zongo." In *West African Chiefs: Their Changing Status under Colonial Rule and Independence.* M. Crowder and O. Ikime, eds., 370–392. New York: Africana.

————. 1978. *People of the Zongo: The Transformation of Ethnic Identities in Ghana.* Cambridge: Cambridge University Press.

———. 1983. "Dependence and Autonomy: The Economic Activities of Secluded Hausa Women in Kano." In *Female and Male in West Africa*. C. Oppong, ed., 107–126. London: George Allen & Unwin.

———. 1986. "Widows in Hausa Society: Ritual Phase or Social Status." In *Widows in African Societies: Choices and Constraints*. B. Potash, ed., 131–152. Stanford: Stanford University Press.

Schwerdtfeger, Friedrich W. 1982. *Traditional Housing in African Cities: A Comparative Study of Houses in Zaria, Ibadan, and Marrakech*. New York: John Wiley & Sons.

Skinner, Elliott P. 1963. "Strangers in West African Societies." *Africa* 33:307–320.

Smart, Josephine and Alan Smart. 1999. "Personal Relations and Divergent Economies: A Case Study of Hong Kong Investment in South China." In *Theorizing the City: The New Urban Anthropology Reader*. S. Low, ed., 169–200. New Brunswick, NJ: Rutgers University Press.

Smith, Abdullahi. 1976. "The Early States of the Central Sudan." In *History of West Africa*. J.F.A. Ajayi and M. Crowder, eds., Vol. I, 152–195. New York: Columbia University Press.

Smith, Mary F. 1981 (1954). *Baba of Karo*. New Haven, CT: Yale University Press.

Smith, M.G. 1957. "The Social Functions and Meanings of Hausa Praise-Singing." *Africa* 27(1):26–43.

———. 1959. "The Hausa System of Social Status." *Africa* 29(3):239–251.

———. 1960. *Government in Zazzau, 1800–1950*. London: Oxford University Press. For the International African Institute.

———. 1961. "Field Histories among the Hausa." *Journal of African History* 11(1): 87–101.

———. 1965. "The Hausa of Northern Nigeria." In *Peoples of Africa*. J.L. Gibbs, ed., 119–156. New York: Holt, Rinehart, Winston.

———. 1978. *The Affairs of Daura: History and Change in a Hausa State 1800–1958*. Los Angeles: University of California Press.

———. 1997. *Government in Kano, 1350–1950*. Boulder: Westview Press.

Spitzer, Leo. 1974. *The Creoles of Sierra Leone*. Madison: University of Wisconsin Press.

Tipple, A.G. 1999. "Housing Supply in Ghana." *Progress in Planning* 51(4):255–324.

Turner, Victor. 1969. *The Ritual Process: Structure and Anti-Structure*. Chicago: Aldine Pub. Co.

Twum-Baah, K.A. 2000. Population Growth of Mega Accra: Emerging Issues. Visions of the City: Accra in the 21st Century. International Seminar, Ghana Institute of Architects and the Goethe Institute. Accra, Ghana.

Van Ham, Nana Apt, E.Q. Blavo, and S.K. Opoku. 1991. *Street Children in Accra: A Survey Report*. Legon: Department of Sociology, University of Ghana.

Vatuk, Sylvia. 1982. "Purdah Revisited: A Comparison of Hindu and Muslim Interpretations of the Cultural Meaning of Purdah in South Asia." In *Separate Worlds: Studies of Purdah in South Asia*. H. Papanek and G. Minault, eds., 54–78. Columbia, MO: South Asia Books.

VerEcke, Catherine. 1993. "It is Better to Die than to Be Shamed: Cultural and Moral Dimensions of Women's Trading in an Islamic Nigerian Society." *Anthropos* 88: 403–417.

Vestbro, Dick Urban. 1975. *Social Life and Dwelling Space*. Stockholm: University of Lund, College of Architecture.

Ward, W.E.F. 1948. *A History of the Gold Coast*. London: George Allen & Unwin.

Weiner, Annette B. 1992. *Inalienable Possessions: The Paradox of Keeping While Giving*. Berkeley: University of California Press.

Weisman, Leslie. 1981. "Women's Environmental Rights: A Manifesto." *Heresies* V(3): 6–8.

Weiss, Brad. 1996. *The Making and Unmaking of the Haya Lived World: Consumption, Commoditization, and Everyday Practice*. Durham: Duke University Press.

Wilks, Ivor. 1971. "Asante Policy Towards the Hausa Trade in the 19th Century." In *The Development of Indigenous Trade and Markets in West Africa*. C. Meillasoux, ed., 124–144. London: Oxford University Press for the International African Institute.

———. 1975. *Asante in the Nineteenth Century: The Structure and Evolution of a Political Order*. London: Cambridge University Press.

Works and Housing, Ministry of. 1992. *Urban II Preparatory Studies: Accra Residential and Market Upgrading Study*. Accra: Government of Ghana.

Works, John A., Jr. 1976. *Pilgrims in a Strange Land: Hausa Communities in Chad*. New York: Columbia.

Wright, S. 1981. "Place and Face: Of Women in Doshman Ziari, Iran." In *Women and Space: Ground Rules and Social Maps*. S. Ardener, ed., 136–157. New York: St. Martin's.

Yeld, E.R. 1966. "Islam and Social Stratification in Northern Nigeria." *British Journal of Sociology* 2:124–131.

Zukin, Sharon. 1995. *The Cultures of Cities*. Cambridge, MA: Blackwells.

INDEX

("n" indicates a note)

www.ingramcontent.com/pod-product-compliance
Lightning Source LLC
Chambersburg PA
CBHW032122020426
42334CB00016B/1036